The *New* Daily Study Bible

The Gospel of
Matthew
Volume I

D1324324

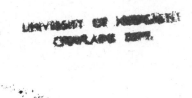

The *New* Daily Study Bible

The full range of titles available in this series

The *New* Daily Study Bible

The Gospel of
Matthew

Volume 1

William Barclay

SAINT ANDREW PRESS
Edinburgh

Published by
SAINT ANDREW PRESS
121 George Street, Edinburgh EH2 4YN

First edition published in 1956 as *The Daily Study Bible: The Gospel of Matthew*
Revised edition published in 1975
This third edition fully revised and updated by Saint Andrew Press and published as
The New Daily Study Bible: The Gospel of Matthew in 2001

Reprinted 2005

ISBN 0 7152 0780 6

British Library Cataloguing in Publication Data
A CIP record for this book is available from the British Library

Cover design by McColl Productions Ltd, by courtesy of Saint Andrew Press

Typeset by Waverley Typesetters, Galashiels
Manufactured in Germany by Bercker GmbH

CONTENTS

MATTHEW

MATTHEW

SERIES FOREWORD
(by Ronnie Barclay)

My father always had a great love for the English language and its literature. As a student at the University of Glasgow, he won a prize in the English class – and I have no doubt that he could have become a Professor of English instead of Divinity and Biblical Criticism. In a pre-computer age, he had a mind like a computer that could store vast numbers of quotations, illustrations, anecdotes and allusions; and, more remarkably still, he could retrieve them at will. The editor of this revision has, where necessary, corrected and attributed the vast majority of these quotations with considerable skill and has enhanced our pleasure as we read quotations from Plato to T. S. Eliot.

There is another very welcome improvement in the new text. My mother was one of five sisters, and my grandmother was a commanding figure as the Presbyterian minister's wife in a small village in Ayrshire in Scotland. She ran that small community very efficiently, and I always felt that my father, surrounded by so many women, was more than somewhat overawed by it all! I am sure that this is the reason why his use of English tended to be dominated by the words 'man', 'men' and so on, with the result that it sounded very male-orientated. Once again, the editor has very skilfully improved my father's English and made the text much more readable for all of us by amending the often one-sided language.

It is a well-known fact that William Barclay wrote at breakneck speed and never corrected anything once it was on paper – he took great pride in mentioning this at every possible opportunity! This revision, in removing repetition and correcting the inevitable errors that had slipped through, has produced a text free from all the tell-tale signs of very rapid writing. It is with great pleasure that I commend this revision to readers old and new in the certainty that William Barclay speaks even more clearly to us all with his wonderful appeal in this new version of his much-loved *Daily Study Bible*.

Ronnie Barclay
Bedfordshire
2001

GENERAL INTRODUCTION

(by William Barclay, from the 1975 edition)

The Daily Study Bible series has always had one aim – to convey the results of scholarship to the ordinary reader. A. S. Peake delighted in the saying that he was a 'theological middle-man', and I would be happy if the same could be said of me in regard to these volumes. And yet the primary aim of the series has never been academic. It could be summed up in the famous words of Richard of Chichester's prayer – to enable men and women 'to know Jesus Christ more clearly, to love him more dearly, and to follow him more nearly'.

It is all of twenty years since the first volume of *The Daily Study Bible* was published. The series was the brain-child of the late Rev. Andrew McCosh, MA, STM, the then Secretary and Manager of the Committee on Publications of the Church of Scotland, and of the late Rev. R. G. Macdonald, OBE, MA, DD, its Convener.

It is a great joy to me to know that all through the years *The Daily Study Bible* has been used at home and abroad, by minister, by missionary, by student and by layman, and that it has been translated into many different languages. Now, after so many printings, it has become necessary to renew the printer's type and the opportunity has been taken to restyle the books, to correct some errors in the text and to remove some references which have become outdated. At the same time, the Biblical quotations within the text have been changed to use the Revised Standard Version, but my own original translation of the New Testament passages has been retained at the beginning of each daily section.

There is one debt which I would be sadly lacking in courtesy if I did not acknowledge. The work of revision and correction has been done entirely by the Rev. James Martin, MA, BD, Minister of High Carntyne Church, Glasgow. Had it not been for him this task would never have been undertaken, and it is impossible for me to thank him enough for the selfless toil he has put into the revision of these books.

It is my prayer that God may continue to use *The Daily Study Bible* to enable men better to understand His word.

William Barclay
Glasgow
1975
(Published in the 1975 edition)

GENERAL FOREWORD

(by John Drane)

I only met William Barclay once, not long after his retirement from the chair of Biblical Criticism at the University
of Glasgow. Of course I had known about him long before
that, not least because his theological passion – the Bible
– was also a significant formative influence in my own life
and ministry. One of my most vivid memories of his influence goes back to when I was working on my own doctoral
research in the New Testament. It was summer 1971, and I
was a leader on a mission team working in the north-east of
Scotland at the same time as Barclay's Baird Lectures were
being broadcast on national television. One night, a young
Ph.D. scientist who was interested in Christianity, but still
unsure about some things, came to me and announced: 'I've
just been watching William Barclay on TV. He's convinced
me that I need to be a Christian; when can I be baptized?'
That kind of thing did not happen every day. So how could it
be that Barclay's message was so accessible to people with
no previous knowledge or experience of the Christian faith?

I soon realised that there was no magic ingredient that
enabled this apparently ordinary professor to be a brilliant
communicator. His secret lay in who he was, his own sense
of identity and purpose, and above all his integrity in being
true to himself and his faith. Born in the far north of Scotland,
he was brought up in Motherwell, a steel-producing town
south of Glasgow where his family settled when he was only
five, and this was the kind of place where he felt most at

home. Though his association with the University of Glasgow provided a focus for his life over almost fifty years, from his first day as a student in 1925 to his retirement from the faculty in 1974, he never became an ivory-tower academic, divorced from the realities of life in the real world. On the contrary, it was his commitment to the working-class culture of industrial Clydeside that enabled him to make such a lasting contribution not only to the world of the university but also to the life of the Church.

He was ordained to the ministry of the Church of Scotland at the age of twenty-six, but was often misunderstood even by other Christians. I doubt that William Barclay would ever have chosen words such as 'missionary' or 'evangelist' to describe his own ministry, but he accomplished what few others have done, as he took the traditional Presbyterian emphasis on spirituality-through-learning and transformed it into a most effective vehicle for evangelism. His own primary interest was in the history and language of the New Testament, but William Barclay was never only a historian or literary critic. His constant concern was to explore how these ancient books, and the faith of which they spoke, could continue to be relevant to people of his own time. If the Scottish churches had known how to capitalize on his enormous popularity in the media during the 1960s and 1970s, they might easily have avoided much of the decline of subsequent years.

Connecting the Bible to life has never been the way to win friends in the world of academic theology, and Barclay could undoubtedly have made things easier for himself had he been prepared to be a more conventional academic. But he was too deeply rooted in his own culture – and too seriously committed to the gospel – for that. He could see little purpose in a belief system that was so wrapped up in arcane and complicated terminology that it was accessible only to experts. Not only did he demystify Christian theology, but he also did it for working people, addressing the kind of things that mattered to ordinary folks in their everyday lives. In doing so, he also challenged the elitism that has often been deeply ingrained in the twin worlds of academic theology and the Church, with their shared assumption that popular culture is an inappropriate vehicle for serious thinking. Professor Barclay can hardly have been surprised when his predilection for writing books for the masses – not to mention talking to them on television – was questioned by his peers and even occasionally dismissed as being 'unscholarly' or insufficiently 'academic'. That was all untrue, of course, for his work was soundly based in reliable scholarship and his own extensive knowledge of the original languages of the Bible. But like One many centuries before him (and unlike most of his peers, in both Church and academy), 'the common people heard him gladly' (Mark 12:37), which no doubt explains why his writings are still inspirational – and why it is a particular pleasure for me personally to commend them to a new readership in a new century.

John Drane
University of Aberdeen
2001

EDITOR'S PREFACE

(by Linda Foster)

When the first volume of the original *Daily Bible Readings*, which later became *The Daily Study Bible* (the commentary on Acts), was published in 1953, no one could have anticipated or envisaged the revolution in the use of language which was to take place in the last quarter of the twentieth century. Indeed, when the first revised edition, to which William Barclay refers in his General Introduction, was completed in 1975, such a revolution was still waiting in the wings. But at the beginning of the twenty-first century, inclusive language and the concept of political correctness are well-established facts of life. It has therefore been with some trepidation that the editing of this unique and much-loved text has been undertaken in producing *The New Daily Study Bible*. Inevitably, the demands of the new language have resulted in the loss of some of Barclay's most sonorous phrases, perhaps best remembered in the often-repeated words 'many a man'. Nonetheless, this revision is made in the conviction that William Barclay, the great communicator, would have welcomed it. In the discussion of Matthew 9:16–17 ('The Problem of the New Idea'), he affirmed the value of language that has stood the test of time and in which people have 'found comfort and put their trust', but he also spoke of 'living in a changing and expanding world' and questioned the wisdom of reading God's word to twentieth-century men and women in Elizabethan English. It is the intention of this new edition to heed that warning and to bring

William Barclay's message of God's word to readers of the twenty-first century in the language of their own time.

In the editorial process, certain decisions have been made in order to keep a balance between that new language and the familiar Barclay style. Quotations from the Bible are now taken from the New Revised Standard Version, but William Barclay's own translation of individual passages has been retained throughout. Where the new version differs from the text on which Barclay originally commented, because of the existence of an alternative reading, the variant text is indicated by square brackets. I have made no attempt to guess what Barclay would have said about the NRSV text; his commentary still refers to the Authorized (King James) and Revised Standard Versions of the Bible, but I believe that the inclusive language of the NRSV considerably assists the flow of the discussion.

For similar reasons, the dating conventions of BC and AD – rather than the more recent and increasingly used BCE (before the common era) and CE (common era) – have been retained. William Barclay took great care to explain the meanings of words and phrases and scholarly points, but it has not seemed appropriate to select new terms and make such explanations on his behalf.

One of the most difficult problems to solve has concerned monetary values. Barclay had his own system for translating the coinage of New Testament times into British currency. Over the years, these equivalent values have become increasingly out of date, and often the force of the point being made has been lost or diminished. There is no easy way to bring these equivalents up to date in a way that will continue to make sense, particularly when readers come from both sides of the Atlantic. I have therefore followed the only known yardstick that gives any feel for the values concerned, namely that a *denarius* was a day's wage for a working man, and I have made alterations to the text accordingly.

One of the striking features of *The Daily Study Bible* is the range of quotations from literature and hymnody that are used by way of illustration. Many of these passages appeared without identification or attribution, and for the new edition I have attempted wherever possible to provide sources and authors. In the same way, details have been included about scholars and other individuals cited, by way of context and explanation, and I am most grateful to Professor John Drane for his assistance in discovering information about some of the more obscure or unfamiliar characters. It is clear that readers use *The Daily Study Bible* in different ways. Some look up particular passages while others work through the daily readings in a more systematic way. The descriptions and explanations are therefore not offered every time an individual is mentioned (in order to avoid repetition that some may find tedious), but I trust that the information can be discovered without too much difficulty.

Finally, the 'Further Reading' lists at the end of each volume have been removed. Many new commentaries and individual studies have been added to those that were the basis of William Barclay's work, and making a selection from that ever-increasing catalogue is an impossible task. It is nonetheless my hope that the exploration that begins with these volumes of *The New Daily Study Bible* will go on in the discovery of new writers and new books.

Throughout the editorial process, many conversations have taken place – conversations with the British and American publishers, and with those who love the books and find in them both information and inspiration. Ronnie Barclay's contribution to this revision of his father's work has been invaluable. But one conversation has dominated the work, and that has been a conversation with William Barclay himself through the text. There has been a real sense of listening to his voice in all the questioning and in the searching for new words to convey the meaning of that text. The aim of *The New Daily Study Bible* is to make clear his message, so that the distinctive voice, which has spoken to so many in past years, may continue to be heard for generations to come.

Linda Foster
London
2001

INTRODUCTION
(by John Drane)

William Barclay was always concerned to ensure that people had a clear understanding of the relevance of the Christian faith to today's world, and to persuade them that it would be worth ordering their lives according to its values. The writer of Matthew's gospel focuses on much the same issues, which probably goes a long way towards explaining why Barclay produced such a vigorous commentary on this book. His comments on the Sermon on the Mount (chapters 5–7) have to be some of the best passages to be found anywhere in the Barclay canon. Even now, the reader cannot fail to recognize the sense of excitement and joyous discovery as Barclay shares what he himself had learned through his study of the Scriptures in their original languages, combined with stories from history and informative insights into life in ancient Palestine.

But Barclay never left such insights in the past, or at a merely theoretical level. His comment on the passage about disciples being the light of the world (5:14–15) is as relevant and meaningful today, in vastly changed social circumstances, as it was when he first penned it. He makes it clear that he himself saw no distinction between the secular and the sacred, and he was convinced that this was an attitude that he had learned from Jesus. He had a strong sense of what we might nowadays call a creation-centred spirituality – rooted in the conviction that all people are of value because they are made in God's image – though the idea of using such a term to describe it would never have occurred to him.

Inevitably, some aspects of this volume seem a little dated, because of either scientific advances or cultural changes. In an age of genetically modified crops, he could not be quite so confident in claiming that 'no synthetic seed would ever grow' (6:11). Nor would he need to be so defensive about the fact that the Magi were apparently astrologers. He never quite knew what to make of anything mystical, and so we find him happily explaining 8:5–13 in terms of extra-sensory perception, while struggling to comprehend ancient beliefs in spiritual forces (8:28–34). In today's world of 'New Age' spirituality, Christian apologists find they have to engage with such matters more robustly, and perhaps this is one of the few topics on which Barclay remains very definitely a person of his time.

John Drane
University of Aberdeen
2001

INTRODUCTION TO
THE GOSPEL OF MATTHEW

The Synoptic Gospels

Matthew, Mark and Luke are usually known as the *synoptic gospels*. *Synoptic* comes from two Greek words which mean *to see together*, and literally means *able to be seen together*. The reason for that name is this. These three gospels each give an account of the same events in Jesus' life. There are in each of them additions and omissions; but broadly speaking their material is the same and their arrangement is the same. It is therefore possible to set them down in parallel columns, and so to compare the one with the other.

When that is done, it is quite clear that there is the closest possible relationship between them. If, for instance, we compare the story of the feeding of the 5,000 (Matthew 14:12–21; Mark 6:30–44; Luke 9:10–17), we find exactly the same story told in almost exactly the same words.

Another instance is the story of the healing of the man who was sick with the palsy (Matthew 9:1–8; Mark 2:1–12; Luke 5:17–26). These three accounts are so similar that even a small explanatory remark – 'he then said to the paralytic' – occurs in all three as an explanation in exactly the same place. The correspondence between the three gospels is so close that we are bound to come to the conclusion either that all three are drawing their material from a common source, or that two of them must be based on the third.

The Earliest Gospel

When we examine the matter more closely, we see that there is every reason for believing that Mark must have been the first of the gospels to be written, and that the other two, Matthew and Luke, are using Mark as a basis.

Mark can be divided into 105 sections. Of these sections, 93 occur in Matthew and 81 in Luke. Of Mark's 105 sections, there are only four which do not occur either in Matthew or in Luke.

Mark has 661 verses; Matthew has 1,068 verses; Luke has 1,149 verses. Matthew reproduces no fewer than 606 of Mark's verses, and Luke reproduces 320. Of the 55 verses of Mark which Matthew does not reproduce, Luke reproduces 31; so there are only 24 verses in the whole of Mark which are not reproduced somewhere in Matthew or Luke.

It is not only the substance of the verses which is reproduced; the very words are reproduced. Matthew uses 51 per cent of Mark's words; and Luke uses 53 per cent.

Both Matthew and Luke as a general rule follow Mark's order of events. Occasionally either Matthew or Luke differs from Mark; but they never *both* differ against him; always at least one of them follows Mark's order.

Improvements on Mark

Since Matthew and Luke are both much longer than Mark, it might just possibly be suggested that Mark is a summary of Matthew and Luke; but there is one other set of facts which shows that Mark is earlier. It is the custom of Matthew and Luke to improve and to polish Mark, if we may put it in such a way. Let us take some instances.

Sometimes Mark seems to limit the power of Jesus; at least, an ill-disposed critic might try to prove that he was doing so. Here are three accounts of the same incident:

> Mark 1:34: And he cured *many* who were sick with various diseases, and cast out *many* demons;
>
> Matthew 8:16: And he cast out the spirits with a word, and cured *all* who were sick;
>
> Luke 4:40: And he laid his hands on *each* of them and cured them.

Let us take three other similar examples:

> Mark 3:10: For he had cured *many*;
>
> Matthew 12:15: And he cured *all* of them;
>
> Luke 6:19: And healed *all* of them.

Matthew and Luke both change Mark's *many* into *all* so that there may be no suggestion of any limitation of the power of Jesus Christ.

There is a very similar change in the account of the events of Jesus' visit to Nazareth. Let us compare the account of Mark and of Matthew.

> Mark 6:5–6: And *he could do* no deed of power there ... and he was amazed at their unbelief;
>
> Matthew 13:58: And *he did not do* many deeds of power there, because of their unbelief.

Matthew shrinks from saying that Jesus *could not* do any deeds of power, and changes the form of the expression accordingly.

Sometimes Matthew and Luke leave out little touches in Mark in case they could be taken to belittle Jesus. Matthew and Luke omit three statements in Mark:

> Mark 3:5: He looked around at them with anger, he
> was grieved at their hardness of heart;
>
> Mark 3:21: And when his family heard it, they went
> out to restrain him for people were saying, '*He
> has gone out of his mind*';
>
> Mark 10:14: He was indignant.

Matthew and Luke hesitate to attribute human emotions of anger and grief to Jesus, and shudder to think that anyone should even have suggested that Jesus was mad.

Sometimes Matthew and Luke slightly alter things in Mark to get rid of statements which might seem to show the apostles in a bad light. We take but one instance, from the occasion on which James and John sought to ensure themselves of the highest places in the coming kingdom. Let us compare the introduction to that story in Mark and in Matthew:

> Mark 10:35: *James and John*, the sons of Zebedee, came
> forward to him, and said to him . . .;
>
> Matthew 20:20: Then the mother of the sons of Zebedee
> came to him with her sons, and kneeling before
> him, she asked a favour of him.

Matthew hesitates to ascribe motives of ambition directly to the two apostles, and so he ascribes them to their mother.

All this makes it clear that Mark is the earliest of the gospels. Mark gives a simple, vivid, direct narrative; but Matthew and Luke have already begun to be affected by doctrinal and theological considerations which make them much more careful of what they say.

The Teaching of Jesus

We have seen that Matthew has 1,068 verses; and that Luke has 1,149 verses; and that between them they reproduce 582 of Mark's 661 verses. That means that in Matthew and Luke there is much more material than Mark supplies. When we examine that material, we find that more than 200 verses of it are almost identical. For instance, such passages as Luke 6:41–2 and Matthew 7:3, 5; Luke 10:21–2 and Matthew 11:25–7; Luke 3:7–9 and Matthew 3:7–10 are almost exactly the same.

But here we notice a difference. The material which Matthew and Luke drew from Mark was almost entirely material dealing with the events of Jesus' life; but these 200 additional verses common to Matthew and Luke tell us not what Jesus *did*, but what Jesus *said*. Clearly in these verses Matthew and Luke are drawing from *a common source book of the sayings of Jesus*.

That book does not now exist; but to it scholars have given the letter Q which stands for *Quelle*, which is the German word for *source*. In its day it must have been an extraordinarily important book, for it was the first handbook of the teaching of Jesus.

Matthew's Place in the Gospel Tradition

It is here that we come to Matthew the apostle. Scholars are agreed that the first gospel as it stands does not come directly from the hand of Matthew. One who had himself been an eyewitness of the life of Christ would not have needed to use Mark as a source book for the life of Jesus in the way Matthew does. But one of the earliest Church historians, a man called Papias, gives us this intensely important piece of information: 'Matthew collected the sayings of Jesus in the Hebrew tongue.'

So, we can believe that it was none other than Matthew who wrote that book which was the source from which everyone who wished to know what Jesus taught must draw. And it was because so much of that source book is incorporated in the first gospel that Matthew's name was attached to it. We must be forever grateful to Matthew, when we remember that it is to him that we owe the Sermon on the Mount and nearly all we know about the teaching of Jesus. Broadly speaking, to Mark we owe our knowledge of the *events* of Jesus' life; to Matthew we owe our knowledge of the substance of Jesus' *teaching*.

Matthew the Tax-gatherer

About Matthew himself we know very little. We read of his call in Matthew 9:9. We know that he was a tax-gatherer and that he must therefore have been a bitterly hated man, for the Jews hated the members of their own race who had entered the civil service of their conquerors. Matthew would be regarded as nothing better than a collaborator.

But there was one gift which Matthew would possess. Most of the disciples were fishermen. They would have little skill and little practice in putting words together and writing them down; but Matthew would be an expert in that. When Jesus called Matthew, as he sat in the office where he collected the customs duty, Matthew rose up and followed him and left everything behind him except one thing – his pen. And Matthew nobly used his literary skill to become the first man ever to compile an account of the teaching of Jesus.

The Gospel of the Jews

Let us now look at the chief characteristics of Matthew's gospel so that we may watch for them as we read it.

First and foremost, Matthew *is the gospel which was written for the Jews*. It was written by a Jew in order to convince Jews.

One of the great objects of Matthew is to demonstrate that all the prophecies of the Old Testament are fulfilled in Jesus, and that, therefore, he must be the Messiah. It has one phrase which runs through it like an ever-recurring theme: 'This was to fulfil what the Lord had spoken by the prophet.' That phrase occurs in the gospel as often as sixteen times. Jesus' birth and Jesus' name are the fulfilment of prophecy (1:21–3); so are the flight to Egypt (2:14–15); the slaughter of the children (2:16–18); Joseph's settlement in Nazareth and Jesus' upbringing there (2:23); Jesus' use of parables (3:34–5); the triumphal entry (21:3–5); the betrayal for thirty pieces of silver (27:9); and the casting of lots for Jesus' garments as he hung on the cross (27:35). It is Matthew's primary and deliberate purpose to show how the Old Testament prophecies received their fulfilment in Jesus; how every detail of Jesus' life was foreshadowed in the prophets; and thus to compel the Jews to admit that Jesus was the Messiah.

The main interest of Matthew is in the Jews. Their conversion is especially near and dear to the heart of its writer. When the Syro-Phoenician woman seeks his help, Jesus' first answer is: 'I was sent only to the lost sheep of the house of Israel' (15:24). When Jesus sends out the Twelve on the task of evangelization, his instruction is: 'Go nowhere among the Gentiles, and enter no town of the Samaritans, but go rather to the lost sheep of the house of Israel' (10:5–6). Yet it is not to be thought that this gospel by any means excludes the Gentiles. Many are to come from the east and the west to sit down in the kingdom of God (8:11). The gospel is to be preached to the whole world (24:14). And it is Matthew which gives us the marching orders of the Church: 'Go therefore and make disciples of all nations' (28:19). It is clear that Matthew's first interest is in the Jews, but that it foresees the day when all nations will be gathered in.

The Jewishness of Matthew is also seen in its attitude to the law. Jesus came not to destroy, but to fulfil the law. The least part of the law will not pass away. People must not be taught to break the law. The righteousness of the Christian must exceed the righteousness of the scribes and Pharisees (5:17–20). Matthew was written by one who knew and loved the law and who saw that even the law has its place in Christian life.

Once again there is an apparent paradox in the attitude of Matthew to the scribes and Pharisees. They are given a very special authority: 'The scribes and the Pharisees sit on Moses' seat; therefore, do whatever they teach you and follow it' (23:2). But at the same time there is no gospel which so sternly and consistently condemns them.

Right at the beginning, there is John the Baptist's savage denunciation of them as a brood of vipers (3:7–12). They complain that Jesus eats with tax-collectors and sinners (9:11). They ascribe the power of Jesus, not to God, but to the prince of devils (12:24). They plot to destroy him (12:14). The disciples are warned against the leaven, the evil teaching, of the scribes and Pharisees (16:12). They are like evil plants doomed to be rooted up (15:13). They are quite unable to read the signs of the times (16:3). They are the murderers of the prophets (21:41). There is no chapter of condemnation in the whole New Testament like Matthew 23, which is condemnation not of what the scribes and the Pharisees teach, but of what they are. He condemns them for falling so far short of their own teaching, and far below the ideal of what they ought to be.

There are certain other special interests in Matthew. Matthew *is especially interested in the Church*. It is in fact the only one of the synoptic gospels which uses the word Church at all. Only Matthew introduces the passage about the Church after Peter's confession at Caesarea Philippi (Matthew 16:13–23; cf. Mark 8:27–33; Luke 9:18–22). Only Matthew says that disputes are to be settled by the Church (18:17). By the time Matthew came to be written, the Church had become a great organization and institution, and indeed the dominant factor in the life of the Christian.

Matthew *has a specially strong apocalyptic interest.* That is to say, Matthew has a specially strong interest in all that Jesus said about his own second coming, about the end of the world, and about the judgment. Matthew 24 gives us a fuller account of Jesus' apocalyptic discourse than any of the other gospels. Matthew alone has the parables of the talents (25:14–30), the wise and the foolish virgins (25:1–13), and the sheep and the goats (25:31–46). Matthew has a special interest in the last things and in judgment.

But we have not yet come to the greatest of all the characteristics of Matthew. *It is supremely the teaching gospel.*

We have already seen that the apostle Matthew was responsible for the first collection and the first handbook of the teaching of Jesus. Matthew was the great systematizer. It was his habit to gather together in one place all that he knew about the teaching of Jesus on any given subject. The result is that in Matthew we find five great blocks in which the teaching of Jesus is collected and systematized. All these sections have to do with the kingdom of God. They are as follows:

(a) The Sermon on the Mount, or the law of the kingdom (5–7).

(b) The duties of the leaders of the kingdom (10).

(c) The parables of the kingdom (13).

(d) Greatness and forgiveness in the kingdom (18).

(e) The coming of the King (24–5).

Matthew does more than collect and systematize. It must be remembered that Matthew was writing in an age when printing had not been invented, when books were few and far between because they had to be handwritten. In an age like that, comparatively few people could possess a book; and, therefore, if they wished to know and to use the teaching and the story of Jesus, they had to carry them in their memories.

Matthew therefore always arranges things in a way that is easy for the reader to memorize. He arranges things in threes and sevens. There are three messages to Joseph; three denials of Peter; three questions of Pilate; seven parables of the kingdom in chapter 13; and seven woes to the scribes and Pharisees in chapter 23.

The genealogy of Jesus with which the gospel begins is a good example of this. The genealogy is to prove that Jesus is the Son of David. In Hebrew there are no figures; when figures are necessary, the letters of the alphabet stand for the figures. In Hebrew there are no written vowels. The Hebrew letters for David are DWD; if these letters are taken as figures and not as letters, they add up to fourteen; and the genealogy consists of three groups of names, and in each group there are fourteen names. Matthew does everything possible to arrange the teaching of Jesus in such a way that people will be able to assimilate and to remember it.

Every teacher owes a debt of gratitude to Matthew, for Matthew wrote what is above all the teacher's gospel.

Matthew has one final characteristic. Matthew's *dominating idea is that of Jesus as King*. He writes to demonstrate the royalty of Jesus.

Right at the beginning, the genealogy is to prove that Jesus is the Son of David (1:1–17). The title, Son of David, is used more often in Matthew than in any other gospel (15:22,

21:9, 21:15). The wise men come looking for him who is King of the Jews (2:2). The triumphal entry is a deliberately dramatized claim to be King (21:1–11). Before Pilate, Jesus deliberately accepts the name of King (27:11). Even on the cross, the title of King is affixed, even if it is in mockery, over his head (27:37). In the Sermon on the Mount, Matthew shows us Jesus quoting the law and five times abrogating it with a regal: 'But I say to you . . .' (5:22, 28, 34, 39, 44). The final claim of Jesus is: 'All authority . . . has been given to me' (28:18).

Matthew's picture of Jesus is of the man born to be King. Jesus walks through his pages as if in the purple and gold of royalty.

MATTHEW

THE LINEAGE OF THE KING

Matthew 1:1–17

This is the record of the lineage of Jesus Christ, the Son of David, the son of Abraham.

Abraham begat Isaac, and Isaac begat Jacob. Jacob begat Judah and his brothers. Judah begat Phares and Zara, whose mother was Thamar. Phares begat Esrom. Esrom begat Aram. Aram begat Aminadab. Aminadab begat Naasson. Naasson begat Salmon. Salmon begat Booz, whose mother was Rachab. Booz begat Obed, whose mother was Ruth. Obed begat Jesse. Jesse begat David, the king.

David begat Solomon, whose mother was Uriah's wife. Solomon begat Roboam. Roboam begat Abia. Abia begat Asaph. Asaph begat Josaphat. Josaphat begat Joram. Joram begat Ozias. Ozias begat Joatham. Joatham begat Achaz. Achaz begat Ezekias. Ezekias begat Manasses. Manasses begat Amos. Amos begat Josias. Josias begat Jechonias, and his brothers, in the days when the exile to Babylon took place.

After the exile to Babylon Jechonias begat Salathiel. Salathiel begat Zorobabel. Zorobabel begat Abioud. Abioud begat Eliakim. Eliakim begat Azor. Azor begat Zadok. Zadok begat Acheim. Acheim begat Elioud. Elioud begat Eleazar. Eleazar begat Matthan. Matthan begat Jacob. Jacob begat Joseph, the husband of Mary, who was the mother of Jesus, who is called Christ.

From Abraham to David there were in all fourteen generations. From David to the exile to Babylon there were also fourteen generations. From the exile to Babylon to the coming of Christ there were also fourteen generations.

It might seem to a modern reader that Matthew chose an extraordinary way in which to begin his gospel; and it might seem daunting to present right at the beginning a long list of names to wade through. But to a Jew this was the most natural, and the most interesting, and indeed the most essential way to begin the story of any man's life.

The Jews were exceedingly interested in genealogies. Matthew calls this *the book of the generation (biblos geneseōs)* of Jesus Christ. That to the Jews was a common phrase; and it means the record of a man's lineage, with a few explanatory sentences, where such comment was necessary. In the Old Testament, we frequently find lists of the *generations* of famous men (Genesis 5:1, 10:1, 11:10, 11:27). When Josephus, the great Jewish historian, wrote his own autobiography, he began it with his own pedigree, which, he tells us, he found in the public records.

The reason for this interest in pedigrees was that the Jews set the greatest possible store on purity of lineage. If in any man there was the slightest element of foreign blood, he lost his right to be called a Jew and a member of the people of God. A priest, for instance, was bound to produce an unbroken record of his pedigree stretching back to Aaron; and, if he married, the woman he married must produce her pedigree for at least five generations back. When Ezra was reorganizing the worship of God after the people returned from exile, and was setting the priesthood to function again, the children of

Habaiah, the children of Koz and the children of Barzillai were debarred from office and were labelled as polluted because 'These looked for their entries in the genealogical records, but they were not found there' (Ezra 2:62).

These genealogical records were actually kept by the Sanhedrin. Herod the Great was always despised by the pure-blooded Jews because he was half-Edomite; and we can see the importance that even Herod attached to these genealogies from the fact that he had the official registers destroyed, so that no one could prove a purer pedigree than his own. This may seem to us an uninteresting passage, but to a Jew it would be a most impressive matter that the pedigree of Jesus could be traced back to Abraham.

It is further to be noted that this pedigree is most carefully arranged. It is arranged in three groups of fourteen people each. It is in fact what is technically known as a mnemonic, that is to say a thing so arranged that it is easy to memorize. It is always to be remembered that the gospels were written hundreds of years before there was any such thing as a printed book. Very few people would be able to own actual copies of them; and so, if they wished to possess them, they would be compelled to memorize them. This pedigree, therefore, is arranged in such a way that it is easy to memorize. It is meant to prove that Jesus was the Son of David, and is so arranged as to make it easy for people to carry it in their memories.

THE THREE STAGES

Matthew 1:1–17 (contd)

THERE is something symbolic of the whole of human life in the way in which this pedigree is arranged. It is arranged in three sections, and the three sections are based on three great stages in Jewish history.

The first section takes the history down to David. David was the man who welded Israel into a nation and made the Jews a power in the world. The first section takes the story down to the rise of Israel's greatest king.

The second section takes the story down to the exile to Babylon. It is the section which tells of the nation's shame, tragedy and disaster.

The third section takes the story down to Jesus Christ. Jesus Christ was the person who liberated men and women from their slavery, who rescued them from their disaster, and in whom the tragedy was turned into triumph.

These three sections stand for three stages in the spiritual history of the world.

(1) *Human beings were born for greatness*. God created them in his own image (cf. Genesis 1:27). As the Revised Standard Version has it, God said: 'Let us make man in our image, after our likeness' (Genesis 1:26). Human beings were created in the image of God. God's dream for them was a dream of greatness. They were designed for fellowship with God; created that they might be nothing less than kin to God. As Cicero, the Roman thinker, saw it, 'The only difference between man and God is in point of time.' Human destiny was for greatness.

(2) *Human beings lost their greatness*. Instead of being the servants of God, they became slaves of sin. As the writer G. K. Chesterton said, 'whatever else is true of man, man is not what he was meant to be'. Men and women used their free will to defy and to disobey God, rather than to enter into friendship and fellowship with him. Left to themselves, they had frustrated the design and plan of God in his creation.

(3) *Human beings can regain their greatness*. Even then, God did not abandon men and women to themselves and to their own devices. God did not allow them to be destroyed by their own folly. The end of the story was not left to be tragedy. Into this world God sent his Son, Jesus Christ, that he might rescue men and women from the morass of sin in which they had lost themselves, and liberate them from the chains of sin with which they had bound themselves so that through him they might regain the fellowship with God which they had lost.

In his genealogy, Matthew shows us the royalty of kingship gained; the tragedy of freedom lost; the glory of liberty restored. And that, in the mercy of God, is the story of all humanity, and of every individual.

THE REALIZATION OF PEOPLE'S DREAMS

Matthew 1:1–17 (*contd*)

THIS passage stresses two special things about Jesus.

(1) It stresses the fact that he was the Son of David. It was, indeed, mainly to prove this that the genealogy was composed. The New Testament stresses this again and again.

Peter states it in the first recorded sermon of the Christian Church (Acts 2:29–36). Paul speaks of Jesus Christ descended from David according to the flesh (Romans 1:3). The writer of the Pastoral Epistles urges people to remember that Jesus Christ, descended from David, was raised from the dead (2 Timothy 2:8). The writer of the Revelation hears the risen Christ say: 'I am the root and the descendant of David' (Revelation 22:16).

Repeatedly, Jesus is addressed in this way in the gospel story. After the healing of the blind and dumb man, the people

exclaim: 'Can this be the Son of David?' (Matthew 12:23).
The woman of Tyre and Sidon, who wished for Jesus' help
for her daughter, calls him 'Son of David' (Matthew 15:22).
The blind men cry out to Jesus as Son of David (Matthew
20:30–1). It is as Son of David that the crowds greet Jesus when
he enters Jerusalem for the last time (Matthew 21:9, 15).

There is something of great significance here. It is clear
that it was the crowd, the ordinary men and women, who
addressed Jesus as Son of David. The Jews were a waiting
people. They never forgot, and never could forget, that they
were the chosen people of God. Although their history was
one long series of disasters, although at this very time they
were a subject people, they never forgot their destiny. And it
was their dream that into this world would come a descendant
of David who would lead them to the glory which they
believed to be theirs by right.

That is to say, Jesus is the answer to the dreams of men
and women. It is true that so often people do not see it so.
They see the answer to their dreams in power, in wealth, in
material plenty, and in the realization of the ambitions which
they cherish. But if ever their dreams of peace and loveliness,
and greatness and satisfaction, are to be realized, they can
find their realization only in Jesus Christ.

Jesus Christ and the life he offers is the answer to the
dreams of men and women. In the old Joseph story, there is a
text which goes far beyond the story itself. When Joseph was
in prison, Pharaoh's chief butler and chief baker were
prisoners along with him. They had their dreams, and their
dreams troubled them, and their bewildered cry is: 'We have
had dreams, and there is no one to interpret them' (Genesis
40:8). Because we are human, because we are children of
eternity, we are always haunted by our dreams; and the only
way to their realization lies in Jesus Christ.

(2) This passage also stresses that Jesus was the fulfilment of prophecy. In him, the message of the prophets came true. We tend nowadays to make very little of prophecy. We are not really interested, for the most part, in searching for sayings in the Old Testament which are fulfilled in the New Testament. But prophecy does contain this great and eternal truth: that in this universe there is purpose and design and that God is meaning and willing certain things to happen.

In Gerald Healy's play *The Black Stranger*, there is a telling scene. The setting is in Ireland, in the terrible days of famine in the mid-nineteenth century. For want of something better to do, and for lack of some other solution, the government had set men to digging roads to no purpose and to no destination. Michael finds out about this and comes home one day, and says in poignant wonder to his father: 'They're makin' roads that lead to nowhere.'

If we believe in prophecy, that is what we can never say. History can never be a road that leads to nowhere. We may not use prophecy in the same way as our ancestors did, but at the back of the fact of prophecy lies the eternal fact that life and the world are not on the way to nowhere, but on the way to the goal of God.

NOT THE RIGHTEOUS, BUT SINNERS

Matthew 1:1-17 (*contd*)

BY far the most amazing thing about this pedigree is the names of the women who appear in it.

It is not normal to find the names of women in Jewish pedigrees at all. Women had no legal rights; a woman was regarded not as a person, but as a thing. She was merely the possession of her father or of her husband, and therefore his to do with as he liked. In the regular form of morning prayer, the Jew thanked God that he had not made him a Gentile, a slave or a woman. The very existence of these names in any pedigree at all is a most surprising and extraordinary phenomenon.

But when we look at who these women were, and at what they did, the matter becomes even more amazing. Rachab, or as the Old Testament calls her, Rahab, was a harlot of Jericho (Joshua 2:1–7). Ruth was not even a Jewess; she was a Moabitess (Ruth 1:4); and does not the law itself lay it down, 'No Ammonite or Moabite shall be admitted to the assembly of the Lord. Even to the tenth generation, none of their descendants shall enter the assembly of the Lord' (Deuteronomy 23:3)? Ruth belonged to an alien and a hated people. Tamar was a deliberate seducer and an adulteress (Genesis 38). Bathsheba, the mother of Solomon, was the woman whom David seduced from Uriah, her husband, with an unforgivable cruelty (2 Samuel 11 and 12). If Matthew had ransacked the pages of the Old Testament for improbable candidates, he could not have discovered four more incredible ancestors for Jesus Christ. But, surely, there is something very lovely in this. Here, at the very beginning, Matthew shows us in symbol the essence of the gospel of God in Jesus Christ, for here he shows us the barriers going down.

(1) *The barrier between Jew and Gentile is down.* Rahab, the woman of Jericho, and Ruth, the woman of Moab, find their place within the pedigree of Jesus Christ. Already the great truth is there that in Christ there is neither Jew nor Greek. Here, at the very beginning, there is the universalism of the gospel and of the love of God.

(2) *The barriers between male and female are down.* In no ordinary pedigree would the name of any woman be found;

but such names are found in Jesus' pedigree. The old contempt is gone; and men and women stand equally dear to God, and equally important to his purposes.

(3) *The barrier between saint and sinner is down.* Somehow God can use for his purposes, and fit into his scheme of things, those who have sinned greatly. 'I have come', said Jesus, 'to call not the righteous, but sinners' (Matthew 9:13).

Here at the very beginning of the gospel, we are given a hint of the all-embracing width of the love of God. God can find his servants among those from whom the respectable orthodox would shrink away in horror.

THE SAVIOUR'S ENTRY INTO THE WORLD

Matthew 1:18–25

> The birth of Jesus Christ happened in this way. Mary, his mother, was betrothed to Joseph, and, before they became man and wife, it was discovered that she was carrying a child in her womb through the action of the Holy Spirit. Although Joseph, her husband, was a man who kept the law, he did not wish publicly to humiliate her, so he wished to divorce her secretly. When he was planning this, behold, an angel of the Lord came to him in a dream. 'Joseph, Son of David,' said the angel, 'do not hesitate to take Mary as your wife; for that which has been begotten within her has come from the Holy Spirit. She will bear a son, and you must call his name Jesus, for it is he who will save his people from their sins. All this has happened that there might be fulfilled that which was spoken by the Lord through the prophet, "Behold, the maiden will conceive and bear a son, and you must call his name Emmanuel, which is translated: God with us."' So Joseph woke from his sleep, and did

as the angel of the Lord had commanded him; and he
accepted his wife; and he did not know her until she
had borne a son; and he called his name Jesus.

To our western ways of thinking, the relationships in this
passage are very bewildering. First, Joseph is said to be
betrothed to Mary; then he is said to be planning quietly to
divorce her; and then she is called his *wife*. But the relationships represent normal Jewish marriage procedure, in which
there were three steps.

(1) There was the *engagement*. The engagement was often
made when the couple were only children. It was usually
made through the parents, or through a professional matchmaker. And it was often made without the couple involved
ever having seen each other. Marriage was held to be far too
serious a step to be left to the dictates of the human heart.

(2) There was the *betrothal*. The betrothal was what we
might call the ratification of the engagement into which the
couple had previously entered. At this point the engagement,
entered into by the parents or the matchmaker, could be
broken if the girl was unwilling to go on with it. But once the
betrothal was entered into, it was absolutely binding. It lasted
for one year. During that year, the couple were known as
husband and wife, although they had not the rights of husband
and wife. It could not be terminated in any other way than by
divorce. In the Jewish law, we frequently find what is to us a
curious phrase. A girl whose fiancé had died during the year
of betrothal is called 'a virgin who is a widow'. It was at this
stage that Joseph and Mary were. They were betrothed; and
if Joseph wished to end the betrothal, he could do so in no
other way than by divorce; and in that year of betrothal, Mary
was legally known as his wife.

(3) The third stage was *the marriage proper*, which took
place at the end of the year of betrothal.

If we remember the normal Jewish wedding customs, then the relationships in this passage are perfectly usual and perfectly clear.

So at this stage it was told to Joseph that Mary was to bear a child, that that child had been begotten by the Holy Spirit, and that he must call the child by the name Jesus. *Jesus* is the Greek form of the Jewish name *Joshua*, and *Joshua* means *Yahweh is salvation*. Long ago, the psalmist had heard God say: 'It is he who will redeem Israel from all its iniquities' (Psalm 130:8). And Joseph was told that the child to be born would grow into the Saviour who would save God's people from their sins. Jesus was not so much the Man born to be King as the Man born to be Saviour. He came to this world, not for his own sake, but for us and for our salvation.

BORN OF THE HOLY SPIRIT

Matthew 1:18–25 (*contd*)

THIS passage tells us how Jesus was born by the action of the Holy Spirit. It tells us of what we call the virgin birth. This is a doctrine which presents us with many difficulties; and we are not compelled to accept it in the literal and the physical sense. This is one of the doctrines on which the Church says that we have full liberty to come to our own conclusion. At the moment, we are concerned only to find out what this means for us.

If we come to this passage with fresh eyes, and read it as if we were reading it for the first time, we will find that what it stresses is not so much that Jesus was born of a woman who was a virgin, as that the birth of Jesus is the work of the Holy Spirit. Mary 'was found to be with child from the Holy Spirit'. 'The child conceived in her is from the Holy Spirit.' It is as if these sentences were underlined, and printed large. That is what Matthew wishes to say to us in this passage. What then does it mean to say that in the birth of Jesus the Holy Spirit of God was specially operative? Let us leave aside all the doubtful and debatable things, and concentrate on that great truth, as Matthew would wish us to do.

In Jewish thought, the Holy Spirit had certain very definite functions. We cannot bring to this passage the *Christian* idea of Holy Spirit in all its fullness, because Joseph would know nothing about that. We must interpret it in the light of the *Jewish* idea of the Holy Spirit, for it is that idea that Joseph would inevitably bring to this message, for that was all he knew.

(1) According to the Jewish idea, *the Holy Spirit was the person who brought God's truth to men and women*. It was the Holy Spirit who taught the prophets what to say; it was the Holy Spirit who taught people of God what to do; it was the Holy Spirit who, throughout the ages and the generations, brought God's truth to men and women. So, Jesus is the one person who brings God's truth to them.

Let us put it in another way. Jesus is the one person who can tell us what God is like and what God means us to be. In him alone, we see what God is and what we ought to be. Before Jesus came, people had only vague and shadowy, and often quite wrong, ideas about God; they could only at best guess and grope; but Jesus could say: 'Whoever has seen me has seen the Father' (John 14:9). In Jesus we see the love, the compassion, the mercy, the seeking heart and the purity of God as nowhere else in all this world. With the coming of Jesus, the time of guessing is gone and the time of certainty is come. Before Jesus came, people did not really know what goodness was. In Jesus alone, we see true humanity, true goodness and true obedience to the will of God. Jesus came to tell us the truth about God and the truth about ourselves.

(2) The Jews believed that the Holy Spirit not only brought God's truth to men and women, but also *enabled them to recognize that truth when they saw it*. So Jesus opens people's eyes to the truth. We are often blinded by our own ignorance; we are led astray by our own prejudices; our minds and eyes are darkened by our own sins and our own passions. Jesus can open our eyes until we are able to see the truth.

In one of William J. Locke's novels, there is a picture of a woman who has any amount of money, and who has spent half a lifetime on a tour of the sights and art galleries of the world. She is weary and bored. Then she meets a Frenchman who has little of this world's goods, but who has a wide knowledge and a great love of beauty. He comes with her, and in his company things are completely different. 'I never knew what things were like,' she said to him, 'until you taught me how to look at them.'

Life is quite different when Jesus teaches us how to look at things. When Jesus comes into our hearts, he opens our eyes to see things truly.

CREATION AND RE-CREATION

Matthew 1:18–25 (*contd*)

(3) The Jews specially *connected the Spirit of God with the work of creation*. It was through his Spirit that God performed his creating work. In the beginning, the Spirit of God moved upon the face of the waters, and chaos became a world (Genesis 1:2). 'By the word of the Lord the heavens were made,' said the psalmist, 'and all their host by the breath of his mouth' (Psalm 33:6). (Both in Hebrew, *ruach*, and in

Greek, *pneuma*, the word for *breath* and *spirit* is the same word.) 'When you send forth your spirit, they are created' (Psalm 104:30). 'The spirit of God has made me,' said Job, 'and the breath of the Almighty gives me life' (Job 33:4).

The Spirit is the Creator of the World and the Giver of Life. So, in Jesus there came into the world God's life-giving and creating power. That power, which reduced the primal chaos to order, came to bring order to our disordered lives. That power, which breathed life where there was no life, has come to breathe life into our weaknesses and frustrations. We could put it this way – we are not really alive until Jesus enters into our lives.

(4) The Jews specially connected the Spirit not only with the work of creation but *with the work of re-creation*. Ezekiel draws his grim picture of the valley of dry bones. He goes on to tell how the dry bones came alive; and then he hears God say: 'I will put my spirit within you, and you shall live' (Ezekiel 37:14). The Rabbis had a saying: 'God said to Israel: "In this world my Spirit has put wisdom in you, but in the future my Spirit will make you to live again."' When people are dead in sin and in lethargy, it is the Spirit of God which can waken them to life anew.

So, in Jesus there came to this world the power which can re-create life. He can bring to life again the soul which is dead in sin; he can revive again the ideals which have died; he can make strong again the will to goodness which has perished. He can renew life when people have lost all that life means.

There is much more in this chapter than the crude fact that Jesus Christ was born of a virgin mother. The essence of Matthew's story is that in the birth of Jesus the Spirit of God was operative as never before in this world. It is the Spirit who brings God's truth to men and women; it is the Spirit who enables them to recognize that truth when they see it; it is the Spirit who was God's agent in the creation of the world; it is the Spirit who alone can re-create the human soul when it has lost the life it ought to have.

Jesus enables us to see what God is and what we ought to be; Jesus opens the eyes of our minds so that we can see the truth of God for us; Jesus is the creating power come among us; Jesus is the re-creating power which can release the souls of men and women from the death of sin.

THE BIRTHPLACE OF THE KING

Matthew 2:1–2

> When Jesus was born in Bethlehem in Judaea, in the days of Herod the king, behold there came to Jerusalem wise men from the east. 'Where', they said, 'is the newly born King of the Jews? For we have seen his star in its rising and we have come to worship him.'

IT was in Bethlehem that Jesus was born. Bethlehem was a small town six miles to the south of Jerusalem. In the past, it had been called Ephrath or Ephratah. The name *Bethlehem* means *the House of Bread*, and Bethlehem stood in fertile countryside, which made its name a fitting name. It stood high up on a grey limestone ridge more than 2,500 feet in height. The ridge had a summit at each end, and a hollow like a saddle between them. So, from its position, Bethlehem looked like a town set in an amphitheatre of hills.

Bethlehem had a long history. It was there that Jacob had buried Rachel and had set up a pillar of memory beside her grave (Genesis 48:7, 35:20). It was there that Ruth had lived when she married Boaz (Ruth 1:22), and from Bethlehem Ruth could see the land of Moab, her native land, across the

Jordan valley. But above all, Bethlehem was the home and the city of David (1 Samuel 16:1, 17:12, 20:6); and it was for the water of the well of Bethlehem that David longed when he was a hunted fugitive upon the hills (2 Samuel 23:14–15).

In later days, we read that Rehoboam fortified the town of Bethlehem (2 Chronicles 11:6). But in the history of Israel, and to the minds of the people, Bethlehem was uniquely the city of David. It was from the line of David that God was to send the great deliverer of his people. As the prophet Micah had it: 'But you, O Bethlehem of Ephrathah, who are one of the little clans of Judah, from you shall come forth for me one who is to rule in Israel, whose origin is from of old, from ancient days' (Micah 5:2).

It was in Bethlehem, David's city, that the Jews expected great David's greater son to be born; it was there that they expected God's Anointed One to come into the world. And it was so.

The picture of the stable and the manger as the birthplace of Jesus is a picture indelibly etched in our minds; but it may well be that that picture is not altogether correct. Justin Martyr, one of the greatest of the early fathers, who lived about AD 150, and who came from the district near Bethlehem, tells us that Jesus was born in a cave near the village of Bethlehem (Justin Martyr, *Dialogue with Trypho*, 78, 304); and it may well be that Justin's information is correct. The houses in Bethlehem are built on the slope of the limestone ridge; and it is very common for them to have a cave-like stable hollowed out in the limestone rock below the house itself; and very likely it was in such a cave-stable that Jesus was born.

To this day, such a cave is shown in Bethlehem as the birthplace of Jesus, and above it the Church of the Nativity has been built. For a very long time, that cave has been shown as the birthplace of Jesus. It was so in the days of the Roman emperor, Hadrian, who, in a deliberate attempt to desecrate the place, erected a shrine to the heathen god Adonis above it. When the Roman Empire became Christian, early in the fourth century, the first Christian emperor, Constantine, built a great church there, and that church, much altered and often restored, still stands.

The travel writer H. V. Morton tells how he visited the Church of the Nativity in Bethlehem. He came to a great wall, and in the wall there was a door so low that he had to stoop to enter it; and through the door, and on the other side of the wall, there was the church. Beneath the high altar of the church is the cave, and when pilgrims descend into it they find a little cavern about fourteen yards long and four yards wide, lit by silver lamps. In the floor there is a star, and round it a Latin inscription: 'Here Jesus Christ was born of the Virgin Mary.'

When the Lord of Glory came to this earth, he was born in a cave where animals were sheltered. The cave in the Church of the Nativity in Bethlehem may be that same cave, or it may not be. That we will never know for certain. But there is something beautiful in the symbolism that the church where the cave is has a door so low that all must stoop to enter. It is supremely fitting that people should approach the infant Jesus upon their knees.

THE HOMAGE OF THE EAST

Matthew 2:1-2 (*contd*)

WHEN Jesus was born in Bethlehem, there came to do him homage wise men from the east. The name given to these men is *Magi*, and that is a word which is difficult to translate.

The Greek historian Herodotus (1:101, 132) has certain information about the Magi. He says that they were originally a Median tribe. The Medes were part of the empire of the Persians. They tried to overthrow the Persians and substitute the power of the Medes. The attempt failed. From that time, the Magi ceased to have any ambitions for power or prestige, and became a tribe of priests. They became in Persia almost exactly what the Levites were in Israel. They became the teachers and instructors of the Persian king. In Persia, no sacrifice could be offered unless one of the Magi was present. They became men of holiness and wisdom.

These Magi were men who were skilled in philosophy, medicine and natural science. They were soothsayers and interpreters of dreams. In later times, the word Magus developed a much lower meaning, and came to mean little more than a fortune-teller, a sorcerer, a magician and a charlatan. Such was Elymas, the sorcerer (Acts 13:6, 8), and Simon who is commonly called Simon Magus (Acts 8:9, 11). But at their best the Magi were good and holy men, who sought for truth.

In those ancient days, everyone believed in astrology. People believed that they could foretell the future from the stars, and they believed that a person's destiny was settled by the star under which he or she was born. It is not difficult to see how that belief arose. The stars pursue their unvarying courses; they represent the order of the universe. If then there suddenly appeared some brilliant star, if the unvarying order of the heavens was broken by some special phenomenon, it did look as if God was breaking into his old order and announcing some special thing.

We do not know what brilliant star those ancient Magi saw. Many suggestions have been made. About 11 BC, Halley's

comet was visible shooting brilliantly across the skies. About
7 BC, there was a brilliant conjunction of Saturn and Jupiter.
In the years 5–2 BC, there was an unusual astronomical
phenomenon. In those years, on the first day of the Egyptian
month Mesori, Sirius, the dog star, rose heliacally, that is at
sunrise, and shone with extraordinary brilliance. Now the
name *Mesori* means *the birth of a prince*, and to those ancient
astrologers such a star would undoubtedly mean the birth of
some great king. We cannot tell what star the Magi saw; but
it was their profession to watch the heavens, and some
heavenly brilliance spoke to them of the entry of a king into
the world.

It may seem to us extraordinary that those men should set
out from the east to find a king; but the strange thing is that,
just about the time Jesus was born, there was in the world a
strange feeling of expectation of the coming of a king. Even
the Roman historians knew about this. Not so very much
later than this, Suetonius could write: 'There had spread over
all the Orient an old and established belief, that it was fated
at that time for men coming from Judaea to rule the world'
(Suetonius, *Life of Vespasian*, 4:5). Tacitus tells of the same
belief that 'there was a firm persuasion . . . that at this very
time the East was to grow powerful, and rulers coming from
Judaea were to acquire universal empire' (Tacitus, *Histories*,
5:13). The Jews had the belief that 'about that time one from
their country should become governor of the habitable earth'
(Josephus, *The Jewish Wars*, 6:5, 4). At a slightly later time,
we find Tiridates, King of Armenia, visiting Nero at Rome
with his Magi along with him (Suetonius, *Life of Nero*, 13:1).
We find the Magi in Athens sacrificing to the memory of
Plato (Seneca, *Epistles*, 58:31). Almost at the same time as
Jesus was born, we find Augustus, the Roman emperor, being
hailed as the Saviour of the world, and Virgil, the Roman

poet, writing his Fourth Eclogue, which is known as the Messianic Eclogue, about the golden days to come.

There is not the slightest need to think that the story of the coming of the Magi to the cradle of Christ is only a lovely legend. It is exactly the kind of thing that could easily have happened in that ancient world. When Jesus Christ came, the world was in an eagerness of expectation. Men and women were waiting for God, and the desire for God was in their hearts. They had discovered that they could not build the golden age without God. It was to a waiting world that Jesus came; and, when he came, the ends of the earth were gathered at his cradle. It was the first sign and symbol of the world conquest of Christ.

THE CRAFTY KING

Matthew 2:3–9

> When Herod the king heard of this he was disturbed, and so was all Jerusalem with him. So he collected all the chief priests and scribes of the people, and asked them where the Anointed One of God was to be born. They said to him, 'In Bethlehem in Judaea. For so it stands written through the prophets, "And you Bethlehem, land of Judah, are by no means the least among the leaders of Judah. For there shall come forth from you the leader, who will be a shepherd to my people Israel."' Then Herod secretly summoned the wise men, and carefully questioned them about the time when the star appeared. He sent them to Bethlehem. 'Go,' he said, 'and make every effort to find out about the little child. And, when you have found him, send news to me, that I too, may come and worship him.' When they had listened to the king they went on their way.

IT came to the ears of Herod that the wise men had come
from the east, and that they were searching for the little
child who had been born to be King of the Jews. Any king
would have been worried at the report that a child had been
born who was to occupy his throne. But Herod was doubly
disturbed.

Herod was half-Jew and half-Idumaean. There was
Edomite blood in his veins. He had made himself useful to
the Romans in the wars and civil wars of Palestine, and they
trusted him. He had been appointed governor in 47 BC; in 40
BC he had received the title of king; and he was to reign until
4 BC. He had wielded power for a long time. He was called
Herod the Great, and in many ways he deserved the title. He
was the only ruler of Palestine who ever succeeded in keeping
the peace and in bringing order to a situation of disorder. He
was a great builder; he was indeed the builder of the Temple
in Jerusalem. He could be generous. In times of difficulty he
cancelled the taxes to make things easier for the people; and
in the famine of 25 BC he had actually melted down his own
gold plate to buy corn for the starving people.

But Herod had one terrible flaw in his character. He was
almost insanely suspicious. He had always been suspicious,
and the older he became the more suspicious he grew, until,
in his old age, he was, as someone said, 'a murderous old
man'. If he suspected anyone as a rival to his power, that
person was promptly eliminated. He murdered his wife
Mariamne and her mother Alexandra. His eldest son,
Antipater, and two other sons, Alexander and Aristobulus,
were all assassinated by him. Augustus, the Roman emperor,
had said, bitterly, that it was safer to be Herod's pig than
Herod's son. (The saying is even more epigrammatic in
Greek, for in Greek *hus* is the word for a *pig*, and *huios* is the
word for a *son*.)

Something of Herod's savage, bitter, warped nature can be seen from the provisions he made when death came near. When he was seventy, he knew that he must die. He retired to Jericho, the loveliest of all his cities. He gave orders that a collection of the most distinguished citizens of Jerusalem should be arrested on trumped-up charges and imprisoned. And he ordered that the moment he died, they should all be killed. He said grimly that he was well aware that no one would mourn for his death, and that he was determined that some tears should be shed when he died.

It is clear how such a man would feel when news reached him that a child was born who was destined to be king. Herod was troubled, and Jerusalem was troubled, too, for Jerusalem knew well the steps that Herod would take to pin down this story and to eliminate this child. Jerusalem knew Herod, and Jerusalem shivered as it waited for his inevitable reaction.

Herod summoned the chief priests and the scribes. The scribes were the experts in Scripture and in the law. The chief priests consisted of two kinds of people. They consisted of ex-high priests. The high priesthood was confined to a very few families. They were the priestly aristocracy, and the members of these select families were called the chief priests. So Herod summoned the religious aristocracy and the theological scholars of his day, and asked them where, according to the Scriptures, the Anointed One of God should be born. They quoted the text in Micah 5:2 to him. Herod sent for the wise men, and despatched them to search diligently for the little child who had been born. He said that he, too, wished to come and worship the child, but his one desire was to murder the child born to be king.

No sooner was Jesus born than we see people grouping themselves into the three groups in which they are always to be found in regard to Jesus Christ. Let us look at the three reactions.

(1) There was the reaction of Herod, *the reaction of hatred and hostility*. Herod was afraid that this little child was going to interfere with his life, his place, his power and his influence, and therefore his first instinct was to destroy him.

There are still those who would gladly destroy Jesus Christ, because they see in him the one who interferes with their lives. They wish to do what they like, and Christ will not let them do what they like; and so they would kill him. People whose one desire is to do what they like never have any use for Jesus Christ. Christians are men and women who have ceased to do what they like, and have dedicated their lives to do as Christ likes.

(2) There was the reaction of the chief priests and scribes, *the reaction of complete indifference*. It did not make the slightest difference to them. They were so engrossed in their Temple ritual and their legal discussions that they completely disregarded Jesus. He meant nothing to them.

There are still those who are so interested in their own affairs that Jesus Christ means nothing to them. The prophet's poignant question can still be asked: 'Is it nothing to you, all you who pass by?' (Lamentations 1:12).

(3) There was the reaction of the wise men, *the reaction of adoring worship*, the desire to lay at the feet of Jesus Christ the noblest gifts which they could bring.

Surely, when we become aware of the love of God in Jesus Christ, we, too, should be lost in wonder, love and praise.

GIFTS FOR CHRIST

Matthew 2:9–12

> And, behold, the star, which they had seen in its rising,
> led them on until it came and stood over the place where

the little child was. When they saw the star, they rejoiced
with exceeding great joy. When they came into the
house, they saw the little child with Mary, his mother,
and they fell down and worshipped him; and they
opened their treasures, and offered to him gifts, gold,
frankincense and myrrh. And because a message from
God came to them in a dream, telling them not to go
back to Herod, they returned to their own country by
another way.

So the wise men found their way to Bethlehem. We need not
think that the star literally moved like a guide across the sky.
There is poetry here, and we must not turn lovely poetry into
crude and lifeless prose. But over Bethlehem the star was
shining. There is a lovely legend which tells how the star, its
work of guidance completed, fell into the well at Bethlehem,
and that it is still there and can still be seen sometimes by
those whose hearts are pure.

Later legends have been busy with the wise men. In the
early days, tradition said that there were twelve of them. But
now the tradition that there were three is almost universal.
The New Testament does not say that there were three, but
the idea that there were three no doubt arose from the
threefold gift which they brought.

Later legend made them kings. And still later legend gave
them names, Caspar, Melchior and Balthasar. Still later legend
assigned to each a personal description, and distinguished
the gift which each of them gave to Jesus. Melchior was
an old man, grey-haired, and with a long beard, and it was
he who brought the gift of gold. Caspar was young and beard-
less, and flushed with youth, and it was he who brought the
gift of frankincense. Balthasar was swarthy, with the beard
newly grown upon him, and it was he who brought the gift of
myrrh.

From very early times, the gifts the wise men brought have been seen as particularly fitting. Each gift has been seen as representing something which specially matched some characteristic of Jesus and his work.

(1) *Gold is the gift of a king.* Seneca, the Roman philosopher, tells us that in Parthia it was the custom that no one could ever approach the king without a gift. And gold, the king of metals, is the fit gift for a king.

So, Jesus was 'the Man born to be King'. But he was to reign not by force but by love; and he was to rule over human hearts, not from a throne, but from a cross.

We do well to remember that Jesus Christ is King. We can never meet Jesus on equal terms. We must always meet him on terms of complete submission. Nelson, the great British admiral, always treated his vanquished opponents with the greatest kindness and courtesy. After one of his naval victories, the defeated admiral was brought aboard Nelson's flagship and on to Nelson's quarterdeck. Knowing Nelson's reputation for courtesy, and thinking to trade upon it, he advanced across the quarterdeck with hand outstretched as if he was advancing to shake hands with an equal. Nelson's hand remained by his side. 'Your sword first,' he said, 'and then your hand.' Before we can be friends with Christ, we must submit to Christ.

(2) *Frankincense is the gift for a priest.* It was in the Temple worship and at the Temple sacrifices that the sweet perfume of frankincense was used. The function of a priest is to open the way to God for men and women. The Latin word for *priest* is *pontifex*, which means a *bridge-builder*. The priest is the one who builds a bridge between human beings and God.

That is what Jesus did. He opened the way to God; he made it possible for us to enter into the very presence of God.

(3) *Myrrh is the gift for one who is to die*. Myrrh was used to embalm the bodies of the dead.

Jesus came into the world to die. Holman Hunt painted a famous picture of Jesus. It shows Jesus at the door of the carpenter's shop in Nazareth. He is still only a boy and has come to the door to stretch his limbs, which have grown cramped over the bench. He stands there in the doorway with arms outstretched, and behind him, on the wall, the setting sun throws his shadow, and it is the shadow of a cross. In the background there stands Mary, and as she sees that shadow there is the fear of coming tragedy in her eyes.

Jesus came into the world to live for men and women, and, in the end, to die for them. He came to give for us his life and his death.

Gold for a king, frankincense for a priest, myrrh for one who was to die – these were the gifts of the wise men, and, even at the cradle of Christ, they foretold that he was to be the true king, the perfect high priest, and in the end the supreme Saviour of the world.

ESCAPE TO EGYPT

Matthew 2:13–15

> When they had gone away, behold, an angel of the Lord appeared in a dream to Joseph. 'Rise,' he said, 'and take the little child and his mother, and flee into Egypt, and stay there until I tell you; for Herod is about to search for the little child, in order to kill him.' So he arose and took the little child and his mother by night and went away into Egypt, and he remained there until the death of Herod. This happened that the word spoken by the Lord through the prophet might be fulfilled: 'Out of Egypt have I called my son.'

THE ancient world had no doubt that God sent his messages to men and women in dreams. So Joseph was warned in a dream to flee into Egypt to escape Herod's murderous intentions. The flight into Egypt was entirely natural. Often, throughout the troubled centuries before Jesus came, when some peril and some tyranny and some persecution made life intolerable for the Jews, they sought refuge in Egypt. The result was that every city in Egypt had its colony of Jews; and in the city of Alexandria there were actually more than 1,000,000 Jews, and certain districts of the city were entirely handed over to them. Joseph in his hour of peril was doing what many Jews had done before; and when Joseph and Mary reached Egypt they would not find themselves altogether among strangers, for in every town and city they would find Jews who had sought refuge there.

It is an interesting fact that, later on, the enemies of Christianity and the enemies of Jesus used the stay in Egypt as a peg to attach their slanders to him. Egypt was proverbially the land of sorcery, of witchcraft and of magic. The *Talmud* says: 'Ten measures of sorcery descended into the world; Egypt received nine, the rest of the world one.' So the enemies of Jesus declared that it was in Egypt that Jesus had learned a magic and a sorcery which made him able to work miracles and to deceive people.

When the pagan philosopher Celsus directed his attack against Christianity in the third century, an attack that Origen met and defeated, he said that Jesus was brought up as an illegitimate child, that he served for hire in Egypt, that he came to the knowledge of certain miraculous powers, and returned to his own country and used these powers to proclaim himself God (Origen, *Contra Celsum*, 1:38). A certain Rabbi, Eliezer ben Hyrcanus, said that Jesus had the necessary magical formulae tattooed upon his body so that he would not forget them. Such were the slanders that twisted minds connected with the flight to Egypt; but they are obviously false, for it was as a little baby that Jesus was taken to Egypt, and it was as a little child that he was brought back.

Two of the loveliest New Testament legends are connected with the flight into Egypt. The first is about the penitent thief. Legend calls the penitent thief Dismas, and tells that he did not meet Jesus for the first time when they both hung on their crosses on Calvary. The story runs like this. When Joseph and Mary were on their way to Egypt, they were waylaid by robbers. One of the robber chiefs wished to murder them at once and to steal their little store of goods. But something about the baby Jesus went straight to Dismas' heart, for Dismas was one of these robbers. He refused to allow any harm to come to Jesus or his parents. He looked at Jesus and said: 'O most blessed of children, if ever there come a time for having mercy on me, then remember me, and forget not this hour.' So, the legend says, Jesus and Dismas met again at Calvary, and Dismas on the cross found forgiveness and mercy for his soul.

The other legend is a child's story, but it is very lovely. When Joseph and Mary and Jesus were on their way to Egypt, the story runs, as the evening came they were weary, and they sought refuge in a cave. It was very cold, so cold that the ground was white with hoar frost. A spider saw the little baby Jesus, and it wished so much that it could do something to keep him warm in the cold night. It decided to do the only thing it could and spin its web across the entrance of the cave, to make, as it were, a curtain there.

Along the path came a detachment of Herod's soldiers, seeking for children to kill to carry out Herod's bloodthirsty order. When they came to the cave, they were about to burst in to search it, but their captain noticed the spider's web, covered with the white hoar frost and stretched right across the entrance to the cave. 'Look', he said, 'at the spider's web there. It is quite unbroken and there cannot possibly be anyone in the cave, for anyone entering would certainly have torn the web.'

So the soldiers passed on, and left the holy family in peace, because a little spider had spun its web across the entrance to the cave. And that, so they say, is why to this day we put tinsel on our Christmas trees, for the glittering tinsel streamers stand for the spider's web, white with the hoar frost, stretched across the entrance of the cave on the way to Egypt. It is a lovely story; and this much, at least, is true, that no gift which Jesus receives is ever forgotten.

The last words of this passage introduce us to a custom which is characteristic of Matthew. He sees in the flight to Egypt a fulfilment of the word spoken by Hosea. He quotes it in the form: 'Out of Egypt I have called my son.' That is a quotation from Hosea 11:1, which reads: 'When Israel was a child, I loved him, and out of Egypt I called my son.'

It can be seen at once that in its original form this saying of Hosea had nothing to do with Jesus, and nothing to do with the flight to Egypt. It was nothing more than a simple statement of how God had delivered the nation of Israel from slavery and from bondage in the land of Egypt.

We shall see, again and again, that this is typical of Matthew's use of the Old Testament. He is prepared to use as a prophecy about Jesus any text at all which can be made verbally to fit, even though originally it had nothing to do with the question in hand, and was never meant to have anything to do with it. Matthew knew that almost the only way to convince the Jews that Jesus was the promised Anointed One of God was to prove that he was the fulfilment of Old Testament prophecy. And in his eagerness to do that, he finds prophecies in the Old Testament where no prophecies were ever meant. When we read a passage like this, we must remember that, though it seems strange and unconvincing to us, it would appeal to those Jews for whom Matthew was writing.

THE SLAUGHTER OF THE CHILDREN

Matthew 2:16–18

> Then Herod saw that he had been tricked by the wise men, and he sent and slew all the children in Bethlehem, and in all the districts near by. He slew every child of two years and under, reckoning from the time when he had made his inquiries from the wise men. Then the word which was spoken through Jeremiah the prophet was fulfilled: 'A voice was heard in Rama, weeping and much lamenting, Rachel weeping for her children, and she refused to be comforted, for they were no more.'

WE have already seen that Herod was a past master in the art of assassination. He had no sooner come to the throne than he began by annihilating the Sanhedrin, the supreme court of the Jews. Later he slaughtered 300 court officers out of hand. Later still he murdered his wife Mariamne, and her mother Alexandra, his eldest son Antipater, and two other sons, Alexander and Aristobulus. And in the hour of his death he arranged for the slaughter of the notable men of Jerusalem.

It was not to be expected that Herod would calmly accept the news that a child had been born who was going to be king. We have read how he had carefully inquired of the wise men when they had seen the star. Even then, he was craftily working out the age of the child so that he might take steps towards murder; and now he put his plans into swift and savage action. He gave orders that every child under two years of age in Bethlehem and the surrounding district should be slaughtered.

There are two things which we must note. First, Bethlehem was not a large town, and the number of the children would not be greater than twenty to thirty babies. We must not think in terms of hundreds. It is true that this does not make Herod's crime any the less terrible, but we must get the picture right.

Second, there are certain critics who hold that this slaughter cannot have taken place because there is no mention of it in any writer outside this one passage of the New Testament. The Jewish historian Josephus, for instance, does not mention it. There are two things to be said. First, as we have just seen, Bethlehem was a comparatively small place, and in a land where murder was so widespread the slaughter of twenty or thirty babies would cause little stir, and would mean very little except to the broken-hearted mothers of Bethlehem. Second, the nineteenth-century historian Thomas Macaulay, in his famous *History of England*, points out that John Evelyn, the well-known seventeenth-century diarist, who was a most assiduous and voluminous recorder of contemporary events, never mentions the massacre of Glencoe. The fact that a thing is not mentioned, even in the places where one might expect it to be mentioned, is no proof at all that it did not happen. The whole incident is so typical of Herod that we need not doubt that Matthew is passing the truth down to us.

Here is a terrible illustration of what some people will do to get rid of Jesus Christ. If they are set on their own course, if they see in Christ someone who is liable to interfere with their ambitions and rebuke their ways, their one desire is to eliminate Christ; and then they are driven to the most terrible things, for if they do not break others physically, they will break their hearts.

Again, at the end of this passage, we see Matthew's characteristic way of using the Old Testament. He quotes Jeremiah 31:15, 'Thus says the Lord: A voice is heard in Ramah, lamentation and bitter weeping. Rachel is weeping for her children; she refuses to be comforted for her children, because they are no more.'

The verse in Jeremiah has no connection with Herod's slaughter of the children. The picture in Jeremiah was this. Jeremiah was picturing the people of Jerusalem being led away in exile. On their sad way to an alien land, they pass Ramah, and Ramah was the place where Rachel lay buried (1 Samuel 10:2); and Jeremiah pictures Rachel weeping, even in the tomb, for the fate that had befallen the people.

Matthew is doing what he so often did. In his eagerness, he is finding a prophecy where no prophecy is. But, again, we must remind ourselves that what seems strange to us seemed in no way strange to those for whom Matthew was writing in his day.

RETURN TO NAZARETH

Matthew 2:19–23

> When Herod died, behold, the angel of the Lord appeared in a dream to Joseph in Egypt. 'Rise,' he said, 'and take the little child and his mother, and go into the land of Israel. For those who seek the little child's life are dead.' So he rose and took the little child and his mother, and went into the land of Israel. When he heard that Archelaus was king in Judaea instead of Herod, his father, he was afraid to go there. So, when he had

received a message from God in a dream, he withdrew
to the districts of Galilee, and he came and settled in a
town called Nazareth. This happened so that the word
spoken through the prophets might be fulfilled: 'He shall
be called a Nazarene.'

In due time Herod died, after which the whole kingdom over
which he had ruled was split up. The Romans had trusted
Herod, and they had allowed him to reign over a very considerable territory; but Herod knew perfectly well that none
of his sons would be allowed the same degree of power. So
he had divided his kingdom into three, and in his will he had
left a part to each of three of his sons. He had left Judaea to
Archelaus, Galilee to Herod Antipas, and the region away to
the north-east and beyond Jordan to Philip.

But the death of Herod did not solve the problem.
Archelaus was a bad king, and he was not to last long upon
the throne. In fact, he had begun his reign with an attempt to
out-Herod Herod, for he had opened his rule with the
deliberate slaughter of 3,000 of the most influential people in
the country. Clearly, even now that Herod was dead, it was
still unsafe to return to Judaea with the savage and reckless
Archelaus on the throne. So Joseph was guided to go to
Galilee, where Herod Antipas, a much better king, reigned.

It was in Nazareth that Joseph settled, and it was in
Nazareth that Jesus was brought up. It must not be thought
that Nazareth was a quiet little backwater, quite out of touch
with life and with events.

Nazareth lay in a hollow in the hills in the south of Galilee.
But a young boy had only to climb the hills for half the world
to be at his door. He could look west and the waters of the
Mediterranean, blue in the distance, would meet his eyes;
and he would see the ships going out to the ends of the earth.
He had only to look at the plain which skirted the coast, and

he would see, slipping round the foot of the very hill on which he stood, the road from Damascus to Egypt, the land bridge to Africa. It was one of the greatest caravan routes in the world.

It was the road by which, centuries before, Joseph had been sold down into Egypt as a slave. It was the road that, 300 years before, Alexander the Great and his legions had followed. It was the road by which, centuries later, Napoleon was to march. It was the road which, in the twentieth century, General Sir Edmund Allenby was to take. Sometimes it was called the Way of the South, and sometimes the Road of the Sea. On it, Jesus would see all kinds of travellers from all kinds of nations on all kinds of errands, coming and going from the ends of the earth.

But there was another road. There was the road which left the sea coast at Acre or Ptolemais and went out to the east. It was the Road of the East. It went out to the eastern bounds and frontiers of the Roman Empire. Once again, the cavalcade of the caravans and their silks and spices would be continually on it; and on it also the Roman legions clanked out to the frontiers.

Nazareth indeed was no backwater. Jesus was brought up in a town where the ends of the earth passed the foot of the hilltop. From his boyhood days, he was confronted with scenes which must have spoken to him of a world for God.

We have seen how Matthew clinches each event in the early life of Jesus with a passage from the Old Testament which he regards as a prophecy. Here, Matthew cites a prophecy: 'He shall be called a Nazarene'; and here Matthew has set us an insoluble problem, for there is no such text in the Old Testament. In fact, Nazareth is never mentioned in the Old Testament. No one has ever satisfactorily solved the problem of what part of the Old Testament Matthew has in mind.

The ancient writers liked puns and plays on words. It has been suggested that Matthew is playing on the words of Isaiah in Isaiah 11:1: 'A shoot shall come out from the stock of Jesse, and a branch shall grow out of his roots.' The word for *branch* is *nezer*; and it is just possible that Matthew is playing on the word *Nazarene* and the word *nezer*; and that he is saying at one and the same time that Jesus was from *Nazareth* and that Jesus was the *nezer*, the promised branch from the stock of Jesse, the descendant of David, the promised anointed king of God. No one can tell. What prophecy Matthew had in mind must remain a mystery.

So now the stage is set: Matthew has brought Jesus to Nazareth, and in a very real sense Nazareth was the gateway to the world.

THE YEARS BETWEEN

BEFORE we move on to the third chapter of Matthew's gospel, there is something at which we would do well to look. The second chapter of the gospel closes with Jesus as a little child; the third chapter of the gospel opens with Jesus as a man of thirty (cf. Luke 3:23). That is to say, between the two chapters there are thirty silent years. Why should it have been so? What was happening in those silent years? Jesus came into the world to be the Saviour of the world, and for thirty years he never moved beyond the bounds of Palestine, except to the Passover at Jerusalem. He died when he was thirty-three, and of these thirty-three years thirty were spent without record in Nazareth. To put it in another way, ten-elevenths of Jesus' life were spent in Nazareth. What was happening then?

(1) Jesus was growing up to boyhood, and then to manhood, in a good home; and there can be no greater start to life than that. J. S. Blackie, the famous Edinburgh professor, once

said in public: 'I desire to thank God for the good stock-in-trade, so to speak, which I inherited from my parents for the business of life.' The poet George Herbert once said: 'A good mother is worth 100 schoolmasters.' So for Jesus the years passed, silently but in a formative way, in the circle of a good home.

(2) Jesus was fulfilling the duties of an eldest son. It seems most likely that Joseph died before the family had grown up. Maybe he was already much older than Mary when they married. In the story of the wedding feast at Cana of Galilee there is no mention of Joseph, although Mary is there, and it is natural to suppose that Joseph had died.

So Jesus became the village craftsman of Nazareth to support his mother and his younger brothers and sisters. A world was calling him, and yet he first fulfilled his duty to his mother and to his own family and to his own home. When his mother died, the writer J. M. Barrie could write: 'I can look back, and I cannot see the smallest thing undone.' There lies happiness. It is on those who faithfully and ungrudgingly accept the simple duties that the world is built.

One of the great examples of that is the great doctor Sir James Y. Simpson, the discoverer of chloroform. He came from a poor home. One day, his mother took him on her knee and began to darn his stockings. When she had finished, she looked at her neat handiwork. 'My, Jamie,' she said, 'mind when your mither's awa' that she was a grand darner.' Jamie was the 'wise wean [child], the little box of brains', and his family knew it. They had their dreams for him. His brother Sandy said: 'I aye felt he would be great some day.' And so, willingly and without jealousy, his brothers worked in the bakery and at their jobs that the boy might have his college education and his chance. There would have been no Sir James Simpson had there not been others willing to do simple things and to deny themselves so that the brilliant child might have his chance.

Jesus is the great example of one who accepted the simple duties of the home.

(3) Jesus was learning what it was like to be a working man. He was learning what it was like to have to earn a living, to save to buy food and clothes, and maybe sometimes a little pleasure; to meet the dissatisfied and the critical customer, and the customer who would not pay his debts. If Jesus was to help men and women, he must first know what their lives were like. He did not come into a protected, cushioned life; he came into the life that all must live. He had to do that, if he was ever to understand the life of ordinary people.

There is a famous story of Marie Antoinette, the queen of France, in the days when the storm of the French Revolution was brooding over the country before it broke. People were starving; the mob was rioting. The queen asked what all the uproar was about. She was told: 'They have no bread.' 'If they have no bread,' she said, 'let them eat cake.' The idea of a life without plenty was an idea which did not come within her horizon. She did not understand.

Jesus worked in Nazareth for all the silent years in order that he might know what our life was like, and that, understanding, he might be able to help.

(4) Jesus was faithfully performing the lesser task before the greater task was given to him to do. The great fact is that, if Jesus had failed in the smaller duties, the mighty task of being the Saviour of the world could never have been given to him to do. He was faithful in little so that he might become master of much. It is a thing never to be forgotten that in the everyday duties of life we make or mar a destiny, and we win or lose a crown.

THE EMERGENCE OF JOHN THE BAPTIZER

Matthew 3:1–6

> In those days John the Baptizer arrived on the scene, preaching in the wilderness of Judaea. 'Repent,' he said, 'for the kingdom of the heavens has come near.' It was this man who was spoken of by Isaiah the prophet when he said, 'The voice of one crying in the wilderness: "Make ready the road by which the Lord is coming, and make straight the paths which he must travel!"' John himself wore a garment made from camel's hair, and he had a leather belt round his waist; and his food was locusts and wild honey. Then Jerusalem and all Judaea, and all the district around the Jordan, went out to him. They were baptized in the River Jordan, and, as they were baptized, they confessed their sins.

THE emergence of John was like the sudden sounding of the voice of God. At this time, the Jews were sadly conscious that the voice of the prophets spoke no more. They said that for 400 years there had been no prophet. Throughout long centuries, the voice of prophecy had been silent. As they put it themselves, 'There was no voice, nor any that answered.' But in John the prophetic voice spoke again. What then were the characteristics of John and his message?

(1) He fearlessly denounced evil wherever he might find it. If Herod the king sinned by contracting an evil and unlawful marriage, John rebuked him. If the Sadducees and Pharisees, the leaders of orthodox religion, the 'church' leaders of their day, were sunk in ritualistic formalism, John never hesitated to say so. If the ordinary people were living lives which were unaware of God, John would tell them so.

Wherever John saw evil – in the state, in the religious establishment, in the crowd – he fearlessly rebuked it. He

was like a light which lit up the dark places; he was like
a wind which swept from God throughout the country. It
was said of a famous journalist who was great, but who
never quite fulfilled the work he might have done, 'He was
perhaps not easily enough disturbed.' There is still a place
in the Christian message for warning and denunciation.
'The truth', said Diogenes, 'is like the light to sore eyes.' 'He
who never offended anyone', he said, 'never did anyone any
good.'

It may be that there have been times when the Church was
too careful not to offend. There come occasions when the
time for smooth politeness has gone, and the time for blunt
rebuke has come.

(2) He urgently summoned men and women to righteousness. John's message was not a mere negative denunciation; it was a positive erecting of the moral standards of God.
He not only denounced people for what they had done; he
summoned them to what they ought to do. He not only
condemned them for what they were; he challenged them to
be what they could be. He was like a voice calling people to
higher things. He not only rebuked evil, he also set before
men and women the good.

It may well be that there have been times when the Church
was too occupied in telling people what not to do, and too
little occupied in setting before them the height of the
Christian ideal.

(3) John came from God. He came out of the desert. He
came among the people only after he had undergone years of
lonely preparation by God. As the Baptist minister Alexander
Maclaren said, 'John leapt, as it were, into the arena full-
grown and full-armed.' He came, not with some opinion of
his own, but with a message from God. For a long time before
he spoke to the world, he had kept company with God.

The preacher, the teacher with the prophetic voice, must always come into the presence of others out of the presence of God.

(4) John pointed beyond himself. The man was not only a light to shine on all that was evil, a voice to rebuke sin, he was also a signpost to God. It was not himself whom he wished people to see; he wished to prepare them for the one who was to come.

It was the Jewish belief that Elijah would return before the Messiah came, and that he would be the herald of the coming King. 'Lo, I will send you the prophet Elijah before the great and terrible day of the Lord comes' (Malachi 4:5). John wore a garment of camel's hair, and a leather belt around his waist. That is the very description which the Revised Standard Version gives of the clothing that Elijah had worn (2 Kings 1:8).

Matthew connects him with a prophecy from Isaiah (Isaiah 40:3). In ancient times in the middle east, the roads were bad. There was a proverb which said: 'There are three states of misery – sickness, fasting and travel.' A traveller setting out upon a journey was advised 'to pay all debts, provide for dependants, give parting gifts, return all articles under trust, take money and good-temper for the journey; then bid farewell to all'. The ordinary roads were no better than tracks. They were not surfaced at all because the soil of Palestine is hard and will bear the traffic of mules, donkeys, oxen and carts. A journey along such a road was an adventure, and indeed an undertaking to be avoided.

There were a few surfaced and artificially made roads. Josephus, for instance, tells us that Solomon laid a causeway of black basalt stone along the roads that led to Jerusalem to make them easier for the pilgrims, and 'to manifest the grandeur of his riches and government'. All such surfaced and artificially made roads were originally built by the king and for the use of the king. They were called 'the king's highway'. They were kept in repair only as the king needed them for any journey that he might make. Before the king was due to arrive in any area, a message was sent out to the people to get the king's roads in order for the king's journey.

John was preparing the way for the king. Preachers, teachers with prophetic voices, point not at themselves, but at God. Their aim is not to focus their eyes on their own cleverness, but on the majesty of God. True preachers are obliterated in their message.

The people recognized John as a prophet, even after years when no prophetic voice had spoken, because he was a *light* to light up evil things, a *voice* to summon men and women to righteousness, and a *signpost* to point them to God, and because he had in him that unanswerable authority which clings to anyone who comes into the presence of others out of the presence of God.

THE MESSAGE OF JOHN – THE THREAT

Matthew 3:7–12

> When he saw many of the Pharisees and Sadducees coming to his baptism, he said to them, 'Brood of vipers! Who put it into your minds to flee from the coming wrath? Produce fruit to fit repentance. Do not think that you can say to yourselves, "We have Abraham as a father." For I tell you that God can raise up children to Abraham from these stones. The axe is already applied to the root of the trees. Therefore every tree which does not produce good fruit is on the point of being cut down and thrown into the fire. I baptize you with water that

> you may repent. He who is coming after me is stronger
> than I. I am not fit to carry his sandals. He will baptize
> you with the Holy Spirit and with fire. His fan is in
> his hand, and he will thoroughly cleanse his threshing-
> floor; and he will gather the corn into his storehouse,
> but he will burn the chaff with a fire that no man can
> quench.'

In John's message, there is both a threat and a promise. This whole passage is full of vivid pictures.

John calls the Pharisees and the Sadducees a brood of vipers, and asks them who has suggested to them to flee from the coming wrath. There may be one of two pictures there.

John knew the desert. The desert had in places thin, short, dried-up grass, and stunted thorn bushes, brittle for want of moisture. Sometimes a desert fire would break out. When that happened, the fire swept like a river of flame across the grass and the bushes, for they were as dry as tinder. And in front of the fire there would come scurrying and hurrying the snakes, the scorpions and the other living creatures that found their shelter in the grass and in the bushes. They were driven from their lairs by this river of flame, and they ran for their lives before it.

But it may be that there is another picture here. There are many little creatures in a standing field of corn – the field mice, the rats, the rabbits, the birds. But when the reaper comes, they are driven from their nests and their shelters, and as the field is laid bare, they have to flee for their lives.

It is in terms of these pictures that John is thinking. If the Pharisees and Sadducees are really coming for baptism, they are like the animals scurrying for life before a desert fire or in front of the sickle of the harvester.

He warns them that pleading that Abraham is their father will not get them anywhere. To orthodox Jews, that was an incredible statement. To Jews, Abraham was unique. So unique was he in his goodness and in his favour with God that his merits sufficed not only for himself but for all his descendants also. He had built up a treasury of merit which not all the claims and needs of his descendants could exhaust. So the Jews believed that simply because they were Jews, and not for any merits of their own, they were safe in the life to come. They said: 'All Israelites have a portion in the world to come.' They talked about 'the delivering merits of the fathers'. They said that Abraham sat at the gates of Gehenna to turn back any Israelite who might by chance have been consigned to its terrors. They said that it was the merits of Abraham which enabled the ships to sail safely on the seas, that it was because of the merits of Abraham that the rain descended on the earth, that it was the merits of Abraham which enabled Moses to enter into heaven and to receive the law, that it was because of the merits of Abraham that David was heard. Even for the wicked, these merits sufficed. 'If thy children', they said of Abraham, 'were mere dead bodies, without blood vessels or bones, thy merits would avail for them!'

It is that spirit which John is rebuking. Maybe the Jews carried it to an unparalleled distance, but there is always need of a warning that we cannot live on the spiritual capital of the past. A degenerate age cannot hope to claim salvation for the sake of a heroic past; and an evil son cannot hope to plead the merits of a saintly father.

Then, once again, John returns to his harvest picture. At the end of the season, the keeper of the vineyards and the fig trees would look at his vines and his trees; and those which were fruitless and useless would be rooted out. They only took up much-needed space. Uselessness always invites disaster. Those who are useless to God and to others are in grave peril, and are under condemnation.

THE MESSAGE OF JOHN – THE PROMISE

Matthew 3:7–12 (*contd*)

BUT after John's threat there came the promise – which had also a threat within it. As we have said, John pointed beyond himself to the one who was to come. At the moment he was enjoying a vast reputation, and he was wielding a most powerful influence. Yet he said that he was not fit to carry the sandals of the one who was to come – and to carry sandals was the duty of a slave. John's whole attitude was self-obliteration, not self-importance. His only importance was, as he saw it, as a signpost pointing to the one who was to come.

He said that the one who was to come would baptize them with the Holy Spirit and with fire.

All through their history, the Jews had looked for the time when the Spirit would come. Ezekiel heard God say: 'A new heart I will give you, and a new spirit I will put within you . . . I will put my spirit within you, and make you follow my statutes and be careful to observe my ordinances' (Ezekiel 36:26–7). 'I will put my spirit within you, and you shall live' (Ezekiel 37:14). 'And I will never again hide my face from them, when I pour out my spirit upon the house of Israel, says the Lord God' (Ezekiel 39:29). 'For I will pour water on the thirsty land, and streams on the dry ground; I will pour my spirit upon your descendants, and my blessing on your offspring' (Isaiah 44:3). 'Then afterwards I will pour out my spirit on all flesh' (Joel 2:28).

What then is the gift and work of this Spirit of God? When we try to answer that question, we must remember to answer it in Hebrew terms. John was a Jew, and it was to Jews that he was speaking. He is thinking and speaking, not in terms of the Christian doctrine of the Holy Spirit, but in terms of the Jewish doctrine of the Spirit.

(1) The word for *spirit* is *ruach*, and *ruach*, like *pneuma* in Greek, means not only *spirit*; it also means *breath*. *Breath is life*; and therefore the promise of the Spirit is *the promise of life*. The Spirit of God breathes God's life into human beings. When the Spirit of God enters us, the tired, lacklustre, weary defeatedness of life is gone, and a surge of new life enters us.

(2) This word *ruach* not only means *breath*; it also means *wind*. It is the word for the storm wind, the mighty rushing wind that once Elijah heard. *Wind means power*. The gale of wind sweeps the ship before it and uproots the tree. The wind has an irresistible power. *The Spirit of God is the Spirit of power*. When the Spirit of God enters into us, our weakness is covered with the power of God. We are enabled to do the undoable, to face the unfaceable and to bear the unbearable. Frustration is banished; victory arrives.

(3) The Spirit of God is connected with *the work of creation*. It was the Spirit of God who moved upon the face of the waters and made the chaos into a cosmos, turned disorder into order, and made a world out of the uncreated mists. The Spirit of God can re-create us. When the Spirit of God enters into us, the disorder of human nature becomes the order of God; our dishevelled, disorderly, uncontrolled lives are moulded by the Spirit into the harmony of God.

(4) To the Spirit, the Jews assigned special functions. *The Spirit brought God's truth to men and women*. Every new discovery in every realm of thought is the gift of the Spirit. The Spirit enters into our minds and turns our human guesses into divine certainty, and changes our human ignorance into divine knowledge.

(5) *The Spirit enables people to recognize God's truth when they see it*. When the Spirit enters our hearts, our eyes

are opened. The prejudices which blinded us are taken away. The self-will which darkened us is removed. The Spirit enables us to see.

Such are the gifts of the Spirit, and, as John saw it, such were the gifts that the one who was to come would bring.

THE MESSAGE OF JOHN –
THE PROMISE AND THE THREAT

Matthew 3:7–12 (*contd*)

THERE is a word and a picture in John's message which combine both *promise* and *threat*.

John says that the baptism of the one who is to come will be with *fire*. In the thought of a baptism with fire, there are three ideas.

(1) There is the idea of *illumination*. The blaze of a flame sends a light through the night and illuminates the darkest corners. In the past, the flame of the beacon guided sailors to the harbour and travellers to their goal. In fire, there is light and guidance. Jesus is the beacon light to lead us into truth and to guide us home to God.

(2) There is the idea of *warmth*. A great and kindly man was described as one who lit fires in cold rooms. When Jesus comes into our lives, he kindles our hearts with the warmth of love towards God and towards one another. Christianity is always the religion of the kindled heart.

(3) There is the idea of *purification*. In this sense, purification involves destruction; for the purifying flame burns away the false and leaves the true. The flame tempers and strengthens and purifies the metal. When Christ comes into our hearts, the evil dross is purged away. Sometimes that has to happen through painful experiences; but, if throughout all

the experiences of life we believe that God is working together all things for good, we will emerge from them with a character which is cleansed and purified, until, being pure in heart, we can see God.

So, the word *fire* has in it the illumination, the warmth and the purification of the entry of Jesus Christ into our hearts.

But there is also a picture which has in it a promise and a threat – the picture of the threshing-floor. The fan was the great wooden winnowing shovel. With it, the grain was lifted from the threshing-floor and tossed into the air. When that was done, the heavy grain fell to the ground, but the light chaff was blown away by the wind. The grain was then collected and stored in the barns, while any chaff which remained was used as fuel for the fire.

The coming of Christ necessarily involves a separation. People either accept him or reject him. When they are confronted with him, they are confronted with a choice which cannot be avoided. They are either for or against. And it is precisely that choice which settles destiny. People are separated by their reaction to Jesus Christ.

In Christianity, there is no escape from the eternal choice. On the village green in Bedford, John Bunyan heard the voice which drew him up all of a sudden and left him looking at eternity: 'Wilt thou leave thy sins and go to heaven, or wilt thou have thy sins and go to hell?' In the last analysis, that is the choice which no one can evade.

THE MESSAGE OF JOHN – THE DEMAND

Matthew 3:7–12 (*contd*)

In all John's preaching, there was one basic demand – and that basic demand was: 'Repent!' (Matthew 3:2). That was also the basic demand of Jesus himself, for Jesus came saying: 'Repent, and believe in the good news' (Mark 1:15). We will do well to seek to understand what this repentance is, and what this basic demand of the King and his herald means.

It is to be noted that both Jesus and John use the word *repent* without any explanation of its meaning. They use it as a word which they were sure their hearers would know and understand.

Let us then look at the Jewish teaching about repentance.

To Jews, repentance was central to all religious faith and to all relationship with God. The Jewish scholar G. F. Moore writes: 'Repentance is the sole, but inexorable, condition of God's forgiveness and the restoration of his favour, and the divine forgiveness and favour are never refused to genuine repentance.' He writes: 'That God fully and freely remits the sins of the penitent is a cardinal doctrine of Judaism.' The Rabbis said: 'Great is repentance for it brings healing upon the world. Great is repentance for it reaches to the throne of glory.' The Jewish scholar C. G. Montefiore wrote: 'Repentance is the great mediatorial bond between God and man.'

The law was created 2,000 years after creation; but, the Rabbis taught, repentance was one of the six things created even before the law. These things are repentance, paradise, hell, the glorious throne of God, the celestial temple and the name of the Messiah. 'A man', they said, 'can shoot an arrow for a few furlongs, but repentance reaches even to the throne of God.'

There is a famous Rabbinic passage which sets repentance in the first of all places: 'Who is like God a teacher of sinners that they may repent?' They asked Wisdom: 'What shall be the punishment of the sinner?' Wisdom answered: 'Misfortune pursues sinners' (Proverbs 13:21). They asked Prophecy. It replied: 'The person that sins . . . shall die'

(Ezekiel 18:4). They asked the law. It replied: 'Let him bring a sacrifice' (cf. Leviticus 1:4). They asked God, and he replied: 'Let him repent and obtain his atonement. My children, what do I ask of you? *Seek me and live.*' So, to Jews, the one gateway back to God is the gateway of repentance.

The Jewish word commonly used for repentance is itself interesting. It is the word *teshubah*, which is the noun for the verb *shub*, which means *to turn*. Repentance is a turning away from evil and a turning towards God. G. F. Moore writes: 'The transparent primary meaning of repentance in Judaism is always a change in man's attitude towards God, and in the conduct of life, a religious and moral reformation of the people or the individual.' C. G. Montefiore writes: 'To the Rabbis the essence of repentance lay in such a thorough change of mind that it issues in a change of life and a change of conduct.' Maimonides, the great medieval Jewish scholar, defines repentance thus: 'What is repentance? Repentance is that the sinner forsakes his sin and puts it away out of his thoughts and fully resolves in his mind that he will not do it again; as it is written, "Let the wicked forsake his way, and the bad man his plans."'

G. F. Moore very interestingly and very truly points out that, with the single exception of the two words in brackets, the Westminster Confession definition of repentance would be entirely acceptable to a Jew: 'Repentance unto life is a saving grace, whereby a sinner, out of a true sense of sin, and apprehension of the mercy of God (in Christ), doth, with grief and hatred of his sin, turn from it unto God, with full purpose of and endeavour after new obedience.' Again and again, the Bible speaks of this *turning away* from sin and this *turning towards* God. Ezekiel had it: 'As I live, says the Lord God, I have no pleasure in the death of the wicked, but that the wicked turn from their ways and live; turn back, turn back

from your evil ways; for why will you die, O house of Israel?'
(Ezekiel 33:11). Jeremiah had it: 'Bring me back, let me come
back, for you are the Lord my God' (Jeremiah 31:18). Hosea
had it: 'Return, O Israel, to the Lord your God . . . Take
words with you and return to the Lord' (Hosea 14:1–2).

From all this, it is quite clear that in Judaism repentance
has in it an ethical demand. It is a turn from evil to God, with
a corresponding change in action. John was fully within the
tradition of his people when he demanded that his hearers
should bring forth fruit suitable for repentance. There is a
beautiful synagogue prayer which runs: 'Cause us to return,
O Father, unto thy law; draw us near, O King, unto thy service;
bring us back in perfect repentance unto thy presence. Blessed
art thou, O Lord, who delightest in repentance.' But that
repentance had to be shown in a real change of life.

A Rabbi, commenting on Jonah 3:10, wrote: 'My brethren,
it is not said of the Ninevites that God saw their sackcloth
and their fasting, but that God saw their *works*, that they
turned from their evil way.' The Rabbis said: 'Be not like
fools, who, when they sin, bring a sacrifice but do not repent.
If a man says, "I will sin and repent, I will sin and repent," he
is not allowed to repent.' Five unforgivable sinners are listed,
and the list includes 'Those who sin in order to repent, and
those who repent much and always sin afresh.' They said: 'If
a man has an unclean thing in his hands, he may wash them
in all the seas of the world, and he will never be clean; but if
he throws the unclean thing away, a little water will suffice.'
The Jewish teachers spoke of what they called 'the nine norms
of repentance', the nine necessities of real repentance. They
found them in the series of commandments in Isaiah 1:16–
17: 'Wash yourselves; make yourselves clean; remove the
evil of your doings from before my eyes; cease to do evil,
learn to do good, seek justice, rescue the oppressed; defend

the orphan, plead for the widow.' The son of Sirach writes in Ecclesiasticus: 'Do not say, "I sinned, yet what has happened to me?" for the Lord is slow to anger. Do not be so confident of forgiveness that you add sin to sin. Do not say, "His mercy is great, he will forgive the multitude of my sins, for both mercy and wrath and his anger will rest on sinners. Do not delay to turn back to the Lord, and do not postpone it from day to day"' (Ecclesiasticus 5:4–7). He writes again: 'If one washes after touching a corpse, and touches it again, what has been gained by washing? So if one fasts for his sins, and goes again and does the same things, who will listen to his prayer? And what has he gained by humbling himself?' (Ecclesiasticus 34:30–1).

Jews held that true repentance issues, not merely in a sentimental sorrow, but in a real change in life – and so do Christians. Jews had a holy horror of seeking to trade on the mercy of God – and so do Christians. Jews held that true repentance brings forth fruits which demonstrate the reality of the repentance – and so do Christians.

But the Jews had still more things to say about repentance, and we must go on to look at them.

THE MESSAGE OF JOHN – THE DEMAND

Matthew 3:7–12 (*contd*)

THERE is an almost terrifying note in the ethical demand of the Jewish idea of repentance, but there are other comforting things.

Repentance is always available. 'Repentance', they said, 'is like the sea – a man can bathe in it at any hour.' There may be times when even the gates of prayer are shut; but the gates of repentance are never closed.

Repentance is completely essential. There is a story of a kind of argument that Abraham had with God. Abraham said to God: 'Thou canst not lay hold of the cord at both ends at once. If Thou desirest strict justice, the world cannot endure. If Thou desirest the preservation of the world, strict justice cannot endure.' The world cannot continue to exist without the mercy of God and the gateway of repentance. If there was nothing but the justice of God, it would be the end of all humanity and of all things. So essential is repentance that in order to make it possible God cancels his own demands: 'Beloved is repentance before God, for he cancels his own words for its sake.' The threat of the destruction of the sinner is cancelled by the acceptance of repentance for the sinner's sins.

Repentance lasts as long as life. As long as life remains, there remains the possibility of repentance. 'God's hand is stretched out under the wings of the heavenly chariot to snatch the penitent from the grasp of justice.' Rabbi Simeon ben Yohai said: 'If a man has been completely righteous all his days, and rebels at the end, he destroys it all, for it is said, "The righteousness of the righteous shall not deliver him when he transgresses" [Ezekiel 33:12]; if a man has been completely wicked all his days, and repents at the end, God receives him, for it is said, "And as for the wickedness of the wicked, he shall not fall by it when he turns from his wickedness" [Ezekiel 33:12].' 'Many', they said, 'can go into the world to come only after years and years; while another gains it in an hour.' As the poet said of the man who gained the mercy of God in the instant of death:

> Betwixt the stirrup and the ground,
> Mercy I asked, mercy I found.

Such is the mercy of God that he will receive even secret
repentance. Rabbi Eleazar said: 'It is the way of the world,
when a man has insulted his fellow in public, and after a time
seeks to be reconciled to him, that the other says, "You insult
me publicly, and now you would be reconciled to me between
us two alone! Go bring the men in whose presence you
insulted me, and I will be reconciled to you." But God is not
so. A man may stand and rail and blaspheme in the market
place, and the Holy One says, "Repent between us two alone,
and I will receive you."' God's mercy is open to those who
are so ashamed that they can tell their shame to no one except
God.

There is no forgetfulness in God, because he is God; but
such is the mercy of God that he not only forgives, but,
incredible as it may sound, he even forgets the sin of the
penitent: 'Who is a God like you, pardoning iniquity and
passing over the transgression of the remnant of your
possession?' (Micah 7:18). 'You forgave the iniquity of your
people; you pardoned all their sin' (Psalm 85:2).

Loveliest of all, God comes half-way and more to meet the
penitent: 'Return as far as you can, and I will come to you the
rest of the way.' The Rabbis at their highest had a glimpse of
the Father, who in his love ran to meet the prodigal son.

Yet, even remembering all this mercy, it remains the case
that in true repentance reparation is necessary in so far as it
can be made. The Rabbis said: 'Injury must be repaired, and
pardon sought and forgiven. The true penitent is he who has
the opportunity to do the same sin again, in the same
circumstances, and who does not do it.' The Rabbis stressed
again and again the importance of human relationships, and
of setting them right.

There is one curious Rabbinic passage. (A *zadik* is *a
righteous man*.) 'He who is good towards heaven and towards

his fellow men is a good *zadik*. He who is good towards heaven and not towards his fellow men is a bad *zadik*. He who is wicked against heaven and wicked against his fellow men is a bad sinner. He who is wicked against heaven, but not wicked against his fellow men, is not a bad sinner.'

It is because reparation is so necessary that those who teach others to sin are the worst of sinners; for they cannot make reparation because they can never tell how far their sins have gone out and how many they have gone on to influence.

Not only is reparation necessary for true repentance; confession is equally necessary. Again and again, we find that demand within the Bible itself. 'When a man or a woman wrongs another . . . that person . . . shall confess the sin that has been committed' (Numbers 5:6–7). 'No one who conceals transgressions will prosper, but one who confesses and forsakes them will obtain mercy' (Proverbs 28:13). 'Then I acknowledged my sin to you, and I did not hide my iniquity; I said, "I will confess my transgressions to the Lord"; and you forgave the guilt of my sin' (Psalm 32:5). It is the person who claims to be innocent and who refuses to admit sinning who is condemned (Jeremiah 2:35). The Jewish philosopher Maimonides gives the formula which may be used to confess a sin: 'O God, I have sinned, I have done iniquity, I have transgressed before thee, and have done thus and so. I am sorry and ashamed for my deed, and I will never do it again.' True repentance necessitates the humility to admit and to confess our sin.

No case is hopeless for repentance, and no one is beyond repentance. The Rabbis said: 'Let not a man say, "Because I have sinned, no repair is possible for me," but let him trust in God and repent, and God will receive him.' The classical example of a seemingly impossible reformation was the case of Manasseh. He worshipped the Baals; he brought strange gods into Jerusalem, he even sacrificed children to Moloch in the valley of Hinnom. Then he was taken away captive to Assyria, and there in fetters he lay upon the thorns. Then he prayed to God in his distress, and God heard his supplication and brought him again to Jerusalem. 'Then Manasseh knew that the Lord indeed was God' (2 Chronicles 33:13). Sometimes it takes God's threat and God's discipline to do it, but none of us is beyond the power of God to bring us home.

There is one last Jewish belief about repentance, and it is a belief which must have been in John's mind. Certain, at least, of the Jewish teachers taught that if Israel could repent perfectly for even one day, the Messiah would come. It was only the hardness of human hearts which delayed the sending of God's Redeemer into the world.

Repentance was the very centre of the Jewish faith as it is the very centre of the Christian faith, for repentance is the turning away from sin and the turning towards God, and towards the life that God means us to live.

JESUS AND HIS BAPTISM

Matthew 3:13–17

> Then Jesus came from Galilee to the Jordan to John to
> be baptized by him. But John tried to prevent him. 'It is
> I', he said, 'who need to be baptized by you, and are
> you coming to me?' Jesus answered him, 'Let it be just
> now, for so it befits us to fulfil all righteousness.' Then
> he allowed Jesus to be baptized. After Jesus had been
> baptized he came up immediately from the water and,
> lo, the heavens were opened for John, and he saw the
> Spirit of God descending, like a dove, and coming upon

him. And, lo, there came a voice from heaven, saying, 'This is my Son, the Beloved One, in whom I am well pleased.'

WHEN Jesus came to John to be baptized, John was startled and unwilling to baptize him. It was John's conviction that it was he who needed what Jesus could give, not Jesus who needed what he could give.

From the very beginning of study of the gospel story, people have found the baptism of Jesus difficult to understand. In John's baptism, there was a summons to repentance and the offer of a way to the forgiveness of sins. But, if Jesus is who we believe him to be, he did not stand in need of repentance, and did not need forgiveness from God. John's baptism was for sinners conscious of their sin, and therefore it does not seem applicable to Jesus at all.

A very early writer suggested that Jesus came to be baptized only to please his mother and his brothers, and that it was in answer to their entreaties that he was almost compelled to let this thing be done. The Gospel according to the Hebrews, which is one of the gospels which failed to be included in the New Testament, has a passage like this: 'Behold the mother of the Lord and his brethren said to him, "John the Baptist baptizeth for the remission of sins; let us go and be baptized by him." But he said to them, "What sin have I committed, that I should go and be baptized by him? Except perchance this very thing that I have said is ignorance."'

From the earliest times, thinkers were puzzled by the fact that Jesus submitted to be baptized. But there were reasons, and good reasons, why he did.

(1) For thirty years, Jesus had waited in Nazareth, faithfully performing the simple duties of the home and of the carpenter's shop. All the time, he knew that a world was

waiting for him. All the time, he grew increasingly conscious of his waiting task. The success of any undertaking is determined by the wisdom with which the moment to embark upon it is chosen. Jesus must have waited for the hour to strike, for the moment to come, for the summons to sound. And when John emerged, Jesus knew that the time had arrived.

(2) Why should that be so? There was one very simple and very vital reason. It is the fact that never in all history before this had any Jew submitted to being baptized. The Jews knew and used baptism, but only for converts who came into Judaism from some other faith. It was natural that sin-stained, polluted converts should be baptized; but the Jews had never conceived that they, the chosen people, children of Abraham, assured of God's salvation, could ever need baptism. Baptism was for sinners, and the Jews never conceived of themselves as sinners shut out from God. Now, for the first time in their national history, they became aware of their own sin and their own urgent need of God. Never before had there been such a unique national movement of penitence and of search for God.

This was the very moment for which Jesus had been waiting. Men and women were conscious of their sin and conscious of their need of God as never before. This was his opportunity, and in his baptism he identified himself with those he came to save, in the hour of their new consciousness of their sin, and of their search for God.

The voice which Jesus heard at the baptism is of supreme importance. 'This is my Son, the Beloved,' it said, 'with whom I am well pleased.' That sentence is composed of two quotations. 'This is my Son' is a reference to Psalm 2:7. Every Jew accepted that Psalm as a description of the Messiah, the mighty King of God who was to come. 'With whom I am well pleased' is a reference to Isaiah 42:1, which is a description of the Suffering Servant, a description which culminates in Isaiah 53.

So, in the baptism there came to Jesus two certainties – the certainty that he was indeed the chosen one of God, and the certainty that the way in front of him was the way of the cross. In that moment, he knew that he was chosen to be King, but he knew also that his throne must be a cross. In that moment, he knew that he was destined to be a conqueror, but that his conquest must have as its only weapon the power of suffering love. In that moment, there was set before Jesus both his task and the only way to the fulfilling of it.

THE TESTING TIME

STEP by step, Matthew unfolds the story of Jesus. He begins by showing us how Jesus was born into this world. He goes on to show us, at least by implication, that Jesus had to perform faithfully his duties to his home before he began on his duty to the world; he had to show himself faithful in the smaller tasks before God gave him the greatest task in all the world.

He goes on to show us how, with the emergence of John the Baptist, Jesus knew that the hour had struck and that the time had come to enter upon his work. He shows us Jesus identifying himself with a people's unprecedented search for God. In that moment, he shows us Jesus' realization that he was indeed the chosen one of God, but that his way to victory lay through the cross.

If anyone has a vision, the immediate problem is how to turn that vision into fact; some way has to be found to turn the dream into reality. That is precisely the problem which faced Jesus. He had come to lead men and women home to God. How was he to do it? What method was he to adopt? Was he to adopt the method of a mighty conqueror, or was he to adopt the method of patient, sacrificial love? That was the problem which faced Jesus in his temptations. The task had been committed into his hands. What method was he to choose to work out the task which God had given him to do?

THE TEMPTATIONS OF CHRIST

Matthew 4:1–11

> Then Jesus was led by the Spirit into the wilderness to be tempted by the devil. After he had deliberately gone without food for forty days and forty nights he was hungry. So the tempter came and said to him, 'If you really are the Son of God, tell these stones to become bread.' He answered: 'It stands written, "Man shall not live by bread alone, but by every word which proceeds through the mouth of God."' Then the devil took him to the holy city, and set him on the pinnacle of the Temple. 'If you really are the Son of God,' he said to him, 'fling yourself down, for it stands written, "He will give his angels orders to care for you, and they will lift you upon their hands, lest at any time you should strike your foot against a stone."' Jesus said to him, 'Again it stands written, "You must not try to put the Lord your God to the test."' Again the devil took him to a very lofty mountain, and showed him all the kingdoms of the world, and their glory, and said to him, 'I will give you all these things, if you will fall down and worship me.' Then Jesus said to him, 'Begone, Satan! For it stands written, "You shall worship the Lord your God, and him alone you will serve."' Then the devil left him alone, and behold, angels came and gave him their service.

THERE is one thing which we must carefully note right at the beginning of our study of the temptations of Jesus, and that is the meaning of the word *to tempt*. The Greek word is *peirazein*. In English, the word *tempt* has a uniformly and consistently bad meaning. It always means to entice people to do wrong, to seek to seduce them into sin, to try to persuade them to take the wrong way. But *peirazein* has a quite different element in its meaning. It means *to test* far more than it means *to tempt* in our sense of the word.

One of the great Old Testament stories is the story of how narrowly Abraham escaped sacrificing his only son Isaac. Now that story begins like this in the Authorized Version: 'And it came to pass after these things that God did *tempt* Abraham' (Genesis 22:1). Quite clearly the word *to tempt* cannot there mean *to seek to seduce into evil*. It is unthinkable that God should try to make anyone a wrong-doer. But the point is quite clear when we understand that it means: 'After these things, God *tested* Abraham.' The time had come for a supreme test of the loyalty of Abraham. Just as metal has to be tested far beyond any stress and strain that it will ever be called upon to bear, before it can be put to any useful purpose, so people have to be tested before God can use them for his purposes. The Jews had a saying: 'The Holy One, blessed be his name, does not elevate a man to dignity till he has first tried and searched him; and if he stands in temptation, then he raises him to dignity.'

Now here is a great and uplifting truth. What we call temptation is not meant to make us sin; it is meant to enable us to conquer sin. It is not meant to make us bad, it is meant to make us good. It is not meant to weaken us, it is meant to make us emerge stronger and finer and purer from the ordeal. Temptation is not the penalty of being human, temptation is the glory of being human. It is the test which comes to those whom God wishes to use. So, we must think of this whole incident as being not so much the *tempting* as the *testing* of Jesus.

We have to note further where this test took place. It took place in *the wilderness*. Between Jerusalem, on the central plateau which is the backbone of Palestine, and the Dead Sea there stretches the wilderness. The Old Testament calls it Jeshimmon, which means the Devastation, and it is a fitting name. It stretches over an area of thirty-five by fifteen miles.

The much-travelled biblical scholar George Adam Smith, who crossed it, describes it. It is an area of yellow sand, of crumbling limestone and of scattered shingle. It is an area of contorted strata, where the ridges run in all directions as if they were warped and twisted. The hills are like dust-heaps; the limestone is blistered and peeling; rocks are bare and jagged; often the very ground sounds hollow when a foot or a horse's hoof falls upon it. It glows and shimmers with heat like some vast furnace. It runs right out to the Dead Sea, and then there comes a drop of 1,200 feet, a drop of limestone, flint and marl, through crags and corries and precipices down to the Dead Sea.

In that wilderness, Jesus could be more alone than anywhere else in Palestine. Jesus went into the wilderness to be alone. His task had come to him; God had spoken to him; he must think how he was to attempt the task which God had given him to do; he had to get things straightened out before he started; and he had to be alone.

It may well be that we often go wrong simply because we never try to be alone. There are certain things which can only be worked out alone. There are times when no one else's advice is any good. There are times when it becomes necessary to stop acting and start thinking. It may be that we often make mistakes because we do not give ourselves a chance to be alone with God.

THE SACRED STORY

Matthew 4:1-11 (*contd*)

THERE are certain further things we must note before we proceed to detailed study of the story of the temptations of Christ.

(1) All three gospel writers seem to stress the immediacy with which the temptations followed the baptism of Jesus. As Mark has it: 'The Spirit *immediately* drove him out into the wilderness' (Mark 1:12).

It is one of the truths of life that after every great moment there comes a moment of reaction – and again and again it is in the reaction that the danger lies. That is what happened to Elijah. With magnificent courage, Elijah in all his loneliness faced and defeated the prophets of Baal on Mount Carmel (1 Kings 18:17-40). That was Elijah's greatest moment of courage and of witness. But the slaughter of the prophets of Baal provoked the wicked Jezebel to wrath, and she threatened Elijah's life. 'Then he was afraid; he got up and fled for his life, and came to Beer-sheba' (1 Kings 19:3). The man who had stood fearlessly against all comers is now fleeing for his life with terror at his heels. The moment of reaction had come.

It seems to be the law of life that just after our resistance power has been at its highest, it nosedives until it is at its lowest. The tempter carefully, subtly and skilfully chose his time to attack Jesus – but Jesus conquered him. We will do well to be specially on our guard whenever life has brought us to the heights, for it is just then that we are in gravest danger of the depths.

(2) We must not regard this experience of Jesus as an outward experience. It was a struggle that went on in his own

heart and mind and soul. The proof is that there is no possible mountain from which all the kingdoms of the earth could be seen. This is an inner struggle.

It is through our inmost thoughts and desires that the tempter comes to us. His attack is launched in our own minds. It is true that that attack can be so real that we almost see the devil. To this day you can see the ink stain on the wall of Martin Luther's room in the Castle of Wartburg in Germany; Luther caused that ink stain by throwing his ink pot at the devil as he tempted him. But the very power of the devil lies in the fact that he breaches our defences and attacks us from within. He finds his allies and his weapons in our own inmost thoughts and desires.

(3) We must not think that in one campaign Jesus conquered the tempter forever and that the tempter never came to him again. The tempter spoke again to Jesus at Caesarea Philippi when Peter tried to dissuade him from taking the way to the cross, and when he had to say to Peter the very same words he had said to the tempter in the wilderness, 'Begone Satan' (cf. Matthew 16:23). At the end of the day, Jesus could say to his disciples: 'You are those who have stood by me in my trials' (Luke 22:28). And never in all history was there such a fight with temptation as Jesus waged in Gethsemane when the tempter sought to deflect him from the cross (Luke 22:42–4).

Eternal vigilance is the price of freedom. In the Christian warfare, there is no release. Sometimes people grow worried because they think that they should reach a stage when they are beyond temptation, a stage at which the power of the tempter is forever broken. Jesus never reached that stage. From the beginning to the end of the day, he had to fight his own battle against temptation; that is why he can help us to fight ours.

(4) One thing stands out about this story – the temptations are such as could only come to a person who had very special powers and who knew that he had them. The New Testament scholar W. Sanday described the temptations as 'the problem of what to do with supernatural powers'. The temptations which came to Jesus could only have come to one who knew that there were amazing things which he could do.

We must always remember that again and again we are tempted *through our gifts*. The person who is gifted with charm will be tempted to use that charm 'to get away with anything'. Those who are gifted with the power of words will be tempted to use their command of words to produce glib excuses to justify their own conduct. The person with a vivid and sensitive imagination will undergo agonies of temptation that a more stolid person will never experience. Those with great gifts of mind will be tempted to use these gifts for themselves and not for others, to control and not to serve others. It is the grim fact of temptation that it is just where we are strongest that we must be forever on the watch.

(5) No one can ever read this story without remembering that its source must have been Jesus himself. In the wilderness, he was alone. No one was with him when this struggle was being fought out. And we know about it only because Jesus himself must have told his disciples about it. It is Jesus telling us his own spiritual autobiography.

We must always approach this story with a unique and special reverence, for in it Jesus is laying bare his inmost heart and soul. He is telling us what he went through. It is the most sacred of all stories, for in it Jesus is saying to us that he can help others who are tempted because he himself was tempted. He draws the veil from his own struggles to help us in our struggle.

THE ATTACK OF THE TEMPTER

Matthew 4:1–11 (*contd*)

THE tempter launched his attack against Jesus along three lines, and in every one of them there was a certain inevitability.

(1) There was the temptation to turn the stones into bread. The desert was littered with little round pieces of limestone rock which were exactly like little loaves; even they would suggest this temptation to Jesus.

This was a double temptation. It was a temptation to Jesus *to use his powers selfishly and for his own use*, and that is precisely what Jesus always refused to do. There is always the temptation to use selfishly whatever powers God has given to us.

God has given each of us a gift, and we can ask one of two questions. We can ask: 'What can I make for myself out of this gift?' or: 'What can I do for others with this gift?' This kind of temptation can come out in the simplest thing. A person may possess, for instance, a voice which is good to hear, and may thereupon 'cash in on it' and refuse to use it unless some payment is made. There is no reason why that person should not use the talent for payment, but there is every reason why payment should not be the only reason for sharing it. There will always be a temptation to use selfishly the gifts which God has given us.

But there was another side to this temptation. Jesus was God's Messiah, and he knew it. In the wilderness, he was facing the choice of a method whereby he could win men and women to God. What method was he to use for the task which God had given him to do? How was he to turn the vision into actuality, and the dream into fact?

One sure way to persuade people to follow him was to give them bread, to give them material things. Did not history justify that? Had not God given his people manna in the wilderness? Had not God said: 'I will rain bread from heaven for you'? Did not the visions of the future golden age include that very dream? Had not Isaiah said: 'They shall not hunger or thirst' (Isaiah 49:10)? Was the messianic banquet not a settled feature in the dreams of the kingdom between the Testaments? If Jesus had wished to give people bread, he could have produced justification enough for it.

But to give them bread would have been a double mistake. First, it would have been to bribe people to follow him. It would have been to persuade them to follow him for the sake of what they could get out of it, whereas the reward Jesus had to offer was a cross. He called men and women to a life of giving, not of getting. To bribe them with material things would have been the denial of all he came to say and would have been ultimately to defeat his own ends.

Second, it would have been to remove the symptoms without dealing with the disease. People are hungry. But the question is, *why are they hungry*? Is it because of their own foolishness, and their own shiftlessness, and their own carelessness? Is it because there are some who selfishly possess too much while others possess too little? The real way to cure hunger is to remove the causes – and these causes are in human souls. And above all, there is a hunger of the heart which it is not in material things to satisfy.

So Jesus answered the tempter in the very words which express the lesson which God had sought to teach his people in the wilderness, that one 'does not live by bread alone, but by every word that comes from the mouth of the Lord' (Deuteronomy 8:3). The only way to true satisfaction is the way which has learned complete dependence on God.

(2) So the tempter renewed his attack from another angle. In a vision, he took Jesus to the *pinnacle of the Temple*. That may mean one of two things.

The Temple was built on the top of Mount Zion. The top of the mountain was levelled out into a plateau, and on that plateau the whole area of the Temple buildings stood. There was one corner at which Solomon's porch and the Royal porch met, and at that corner there was a sheer drop of 450 feet into the valley of the Kedron. Why should Jesus not stand on that pinnacle, and leap down, and land unharmed in the valley beneath? People would be startled into following someone who could do a thing like that.

On the top of the roof of the Temple itself, there was a stance where every morning a priest stood with a trumpet in his hands, waiting for the first flush of the dawn across the hills of Hebron. At the first dawn light, he sounded the trumpet to tell everyone that the hour of morning sacrifice had come. Why should Jesus not stand there, and leap down right into the Temple court, and amaze people into following him? Had not Malachi said: 'The Lord whom you seek will suddenly come to his temple' (Malachi 3:1)? Was there not a promise that the angels would bear God's servant upon their hands lest any harm should come to him (Psalm 91:11-12)?

This was the very method that the false Messiahs who were continually arising promised. Theudas had led the people out, and had promised with a word to split the waters of Jordan in two. The famous Egyptian pretender (Acts 21:38) had promised that with a word he would lay flat the walls of Jerusalem. Simon Magus, so it is said, had promised to fly through the air, and had perished in the attempt. These pretenders had offered sensational acts which they could not perform. Jesus could perform anything he promised. Why should he not do it?

There were two good reasons why Jesus should not adopt that course of action. First, those who seek to attract people to them by the offer of sensational acts have adopted a way in which there is literally no future. The reason is simple. To retain their power, they must produce greater and greater spectacles. Wonders are apt to be short-lived. This year's sensation is next year's commonplace. A gospel founded on sensation-mongering is doomed to failure. Second, that is not the way to use the power of God. 'You shall not put the Lord your God to the test,' said Jesus (cf. Deuteronomy 6:16). He meant this: there is no good in seeing how far you can go with God; there is no good in putting yourself deliberately into a threatening situation, and doing it quite recklessly and needlessly, and then expecting God to rescue you from it.

God expects us to take risks in order to be true to him, but he does not expect us to take risks to enhance our own prestige. The very faith which is dependent on signs and wonder is not faith. If faith cannot believe without sensational actions, it is not really faith; it is doubt looking for proof and looking in the wrong place. God's rescuing power is not something to be played and experimented with; it is something to be quietly trusted in everyday life.

Jesus refused the way of the sensational because he knew that it was the way to failure – it still is – and because to long for something sensational is not to trust but to distrust God.

(3) So the tempter tried his third avenue of attack. It was the world that Jesus came to save, and into his mind there came a picture of the world. The tempting voice said: 'Fall down and worship me, and I will give you all the kingdoms of this world.' Had not God himself said to his chosen one: 'Ask of me, and I will make the nations your heritage, and the ends of the earth your possession' (Psalm 2:8)?

What the tempter was saying was: 'Compromise! Come to terms with me! Don't pitch your demands quite so high! Wink just a little at evil and questionable things – and then people will follow you in their hordes.' This was the temptation to come to terms with the world, instead of uncompromisingly presenting God's demands to it. It was the temptation to try to advance by retreating, to try to change the world by becoming like the world.

Back came Jesus' answer: 'The Lord your God you shall fear; him you shall serve, and by his name alone you shall swear' (Deuteronomy 6:13). Jesus was quite certain that we can never defeat evil by compromising with evil. He made it quite clear that Christian faith does not compromise. Christianity cannot stoop to the level of the world; it must lift the world to its own level. Nothing less will do.

So Jesus made his decision. He decided that he must never bribe people into following him; he decided that the sensational way was not for him; he decided that there could be no compromise in the message he preached and in the faith he demanded. That choice inevitably meant the cross – but the cross just as inevitably meant the final victory.

THE SON OF GOD GOES FORTH

Matthew 4:12–17

> When Jesus heard that John had been delivered into the hands of the authorities, he withdrew into Galilee. He left Galilee and came and made his home in Capernaum, which is on the lakeside, in the districts of Zebulun and Naphtali. This was done that there might be fulfilled that which was spoken through Isaiah the prophet, when he said, 'Land of Zebulun, land of Naphtali, by the way

> of the sea, beyond Jordan, Galilee of the Gentiles – the people who sat in darkness have seen a great light, and a light has risen for those who sat in the land and in the shadow of death.' From that time Jesus began to proclaim his message and to say, 'Repent, for the kingdom of the heavens has come near!'

BEFORE very long, disaster came to John. He was arrested and imprisoned in the dungeons of the fortress of Machaerus by Herod the king. His crime was that he had publicly denounced Herod for seducing his brother's wife, and making her his own wife, after he had put away the wife he had. It is never safe to rebuke a tyrant, and John's courage brought him first imprisonment and then death. We shall come later to the details of that story, which is not told until Matthew 14:3–12.

For Jesus, the time had come when he must go forth to his task.

Let us note what he did first of all. He left Nazareth and took up residence in the town of Capernaum. There was a kind of symbolic finality in that move. In that moment, Jesus left his home, never again to return to live in it. It is as if he shut the door that lay behind him before he opened the door that stood in front of him. It was a clean surgical cut between the old and the new. One chapter was ended and another had begun. Into life, there come these moments of decision. It is always better to meet them with an even surgical cut than to waver undecided between two courses of action.

Let us note where Jesus went. He went into Galilee. When Jesus went into Galilee to begin his mission and his ministry, he knew what he was doing. Galilee was the most northerly district of Palestine. It stretched from the Litany River in the north to the Plain of Esdraelon in the south. On the west, it did not reach the sea coast of the Mediterranean, because the coastal strip was in the possession of the Phoenicians. On the north-east it was bounded by Syria, and its eastern limit was the waters of the Sea of Galilee. Galilee was not large; it was only fifty miles from north to south, and twenty-five miles from east to west.

But, small as it was, Galilee was densely populated. It was by far the most fertile region of Palestine; its fertility was indeed phenomenal and proverbial. There was a saying that it was easier to raise a legion of olives in Galilee than it was to bring up one child in Judaea. Josephus, who was at one time governor of the province, says: 'It is throughout rich in soil and pasturage producing every variety of tree, and inviting by its productiveness even those who have the least inclination for agriculture; it is everywhere tilled; no part is allowed to be idle, and everywhere it is productive.' The result of this was that for its size Galilee had an enormous population. Josephus tells us that in it there were 204 villages, none with a population of fewer than 15,000 people. So, Jesus began his mission in that part of Palestine where there were most people to hear him; he began his work in an area teeming with people to whom the gospel proclamation might be made.

But not only was Galilee a populous district; its people were people of a certain kind. Of all parts of Palestine, Galilee was most open to new ideas. Josephus says of the Galilaeans: 'They were ever fond of innovations, and by nature disposed to changes, and delighted in seditions.' They were always ready to follow a leader and to begin an insurrection. They were notoriously quick in temper and given to quarrelling. Yet for all that, they were the most brave and honourable people. 'The Galilaeans', said Josephus, 'have never been destitute of courage.' 'Cowardice was never a characteristic of the Galilaeans.' 'They were ever more anxious for honour than for gain.' The inborn characteristics of the Galilaeans were such as to make them most fertile ground for a new gospel to be preached to them.

This openness to new ideas was due to certain facts.

(1) The name *Galilee* comes from the Hebrew word *galil* which means a *circle*. The full name of the area was *Galilee of the Gentiles*. In his commentary on Matthew, A. Plummer wishes to take that to mean 'heathenish Galilee'. But the phrase came from the fact that Galilee was literally surrounded by Gentiles. On the west, the Phoenicians were its neighbours. To the north and the east, there were the Syrians. And even to the south, there lay the territory of the Samaritans. Galilee was in fact the one part of Palestine that was inevitably in touch with non-Jewish influences and ideas. Galilee was bound to be open to new ideas in a way that no other part of Palestine was.

(2) The great roads of the world passed through Galilee, as we saw when we were thinking of the town of Nazareth. The Way of the Sea led from Damascus through Galilee right down to Egypt and to Africa. The Road to the East led through Galilee away out to the frontiers. The traffic of the world passed through Galilee. Down in the south, Judaea is tucked into a corner, isolated and secluded. As it has been well said, 'Judaea is on the way to nowhere: Galilee is on the way to everywhere.' Judaea could erect a fence and keep all foreign influence and all new ideas out; Galilee could never do that. Into Galilee, the new ideas were bound to come.

(3) Galilee's geographical position had affected its history. Again and again it had been invaded and conquered, and the tides of the other nations had often flowed over it and had sometimes engulfed it.

Originally it had been assigned to the tribes of Asher, Naphtali and Zebulun when the Israelites first came into the land (Joshua 9), but these tribes had never been completely successful in expelling the native Canaanite inhabitants, and from the beginning the population of Galilee was mixed. More than once, foreign invasions from the north and east had swept down on it from Syria, and in the eighth century BC the Assyrians had engulfed it completely, the greater part of its population had been taken away into exile, and strangers had been settled in the land. Inevitably, this brought a very large injection of foreign blood into Galilee.

From the eighth until the second century BC it had been largely in Gentile hands. When the Jews returned from exile under Nehemiah and Ezra, many of the Galilaeans came south to live in Jerusalem. In 164 BC, Simon Maccabaeus chased the Syrians north from Galilee back to their own territory; and on his way back he took with him to Jerusalem the remnants of the Galilaeans who were left.

The most amazing thing of all is that in 104 BC Aristobulus reconquered Galilee for the Jewish nation and proceeded forcibly to circumcise the inhabitants of Galilee and thus to make them Jews whether they liked it or not. History had compelled Galilee to open its doors to new strains of blood and to new ideas and to new influences.

The natural characteristics of the Galilaeans, and the preparation of history, had made Galilee the one place in all Palestine where a new teacher with a new message had any real chance of being heard – and it was there that Jesus began his mission and first announced his message.

THE HERALD OF GOD

Matthew 4:12–17 (*contd*)

BEFORE we leave this passage, there are certain other things which we must note.

It was to the town of Capernaum that Jesus went. The correct form of the name is *Capharnaum*. The form *Capernaum* does not occur at all until the fifth century AD, but it is so fixed in our minds and memories that it would not be wise to try to change it.

There has been much argument about the site of Capernaum. Two places have been suggested. The commonest, and the likeliest, identification is that Capernaum is Tell Hum, which is on the west side of the extreme north of the Sea of Galilee; the alternative, and the less likely, identification is that Capernaum is Khan Minyeh, which is about two and a half miles to the south-west of Tell Hum. In any event, there is now nothing but ruins left to show where Capernaum once stood.

It was Matthew's habit to find in the Old Testament something which he could use as a prophecy about every event in Jesus' life. He finds such a prophecy in Isaiah 9:1–2. In fact, that is another of the prophecies which Matthew tears violently from its context and uses in his own extraordinary way. It is a prophecy which dates back to the reign of Pekah over the Northern Kingdom of Israel. In those days, the northern parts of Palestine, including Galilee, had been despoiled by the invading armies of the Assyrians; and this was originally a prophecy of the deliverance which would some day come to these conquered territories. Matthew finds in it a prophecy which foretold of the light that Jesus was to bring.

Finally, Matthew gives us a brief one-sentence summary of the message which Jesus brought. The Authorized Version and Revised Standard Version both say that Jesus began to *preach*. The word *preach* has come down in the world; it is all too unfortunately connected in the minds of many people with boredom. The word in Greek is *kērussein*, which is the word for a herald's proclamation from a king. *Kērux* is the Greek word for herald, and the herald was the man who brought a message direct from the king.

This word tells us of certain characteristics of the preaching of Jesus, and these are characteristics which should be in all preaching.

(1) The herald had in his voice a note of *certainty*. There was no doubt about his message; he did not come with perhapses and maybes and probablys; he came with a definite message. The German poet Goethe had it: 'Tell me of your certainties: I have doubts enough of my own.' Preaching is the proclamation of certainties, and we cannot make others sure of that about which we ourselves are in doubt.

(2) The herald had in his voice the note of *authority*. He was speaking for the king; he was laying down and announcing the king's law, the king's command and the king's decision. As was said of a great preacher, 'He did not cloudily guess; he knew.' Preaching, as it has been put, is the application of prophetic authority to the present situation.

(3) The herald's message came from a *source beyond himself*; it came from the king. Preaching speaks from a source beyond the preacher. It is not the expression of one individual's personal opinions; it is the voice of God transmitted through that person to the people. It was with the voice of God that Jesus spoke to men and women.

The message of Jesus consisted of a command which was the consequence of a new situation. 'Repent!' he said. 'Turn from your own ways, and turn to God. Lift your eyes from earth and look to heaven. Reverse your direction, and stop walking away from God and begin walking towards God.' That command had become urgently necessary because the reign of God was about to begin. Eternity had invaded time; God had invaded earth in Jesus Christ, and therefore it was of paramount importance that each man and each woman should choose the right side and the right direction.

CHRIST CALLS THE FISHERMEN

Matthew 4:18–22

> While he was walking beside the Sea of Galilee, he saw two brothers, Simon, who is called Peter, and Andrew, his brother, casting their net into the sea, for they were fishermen. He said to them, 'Follow me, and I will make you fishers of men.' They immediately left their nets and followed him. He went on from there and saw other two brothers, James, Zebedee's son, and John, his brother. They were in the boat with Zebedee, their father, getting ready their nets for use. So he called them. They immediately left their boat and their father, and followed him.

ALL Galilee centred round the Sea of Galilee. It is thirteen miles long from north to south, and eight miles across from east to west. The Sea of Galilee is therefore small, and it is interesting to note that Luke, the Gentile, who had seen so much more of the world, never calls it the *sea* (*thalassa*), but always the *lake* (*limnē*). It is in the shape of an oval, wider at the top than at the bottom. It lies in that great rift in the earth's surface in which the Jordan valley runs, and the surface of the Sea of Galilee is 680 feet below sea level. The fact that it lies in this dip in the earth's surface gives it a very warm climate and makes the surrounding countryside phenomenally fertile. It is one of the loveliest lakes in the world. In *The Land and the Book*, W. M. Thomson describes it: 'Seen from any point of the surrounding heights it is a fine sheet of water – a burnished mirror set in a framework of rounded hills and rugged mountains, which rise and roll backward and upward to where [Mount] Hermon hangs the picture against the blue vault of heaven.'

In the days of Josephus, there were no fewer than nine populous cities on its shore. In the 1930s, when the travel writer H. V. Morton saw it, only Tiberias was left, and it was little more than a village. Today it is the largest town in Galilee and steadily growing.

In the time of Jesus, the Sea of Galilee was thick with fishing boats. Josephus on a certain expedition had no difficulty in assembling 240 fishing boats to set out from Tarichaea; but nowadays the fishermen are few and far between.

There were three methods of fishing. There was fishing by line.

There was fishing with the casting net. The casting net was circular, and might be as much as nine feet across. It was skilfully cast into the water from the land, or from the shallow water at the edge of the lake. It was weighted with pellets of lead round the circumference. It sank into the sea and surrounded the fish; it was then drawn through the water as if the top of a bell tent were being drawn to land, and in it the fish were caught. That was the kind of net that Peter and Andrew, and James and John, were handling when Jesus saw them. Its name was the *amphiblēstron*.

The dragnet was used from a boat, or better from two boats. It was cast into the water with ropes at each of the four corners. It was weighted at the foot so that, as it were, it stood upright in the water. When the boats were rowed along with the net behind them, the effect was that the net became a great cone, and in the cone the fish were caught and brought into the boat. This kind of net is the net in the parable of the dragnet, and is called the *sagēnē*.

So Jesus was walking by the lakeside; and as he walked he called Peter and Andrew, and James and John. It is not to be thought that this was the first time that he had seen them, or they him. As John tells the story, at least some of them were already disciples of John the Baptist (John 1:35). No doubt they had already talked with Jesus and had already listened to him, but in this moment there came to them the challenge once and for all to throw in their lot with him.

The Greeks used to tell how Xenophon first met Socrates. Socrates met him in a narrow lane and barred his path with his stick. First of all, Socrates asked him if he knew where he could buy this and that, and if he knew where this and that were made. Xenophon gave the required information. Then Socrates asked him: 'Do you know where men are made good and virtuous?' 'No,' said the young Xenophon. 'Then,' said Socrates, 'follow me and learn!'

Jesus, too, called on these fishermen to follow him. It is interesting to note what kind of men they were. They were not men of great scholarship, or influence, or wealth, or social background. They were not poor; they were simple, working people with no great background, and certainly, anyone would have said, with no great future.

It was these ordinary men whom Jesus chose. Once there came to Socrates a very ordinary man called Aeschines. 'I am a poor man,' said Aeschines. 'I have nothing else, but I give you myself.' 'Do you not see', said Socrates, 'that you are giving me the most precious thing of all?' What Jesus needs is ordinary men and women who will give him themselves. He can do anything with people like that.

Further, these men were fishermen. It has been pointed out by many scholars that those who are good at fishing must possess these very qualities which will make them equally good at 'catching' people.

(1) They must have *patience*. They must learn to wait patiently until the fish will take the bait. If they are restless and quick to move, they will never catch anything. To become good at bringing people in, we will have need of patience. It is but rarely in preaching or in teaching that we will see quick results. We must learn to wait.

(2) They must have *perseverance*. They must learn never to be discouraged, but always to try again. Good preachers and teachers must not be discouraged when nothing seems to happen. They must always be ready to try again.

(3) They must have *courage*. As the old Greek said when he prayed for the protection of the gods, 'My boat is so small and the sea is so large.' They must be ready to risk and to face the fury of the sea and of the gale. Good preachers and teachers must be well aware that there is always a danger in telling people the truth. Those who tell the truth, more often than not, take their reputation and their lives in their hands.

(4) They must have *an eye for the right moment*. Through experience, they know that there are times when it is hopeless to fish. They know when to cast and when not to cast. Good preachers and teachers chooses the right moment. There are times when people will welcome the truth, and times when they will resent the truth. There are times when the truth will move them, and times when the truth will harden them in their opposition to the truth. Wise preachers and teachers know that there is a time to speak and a time to be silent.

(5) They must *fit the bait to the fish*. One fish will rise to one bait and another to another. Paul said that he became all things to all people if by any chance he might win some (cf. 1 Corinthians 9:22). Wise preachers and teachers know that the same approach will not win everyone. They may even have to know and recognize their own limitations. They may

have to discover that there are certain spheres in which they themselves can work, and others in which they cannot.

(6) They must *keep themselves out of sight*. If they make their presence too obvious or even show their own shadows, the fish will certainly not bite. Wise preachers and teachers will always seek to present men and women not with themselves but with Jesus Christ. Their aim is to fix people's eyes not on themselves but on that figure beyond.

THE METHODS OF THE MASTER

Matthew 4:23–5

> Jesus made a circular tour of Galilee, teaching in the synagogues, proclaiming the good news of the kingdom, and healing all kinds of diseases and ailments among the people; and the report of his activities went out all over Syria. So they brought to him all those who were ill, those who were in the grip of the most varied diseases and pains, those who were possessed by demons, those who were epileptics, and those who were paralysed; and he healed them. And great crowds followed him from Galilee, and from the Decapolis, and from Jerusalem, and from Judaea, and from beyond Jordan.

JESUS had chosen to begin his mission in Galilee; and we have seen how well prepared Galilee was to receive the seed. With Galilee, Jesus chose to launch his campaign in the synagogues.

The synagogue was the most important institution in the life of any Jew. There was a difference between the synagogues and the Temple. There was only one Temple, the Temple in Jerusalem, but wherever there was the smallest colony of Jews there was a synagogue. The Temple existed solely for the offering of sacrifice; in it there was no preaching or teaching. The synagogue was essentially a teaching institution. The synagogues have been defined as 'the popular religious universities of their day'. If a man had any religious teaching or religious ideas to disseminate, the synagogue was unquestionably the place to start.

Further, the synagogue service was such that it gave the new teacher his chance. In the synagogue service, there were three parts. The first part consisted of prayers. The second part consisted of readings from the law and from the prophets, readings in which members of the congregation took part. The third part was the address. The important fact is that there was no one person to give the address. There was no such thing as a professional ministry. The president of the synagogue presided over the arrangements for the service. Any distinguished stranger could be asked to give the address, and anyone with a message to give might volunteer to give it; and, if the ruler or president of the synagogue judged him to be a fit person to speak, he was allowed to speak. Thus, at the beginning, the door of the synagogue and the pulpit of the synagogue were open to Jesus. He began in the synagogue because it was there he would find the most sincerely religious people of his day, and the way to speak to them was open to him. After the address, there came a time for talk, and questions, and discussion. The synagogue was the ideal place in which to get a new teaching across to the people.

But not only did Jesus preach; he also healed the sick. It was little wonder that reports of what he was doing went out and people came crowding to hear him, and to see him, and to benefit from his compassion.

They came from Syria. Syria was the great province of which Palestine was only a part. It stretched away to the north and the north-east with the great city of Damascus as its centre. It so happens that one of the loveliest legends passed down to us by the fourth-century historian Eusebius (*Ecclesiastical History*, 1:13) goes back to this time. The story goes that there was a king called Abgar, in Edessa, and he was ill. So, it is said, he wrote to Jesus: 'Abgar, ruler of Edessa, to Jesus, the most excellent Saviour, who has appeared in the country of Jerusalem – greeting. I have heard of you and of your cures, performed without medicine and without herb; for, it is said, you make the blind to see and the lame to walk, you cleanse the lepers, you cast out evil spirits and demons, you heal those afflicted with lingering diseases, and you raise the dead. Now, as I have heard all this about you, I have concluded that one of two things must be true; either, you are God, and having descended from heaven, you do these things, or else, you are a son of God by what you do. I write to you, therefore, to ask you to come and cure the disease from which I am suffering. For I have heard that the Jews murmur against you, and devise evil things against you. Now, I have a very small but an excellent city which is large enough for both of us.' Jesus was said to have written back: 'Blessed are you for having believed in me without seeing me. For it is written concerning me that those who have seen me will not believe in me, while they who have not seen me will believe and be saved. But, as to your request that I should come to you, I must fulfil all things here for which I have been sent, and, after fulfilling them, be taken up again to him who sent me. Yet, after I am taken up, I will send you one of my disciples to cure your disease, and to give life to you and to yours.' So, the legend goes on, Thaddaeus went to Edessa and cured Abgar. It is only a legend, but it does show how it was believed that even in distant Syria people had heard of Jesus and longed with all their hearts for the help and the healing which he alone could give.

Very naturally they came from Galilee, and the word about Jesus had spread south to Jerusalem and Judaea also, and they came from there. They came from the land across the Jordan, which was known as Peraea, and which stretched from Pella in the north to Arabia Petra in the south. They came from the Decapolis. The Decapolis was a federation of ten independent Greek cities, all of which, except Scythopolis, were on the far side of the Jordan.

This list is symbolic, for in it we see not only the Jews but the Gentiles also coming to Jesus Christ for what he alone could give them. Already the ends of the earth are gathering to him.

THE ACTIVITIES OF JESUS

Matthew 4:23-5 (*contd*)

THIS passage is of great importance because it gives us in brief summary the three great activities of Jesus' life.

(1) He came *proclaiming* the gospel, or, as the Authorized Version and Revised Standard Version have it, he came *preaching*. Now, as we have already seen, preaching is the proclamation of certainties. Therefore, *Jesus came to defeat human ignorance*. He came to tell men and women the truth about God, to tell them something that they could never have found out for themselves. He came to put an end to guessing and to groping, and to show them what God is like.

(2) He came *teaching* in the synagogues. What is the difference between *teaching* and *preaching*? Preaching is the uncompromising proclamation of certainties; teaching is the explanation of the meaning and the significance of them. Therefore, *Jesus came to defeat human misunderstandings*. There are times when we know the truth and misinterpret it.

We know the truth and draw the wrong conclusions from it. Jesus came to tell men and women the meaning of true religion.

(3) He came *healing* all those who had need of healing. That is to say, *Jesus came to defeat human pain*. The important thing about Jesus is that he was not satisfied with simply telling the truth in *words*; he came to turn that truth into deeds. Florence Allshorn, the great missionary teacher, said: 'An ideal is never yours until it comes out of your fingertips.' The ideal is not yours until it is made real in action. Jesus embodied his own teaching in deeds of help and healing.

Jesus came *preaching* that he might defeat all *ignorance*. He came *teaching* that he might defeat all *misunderstandings*. He came *healing* that he might defeat all *pain*. We, too, must proclaim our certainties; we, too, must be ready to explain our faith; we, too, must turn the ideal into action and into deeds.

THE SERMON ON THE MOUNT

As we have already seen, Matthew has a careful pattern in his gospel.

In his story of the baptism of Jesus, he shows us Jesus realizing that the hour has struck, that the call to action has come, and that Jesus must go forth on his crusade. In his story of the temptations, he shows us Jesus deliberately choosing the method he will use to carry out his task, and deliberately rejecting methods which he knew to be against the will of God. Anyone who embarks upon a great task needs helpers, assistants and staff. So Matthew goes on to show us Jesus selecting those who will be his fellow workers.

But if helpers and assistants are to do their work intelligently and effectively, they must first have instruction. And now, in the Sermon on the Mount, Matthew shows us Jesus instructing his disciples in the message which was his and which they were to take to the people. In Luke's account of the Sermon on the Mount, this becomes even clearer. In Luke, the Sermon on the Mount follows immediately after what we might call the official choosing of the Twelve (Luke 6:13ff.).

For that reason, one great scholar called the Sermon on the Mount 'the Ordination Address to the Twelve'. Just as young ministers have their task set out before them, when they are called to take charge of their first churches, so the Twelve received from Jesus their ordination address before they went out to their task. It is for that reason that other scholars have given other titles to the Sermon on the Mount. It has been called 'the Compendium of Christ's Doctrine', 'the Magna Carta [the charter of liberties] of the Kingdom' and 'the Manifesto of the King'. All are agreed that in the Sermon on the Mount we have the essence of the teaching of Jesus to the inner circle of his chosen disciples.

The Summary of the Faith

In actual fact, this is even truer than at first sight appears. We speak of the Sermon on the Mount as if it was one single sermon preached on one single occasion. But it is far more than that. There are good and compelling reasons for thinking that the Sermon on the Mount is far more than one sermon – that it is, in fact, a kind of epitome, a representative summary, of all the sermons that Jesus ever preached.

(1) Anyone who heard it in its present form would be exhausted long before the end. There is far too much in it for one hearing. It is one thing to sit and *read* it, and to pause and linger as we read; it would be entirely another thing to *listen* to it for the first time in spoken words. We can read at our

own pace and with a certain familiarity with the words; but to hear it in its present form for the first time would be to be dazzled with excess of light long before it was finished.

(2) There are certain sections of the Sermon on the Mount which emerge, as it were, without warning; they have no connection with what goes before and no connection with what comes after. For instance, Matthew 5:31–2 and Matthew 7:7–11 are quite detached from their context. There is a certain disconnection in the Sermon on the Mount.

(3) The most important point is this. Both Matthew and Luke give us a version of the Sermon on the Mount. In Matthew's version, there are 107 verses. Of these 107 verses, 29 are found all together in Luke 6:20–49; 44 have no parallel in Luke's version; and 34 are found scattered all over Luke's gospel in different contexts.

For instance, the simile of the salt is in Matthew 5:13 and in Luke 14:34–5; the simile of the lamp is in Matthew 5:15 and in Luke 8:16; the saying that not one jot or tittle of the law shall pass away is in Matthew 5:18 and in Luke 16:17. That is to say, passages which are consecutive in Matthew's gospel appear in widely separated chapters in Luke's gospel.

To take another example, the saying about the speck in one person's eye and the beam in our own is in Matthew 7:1–5 and in Luke 6:37–42; the passage in which Jesus gives the bidding to ask and seek and find is in Matthew 7:7–12 and in Luke 11:9–3.

If we tabulate these things, the matter will become clear:

Matthew 5:13	=	Luke 14:34–5
Matthew 5:15	=	Luke 8:16
Matthew 5:18	=	Luke 16:17
Matthew 7:1–5	=	Luke 6:37–42
Matthew 7:7–12	=	Luke 11:9–13

Now, as we have seen, Matthew is essentially the teaching gospel; it is Matthew's characteristic that he collects the teaching of Jesus under certain great headings; and it is surely far more likely that Matthew collected Jesus' teaching into one whole pattern, than that Luke took the pattern and broke it up and scattered the pieces all over his gospel. The Sermon on the Mount is not one single sermon which Jesus preached on one definite situation; it is the summary of his consistent teaching to his disciples. It has been suggested that, after Jesus definitely chose the Twelve, he may have taken them away into a quiet place for a week or even a longer period of time, and that, during that space, he taught them all the time, and the Sermon on the Mount is the distillation of that teaching.

Matthew's Introduction

In point of fact, Matthew's introductory sentence goes a long way to make that clear.

> Seeing the crowds, Jesus went up on the mountain, and when he sat down his disciples came to him. And he opened his mouth and taught them.

In that brief verse, there are three clues to the real significance of the Sermon on the Mount.

(1) Jesus began to teach *when he had sat down*. When a Jewish Rabbi was teaching officially, he sat to teach. We still speak of a professor's *chair*; the pope still speaks *ex cathedra*, from his seat. Often a Rabbi gave instruction when he was standing or strolling about; but his really official teaching was done when he had taken his seat. So, the very intimation that Jesus sat down to teach his disciples is the indication that this teaching is central and official.

(2) Matthew goes on to say that *when he had opened his mouth*, he taught them. This phrase *he opened his mouth* is

not simply a decoratively roundabout way of saying *he said*.
In Greek, the phrase has a double significance. (a) In Greek,
it is used of a solemn, grave and dignified utterance. It is
used, for instance, of the saying of an oracle. It is the natural
preface for a most weighty saying. (b) It is used when people
really open their hearts and fully pour out their minds. It is
used of intimate teaching with no barriers between. Again,
the very use of this phrase indicates that the material in the
Sermon on the Mount is no chance piece of teaching. It is the
grave and solemn utterance of the central things; it is the
opening of Jesus' heart and mind to those men who were to
be his right-hand men in his task.

(3) The Authorized Version has it that when Jesus had sat
down, he opened his mouth and *taught them saying*. In Greek,
there are two past tenses of the verb. There is the *aorist* tense,
and the aorist tense expresses one particular action, done and
completed in past time. In the sentence, 'He shut the gate,'
shut would be an aorist in Greek because it describes one completed action in past time. There is the *imperfect* tense, and
the imperfect tense describes repeated, continuous or habitual
action in past time. In the sentence, 'It was his custom to go to
church every Sunday,' in Greek *it was his custom to go* would
be expressed by a single verb in the imperfect tense, because
it describes continuous and often-repeated action in the past.

Now the point is that in the Greek of this sentence, which
we are studying, the verb *taught* is not an *aorist* but an
imperfect, and therefore it describes repeated and habitual
action, and the translation should be: ' This is what he used to
teach them.' Matthew has said as plainly as Greek will say it
that the Sermon on the Mount is not one sermon of Jesus,
given at one particular time and on one particular occasion; it
is the essence of all that Jesus continuously and habitually
taught his disciples.

The Sermon on the Mount is greater even than we think. Matthew in his introduction wishes us to see that it is the official teaching of Jesus; that it is the opening of Jesus' whole mind to his disciples; that it is the summary of the teaching which Jesus habitually gave to his inner circle. The Sermon on the Mount is nothing less than the concentrated memory of many hours of heart-to-heart communion between the disciples and their Master.

As we study the Sermon on the Mount, we are going to set at the head of each of the beatitudes the translation of the New Revised Standard Version; and then at the end of our study of each beatitude we shall see what the words mean in modern English.

THE SUPREME BLESSEDNESS

Matthew 5:3

'Blessed are the poor in spirit, for theirs is the kingdom of heaven.'

BEFORE we study each of the beatitudes in detail, there are two general facts which we must note.

(1) It can be seen that every one of the beatitudes has precisely the same form. As they are commonly printed in our Bibles, each one of them in the Authorized Version has the word *are* printed in italic, or sloping, type. When a word appears in italics in the Authorized Version it means that in the Greek, or in the Hebrew, there is no equivalent word, and that that word has had to be added to bring out the meaning of the sentence.

This is to say that in the beatitudes there is no verb, there is no *are*. Why should that be? Jesus did not speak the beatitudes in Greek; he spoke them in Aramaic, which was the kind of Hebrew people spoke in his day. Aramaic and Hebrew have a very common kind of expression, which is in fact an exclamation and which means: 'O the blessedness of . . .'. That expression (*asherē* in the Hebrew) is very common in the Old Testament. For instance, the first Psalm begins in the Hebrew: 'O the blessedness of those who do not follow the advice of the wicked' (cf. Psalm 1:1). That is the form in which Jesus first spoke the beatitudes. The beatitudes are not simple statements; they are exclamations: 'O the blessedness of the poor in spirit!'

That is most important, for it means that the beatitudes are not pious hopes of what shall be; they are not glowing, but vague prophecies of some future bliss; they are con-gratulations on what is. The blessedness which belongs to Christians is not a blessedness which is postponed to some future world of glory; it is a blessedness which exists here and now. It is not something into which Christians *will enter*; it is something into which they *have entered*.

True, it will find its fullness and its consummation in the presence of God; but, for all that, it is a present reality to be enjoyed here and now. The beatitudes in effect say: 'O the bliss of being a Christian! O the joy of following Christ! O the sheer happiness of knowing Jesus Christ as Master, Saviour and Lord!' The very form of the beatitudes is the statement of the joyous thrill and the radiant gladness of the Christian life. In the light of the beatitudes, a gloom-encompassed Christianity is unthinkable.

(2) The word *blessed* which is used in each of the beati-tudes is a very special word. It is the Greek word *makarios*. *Makarios* is the word which specially describes the gods. In Christianity, there is a godlike joy.

The meaning of *makarios* can best be seen from one particular usage of it. The Greeks always called Cyprus *hē makaria* (the feminine form of the adjective), which means *The Happy Isle*, and they did so because they believed that Cyprus was so lovely, so rich and so fertile an island that there was never any need to go beyond its coastline in order to find the perfectly happy life. It had such a climate, such flowers and fruits and trees, such minerals and such natural resources that it contained within itself all the materials for perfect happiness.

Makarios, then, describes that joy which has its secret within itself, that joy which is serene and untouchable, and self-contained, that joy which is completely independent of all the chances and the changes of life. The English word *happiness* gives its own case away. It contains the root *hap*, which means *chance*. Human happiness is something which is dependent on the chances and the changes of life, something which life may give and which life may also destroy. The Christian blessedness is completely untouchable and unassailable. 'No one', said Jesus, 'will take your joy from you' (John 16:22). The beatitudes speak of that joy which seeks us through our pain, that joy which sorrow and loss, and pain and grief, are powerless to touch, that joy which shines through tears, and which nothing in life or death can take away.

The world can win its joys, and the world can equally well lose its joys. A change in fortune, a collapse in health, the failure of a plan, the disappointment of an ambition, even a change in the weather, can take away the fickle joy the world can give. But the Christian has the serene and untouchable joy which comes from walking forever in the company and in the presence of Jesus Christ.

The greatness of the beatitudes is that they are not wistful glimpses of some future beauty; they are not even golden promises of some distant glory; they are triumphant shouts

of bliss for a permanent joy that nothing in the world can
ever take away.

THE BLISS OF THE DESTITUTE

Matthew 5:3 (*contd*)

IT seems a surprising way to begin talking about happiness
by saying: 'Blessed are the poor in spirit.' There are two ways
in which we can come at the meaning of this word *poor*.

As we have them, the beatitudes are in Greek, and the
word that is used for *poor* is the word *ptōchos*. In Greek,
there are two words for poor. There is the word *penēs*. *Penēs*
describes a man who has to work for his living; it is defined
by the Greeks as describing the man who is *autodiakonos*,
that is, *the man who serves his own needs with his own hands*.
Penēs describes the working man, the man who has nothing
superfluous, the man who is not rich, but who is not destitute
either. But, as we have seen, it is not *penēs* that is used in this
beatitude; it is *ptōchos*, which describes *absolute and abject
poverty*. It is connected with the root *ptōssein*, which means
to crouch or *to cower*; and it describes the poverty of those
literally forced to their knees to beg. As has been said, *penēs*
describes the person who has nothing superfluous, while
ptōchos describes the person who has nothing at all. So this
beatitude becomes even more surprising. Blessed are those
who are abjectly and completely poverty-stricken. Blessed
are those who are absolutely destitute.

As we have also seen, the beatitudes were originally spoken
not in Greek but in Aramaic. Now the Jews had a special
way of using the word *poor*. In Hebrew, the word is *'ani* or
ebiōn. These words in Hebrew underwent a four-stage
development of meaning. (1) They began by meaning simply

poor. (2) They went on to mean, *because poor, therefore having no influence or power, or help, or prestige*. (3) They went on to mean, *because having no influence, therefore downtrodden and oppressed*. (4) Finally, they came to describe *those who, because they have no earthly resources whatever, put their whole trust in God*.

So, in Hebrew the word *poor* was used to describe the humble and the helpless people who put their whole trust in God. It is thus that the psalmist uses the word, when he writes: 'This *poor soul* cried, and was heard by the Lord, and was saved from every trouble' (Psalm 34:6). It is in fact true that in the Psalms the poor person, in this sense of the term, is the good person who is dear to God. 'The hope of the poor [shall not] perish for ever' (Psalm 9:18). God delivers the needy (Psalm 35:10). 'In your goodness, O God, you provided for the needy' (Psalm 68:10). 'May he defend the cause of the poor of the people' (Psalm 72:4). 'He raises up the needy out of distress, and makes their families like flocks' (Psalm 107:41). 'I will satisfy its poor with bread' (Psalm 132:15). In all these cases, the *poor* are the humble and helpless who have put their trust in God.

Let us now take the two sides, the Greek and the Aramaic, and put them together. *Ptōchos* describes someone who is absolutely destitute, the person who has nothing at all; *'ani* and *ebiōn* describe the poor, and humble, and helpless who have put their whole trust in God. Therefore, 'Blessed are the poor in spirit' means:

> Blessed are those who have realized their own utter helplessness, and who have put their whole trust in God.

If people have realized their own utter helplessness, and have put their whole trust in God, there will enter into their lives two elements which are opposite sides of the same coin.

They will become completely *detached from material things*, for they will know that things do not have the power to bring happiness or security; and they will become completely *attached to God*, for they will know that God alone can bring them help, hope and strength. Those who are poor in spirit are men and women who have realized that things mean nothing, and that God means everything.

We must be careful not to think that this beatitude calls actual material poverty a good thing. Poverty is not a good thing. Jesus would never have called blessed a state where people live in slums and do not have enough to eat, and where health deteriorates because conditions are all against it. It is the aim of the Christian gospel to remove that kind of poverty. The poverty which is blessed is the poverty *of spirit*, when people realize their own utter lack of resources to meet life, and find their help and strength in God.

Jesus says that to such a poverty belongs the kingdom of heaven. Why should that be so? If we take the two petitions of the Lord's Prayer and set them together:

> Your kingdom come.
> Your will be done in earth as it is in heaven,

we get the definition: the kingdom of God is a society where God's will is as perfectly done in earth as it is in heaven. That means that only those who do God's will are citizens of the kingdom; and we can only do God's will when we realize our own utter helplessness, our own utter ignorance, our own utter inability to cope with life, and when we put our whole trust in God. Obedience is always founded on trust. The kingdom of God is the possession of the poor in spirit, because the poor in spirit have realized their own utter helplessness without God, and have learned to trust and obey.

So, the first beatitude means:

O THE BLISS OF THOSE WHO HAVE REALIZED THEIR OWN UTTER
HELPLESSNESS, AND WHO HAVE PUT THEIR WHOLE TRUST IN
GOD, FOR THUS ALONE CAN THEY RENDER TO GOD THAT
PERFECT OBEDIENCE WHICH WILL MAKE THEM CITIZENS OF
THE KINGDOM OF HEAVEN!

THE BLISS OF THE BROKEN HEART

Matthew 5:4

'Blessed are those who mourn, for they will be comforted.'

IT is first of all to be noted about this beatitude that the Greek
word for *to mourn*, used here, is the strongest word for
mourning in the Greek language. It is the word which is used
for mourning for the dead, for the passionate lament for one
who was loved. In the Septuagint, the Greek version of the
Old Testament, it is the word which is used of Jacob's grief
when he believed that Joseph, his son, was dead (Genesis
37:34). It is defined as the kind of grief which takes such a
hold that it cannot be hidden. It is not only the sorrow
which brings an ache to the heart; it is the sorrow which
brings the unrestrainable tears to the eyes. Here then indeed
is an amazing kind of bliss:

Blessed are those who mourn like those mourning for
the dead.

There are three ways in which this beatitude can be taken.

(1) It can be taken quite literally: blessed are those who
have endured the bitterest sorrow that life can bring. The
Arabs have a proverb: 'All sunshine makes a desert.' The
land on which the sun always shines will soon become an
arid place in which no fruit will grow. There are certain things

which only the rains will produce, and certain experiences which can only come out of sorrow.

Sorrow can do two things for us. It can show us, as nothing else can, the essential kindness of others; and it can show us, as nothing else can, the comfort and the compassion of God. So many people in the hour of their sorrow have discovered other people and God as never before. When things go well, it is possible to live for years on the surface of things; but when sorrow comes, we are driven to the deep things of life, and, if we accept it aright, a new strength and beauty will enter into our souls.

As Robert Browning Hamilton's poem, 'Along the Road', puts it:

> I walked a mile with Pleasure,
> 　　She chattered all the way,
> But left me none the wiser
> 　　For all she had to say.
>
> I walked a mile with Sorrow,
> 　　And ne'er a word said she,
> But, oh, the things I learned from her
> 　　When Sorrow walked with me!

(2) Some people have taken this beatitude to mean:

> Blessed are those who are desperately sorry for the sorrow and the suffering of this world.

When we were thinking of the first beatitude, we saw that it is always right to be detached from *things*, but it is never right to be detached from *people*. This world would have been a very much poorer place if there had not been those who cared intensely about the sorrows and the sufferings of others.

Through his work on the factory and coalmining acts in the nineteenth century, Lord Shaftesbury probably did more for ordinary working men and women and for little children than any social reformer ever did. It all began very simply. When he was a boy at Harrow, he was going along the street one day, and he met a pauper's funeral. The coffin was a shoddy, ill-made box. It was on a hand-barrow. The barrow was being pushed by a quartet of men who were drunk; and as they pushed the barrow along, they were singing ribald songs, and joking and jesting among themselves. As they pushed the barrow up the hill, the box, which was the coffin, fell off the barrow and burst open. Some people would have thought the whole business a good joke; some would have turned away in fastidious disgust; some would have shrugged their shoulders and would have felt that it had nothing to do with them, although it might be a pity that such things should happen. The young Shaftesbury saw it and said to himself: 'When I grow up, I'm going to give my life to see that things like that don't happen.' So he dedicated his life to caring for others.

Christianity *is* caring. This beatitude does mean: blessed are those who care intensely for the sufferings, and for the sorrows, and for the needs of others.

(3) No doubt both these thoughts are in this beatitude, but its main thought undoubtedly is: blessed are those who are desperately sorry for their own sin and their own un-worthiness.

As we have seen, the very first word of the message of Jesus was: 'Repent!' We cannot repent unless we are sorry for our sins. The thing which really changes people is when they suddenly come up against something which opens their eyes to what sin is and to what sin does. A boy or a girl may go his or her own way, and may never think of effects and consequences; and then some day something happens and that boy or girl sees the stricken look in a father's or a mother's eyes, and suddenly sin is seen for what it is.

That is what the cross does for us. As we look at the cross, we are bound to say: 'That is what sin can do. Sin can take the loveliest life in all the world and smash it on a cross.' One of the great functions of the cross is to open the eyes of men and women to the horror of sin. And when they see sin in all its horror, they cannot do anything else but experience intense sorrow for their sin.

Christianity begins with a sense of sin. Blessed are those who are intensely sorry for their sin, those who are heart-broken for what their sin has done to God and to Jesus Christ, those who see the cross and who are appalled by the havoc wrought by sin.

It is the man or woman who has that experience who will indeed be comforted; for that experience is what we call penitence, and the broken and the contrite heart God will never despise (Psalm 51:17). The way to the joy of forgiveness is through the desperate sorrow of the broken heart.

The real meaning of the second beatitude is:

O THE BLISS OF THOSE WHOSE HEARTS ARE BROKEN FOR THE WORLD'S SUFFERING AND FOR THEIR OWN SIN, FOR OUT OF THEIR SORROW THEY WILL FIND THE JOY OF GOD!

THE BLISS OF THE GOD-CONTROLLED LIFE

Matthew 5:5

'Blessed are the meek, for they will inherit the earth.'

IN our modern English idiom, the word *meek* is hardly one of the honourable words of life. Nowadays, it carries with it an idea of spinelessness, subservience and mean-spiritedness. It paints the picture of a submissive and ineffective person. But it so happens that the word *meek* – in Greek *praus* – was one of the great Greek ethical words.

Aristotle has a great deal to say about the quality of *meekness* (*praotēs*). It was Aristotle's fixed method to define every virtue as the happy medium between two extremes. On the one hand there was the extreme of excess; on the other hand there was the extreme of defect; and in between there was the virtue itself, the happy medium. To take an example, on the one extreme there is the spendthrift; on the other extreme there is the miser; and in between there is the generous person.

Aristotle defines *meekness*, *praotēs*, as the balance between *orgilotēs*, which means *excessive anger*, and *aorgēsia*, which means *excessive angerlessness*. *Praotēs*, *meekness*, as Aristotle saw it, is the happy medium between too much and too little anger. And so the first possible translation of this beatitude is:

> Blessed are those who are always angry at the right time, and never angry at the wrong time.

If we ask what the right time and the wrong time are, we may say as a general rule for life that it is never right to be angry for any insult or injury done to ourselves – that is something that no Christian must ever resent – but that it is often right to be angry at injuries done to other people. Selfish anger is always a sin; selfless anger can be one of the great moral dynamics of the world.

But the word *praus* has a second standard Greek usage. It is the regular word for an animal which has been domesticated, which has been trained to obey the word of command, which has learned to respond to the reins. It is the word for an animal which has learned to accept control. So the second possible translation of this beatitude is:

> Blessed are those who have every instinct, every impulse, every passion under control. Blessed are those who are entirely self-controlled.

The moment we have stated that, we see that it needs a change. It is not so much the blessing of those who are *self*-controlled, for such complete self-control is beyond human capacity; rather, it is the blessing of those who are completely *God*-controlled, for only in his service do we find our perfect freedom and, in doing his will, our peace.

But there is still a third possible side from which we may approach this beatitude. The Greeks always contrasted the quality which they called *praotēs*, and which the Authorized Version translates as *meekness*, with the quality which they called *hupsēlokardia*, which means *lofty-heartedness*. In *praotēs*, there is the true humility which banishes all pride.

Without humility we cannot learn, for the first step to learning is the realization of our own ignorance. Quintilian, the great Roman teacher of oratory, said of certain of his scholars: 'They would no doubt be excellent students, if they were not already convinced of their own knowledge.' No one can teach people who know it all already. Without humility there can be no such thing as love, for the very beginning of love is a sense of unworthiness. Without humility there can be no true religion, for all true religion begins with a realization of our own weakness and of our need for God. True humanity can only be reached when we are always conscious that we are the creatures and that God is the Creator, and that without God we can do nothing.

Praotēs describes humility, the acceptance of the necessity to learn and of the necessity to be forgiven. It describes the only proper attitude to God. So, the third possible translation of this beatitude is:

> Blessed are those who have the humility to know their own ignorance, their own weakness, and their own need.

It is this meekness, Jesus says, which will inherit the earth. It is the fact of history that it has always been those who possess this gift of self-control, those with their passions, instincts and impulses under discipline, who have been great. Numbers says of Moses, the greatest leader and the greatest law-giver the world has ever seen: 'Now the man Moses was very humble, more so than anyone else on the face of the earth' (Numbers 12:3). Moses was no milk-and-water character; he was no spineless creature; he could be blazingly angry; but he was a man whose anger was on the leash, only to be released when the time was right. The writer of Proverbs has it: 'One whose temper is controlled [is better] than one who captures a city' (Proverbs 16:32).

It was the lack of that very quality which ruined Alexander the Great, who, in a fit of uncontrolled temper in the middle of a drunken debauch, hurled a spear at his best friend and killed him. We cannot lead others until we have found our own direction in life; we cannot serve others until we have put aside self; we cannot be in control of others until we have learned to control ourselves. But those who give themselves into the complete control of God will gain this meekness, which will indeed enable them to inherit the earth.

It is clear that this word *praus* means far more than the English word *meek* now means; it is, in fact, clear that there is no one English word which will translate it, although perhaps the word *gentle* comes nearest to it. The full translation of this third beatitude must read:

O THE BLISS OF THOSE WHO ARE ALWAYS ANGRY AT THE RIGHT
TIME AND NEVER ANGRY AT THE WRONG TIME, WHO HAVE
EVERY INSTINCT, IMPULSE AND PASSION UNDER CONTROL
BECAUSE THEY THEMSELVES ARE GOD-CONTROLLED, WHO
HAVE THE HUMILITY TO REALIZE THEIR OWN IGNORANCE AND
THEIR OWN WEAKNESS, FOR SUCH PEOPLE CAN INDEED RULE
THE WORLD!

THE BLISS OF THE STARVING SPIRIT

Matthew 5:6

'Blessed are those who hunger and thirst for righteousness, for they will be filled.'

WORDS do not exist in isolation; they exist against a background of experience and of thought; and the meaning of any
word is conditioned by the background of the person who
speaks it. That is particularly true of this beatitude. It would
convey to those who heard it for the first time an impression
quite different from the impression which it conveys to us.

The fact is that very few of us in modern conditions of
life know what it is to be really hungry or really thirsty. In
the ancient world, it was very different. A working man's
wage was one denarius, not a wage on which anyone ever
got fat. A working man in Palestine ate meat only once a
week, and in Palestine the working man and the day labourer
were never far from the borderline of real hunger and actual
starvation.

It was still more so in the case of thirst. It was not possible
for the vast majority of people to turn a tap and find the clear,
cold water pouring into their house. A traveller might be on a
journey, and in the middle of it the hot wind which brought
the sandstorm might begin to blow. There was nothing for

him to do but to wrap his head in his hooded cloak and turn his back to the wind, and wait, while the swirling sand filled his nostrils and his throat until he was likely to suffocate, and until he was parched with an overpowering thirst. In the conditions of modern western life, there is no parallel at all to that.

So, the hunger which this beatitude describes is no genteel hunger which could be satisfied with a mid-morning snack; the thirst of which it speaks is no thirst which could be quenched with a cup of coffee or an iced drink. It is the hunger of someone who is starving for food, and the thirst of someone who will die unless given something to drink.

Since that is so, this beatitude is in reality a question and a challenge. In effect, it demands: 'How much do you want goodness? Do you want it as much as a starving person wants food, and as much as someone dying of thirst wants water?' How intense is our desire for goodness?

Most people have an instinctive desire for goodness, but that desire is wistful and vague rather than sharp and intense; and when the moment of decision comes they are not prepared to make the effort and the sacrifice which real goodness demands. Most people suffer from what the author Robert Louis Stevenson called 'the malady of not wanting'. It would obviously make the biggest difference in the world if we desired goodness more than anything else.

When we approach this beatitude from that side, it is the most demanding, and indeed the most frightening, of them all. But not only is it the most demanding beatitude; in its own way it is also the most comforting. At the back of it, there is the meaning that those who are blessed are not necessarily the people who achieve this goodness, but the people who long for it with their whole heart. If blessedness came only to those who achieved, then none would be blessed. But blessedness comes to all who, in spite of failures and failings, still clutch to themselves the passionate love of the highest.

The writer H. G. Wells somewhere said: 'A man may be a bad musician and yet be passionately in love with music.' Robert Louis Stevenson spoke of even those who have sunk to the lowest depths 'clutching the remnants of virtue to them in the brothel and on the scaffold'. Sir Norman Birkett, the famous lawyer and judge, once, speaking of the criminals with whom he had come into contact in his work, spoke of the inextinguishable something in every individual. Goodness, 'the implacable hunter', is always at their heels. The worst of all people are 'condemned to some kind of nobility'.

The true wonder of human beings is not that we are sinners, but that even in our sin we are haunted by goodness, that even in the mud we can never wholly forget the stars. David had always wished to build the Temple of God; he never achieved that ambition; it was denied and forbidden him; but as the Revised Standard Version has it, God said to him: 'You did well that it was in your heart' (1 Kings 8:18). In his mercy, God judges us not only by our achievements but also by our dreams. Even if we never attain goodness, if to the end of the day we are still hungering and thirsting for it, we are not shut out from blessedness.

There is one further point in this beatitude, a point which only emerges in the Greek. It is a rule of Greek grammar that verbs of hungering and thirsting are followed by the genitive case. The genitive case is the case which, in English, is expressed by the word *of*; *of the people* is the genitive case. The genitive which follows verbs of hungering and thirsting in Greek is called the partitive genitive, that is the genitive of the part. The idea is this. When a Greek said: 'I hunger for of bread,' it was some bread that was desired, a part of the bread, not the whole loaf. When a Greek said: 'I thirst for of water,' it was some water that was desired, a drink of water, not all the water in the tank.

But in this beatitude, most unusually, *righteousness* is in the direct accusative, and not in the normal genitive. Now, when verbs of hungering and thirsting in Greek take the accusative instead of the genitive, the meaning is that the hunger and the thirst are for *the whole thing*. To say I hunger for bread in the accusative means I want the whole loaf. To say I thirst for water in the accusative means I want the whole pitcher. There, the correct translation is:

> Blessed are those who hunger and thirst for the whole
> of righteousness, for complete righteousness.

That is in fact what people seldom do. They are content with a part of righteousness. Some people, for instance, may be good in the sense that, however hard one tried, one could not pin a moral fault on to them. Their honesty, their morality and their respectability are beyond question; but it may be that no one could go to them and pour out a sorry story to them; they would freeze if one tried to do so. There can be a goodness which is accompanied with a hardness, a censoriousness, a lack of sympathy. Such a goodness is a partial goodness.

On the other hand, people may have all kinds of faults; they may drink, swear, gamble and lose their temper; and yet, if anyone is in trouble, they would give the last penny out of their pocket and the very coat off their back. Again, that is a partial goodness.

This beatitude says that it is not enough to be satisfied with a partial goodness. Blessed are those who hunger and thirst for the goodness which is total. Neither an icy faultlessness nor a faulty warm-heartedness is enough.

So, the translation of the fourth beatitude could run:

O THE BLISS OF THOSE WHO LONG FOR TOTAL RIGHTEOUSNESS
AS THE STARVING LONG FOR FOOD, AND THOSE PERISHING OF
THIRST LONG FOR WATER, FOR THEY WILL BE TRULY SATISFIED!

THE BLISS OF PERFECT SYMPATHY

Matthew 5:7

'Blessed are the merciful, for they will receive mercy.'

EVEN as it stands, this is surely a great saying; and it is the
statement of a principle which runs all through the New
Testament. The New Testament is insistent that to be forgiven
we must be forgiving. As James had it: 'For judgement will
be without mercy to anyone who has shown no mercy'
(James 2:13). Jesus finishes the story of the unforgiving debtor
with the warning: 'So my heavenly Father will also do to
every one of you, if you do not forgive your brother or sister
from your heart' (Matthew 18:35). The Lord's Prayer is
followed by the two verses which explain and underline the
petition: 'Forgive us our debts, as we also have forgiven our
debtors.' 'For if you forgive others their trespasses, your
heavenly Father will also forgive you; but if you do not
forgive others, neither will your Father forgive your trespasses' (Matthew 6:12, 14–15). It is the consistent teaching
of the New Testament that indeed only the merciful shall
receive mercy.

But there is even more to this beatitude than that. The
Greek word for *merciful* is *eleēmōn*. But, as we have repeatedly seen, the Greek of the New Testament as we possess
it goes back to an original Hebrew and Aramaic. The Hebrew
word for *mercy* is *chesedh*; and it is an untranslatable word.
It does not mean only to sympathize with a person in the

popular sense of the term; it does not mean simply to feel sorry for someone in trouble. *Chesedh*, *mercy*, means the ability to get right inside other people until we can see things with their eyes, think things with their minds and feel things with their feelings.

Clearly, this is much more than an emotional wave of pity; clearly, this demands a quite deliberate effort of the mind and of the will. It denotes a sympathy which is not given, as it were, from outside, but which comes from a deliberate identification with other people, until we see things as they see them, and feel things as they feel them. This is *sympathy* in the literal sense of the word. *Sympathy* is derived from two Greek words, *syn* which means *together with*, and *paschein* which means *to experience* or *to suffer*. *Sympathy* means *experiencing things together with other people*, literally going through what they are going through.

This is precisely what many people do not even try to do. Most people are so concerned with their own feelings that they are not much concerned with the feelings of anyone else. When they are sorry for someone, it is, as it were, from the outside; they do not make the deliberate effort to get inside the other person's mind and heart, until they see and feel things as that person sees and feels them.

If we did make this deliberate attempt, and if we did achieve this identification with the other person, it would obviously make a very great difference.

(1) It would save us from being kind in the wrong way. There is one outstanding example of insensitive and mistaken kindness in the New Testament. It is in the story of Jesus' visit to the house of Martha and Mary at Bethany (Luke 10:38–42). When Jesus paid that visit, the cross was only a few days ahead. All that he wanted was an opportunity for

so short a time to rest and to relax, and to lay down the terrible tension of living.

Martha loved Jesus; he was her most honoured guest; and because she loved him she would provide the best meal the house could supply. She bustled and scurried here and there with the clatter of dishes and the clash of pans; and every moment was torture to the tense nerves of Jesus. All he wanted was quiet.

Martha meant to be kind, but she could hardly have been more cruel. But Mary understood that Jesus wished only for peace. So often when we wish to be kind, the kindness has to be given in our way, and other people have to put up with it whether they like it or not. Our kindness would be doubly kind, and would be saved from much quite unintentional unkindness, if we would only make the effort to get inside other people.

(2) It would make forgiveness and tolerance so much easier. There is one principle in life which we often forget – there is always a reason why people think and act as they do; and, if we knew that reason, it would be so much easier to understand and to sympathize and to forgive. If someone thinks, as we see it, mistakenly, that person may have come through experiences, and may have a heritage which has shaped that way of thinking. If someone is irritable and discourteous, that person may be worried or in pain. If someone treats us badly, it may be because there is some idea in that person's mind which is quite mistaken.

Truly, as the French proverb has it, 'to know all is to forgive all'; but we will never know all until we make the deliberate attempt to get inside the other person's mind and heart.

(3) In the last analysis, is not that what God did in Jesus Christ? In Jesus Christ, in the most literal sense, God got inside the skin of human beings. He came as a man; he came

seeing things with human eyes, feeling things with human feelings, thinking things with human minds. God knows what life is like, because God came right inside life.

Queen Victoria was a close friend of Principal and Mrs John Tulloch of St Andrews. Prince Albert died, and Victoria was left alone. Just at the same time, Principal Tulloch died and Mrs Tulloch was left alone. Completely unannounced, Queen Victoria came to call on Mrs Tulloch when she was resting on a couch in her room. When the queen was announced, Mrs Tulloch struggled to rise quickly from the couch and to curtsey. The queen stepped forward: 'My dear,' she said, 'don't rise. I am not coming to you today as the queen to a subject, but as one woman who has lost her husband to another.'

That is just what God did; he came to us, not as the remote, detached, isolated, majestic God, but as a man. The supreme instance of *mercy*, *chesedh*, is the coming of God in Jesus Christ.

It is only those who show this mercy who will receive it. This is true on the human side, for it is the great truth of life that in other people we see the reflection of ourselves. If we are detached and show no interest in them, they will be detached and will show no interest in us. If they see that we care, their hearts will respond in caring. It is supremely true on the divine side, for those who show this mercy have become nothing less than like God.

So, the translation of the fifth beatitude might read:

O THE BLISS OF THOSE WHO GET RIGHT INSIDE OTHER PEOPLE, UNTIL THEY CAN SEE WITH THEIR EYES, THINK WITH THEIR THOUGHTS, FEEL WITH THEIR FEELINGS, FOR THOSE WHO DO THAT WILL FIND OTHERS DO THE SAME FOR THEM, AND WILL KNOW THAT THAT IS WHAT GOD IN JESUS CHRIST HAS DONE!

THE BLISS OF THE CLEAN HEART

Matthew 5:8

'Blessed are the pure in heart, for they will see God.'

HERE is the beatitude which demands that all who read it should stop and think, and examine themselves.

The Greek word for *pure* is *katharos*, and it has a variety of usages, all of which have something to add to the meaning of this beatitude for the Christian life.

(1) Originally it simply meant *clean*, and could, for instance, be used of soiled clothes which have been washed clean.

(2) It is regularly used for corn which has been winnowed or sifted and cleansed of all chaff. In the same way, it is used of an army which has been purged of all discontented, cowardly, unwilling and inefficient soldiers, and which is a force composed solely of first-class fighting men.

(3) It very commonly appears in company with another Greek adjective – *akēratos*. *Akēratos* can be used of milk or wine which is unadulterated with water, or of metal which has in it no tinge of alloy.

So, the basic meaning of *katharos* is *unmixed, unadulterated, unalloyed*. That is why this beatitude is so demanding a beatitude. It could be translated:

Blessed are those whose motives are always entirely unmixed, for they shall see God.

It is very seldom indeed that we do even our finest actions from absolutely unmixed motives. If we give generously and liberally to some good cause, it may well be that there lingers in the depths of our hearts some contentment in basking in the sunshine of our own self-approval, some pleasure in the praise and thanks and credit which we will receive. If we do

some fine thing, which demands some sacrifice from us, it
may well be that we are not altogether free from the feeling
that others will see something heroic in us and that we may
regard ourselves as martyrs. Even the most sincere preacher
is not altogether free from the danger of self-satisfaction in
having preached a good sermon. Was it not John Bunyan
who was once told by someone that he had preached well
that day, and who answered sadly: 'The devil already told
me that as I was coming down the pulpit steps'?

This beatitude demands from us the most exacting self-
examination. Is our work done from motives of service or
from motives of pay? Is our service given from selfless
motives or from motives of self-display? Is the work we do
in church done for Christ or for our own prestige? Is our
church-going an attempt to meet God or a fulfilling of a
habitual and conventional respectability? Are even our prayer
and our Bible-reading engaged upon with the sincere desire
to keep company with God or because it gives us a pleasant
feeling of superiority to do these things? Is our religion a
thing in which we are conscious of nothing so much as the
need of God within our hearts, or a thing in which we have
comfortable thoughts of our own piety? To examine one's
own motives is a daunting and a shaming thing, for there are
few things in this world that even the best of us do with
completely unmixed motives.

Jesus went on to say that only the pure in heart will see
God. It is one of the simple facts of life that we see only what
we are able to see; and that is true not only in the physical
sense; it is also true in every other possible sense.

If we go out on a night of stars, our untrained eyes see
only a host of pinpoints of light in the sky; we see what we
are fit to see. But in that same sky the astronomer will call
the stars and the planets by their names, and will move among

them as among friends; and from that same sky the navigator could find the means to bring a ship across the trackless seas to the desired haven.

The ordinary person can walk along a country road and see by the hedgerows nothing but a tangle of weeds and wild flowers and grasses. The trained botanist would see this and that, and call it by name and know its use, and might even see something of infinite value and rarity through having eyes to see.

Put two people into a room filled with ancient pictures. A person with no knowledge and no skill could not tell an old master from a worthless daub, whereas a trained art critic might well discern a picture of immense value in a collection which someone else might dismiss as junk.

There are people with filthy minds who can see in any situation material for sniggering innuendo and a dirty joke. In every sphere of life, we see what we are able to see.

So, says Jesus, it is only the pure in heart who shall see God. It is a warning thing to remember that, as by God's grace we keep our hearts clean, or as by human lust we soil them, we are either fitting or unfitting ourselves some day to see God.

So, this sixth beatitude might read:

O THE BLISS OF THOSE WHOSE MOTIVES ARE ABSOLUTELY PURE,
FOR THEY WILL SOME DAY BE ABLE TO SEE GOD!

THE BLISS OF BRINGING PEOPLE TOGETHER

Matthew 5:9

'Blessed are the peacemakers, for they will be called children of God.'

W E must begin our study of this beatitude by investigating certain matters of meaning in it.

(1) First, there is the word *peace*. In Greek, the word is *eirēnē*, and in Hebrew it is *shalōm*. In Hebrew, *peace* is never only a negative state; it never means only the absence of trouble; in Hebrew, *peace* always means *everything which makes for a person's highest good*. In the middle east, when people say to one another *Salaam* – which is the same word – they do not mean that they wish for the others only the absence of evil things; they wish for them the presence of all good things. In the Bible, peace means not only freedom from all trouble, it means enjoyment of all good.

(2) Second, it must be carefully noted what the beatitude is saying. The blessing is on the peace*makers*, not necessarily on the peace*lovers*. It very often happens that if people love peace in the wrong way, they succeed in making trouble and not peace. We may, for instance, allow a threatening and dangerous situation to develop, and our defence is that for peace's sake we do not want to take any action. There are many people who think that they are loving peace, when in fact they are piling up trouble for the future, because they refuse to face the situation and to take the action which the situation demands. The peace which the Bible calls blessed does not come from the evasion of issues; it comes from facing them, dealing with them and conquering them. What this beatitude demands is not the passive acceptance of things because we are afraid of the trouble of doing anything about them, but the active facing of things, and the *making* of peace, even when the way to peace is through struggle.

(3) The Authorized Version (echoed by the New Revised Standard Version) says that the peacemakers shall be called the *children* of God; the Greek more literally is that the peacemakers will be called the *sons* (*huioi*) of God. This is a

typical Hebrew way of expression. Hebrew is not rich in adjectives, and often when Hebrew wishes to describe something, it uses not an adjective but the phrase *son of . . .* plus an abstract noun. Hence a man may be called *a son of peace* instead of *a peaceful man*. Barnabas is called *a son of consolation* instead of *a consoling and comforting man* (cf. Acts 4:36). This beatitude says: blessed are the peacemakers, for they shall be called the sons of God; what it means is: blessed are the peacemakers, for they shall be doing a Godlike work. Those who make peace are engaged on the very work which the God of peace is doing (Romans 15:33; 2 Corinthians 13:11; 1 Thessalonians 5:23; Hebrews 13:20).

The meaning of this beatitude has been sought along three main lines.

(1) It has been suggested that, since *shalōm* means everything which makes for a person's highest good, this beatitude means: blessed are those who make this world a better place for everyone to live in. Abraham Lincoln once said: 'Die when I may, I would like it to be said of me that I always pulled up a weed and planted a flower where I thought a flower would grow.' This then would be the beatitude of those who have lifted the world a little further on.

(2) Most of the early scholars of the Church took this beatitude in a purely spiritual sense, and held that it meant: blessed are those who make peace in their own hearts and in their own souls. In every one of us, there is an inner conflict between good and evil; we are always tugged in two directions at once; everyone is at least to some extent a walking civil war. Happy indeed are those who have won through to inner peace, in which the inner warfare is over, and whole hearts are given to God.

(3) But there is another meaning for this word *peace*. It is a meaning on which the Jewish Rabbis loved to dwell, and it

is almost certainly the meaning which Jesus had in his mind. The Jewish Rabbis held that the highest task which anyone can perform is to establish *right relationships* with other people. That is what Jesus means.

There are people who are always storm centres of trouble and bitterness and strife. Wherever they are, they are either involved in quarrels themselves or the cause of quarrels between others. They are troublemakers. There are people like that in almost every society and every church, and such people are doing the devil's own work. On the other hand – thank God – there are people in whose presence bitterness cannot live, people who bridge the gulfs, and heal the breaches, and sweeten the bitternesses. Such people are doing a Godlike work, for it is the great purpose of God to bring peace between men and women and himself, and among all people. Anyone who divides people is doing the devil's work; anyone who unites people is doing God's work.

So, this beatitude might read:

> O THE BLISS OF THOSE WHO PRODUCE RIGHT RELATIONSHIPS
> ONE WITH ANOTHER, FOR THEY ARE DOING A GODLIKE WORK!

THE BLISS OF THE SUFFERER FOR CHRIST

Matthew 5:10–12

> 'Blessed are those who are persecuted for righteousness' sake, for theirs is the kingdom of heaven.
>
> 'Blessed are you when people revile you and persecute you and utter all kinds of evil against you falsely on my account. Rejoice and be glad, for your reward is great in heaven, for in the same way they persecuted the prophets who were before you.'

ONE of the outstanding qualities of Jesus was his sheer honesty. He never left people in any doubt what would happen to them if they chose to follow him. He was clear that he had come 'not to make life easy, but to make us great'.

It is hard for us to realize what the first Christians had to suffer. Every department of their life was disrupted.

(1) Their Christianity might well disrupt their *work*. Suppose a man was a stone mason. That seems a harmless enough occupation. But suppose his firm received a contract to build a temple to one of the pagan gods, what was that man to do? Suppose a man was a tailor, and suppose his firm was asked to produce robes for the pagan priests, what was that man to do? In a situation such as that in which the early Christians found themselves, there was hardly any job in which a man might not find a conflict between his business interests and his loyalty to Jesus Christ.

The Church was in no doubt where an individual's duty lay. More than 100 years after this, a man came to Tertullian with this very problem. He told of his business difficulties. He ended by saying: 'What can I do? I must live!' 'Must you?' said Tertullian. If it came to a choice between a loyalty and a living, the real Christian never hesitated to choose loyalty.

(2) Their Christianity would certainly disrupt their *social* life. In the ancient world, most feasts were held in the temple of some god. In very few sacrifices was the whole animal burned upon the altar. It might be that only a few hairs from the forehead of the beast were burned as a symbolic sacrifice. Part of the meat went to the priests as their 'perks'; and part of the meat was returned to the worshipper. With his share, he made a feast for his friends and his relatives. One of the gods most commonly worshipped was Serapis. And when the invitations to the feast went out, they would read:

I invite you to dine with me at the table of our Lord
Serapis.

Could a Christian share in a feast held in the temple of a
pagan god? Even an ordinary meal in an ordinary house began
with a libation, a cup of wine, poured out in honour of the
gods. It was like grace before a meal. Could a Christian
become a sharer in a pagan act of worship like that? Again
the Christian answer was clear. Christians must cut themselves
off from their fellows rather than give approval to such a thing
by their presence. People had to be prepared to be lonely in
order to be Christians.

(3) Worst of all, their Christianity was liable to disrupt
their *home* life. It happened again and again that one member
of a family became a Christian while the others did not. A
wife might become a Christian while her husband did not.
A son or a daughter might become a Christian while the rest
of the family did not. Immediately there was a split in the
family. Often the door was shut forever in the face of the one
who had accepted Christ.

Christianity often came to send not peace but a sword
which divided families in two. It was literally true that a man
might have to love Christ more than he loved father or mother,
wife, or brother or sister. Christianity often involved in those
days a choice between a man's or a woman's nearest and
dearest and Jesus Christ.

Still further, the penalties which a Christian had to suffer
were terrible beyond description. All the world knows of the
Christians who were flung to the lions or burned at the stake;
but these were kindly deaths. Nero wrapped the Christians in
pitch and set them alight, and used them as living torches to
light his gardens. He sewed them in the skins of wild animals
and set his hunting dogs upon them to tear them to death.

They were tortured on the rack; they were scraped with pincers; molten lead was poured hissing upon them; red-hot brass plates were affixed to the tenderest parts of their bodies; eyes were torn out; parts of their bodies were cut off and roasted before their eyes; their hands and feet were burned while cold water was poured over them to lengthen the agony. These things are not pleasant to think about, but these are the things men and women had to be prepared for, if they took their stand with Christ.

We may well ask why the Romans persecuted the Christians. It seems an extraordinary thing that anyone living a Christian life should seem a fit victim for persecution and death. There were two reasons.

(1) There were certain slanders which were circulating about the Christians. (a) The Christians were accused of cannibalism. The words of the Last Supper – 'This is my body,' 'This cup is the New Testament in my blood' – were taken and twisted into a story that the Christians sacrificed a child and ate the flesh. (b) The Christians were accused of immoral practices, and their meetings were said to be orgies of lust. The Christian weekly meeting was called the *Agapē*, the Love Feast; and the name was grossly misinterpreted. Christians greeted each other with the kiss of peace; and the kiss of peace became a ground on which to build the slanderous accusations. (c) The Christians were accused of being fire-raisers. It is true that they spoke of the coming end of the world, and they clothed their message in the apocalyptic pictures of the end of the world in flames. Their slanderers took these words and twisted them into threats of being political and revolutionary agitators. (d) The Christians were accused of tampering with family relationships. Christianity did in fact split families as we have seen; and so Christianity was represented as something which divided husband and

wife, and disrupted the home. There were slanders enough
waiting to be invented by malicious-minded people.

(2) But the great ground of persecution was in fact
political. Let us think of the situation. The Roman Empire
included almost the whole known world, from Britain to the
Euphrates, and from Germany to North Africa. How could
that vast amalgam of peoples be somehow welded into
one? Where could a unifying principle be found? At first
it was found in the worship of the goddess Roma, the spirit
of Rome. This was a worship which the provincial peoples
were happy to give, for Rome had brought them peace
and good government, and civil order and justice. The
roads were cleared of bandits and the seas of pirates; the
despots and tyrants had been banished by impartial Roman
justice. The provincial peoples were very willing to
sacrifice to the spirit of the empire which had done so much
for them.

But this worship of Roma took a further step. There was
one man who personified the empire, one man in whom Roma
might be felt to be incarnated, and that was the emperor; and
so the emperor came to be regarded as a god, and divine
honours came to be paid to him, and temples were raised to
his divinity. The Roman government did not begin this
worship; at first, in fact, it did all it could to discourage it.
Claudius, the emperor, said that he deprecated divine honours
being paid to any human being. But as the years went on, the
Roman government saw in this emperor-worship the one
thing which could unify the vast empire of Rome; here was
the one centre on which they could all come together. So, in
the end, the worship of the emperor became not voluntary
but compulsory. Once a year, people had to go and burn a
pinch of incense to the godhead of Caesar and say: 'Caesar is
Lord.' And that is precisely what the Christians refused to

do. For them Jesus Christ was the Lord, and to no one would they give that title which belonged to Christ.

It can be seen at once that Caesar-worship was far more a test of political loyalty than anything else. In actual fact, when the pinch of incense had been burned, a certificate, a *libellus*, was issued to say that it had been done, and then people could go and worship any god they liked, so long as that worship did not interfere with public order and decency. The Christians refused to conform. Confronted with the choice, 'Caesar or Christ?', they uncompromisingly chose Christ. They utterly refused to compromise. The result was that, however good and however upstanding as citizens Christians were, they were automatically outlaws. In the vast empire, Rome could not afford pockets of disloyalty, and that is exactly what every Christian congregation appeared to the Roman authorities to be. A poet has spoken of

> The panting, huddled flock whose crime was Christ.

The only crime of which Christians were guilty was that they set Christ above Caesar; and for that supreme loyalty the Christians died in their thousands, and faced torture for the sake of the lonely supremacy of Jesus Christ.

THE BLISS OF THE BLOOD-STAINED WAY

Matthew 5:10–12 (*contd*)

When we see how persecution arose, we are in a position to see the real glory of the martyr's way. It may seem an extra-ordinary thing to talk about the bliss of the persecuted; but for those who had eyes to see beyond the immediate present, and minds to understand the greatness of the issues involved, there must have been a glory in that blood-stained way.

(1) To have to suffer persecution was an opportunity to show one's loyalty to Jesus Christ. One of the most famous of all the martyrs was Polycarp, the aged bishop of Smyrna. The mob dragged him to the tribunal of the Roman magistrate. He was given the inevitable choice – sacrifice to the godhead of Caesar or die. 'Eighty and six years', came the immortal reply, 'have I served Christ, and he has done me no wrong. How can I blaspheme my King who saved me?' So they brought him to the stake, and he prayed his last prayer: 'O Lord God Almighty, the Father of thy well-beloved and ever-blessed Son, by whom we have received the knowledge of thee . . . I thank thee that thou hast graciously thought me worthy of this day and of this hour.' Here was the supreme opportunity to demonstrate his loyalty to Jesus Christ.

In the First World War, Rupert Brooke, the poet, was one of those who died too young. Before he went out to the battle, he wrote:

> Now God be thanked who has matched us with his hour.

There are so many of us who have never in our lives made anything like a real sacrifice for Jesus Christ. The moment when Christianity seems likely to cost us something is the moment when it is open to us to demonstrate our loyalty to Jesus Christ in a way that all the world can see.

(2) To have to suffer persecution is, as Jesus himself said, the way to walk the same road as the prophets, the saints and the martyrs have walked. To suffer for the right is to gain a share in a great succession. Those who have to suffer something for their faith can throw back their heads and say:

> We are treading where the saints have trod.

(3) To have to suffer persecution is to share in the great occasion. There is always something thrilling in even being

present on the great occasion, in being there when something memorable and crucial is happening. There is an even greater thrill in having a share, however small, in the actual action. That is the feeling about which Shakespeare wrote so unforgettably in *Henry V* in the words he put into Henry's mouth before the Battle of Agincourt:

> He that shall live this day and see old age,
> Will yearly on the vigil feast his friends,
> And say, 'Tomorrow is Saint Crispin':
> Then will he strip his sleeve and show his scars,
> And say, 'These wounds I had on Crispin's day.'
> [. . .]
> And gentlemen in England now a-bed
> Shall think themselves accurs'd they were not here,
> And hold their manhoods cheap while any speaks
> That fought with us upon Saint Crispin's day.

When someone is called on to suffer something for Christianity, that is always a crucial moment; it is the great occasion; it is the clash between the world and Christ; it is a moment in the drama of eternity. To have a share in such a moment is not a penalty but a glory. 'Rejoice at such a moment,' says Jesus, 'and be glad.' The word for *be glad* is from the verb *agalliasthai*, which has been derived from two Greek words which mean *to leap exceedingly*. It is the joy which leaps for joy. As it has been put, it is the joy of the climber who has reached the summit, and who leaps for joy that the mountain path is conquered.

(4) To suffer persecution is to make things easier for those who are to follow. Today we enjoy the blessing of liberty because men and women in the past were willing to buy it for us at the cost of blood, sweat and tears. They made it easier for us, and by a steadfast and immovable witness

for Christ we may make it easier for others who are still to come.

In the United States, in the great Boulder Dam (now known as the Hoover Dam) scheme of the 1930s, men lost their lives in that project which was to turn a dust-bowl into fertile land. When the scheme was completed, the names of those who had died were put on a tablet and the tablet was put into the great wall of the dam, and on it there was the inscription: 'These died that the desert might rejoice and blossom as the rose.'

The man or woman who fights a battle for Christ will always make things easier for those who follow after. For them there will be one less struggle to be encountered on the way.

(5) Still further, no one ever suffers persecution alone; if people are called upon to bear material loss, the failure of friends, slander, loneliness, even the death of love, for their principles, they will not be left alone. Christ will be nearer to them than at any other time.

The old story in Daniel tells how Shadrach, Meshach and Abednego were thrown into the furnace heated to seven times its normal temperature because of their refusal to move from their loyalty to God. The courtiers watched. 'Was it not three men that we threw bound into the fire?' they asked. The reply was that it was indeed so. Then came the astonished answer: 'But I see four men unbound, walking in the middle of the fire, and they are not hurt; *and the fourth has the appearance of a god*' (Daniel 3:19–25).

As Robert Browning had it in 'Christmas Eve and Easter Day':

> I was born sickly, poor and mean,
> A slave; no misery could screen
> The holders of the pearl of price
> From Caesar's envy; therefore twice

> I fought with beasts, and three times saw
> My children suffer by his law;
> At last my own release was earned;
> I was some time in being burned,
> But at the close a Hand came through
> The fire above my head, and drew
> My soul to Christ, whom now I see.
> Sergius, a brother, writes for me
> This testimony on the wall –
> For me, I have forgot it all.

When people have to suffer something for their faith, that is the way to the closest possible companionship with Jesus Christ.

There remains only one question to ask – why is this persecution so inevitable? It is inevitable because the Church, when it really is the Church, is bound to be the conscience of the nation and the conscience of society. Where there is good the Church must praise; where there is evil the Church must condemn – and inevitably some people will try to silence the troublesome voice of conscience. It is not the duty of individual Christians habitually to find fault, to criticize or to condemn; but it may well be that their every action is a silent condemnation of the un-Christian lives of others, and they will not escape their hatred.

It is not likely that death awaits us because of our loyalty to the Christian faith. But insult awaits those who insist on Christian honour. Mockery awaits those who practise Christian love and Christian forgiveness. Actual persecution may well await Christians who insist on doing an honest day's work. Christ still needs his witnesses; he needs those who are prepared not so much to die for him, as to live for him. The Christian struggle and the Christian glory still exist.

THE SALT OF THE EARTH

Matthew 5:13

> 'You are the salt of the earth; but if salt has lost its taste
> how shall its saltness be restored? It is no longer good
> for anything except to be thrown out and trodden
> underfoot by men.'

WHEN Jesus said this, he provided us with an expression which
has become the greatest compliment that can be paid to
anyone. When we wish to stress someone's solid worth and
usefulness, we say: 'People like that are the salt of the earth.'

In the ancient world, salt was highly valued. The Greeks
called salt *divine* (*theion*). In a phrase, which in Latin is a
kind of jingle, the Romans said: 'There is nothing more useful
than sun and salt.' (*Nil utilius sole et sale.*) In the time of
Jesus, salt was connected in people's minds with three special
qualities.

(1) Salt was connected with *purity*. No doubt its glistening
whiteness made the connection easy. The Romans said that
salt was the purest of all things, because it came from the
purest of all things, the sun and the sea. Salt was indeed the
most primitive of all offerings to the gods, and to the end of
the day the Jewish sacrifices were offered with salt. So, if the
Christians are to be the salt of the earth, they must be *examples
of purity*.

One of the characteristics of the world in which we live is
the lowering of standards. Standards of honesty, standards of
diligence in work, standards of conscientiousness, moral
standards, all tend to be lowered. The Christian must be the
person who holds aloft the standard of absolute purity in
speech, in conduct and even in thought. A certain writer
dedicated a book to a friend 'who makes the best seem easily

credible'. Christians can never depart from the standards of strict honesty. Christians can never think lightly of the lowering of moral standards in a world where the streets of every great city provide their deliberate enticements to sin. Christians can never allow themselves the tarnished and suggestive jests which are so often part of social conversation. Christians cannot withdraw from the world, but they must, as James said, keep themselves 'unstained by the world' (James 1:27).

(2) In the ancient world, salt was the commonest of all *preservatives*. It was used to keep things from going bad, and to hold putrefaction at bay. Plutarch, the Roman historian and philosopher, has a strange way of putting that. He says that meat is a dead body and part of a dead body, and will, if left to itself, go bad; but salt preserves it and keeps it fresh, and is therefore like a new soul inserted into a dead body.

So, salt preserves from corruption. If Christians are to be the salt of the earth, they must have a certain antiseptic influence on life.

We all know that there are certain people in whose company it is easy to be good; and that also there are certain people in whose company it is easy for standards to be relaxed. There are certain people in whose presence a risqué story would be readily told, and there are other people to whom no one would dream of telling such a tale. Christians must be the cleansing antiseptic in any society in which they happen to be; they must be the ones who by their presence defeat corruption and make it easier for others to be good.

(3) But the greatest and the most obvious quality of salt is that *salt lends flavour to things*. Food without salt is a sadly insipid and even a sickening thing. Christianity is to life what salt is to food. Christianity lends flavour to life.

The tragedy is that, so often, people have connected Christianity with precisely the opposite. They have connected Christianity with that which takes the flavour out of life. In his 'Hymn to Proserpine', Swinburne wrote:

> Thou hast conquered, O pale Galilaean; the world has
> grown gray from Thy breath.

Even after Constantine had made Christianity the religion of the Roman Empire, there came to the throne another emperor called Julian, who wished to put the clock back and to bring back the old gods. His complaint, as the playwright Henrik Ibsen puts it, was:

> Have you looked at these Christians closely? Hollow-
> eyed, pale-cheeked, flat-breasted all; they brood their
> lives away, unspurred by ambition: the sun shines
> for them, but they do not see it: the earth offers
> them its fulness, but they desire it not; all their
> desire is to renounce and to suffer that they may come
> to die.

As Julian saw it, Christianity took the vividness out of life.

The American judge Oliver Wendell Holmes once said: 'I might have entered the ministry if certain clergymen I knew had not looked and acted so much like undertakers.' Robert Louis Stevenson once entered in his diary, as if he was recording an extraordinary phenomenon: 'I have been to Church today, and am not depressed.'

We need to discover the lost radiance of the Christian faith. In a worried world, Christians should be the only people who remain serene. In a depressed world, Christians should be the only people who remain full of the joy of life. There should be a sheer sparkle about Christians, but too often they dress like mourners at a funeral, and talk like spectres at a feast. Wherever they are, if they are to be the salt of the earth, Christians must be diffusers of joy.

Jesus went on to say that, if the salt had become insipid, it was fit only to be thrown out and trodden on. This is difficult, because salt does not lose its flavour and its saltness. E. F. F. Bishop in his book *Jesus of Palestine* cites a very likely explanation given by Miss F. E. Newton. In Palestine, the ordinary oven is out of doors and is built of stone on a base of tiles. In such ovens, 'in order to retain the heat, a thick bed of salt is laid under the tiled floor. After a certain length of time the salt perishes. The tiles are taken up, the salt removed and thrown on the road outside the door of the oven . . . It has lost its power to heat the tiles and it is thrown out.' That may well be the picture here.

But the essential point remains whatever the picture, and it is a point which the New Testament makes and remakes again and again – uselessness invites disaster. If Christians are not fulfilling their purpose as Christians, then they are on the way to disaster. We are meant to be the salt of the earth, and if we do not bring to life the purity, the antiseptic power, the radiance that we ought, then we invite disaster.

It remains to be noted that sometimes the early Church made a very strange use of this text. In the synagogue, among the Jews, there was a custom that if a Jew became an unbeliever and then returned to the faith, before he was received back into the synagogue he must in penitence lie across the door of the synagogue and invite people to trample upon him as they entered. In certain places the Christian Church took over that custom, and Christians who had been ejected by discipline from the church were compelled, before they were received back, to lie at the door of the church and to invite people as they entered: 'Trample upon me who am the salt which has lost its savour.'

THE LIGHT OF THE WORLD

Matthew 5:14-15

> 'You are the light of the world. A city set on a hill
> cannot be hid. Nor do men light a lamp and put it under
> a bushel, but on a stand, and it gives light to all in the
> house.'

It may well be said that this is the greatest compliment that
was ever paid to the individual Christian, for in it Jesus
commands the Christian to be what he himself claimed to be.
Jesus said: 'As long as I am in the world, I am the light of the
world' (John 9:5). When Jesus commanded his followers to
be the lights of the world, he demanded nothing less than
that they should be like himself.

When Jesus spoke these words, he was using an expression which was quite familiar to the Jews who heard it for
the first time. They themselves spoke of Jerusalem as 'a
light to the Gentiles', and a famous Rabbi was often called
'a lamp of Israel'. But the way in which the Jews used
this expression will give us a key to the way in which Jesus
also used it.

Of one thing the Jews were very sure – people never
kindled their own light. Jerusalem was indeed a light to the
Gentiles, but 'God lit Israel's lamp.' The light with which the
nation or the people of God shone was a borrowed light. It
must be so with the Christian. It is not the demand of Jesus
that we should, as it were, produce our own light. We must
shine with the reflection of his light. The radiance which
shines from the Christian comes from the presence of Christ
within the Christian's heart. We often speak about *a radiant
bride*, but the radiance which shines from her comes from
the love which has been born within her heart.

When Jesus said that Christians must be the light of the world, what did he mean?

(1) A light is first and foremost something which is meant to be seen. The houses in Palestine were very dark, with only one little circular window perhaps not more than eighteen inches across. The lamp was like a sauce-boat filled with oil with the wick floating in it. It was not so easy to rekindle a lamp in the days before matches existed. Normally the lamp stood on the lamp stand, which would be no more than a roughly shaped branch of wood; but when people went out, for safety's sake, they took the lamp from its stand and put it under an earthen bushel measure, so that it might burn without risk until they came back. The primary duty of the light of the lamp was to be seen.

So, Christianity is something which is meant to be seen. As someone has well said, 'There can be no such thing as secret discipleship, for either the secrecy destroys the discipleship, or the discipleship destroys the secrecy.' Our Christianity should be perfectly visible to everyone.

Further, this Christianity should be visible not only within the Church. A Christianity whose effects stop at the church door is not much use to anyone. It should be even more visible in the ordinary activities of the world. Our Christianity should be visible in the way we treat a shop assistant across the counter, in the way we order a meal in a restaurant, in the way we treat our employees or serve our employer, in the way we play a game or drive or park a car, in the daily language we use, in the daily literature we read. As Christians, we should be just as much a Christian in the factory, the workshop, the shipyard, the mine, the schoolroom, the surgery, the kitchen, the golf course and the playing field as we are in church. Jesus did not say: 'You are the light of the *Church*'; he said: 'You are the light of the *world*' – and in our lives in the world our Christianity should be evident to all.

(2) A light is a guide. On the estuary of any river, we may see the line of lights which marks the channel for the ships to sail in safety. We know how difficult even the city streets are when there are no lights. A light is something to make clear the way.

So, Christians must make the way clear to others. That is to say, Christians must of necessity be examples. One of the things which this world needs more than anything else is people who are prepared to be channels for goodness. Suppose there is a group of people, and suppose it is suggested that some questionable thing should be done. Unless someone makes a protest, the thing will be done. But if someone rises and says: 'I will not be a party to that,' another and another and another will rise to say: 'Neither will I.' But, had they not been given the lead, they would have remained silent.

There are many people in this world who do not have the moral strength and courage to take a stand by themselves, but if someone gives them a lead, they will follow; if they have someone strong enough to lean on, they will do the right thing. It is the Christian's duty to take the stand which the weaker brother or sister will support, to give the lead which those with less courage will follow. The world needs its guiding lights; there are people waiting and longing for a lead to take the stand and to do the thing which they do not dare by themselves.

(3) A light can often be a *warning light*. A light is often the warning which tells us to halt when there is danger ahead.

It is sometimes the duty of Christians to bring to others the necessary warning. That is often difficult, and it is often hard to do it in a way which will not do more harm than good; but one of the most poignant tragedies in life is for someone, especially a young person, to come and say to us: 'I would never have been in the situation in which I now find myself, if you had only spoken in time.'

It was said of Florence Allshorn, the famous teacher and principal, that if she ever had occasion to rebuke her students, she did it 'with her arm round about them'. If our warnings are given not in anger, not in irritation, not in criticism, not in condemnation, not in the desire to hurt, but in love, they will be effective.

The light which can be seen, the light which warns, the light which guides – these are the lights which Christians must be.

SHINING FOR GOD

Matthew 5:16

> 'Let your light so shine before men, that they may see your good works and give glory to your Father who is in heaven.'

THERE are two most important things here.

(1) People are to see our *good* deeds. In Greek, there are two words for *good*. There is the word *agathos*, which simply defines a thing as good in quality; and there is *kalos*, which means that a thing is not only good but that it is also captivating and beautiful and attractive. The word which is used here is *kalos*.

The good deeds of the Christian must be not only *good*; they must be also *attractive*. There must be a certain charm in Christian goodness. The tragedy of so much so-called goodness is that in it there is an element of hardness and coldness and austerity. There is a goodness which attracts and a goodness which repels. There is a charm in true Christian goodness which makes it a lovely thing.

(2) It is further to be noted that our good deeds ought to draw attention not to ourselves but to God. This saying of Jesus is a total prohibition of what someone has called 'theatrical goodness'.

At a conference at which the American evangelist D. L. Moody was present, there were also present some young people who took their Christian faith very seriously. One night, they held an all-night prayer meeting. As they were leaving it in the morning, they met Moody, and he asked them what they had been doing. They told him; and then they went on: 'Mr Moody, see how our faces shine.' Moody answered very gently: 'Moses wist not [did not know] that his face shone.' That goodness which is conscious, which draws attention to itself, is not the Christian goodness.

One of the old historians wrote of Henry V after the Battle of Agincourt: 'Neither would he suffer any ditties to be made and sung by the minstrels of his glorious victory, for that he would wholly have the praise and thanks altogether given to God.' Christians never think of what they have done, but of what God has enabled them to do. They never seek to draw the eyes of others to themselves, but always to direct them to God. As long as people are thinking of the praise, the thanks and the prestige which they will get for what they have done, they have not really even begun on the Christian way.

THE ETERNAL LAW

Matthew 5:17–20

'Do not think that I have come to destroy the law or the prophets. I have not come to destroy them but to fulfil them. This is the truth I tell you – until the heaven and the earth shall pass away, the smallest letter or the smallest part of any letter shall not pass away from the law, until all things in it shall be performed. So then, whoever will break one of the least of these commandments, and will teach others to do so, shall be called least in the kingdom of the heavens; but whoever will do them and will teach others to do them, he will be called great in the kingdom of the heavens. For I tell you, that you will certainly not enter into the kingdom of heaven, unless your righteousness goes beyond that of the scribes and Pharisees.'

AT a first reading, it might well be held that this is the most astonishing statement that Jesus made in the whole Sermon on the Mount. In this statement, Jesus lays down the eternal character of the law; and yet Paul can say: 'Christ is the end of the law' (Romans 10:4).

Again and again, Jesus broke what the Jews called the law. He did not observe the handwashings that the law laid down; he healed sick people on the Sabbath, although the law forbade such healings; he was in fact condemned and crucified as a law-breaker; and yet here he seems to speak of the law with a veneration and a reverence that no Rabbi or Pharisee could exceed. The smallest letter – the letter which the Authorized Version calls the *jot* – was the Hebrew letter *iodh*. In form it was like an apostrophe – ' – ; not even a letter not much bigger than a dot was to pass away. The smallest part of the letter – what the Authorized Version calls the *tittle* – is what we call the *serif*, the little projecting part at the foot of a letter, the little line at each side of the foot of, for example, the letter I. Jesus seems to lay it down that the law is so sacred that not the smallest detail of it will ever pass away.

Some people have been so puzzled by this saying that they have come to the conclusion that Jesus could not have said it. They have suggested that, since Matthew is the most Jewish of the gospels, and since Matthew wrote it specially to convince Jews, this is a saying which Matthew put into Jesus' mouth, and that this is not a saying of Jesus at all. But that is a weak argument, for this is a saying which is indeed so unlikely that no one would have invented it; it is so unlikely a saying that Jesus must have said it; and when we come to see what it really means, we will see that it is inevitable that Jesus should have said it.

The Jews used the expression *the law* in four different ways. (1) They used it to mean the Ten Commandments. (2) They used it to mean the first five books of the Bible. That part of the Bible which is known as the *Pentateuch* – which literally means *The Five Rolls* – was to Jews the law *par excellence* and was to them by far the most important part of the Bible. (3) They used the phrase *the law and the prophets* to mean the whole of Scripture; they used it as a comprehensive description of what we would call the whole Old Testament. (4) They used it to mean the *oral* or the *scribal law*.

In the time of Jesus, it was the last meaning which was commonest; and it was in fact this scribal law which both Jesus and Paul so utterly condemned. What, then, was this scribal law?

In the Old Testament itself, we find very few rules and regulations; what we do find are great, broad principles which people must take and interpret for themselves under God's guidance, and apply to the individual situations in life. In the Ten Commandments, we find no rules and regulations at all; they are each one of them great principles out of which people must find their own rules for life. To the later Jews, these great principles did not seem enough. They held that the law was divine, and that in it God had said his last word, and that therefore everything must be in it. If a thing was not in the law *explicitly*, it must be there *implicitly*. They therefore argued that out of the law it must be possible to deduce a rule and a regulation for every possible situation in life. So there arose a group of men called the scribes who made it the business of their lives to reduce the great principles of the law to literally thousands upon thousands of rules and regulations.

We may best see this in action. The law lays it down that the Sabbath day is to be kept holy, and that on it no work is to be done. That is a great principle. But the Jewish legalists had a passion for definition. So they asked: 'What is work?'

All kinds of things were classified as work. For instance, *to carry a burden* on the Sabbath day is to work. But next a burden has to be defined. So the scribal law lays it down that a burden is 'food equal in weight to a dried fig, enough wine for mixing in a goblet, milk enough for one swallow, honey enough to put upon a wound, oil enough to anoint a small member, water enough to moisten an eye-salve, paper enough to write a custom-house notice upon, ink enough to write two letters of the alphabet, reed enough to make a pen' – and so on endlessly. So they spent endless hours arguing whether a lamp could or could not be lifted from one place to another on the Sabbath, whether a tailor committed a sin if he went out with a needle in his robe, whether a woman might wear a brooch or false hair, even if it was permissible to go out on the Sabbath with false teeth or an artificial limb, or if a parent might lift a child on the Sabbath day. These things to them were the essence of religion. Their religion was a legalism of petty rules and regulations.

To write was to work on the Sabbath. But writing has to be defined. So the definition runs: 'He who writes two letters of the alphabet with his right or with his left hand, whether of one kind or of two kinds, if they are written with different inks or in different languages, is guilty. Even if he should write two letters from forgetfulness, he is guilty, whether he has written them with ink or with paint, red chalk, vitriol, or anything which makes a permanent mark. Also he that writes on two walls that form an angle, or on two tablets of his account book so that they can be read together is guilty . . . But, if anyone writes with dark fluid, with fruit juice, or in the dust of the road, or in sand, or in anything which does not make a permanent mark, he is not guilty . . . If he writes one letter on the ground, and one on the wall of the house, or on two pages of a book, so that they cannot be read together, he is not guilty.' That is a typical passage from the scribal law; and that is what orthodox Jews regarded as true religion and the true service of God.

To heal was to work on the Sabbath. Obviously this has to be defined. Healing was allowed when there was danger to life, and especially in troubles of the ear, nose and throat; but even then, steps could be taken only to keep the patient from becoming worse; no steps might be taken to make the patient get any better. So a plain bandage might be put on a wound, but no ointment; plain wadding might be put into a sore ear, but not medicated wadding.

The *scribes* were the men who worked out these rules and regulations. The *Pharisees*, whose name means *the separated ones*, were the men who had separated themselves from all the ordinary activities of life to keep all these rules and regulations.

We can see the lengths to which this went from the following facts. For many generations, this scribal law was never written down; it was the *oral* law, and it was handed down in the memory of generations of scribes. In the middle of the third century AD, a summary of it was made and codified. That summary is known as the *Mishnah*; it contains sixty-three tractates on various subjects of the law, and in English makes a book of almost 800 pages. Later Jewish scholarship busied itself with making commentaries to explain the *Mishnah*. These commentaries are known as the *Talmuds*. Of the Jerusalem *Talmud* there are twelve printed volumes; and of the Babylonian *Talmud* there are sixty printed volumes.

To strict orthodox Jews, in the time of Jesus, religion, serving God, was a matter of keeping thousands of legalistic rules and regulations; they regarded these petty rules and regulations as literally matters of life and death and eternal destiny. Clearly, Jesus did not mean that not one of these rules and regulations was to pass away; repeatedly he broke them himself, and repeatedly he condemned them; that is certainly not what Jesus meant by the law, for that is the kind of law that both Jesus and Paul condemned.

THE ESSENCE OF THE LAW

Matthew 5:17–20 (*contd*)

WHAT then did Jesus mean by the law? He said that he had come not to destroy the law, but to *fulfil* the law. That is to say, he came really to bring out the real meaning of the law. What was the real meaning of the law? Even behind the scribal and oral law, there was one great principle which the scribes and the Pharisees had imperfectly grasped. The one great principle was that in all things people must seek God's will, and that, when they know it, they must dedicate their whole life to the obeying of it. The scribes and Pharisees were right in seeking God's will, and profoundly right in dedicating their lives to obeying it; they were wrong in finding that will in their man-made hordes of rules and regulations.

What then is the real principle behind the whole law, that principle which Jesus came to fulfil, the true meaning of which he came to show?

When we look at the Ten Commandments, which are the essence and the foundation of all law, we can see that their whole meaning can be summed up in one word – *respect*, or even better, *reverence*. Reverence for God and for the name of God, reverence for God's day, respect for parents, respect for life, respect for property, respect for personality, respect for the truth and for another person's good name, respect for oneself so that wrong desires may never overpower us – these are the fundamental principles behind the Ten Commandments, principles of reverence for God, and respect for our neighbours and for ourselves. Without them there can be no such thing as law. On them all law is based.

That reverence and that respect Jesus came to fulfil. He came to show men and women in actual life what reverence for God and respect for one another are like. Justice, said the Greeks, consists in giving to God and to others that which is their due. Jesus came to show in actual life what it means to give to God the reverence and to other people the respect which are their due.

That reverence and that respect did not consist in obeying a multitude of petty rules and regulations. They consisted not in sacrifice but in mercy; not in legalism but in love; not in prohibitions which demanded that men and women should not do things, but in the instruction to mould their lives on the positive commandment to love.

The reverence and the respect which are the basis of the Ten Commandments can never pass away; they are the permanent stuff of our relationship to God and to one another.

THE LAW AND THE GOSPEL

Matthew 5:17–20 (*contd*)

WHEN Jesus spoke as he did about the law and the gospel, he was implicitly laying down certain broad principles.

(1) He was saying that there is a definite continuation between the past and the present. We must never look on life as a kind of battle between the past and the present. The present grows out of the past.

After Dunkirk, in the Second World War, there was a tendency on all hands to look for someone to blame for the disaster which had befallen the British forces, and there were many who wished to enter into bitter recriminations with those who had guided things in the past. At that time, the Prime Minister, Winston Churchill, said a very wise thing: 'If we open a quarrel between the past and the present, we shall find that we have lost the future.'

There had to be the law before the gospel could come. People had to learn the difference between right and wrong; they had to discover their own human inability to cope with the demands of the law, and to respond to the commands of God; they had to become aware of a sense of sin and unworthiness and inadequacy. We blame the past for many things – and often rightly – but it is equally, and even more, necessary to acknowledge our debt to the past. As Jesus saw it, it is our duty neither to forget nor to attempt to destroy the past, but to build upon the foundation of the past. We have entered into the labours of others, and we must so labour that other people will enter into ours.

(2) In this passage, Jesus definitely warns the disciples not to think that Christianity is easy. People might say: 'Christ is the end of the law; now I can do what I like.' They might

think that all the duties, all the responsibilities and all the demands are gone. But it is Jesus' warning that the righteousness of the Christian must *exceed* the righteousness of the scribes and Pharisees. What did he mean by that?

The motive under which the scribes and Pharisees lived was the motive of law; their one aim and desire was to satisfy the demands of the law. Now, at least theoretically, it is perfectly possible to satisfy the demands of the law; in one sense there can come a time when it is possible for someone to say: 'I have done all that the law demands; my duty is discharged; the law has no more claim on me.' But the motive under which Christians live is the motive of love; the one desire of all Christians is to show their wondering gratitude for the love they have received from God in Jesus Christ. Now, it is not even theoretically possible to satisfy the claims of love. If we love someone with all our hearts, we are bound to feel that if we gave to that person a lifetime's service and adoration, if we offered the sun and the moon and the stars, we would still not have offered enough. For love, the whole realm of nature is an offering far too small.

The Jews aimed to satisfy the *law* of God; and to the demands of the law there is always a limit. Christians aim to show their gratitude for the *love* of God; and to the claims of love there is no limit in time or in eternity. Jesus set before men and women not the law of God, but the love of God. Long ago, St Augustine said that the Christian life could be summed up in the one phrase: 'Love God, and do what you like.' But when we realize how God has loved us, the one desire of life is to answer to that love, and that is the greatest task in all the world, for it presents us with a task the like of which those who think in terms of law never dream of, and with an obligation more binding than the obligation to any law.

THE NEW AUTHORITY

Matthew 5:21–48

THIS section of the teaching of Jesus is one of the most important in the whole New Testament. Before we deal with it in detail, there are certain general things about it which we must note.

In it, Jesus speaks with an authority which no other man had ever dreamed of assuming. The authority which Jesus assumed always amazed those who came into contact with him. Right at the beginning of his ministry, after he had been teaching in the synagogue in Capernaum, it is said of his hearers: 'They were astounded at his teaching, for he taught them as one having authority, and not as the scribes' (Mark 1:22). Matthew concludes his account of the Sermon on the Mount with the words: 'Now when Jesus had finished saying these things, the crowds were astounded at his teaching, for he taught them as one having authority, and not as their scribes' (Matthew 7:28–9).

It is difficult for us to realize just how shocking a thing this authority of Jesus must have seemed to the Jews who listened to him. To the Jews, the law was absolutely holy and absolutely divine; it is impossible to exaggerate the place that the law had in their reverence. The Jewish document *The Letter of Aristeas* says: 'The law is holy and has been given by God.' 'Only Moses' decrees', said Philo, 'are everlasting, unchangeable and unshakable, as signed by nature herself with her seal.' The Rabbis said: 'Those who deny that the law is from heaven have no part in the world to come.' They said: 'Even if one says that the law is from God with the exception of this or that verse, which Moses, not God, spoke from his own mouth, then there applies to him the judgment. He has despised the word of the Lord: he has shown the irreverence which merits the destruction of the soul.' The first act of every synagogue service was the taking of the rolls of the law from the ark in which they were stored, and the carrying of them round the congregation, that the congregation might show their reverence for them.

That is what the Jews thought of the law; and now no fewer than five times (Matthew 5:21, 27, 33, 38, 43) Jesus quotes the law, only to contradict it and to substitute a teaching of his own. He claimed the right to point out the inadequacies of the most sacred writings in the world, and to correct them out of his own wisdom. The Greeks defined *exousia*, authority, as 'the power to add and the power to take away at will'. Jesus claimed that power even with regard to that which the Jews believed to be the unchanging and unchangeable word of God. Nor did Jesus argue about this, or seek in any way to justify himself for so doing, or seek to prove his right to do so. He calmly and without question assumed that right.

No one had ever heard anything like this before. The great Jewish teachers had always had characteristic phrases in their teaching. The characteristic phrase of the prophet was: 'Thus says the Lord.' He claimed no personal authority at all; his only claim was that what he spoke God had told him. The characteristic phrase of the scribe and the Rabbi was: 'There is a teaching that . . .'. The scribe or the Rabbi never dared to express even an opinion of his own unless he could buttress it with supporting quotations from the great teachers of the past. Independence was the last quality that he would claim. But, to Jesus, a statement required no authority other than the fact that he made it. He was his own authority.

Clearly, one of two things must be true – either Jesus was mad, or he was unique; either he was a megalomaniac, or else he was the Son of God. No ordinary person would dare to make such a claim, to take and overturn what up to that point had been regarded as the eternal word of God.

The amazing thing about authority is that it is self-evidencing. No sooner does someone begin to teach than we know at once whether or not that person has the right to teach. Authority is like an atmosphere about people. They do not need to claim it; they either have it, or they do not.

Orchestras which played under Toscanini, that supreme conductor, said that as soon as he mounted the rostrum they could feel a wave of authority flowing from him. Julian Duguid tells how he once crossed the Atlantic in the same ship as the physician and missionary Sir Wilfred Grenfell; and he says that when Grenfell came into one of the ship's public rooms, he could tell (without even looking round) that he had entered the room, for a wave of authority went out from the man. It was supremely so with Jesus.

Jesus took the highest human wisdom and corrected it, because he was who he was. He did not need to argue; it was sufficient for him to speak. No one can honestly face Jesus and honestly listen to him without feeling that this is God's last word beside which all other words are inadequate, and all other wisdom out of date.

THE NEW STANDARD

Matthew 5:21–48 (contd)

BUT startling as was Jesus' accent of authority, the standard which he put before men and women was even more startling. Jesus said that in God's sight it was not only the person who committed murder who was guilty; the person who was angry with another person was also guilty and liable to judgment. It was not only the person who committed adultery who was guilty; anyone who seriously entertained unclean desire was also guilty.

Here was something which was entirely new, something which we have not yet fully grasped. It was Jesus' teaching that it was not enough not to commit murder; the only thing sufficient was never even to wish to commit murder. It was Jesus' teaching that it was not enough not to commit adultery; the only thing sufficient was never even to wish to commit adultery.

It may be that we have never struck another person, but can we say that we never *wished* to strike someone? It may be that we have never committed adultery, but can we say that we have never experienced the desire for the forbidden thing? It was Jesus' teaching that thoughts are just as important as deeds, and that it is not enough not to commit a sin; the only thing that is enough is not to *wish* to commit it. It was Jesus' teaching that we are not judged only by our deeds, but are judged even more by the desires which never emerged in deeds. By the world's standards, people are considered good if they never do a forbidden thing. The world is not concerned to judge people's thoughts. By Jesus' standards, we can only aspire to goodness when we never even desire to do a forbidden thing. Jesus is intensely concerned with our thoughts. Three things emerge from this.

(1) Jesus was profoundly right, for Jesus' way is the only way to safety and security. To some extent, every individual is a split personality. There is part of each of us which is attracted to good, and part which is attracted to evil. As long as we are like that, an inner battle is going on inside us. One voice is inciting us to take the forbidden thing; the other voice is forbidding us to take it.

Plato likened the soul to a charioteer whose task it was to drive two horses. The one horse was gentle and biddable and obedient to the reins and to the word of command; the other horse was wild and untamed and rebellious. The name of the one horse was reason; the name of the other was passion. Life is always a conflict between the demands of the passions and the control of the reason. The reason is the leash which keeps the passions in check. But *a leash may snap at any time*. Self-control may be for a moment off its guard – and then what may happen? As long as there is this inner tension, this inner conflict, life must be insecure. In such circumstances, there can be no such thing as safety. The only way to safety, Jesus said, is to eradicate the desire for the forbidden thing forever. Then and then alone, life is safe.

(2) If that is so, then God alone can judge us. We see only people's outward actions; God alone sees the secret of their hearts. And there will be many whose outward actions are a model of rectitude, whose inward thoughts stand condemned before God. There are many who can stand the judgment of society, which is bound to be a judgment of externals, but whose goodness collapses before the all-seeing eye of God.

(3) And if that is so, it means that every one of us is in default; for no one can stand this judgment of God. Even if we have lived a life of outward moral perfection, none of us can say that we never experienced the forbidden desire for the wrong things. For the inner perfection, it is only necessary to say that we ourselves are dead and Christ lives in us. 'I have been crucified with Christ', said Paul. 'It is no longer I who live, but it is Christ who lives in me' (Galatians 2:19–20).

The new standard kills all pride, and forces us to Jesus Christ, who alone can enable us to rise to that standard which he himself has set before us.

THE FORBIDDEN ANGER

Matthew 5:21–2

> 'You have heard that it was said by the people of the
> old days, "You shall not kill"; and "whoever kills is
> liable to the judgment court". But I say unto you that
> everyone who is angry with his brother is liable to the
> judgment court; and he who says to his brother, "You
> brainless one!" is liable to judgment in the supreme
> court; and he who says to his brother, "You fool!" is
> liable to be cast into the Gehenna of fire.'

HERE is the first example of the new standard which Jesus
takes. The ancient law had laid it down: 'You shall not
murder' (Exodus 20:13); but Jesus lays it down that even
anger against another person is forbidden. In the Authorized
Version, the person who is condemned is the one who is angry
without a cause. But the words *without a cause* are not found
in any of the great manuscripts, and this is nothing less than a
total prohibition of anger. It is not enough not to strike
someone; the only thing that is enough is not even to wish to
strike the blow; not even to have hard feelings against that
person within the heart.

In this passage, Jesus is arguing as a Rabbi might argue.
He is showing that he was skilful in using the debating
methods which the wise men of his time were in the habit of
using. There is in this passage a neat gradation of anger, and
an answering neat gradation of punishment.

(1) There is first the person who is *angry with someone
else*. The verb used here is *orgizesthai*. In Greek, there are
two words for anger. There is *thumos*, which was described
as being like the flame which comes from dried straw. It is
the anger which quickly blazes up and which just as quickly

dies down. It is an anger which rises speedily and which just as speedily passes.

Then there is *orgē*, which was described as anger that has become deep-rooted. It is the long-lived anger; it is the anger of those who nurse their wrath to keep it warm; it is the anger over which people brood, and which they will not allow to die.

That anger is liable to *the judgment court*. The judgment court is the local village council which dispensed justice. That court was composed of the local village elders, and varied in number from three in villages of fewer than 150 inhabitants, to seven in larger towns and twenty-three in still bigger cities.

So, then, Jesus condemns all selfish anger. The Bible is clear that anger is forbidden. 'Your anger', said James, 'does not produce God's righteousness' (James 1:20). Paul orders his people to put off all 'anger, wrath, malice, slander' (Colossians 3:8). Even the highest pagan thought saw the folly of anger. Cicero said that when anger entered into the scene, 'nothing could be done rightly and nothing sensibly'. In a vivid phrase, Seneca called anger 'a brief insanity'.

So, Jesus forbids forever the anger which broods, the anger which will not forget, the anger which refuses to be pacified, the anger which seeks revenge. If we are to obey Jesus, all anger must be banished from life, and especially that anger which lingers too long. It is a warning thing to remember that we cannot call ourselves Christians and lose our temper because of any personal wrong which we have suffered.

(2) Immediately, Jesus goes on to speak of two cases where anger turns into insulting words. The Jewish teachers forbade such anger and such words. These teachers spoke of

'oppression in words' and of 'the sin of insult'. They had a saying: 'Three classes go down to Gehenna and return not – the adulterer, he who puts his neighbour openly to shame, and he who gives his neighbour an insulting name.' Anger in a person's heart and anger in a person's speech are equally forbidden.

WORDS OF INSULT

Matthew 5:21–2 (*contd*)

FIRST of all, the person who calls another *Raca* is condemned. *Raca* is an almost untranslatable word, because it describes a tone of voice more than anything else. Its whole accent is the accent of *contempt*. To call a man *Raca* was to call him a brainless idiot, a silly fool, an empty-headed blunderer. It is the word of one who despises another with an arrogant contempt.

There is a Rabbinic tale of a certain Rabbi, Simon ben Eleazar. He was coming from his teacher's house, and he was feeling uplifted at the thought of his own scholarship and erudition and goodness. A very ill-favoured passer-by gave him a greeting. The Rabbi did not return the greeting, but said, 'You Raca! How ugly you are! Are all the men of your town as ugly as you?' 'That', said the passer-by, 'I do not know. Go and tell the Maker who created me how ugly is the creature he has made.' So, there the sin of contempt was rebuked.

The sin of contempt is liable to an even more severe judgment. It is liable to the judgment of the Sanhedrin (*sunedrion*), the supreme court of the Jews. This of course is not to be taken literally. It is as if Jesus said: 'The sin of deep-rooted anger is bad; the sin of contempt is worse.'

There is no sin quite so un-Christian as the sin of contempt. There is a contempt which comes from pride of birth, and snobbery is in truth an ugly thing. There is a contempt which comes from position and from money; and pride in material things is also an ugly thing. There is a contempt which comes from knowledge, and of all snobberies intellectual snobbery is the hardest to understand, for the wise were never impressed with anything but their own ignorance. We should never look with contempt on anyone for whom Christ died.

(3) Then Jesus goes on to speak of the person who calls someone else *mōros*. *Mōros* also means *fool*, but the person who is *mōros* is a *moral* fool, someone who is *playing the fool*. The psalmist spoke of fools who say in their hearts that there is no God (Psalm 14:1). Such people were moral fools, who lived immoral lives, and who in wishful thinking said that there was no God. To call people *mōros* was not to criticize their mental ability; it was to cast aspersions on their moral character; it was to take their name and reputation from them, and to brand them as loose-living and immoral.

So, Jesus says that anyone who destroys another's name and reputation is liable to the most severe judgment of all, the judgment of the *fire of Gehenna*.

Gehenna is a word with a history; often the Revised Standard Version translates it as *hell*. The word was very commonly used by the Jews (Matthew 5:22, 29, 30, 10:28, 18:9, 23:15, 33; Mark 9:43, 45, 47; Luke 12:5; James 3:6). It really means the Valley of Hinnom. The Valley of Hinnom is a valley to the south-west of Jerusalem. It was notorious as the place where Ahaz had introduced into Israel the fire-worship of the pagan god Molech, to whom little children were burned in the fire. 'He made offerings in the valley of the son of Hinnom, and made his sons pass through fire'

(2 Chronicles 28:3). Josiah, the reforming king, had stamped out that worship, and had ordered that the valley should be forever after an accursed place. 'He defiled Topheth, which is in the valley of Ben-hinnom, so that no one would make a son or a daughter pass through fire as an offering to Molech' (2 Kings 23:10). In consequence of this, the Valley of Hinnom became the place where the refuse of Jerusalem was cast out and destroyed. It was a kind of public incinerator. Always the fire smouldered in it, and a pall of thick smoke lay over it, and it bred a loathsome kind of worm which was hard to kill (Mark 9:44–8). So Gehenna, the Valley of Hinnom, became identified in people's minds with all that was accursed and filthy, the place where useless and evil things were destroyed. That is why it became a synonym for the place of God's destroying power, for hell.

So, Jesus insists that the gravest thing of all is to destroy someone's reputation and to take that person's good name away. No punishment is too severe for those who tell malicious stories, or the idle gossip which murders people's reputations. Such conduct, in the most literal sense, is a hell-deserving sin.

As we have said, all these gradations of punishment are not to be taken literally. What Jesus is saying here is this: 'In the old days, people condemned murder; and truly murder is forever wrong. But I tell you that not only are your outward actions under judgment; your inmost thoughts are also under the scrutiny and the judgment of God. Long-lasting anger is bad; contemptuous speaking is worse, and the careless or the malicious talk which destroys a person's good name is worst of all.' Those who are the slaves of anger, those who speak in the accent of contempt, or who destroy another's good name, may never have committed a murder in action; but they are murderers at heart.

THE INSURMOUNTABLE BARRIER

Matthew 5:23–4

> 'So, then, if you bring your gift to the altar, and if you
> there remember that your brother has something against
> you, leave your gift there before the altar, and go, and
> first be reconciled to your brother, and then come and
> offer your gift.'

WHEN Jesus said this, he was doing no more than reminding
the Jews of a principle which they knew well and ought never
to have forgotten. The idea behind sacrifice was quite simple.
If someone did a wrong thing, that action disturbed the
relationship between that person and God, and the sacrifice
was meant to be the cure which restored that relationship.

But two most important things have to be noted. First, it
was never held that sacrifice could atone for deliberate sin,
for what the Jews called 'the sin of a high hand'. If someone
committed a sin unawares, or was swept into sin in a moment
of passion when self-control broke, then sacrifice was
effective; but if a person deliberately, defiantly, callously and
with open eyes committed sin, then sacrifice was powerless
to atone.

Second, to be effective, sacrifice had to include confession
of sin and true penitence; and true penitence involved the
attempt to rectify any consequences sin might have had. The
great Day of Atonement was held to make atonement for the
sins of the whole nation, but the Jews were quite clear that
not even the sacrifices of the Day of Atonement could avail
unless people were first reconciled to their neighbours. The
breach between human beings and God could not be healed
until human beings could reconcile their differences. If someone was making a sin offering, for instance, to atone for a

theft, the offering was held to be completely unavailing until the thing stolen had been restored; and, if it was discovered that the thing had not been restored, then the sacrifice had to be destroyed as unclean and burned outside the Temple. The Jews were quite clear that people had to do their utmost to put things right themselves before they could be right with God.

In some sense, sacrifice was substitutionary. The symbol of this was that, as the victim was about to be sacrificed, the worshipper placed his hands upon the animal's head and pressed them down upon it, as if to transfer his own guilt to it. As he did so, he said: 'I entreat, O Lord; I have sinned, I have done perversely, I have rebelled; I have committed . . . [here the sacrificer specified his sins]; but I return in penitence, and let this be for my covering.'

If any sacrifice was to be valid, confession and restoration were involved. The picture which Jesus is painting is very vivid. The worshipper, of course, did not make his own sacrifice; he brought it to the priest, who offered it on his behalf. The worshipper has entered the Temple; he has passed through its series of courts, the Court of the Gentiles, the Court of the Women and the Court of the Men. Beyond that, there lay the Court of the Priests, into which the layman could not go. The worshipper is standing at the rail, ready to hand over his victim to the priest; his hands are on it to confess; and then he remembers his breach with his friend, the wrong done to his neighbour. If his sacrifice is to avail, he must go back and mend that breach and undo that wrong, or nothing can happen.

Jesus is quite clear about this basic fact – we cannot be right with God until we are right with one another; we cannot hope for forgiveness until we have confessed our sin, not only to God, but also to others, and until we have done our best to remove the practical consequences of it. We sometimes wonder why there is a barrier between us and God; we sometimes wonder why our prayers seem unavailing. The reason may well be that we ourselves have erected that barrier, through being at variance with our neighbours, or because we have wronged someone and have done nothing to put things right.

MAKE PEACE IN TIME

Matthew 5:25–6

> 'Get on to good terms again with your opponent, while you are still on the road with him, in case your opponent hands you over to the judge, and the judge hands you over to the court officer, and you be cast into prison. This is the truth I tell you – if that happens, you certainly will not come out until you have paid the last penny.'

HERE, Jesus is giving the most practical advice; he is telling people to get trouble sorted out in time, before it piles up still worse trouble for the future.

Jesus draws a picture of two opponents on their way together to the law courts, and he tells them to get things settled and straightened out before they reach the court; for if they do not, and the law takes its course, there will be still worse trouble for one of them at least in the days to come.

The picture of two opponents on the way to court together seems to us very strange, and indeed rather improbable. But in the ancient world it often happened.

Under Greek law, there was a process of arrest called *apagōgē*, which means *summary arrest*. In it, the plaintiff himself arrested the defendant. He caught him by his robe at the throat, and held the robe in such a way that, if the man struggled, he would strangle himself. Obviously the causes for which such an arrest was legal were very few, and the wrongdoer had to be caught red-handed.

The crimes for which a man might be summarily arrested by anyone in this way were thieving, clothes-stealing (clothes-stealers were the curse of the public baths in ancient Greece), picking pockets, housebreaking and kidnapping (the kidnapping of specially gifted and accomplished slaves was very common). Further, a man might be summarily arrested if he was discovered to be exercising the rights of a citizen when he had been disfranchised, or if he returned to his state or city after being exiled. In view of this custom, it was by no means uncommon to see a plaintiff and a defendant on their way to court together in a Greek city.

Clearly, it is much more likely that Jesus would be thinking in terms of Jewish law; and this situation was by no means impossible under Jewish law. This is obviously a case of debt, for if peace is not made, the last penny will have to be paid. Such cases were settled by the local council of elders. A time was appointed when plaintiff and defendant had to appear together; in any small town or village, there was every likelihood of them finding themselves on the way to the court together. When a man was adjudged guilty, he was handed over to the court officer. Matthew calls the officer the *huperētēs*; Luke calls him, in his version of the saying, by the more common term, *praktōr* (Luke 12:58–9). It was the duty of the court officer to see that the penalty was duly paid; and, if it was not paid, he had the power to imprison the defaulter until it was paid. It is, no doubt, of that situation that Jesus was thinking. Jesus' advice may mean one of two things.

(1) It may be a piece of most practical advice. Again and again, it is the experience of life that if a quarrel, or a

difference, or a dispute is not healed immediately, it can go on breeding worse and worse trouble as time goes on. Bitterness breeds bitterness. It has often happened that a quarrel between two people has descended to their families, and has been inherited by future generations, and has in the end succeeded in splitting a church or a society in two.

If at the very beginning one of the parties had had the grace to apologize or to admit fault, a grievous situation need never have arisen. If ever we are at variance with someone else, we must get the situation put right straight away. It may mean that we must be humble enough to confess that we were wrong and to make apology; it may mean that, even if we were in the right, we have to take the first step towards healing the breach. When personal relations go wrong, in nine cases out of ten immediate action will mend them; but if that immediate action is not taken, they will continue to deteriorate, and the bitterness will spread in an ever-widening circle.

(2) It may be that in Jesus' mind there was something even more fundamental than this. It may be that he is saying: 'Put things right with your neighbours *while life lasts*, for some day – you know not when – life will finish, and you will go to stand before God, the final Judge of all.' The greatest of all Jewish days was the Day of Atonement. Its sacrifices were held to atone for sin known and unknown; but even this day had its limitations. The Talmud clearly lays it down: 'The Day of Atonement does atone for the offences between man and God. The Day of Atonement does not atone for the offences between a man and his neighbour, unless the man has first put things right with his neighbour.' Here again we have the basic fact – we cannot be right with God unless we are right with one another. We must so live that the end will find us at peace with all people.

It may well be that we do not need to choose between these two interpretations of this saying of Jesus. It may well be that both were in his mind, and that what Jesus is saying is: 'If you want happiness in time, and happiness in eternity, never leave an unreconciled quarrel or an unhealed breach between yourself and another. Act immediately to remove the barriers which anger has raised.'

THE FORBIDDEN DESIRE

Matthew 5:27–8

> 'You have heard that it has been said, "You must not commit adultery." But I say to you that every one who looks at a woman in such a way as to waken within himself forbidden desires for her has already committed adultery with her within his heart.'

HERE is Jesus' second example of the new standard. The law laid it down: 'You shall not commit adultery' (Exodus 20:14). So serious a view did the Jewish teachers take of adultery that the guilty parties could be punished by nothing less than death (Leviticus 20:10); but once again, Jesus lays it down that not only the forbidden action but also the forbidden thought is guilty in the sight of God.

It is necessary that we should understand what Jesus is saying here. He is not speaking of the natural, normal desire, which is part of human instinct and human nature. According to the literal meaning of the Greek, the man who is condemned is the man who looks at a woman with the deliberate intention of lusting after her. The man who is condemned is the man who deliberately uses his eyes to awaken his lust, the man who looks in such a way that passion is awakened and desire deliberately stimulated.

The Jewish Rabbis knew well the way in which the eyes can be used to stimulate the wrong desire. They had their sayings. 'The eyes and the hand are the two brokers of sin.' 'Eye and heart are the two handmaids of sin.' 'Passions lodge only in him who sees.' 'Woe to him who goes after his eyes for they are adulterous!' As someone has said, 'There is an internal desire of which adultery is only the fruit.'

In a tempting world, there are many things which are deliberately designed to excite desire – books, pictures, plays, even advertisements. The man whom Jesus here condemns is the man who deliberately uses his eyes to stimulate his desires, or who finds a strange delight in things which waken the desire for what is forbidden. To the pure, all things are pure. But the man whose heart is corrupted can look at any scene and find something in it to titillate and excite the wrong desire.

THE SURGICAL CURE

Matthew 5:29–30

> 'If your right eye proves a stumbling-block to you, tear it out and throw it away from you; for it is better that one part of your body should be destroyed than that your whole body should go away to Gehenna. If your right hand proves a stumbling-block to you, cut it off and throw it away from you; for it is better for you that one part of your body should be destroyed than that your whole body should go away to Gehenna.'

HERE Jesus makes a great demand, and it is literally a surgical demand. He insists that anything which is a cause of, or a seduction to, sin should be completely cut out of life.

The word he uses for a *stumbling-block* is interesting. It is the word *skandalon*. *Skandalon* is a form of the word *skandalēthron*, which means the *bait-stick* in a trap. It was the stick or arm on which the bait was fixed and which operated the trap to catch the animal lured to its own destruction. So the word came to mean *anything which causes a person's destruction*.

Behind it there are two pictures. First, there is the picture of a hidden stone in a path against which someone may stumble, or of a cord stretched across a path, deliberately put there to make them trip. Second, there is the picture of a pit dug in the ground and deceptively covered over with a thin layer of branches or of turf, and so arranged that, when unwary travellers set foot on it, they are immediately thrown into the pit. The *skandalon*, the *stumbling-block*, is something which trips people up, something which sends them crashing to destruction, something which lures them to their own ruin.

Of course, the words of Jesus are not to be taken with a crude literalism. What they mean is that anything which helps to seduce us to sin is to be ruthlessly rooted out of life. If there is a habit which can be seduction to evil, if there is an association which can be the cause of wrongdoing, if there is a pleasure which could turn out to be our ruin, then that thing must be surgically excised from our life.

Coming as it does immediately after the passage which deals with forbidden thoughts and desires, this passage compels us to ask: how shall we free ourselves from these unclean desires and corrupting thoughts? It is the fact of experience that thoughts and pictures come unbidden into our minds, and it is the hardest thing on earth to shut the door to them.

There is one way in which these forbidden thoughts and desires cannot be dealt with – and that is to sit down and to say, I will not think of these things. The more we say, I will not think of such and such a thing, the more our thoughts are in fact concentrated on it.

The outstanding example in history of the wrong way to deal with such thoughts and desires was that of the hermits and the monks in the desert in the time of the early Church. They were individuals who wished to free themselves from all earthly things, and especially of the desires of the body. To do so, they went away into the Egyptian desert with the idea of living alone and thinking of nothing but God.

The most famous of them all was Saint Anthony. He lived the hermit's life; he fasted; he did without sleep; he tortured his body. For thirty-five years he lived in the desert, and these thirty-five years were a non-stop battle, without respite, with his temptations. The story is told in his biography. 'First of all the devil tried to lead him away from discipline, whispering to him the remembrance of his wealth, cares for his sister, claims of kindred, love of money, love of glory, the various pleasures of the table, and the other relaxations of life, and, at last, the difficulty of virtue and the labour of it . . . The one would suggest foul thoughts, and the other counter them with prayers; the one fire him with lust, the other, as one who seemed to blush, fortify his body with prayers, faith and fasting. The devil one night even took upon him the shape of a woman, and imitated all her acts simply to beguile Anthony.' So for thirty-five years the struggle went on.

The plain fact is that, if ever anyone was asking for trouble, Anthony and his friends were. It is the inevitable law of human nature that the more we say we will not think of something, the more that something will present itself to our thoughts. There are only two ways to defeat the forbidden thoughts.

The first way is by Christian action. The best way to defeat such thoughts is to do something, to fill life so full with

Christian labour and Christian service that there is no time for these thoughts to enter in; to think so much of others that in the end we entirely forget ourselves; to rid ourselves of a diseased and morbid introspection by concentrating not on ourselves but on other people. The real cure for evil thoughts is good action.

The second way is to fill the mind with good thoughts. There is a famous scene in J. M. Barrie's *Peter Pan*. Peter is in the children's bedroom; they have seen him fly; and they wish to fly too. They have tried it from the floor and they have tried it from the beds and the result is failure. 'How do you do it?' John asked. And Peter answered: 'You just think lovely, wonderful thoughts and they lift you up in the air.' The only way to defeat evil thoughts is to begin to think of something else.

If people are harassed by thoughts of the forbidden and unclean things, they will certainly never defeat the evil things by withdrawing from life and saying, I will not think of these things. They can do so only by plunging into Christian action and Christian thought. They will never do it by trying to save their own lives; they can do it only by flinging their lives away for others.

THE BOND WHICH MUST NOT BE BROKEN

1. *Marriage among the Jews*

Matthew 5:31–2

> 'It has been said, "Let every man who divorces his wife give her a bill of divorcement." But I say to you that everyone who divorces his wife for any other cause than fornication causes her to commit adultery; and anyone who marries a woman who has been so divorced himself commits adultery.'

WHEN Jesus laid down this law for marriage, he laid it down against a very definite situation. There is no time in history when the marriage bond stood in greater peril of destruction than in the days when Christianity first came into this world. At that time, the world was in danger of witnessing the almost total break-up of marriage and the collapse of the home.

Christianity had a double background. It had the background of the Jewish world, and of the world of the Romans and the Greeks. Let us look at Jesus' teaching against these two backgrounds.

Theoretically, no nation ever had a higher ideal of marriage than the Jews had. Marriage was a sacred duty which a man was bound to undertake. He might delay or abstain from marriage for only one reason – to devote his whole time to the study of the law. If a man refused to marry and have children, he was said to have broken the positive commandment which instructed men to be fruitful and to multiply, and he was said to have 'lessened the image of God in the world' and to have 'slain his posterity'.

Ideally, the Jews abhorred divorce. The voice of God had said: 'I hate divorce' (Malachi 2:16). The Rabbis had the loveliest sayings. 'We find that God is long-suffering to every sin except the sin of unchastity.' 'Unchastity causes the glory of God to depart.' 'Every Jew must surrender his life rather than commit idolatry, murder or adultery.' 'The very altar sheds tears when a man divorces the wife of his youth.'

The tragedy was that practice fell so far short of the ideal. One thing detracted from the whole marriage relationship. The woman in the eyes of the law was a thing. She was at the absolute disposal of her father or of her husband. She had virtually no legal rights at all. To all intents and purposes, a woman could not divorce her husband for any reason, and a man could divorce his wife for any cause at all. 'A woman', said the Rabbinic law, 'may be divorced with or without her will; but a man only with his will.'

The matter was complicated by the fact that the Jewish law of divorce was very simple in its expression and very debatable in its meaning. It is stated in Deuteronomy 24:1: 'Suppose a man enters into marriage with a woman, but she does not please him because he finds something objectionable about her, and so he writes her a certificate of divorce, puts it in her hand, and sends her out of his house.' The process of divorce was extremely simple. The bill of divorcement simply ran:

> Let this be from me thy writ of divorce and letter of dismissal and deed of liberation, that thou mayest marry whatsoever man thou wilt.

All that had to be done was to hand that document to the woman in the presence of two witnesses, and she stood divorced.

Clearly, the crux of this matter lies in the interpretation of the phrase *something objectionable*. In all matters of Jewish law, there were two schools. There was the school of Shammai, which was the strict, severe, austere school; and there was the school of Hillel, which was the liberal, broad-minded, generous school. Shammai and his school defined *something objectionable* as meaning unchastity and nothing but unchastity. 'Let a wife be as mischievous as the wife of Ahab,' they said, 'she cannot be divorced except for adultery.' To the school of Shammai, there was no possible ground of divorce except only adultery and unchastity. On the other hand, the school of Hillel defined *something objectionable* in the widest possible way. They said that it meant that a man could divorce his wife if she spoiled his dinner by putting too much salt in his food, if she went in public with her head uncovered, if she talked with men in the streets, if she was a brawling woman, if she spoke disrespectfully of her husband's parents in his presence, if she was troublesome or quarrelsome. A certain Rabbi Akiba said that the phrase translated here as *but she does not find favour in his sight* meant that a man might divorce his wife if he found a woman whom he considered to be more attractive than she.

Human nature being such as it is, it is easy to see which school would have the greater influence. In the time of Jesus, divorce had grown easier and easier, so that a situation had arisen in which girls were actually unwilling to marry, because marriage was so insecure.

When Jesus said this, he was not speaking as some theoretical idealist; he was speaking as a practical reformer. He was seeking to deal with a situation in which the structure of family life was collapsing, and in which national morals were becoming ever more lax.

THE BOND THAT CANNOT BE BROKEN

2. *Marriage among the Greeks*

Matthew 5:31–2 (*contd*)

WE have seen the state of marriage in Palestine in the time of Jesus; but the day was soon to come when Christianity would go out far beyond Palestine, and it is necessary that we should look at the state of marriage in that wider world into which the teachings of Christianity were to go.

First, let us look at marriage among the Greeks. Two things had an adverse effect on the marriage situation in the Greek world.

A. W. Verrall, the great classical scholar, said that one of the chief diseases from which ancient civilization died was a low view of women. The first thing which wrecked the marriage situation among the Greeks was the fact that relationships outside marriage carried no stigma whatsoever, and were in fact the accepted and the expected thing. Such relationships brought not the slightest discredit; they were part of the ordinary routine of life. Demosthenes laid it down as the accepted practice of life: 'We have courtesans for the sake of pleasure; we have concubines for the sake of daily cohabitation; we have wives for the purpose of having children legitimately, and of having a faithful guardian for all our household affairs.'

In later days, when Greek ideas had penetrated into, and had ruined, Roman morality, Cicero in his speech *In defence of Caelius* says: 'If there is anyone who thinks that young men should be absolutely forbidden the love of courtesans he is indeed extremely severe. I am not able to deny the principle that he states. But he is at variance, not only with the licence of his own age, but also from the customs and concessions of our ancestors. When indeed was this not done? When did anyone ever find fault with it? When was permission denied? When was it that that which is now lawful was not lawful?' It is Cicero's plea, as it was the statement of Demosthenes, that relationships outside marriage were the ordinary and the conventional thing.

The Greek view of marriage was an extraordinary paradox. The Greeks demanded that the respectable woman should live such a life of seclusion that she could never even appear on the street alone, and that she did not even have her meals in the apartments of the men. She had no part even in social life. From his wife, a Greek demanded the most complete moral purity; for himself, he demanded the utmost immoral licence. To put it bluntly, the Greeks married a wife for domestic security, but found their pleasure elsewhere. Even

Socrates said: 'Is there anyone to whom you entrust more serious matters than to your wife, and is there anyone to whom you talk less?' Verus, the colleague of the Roman emperor Marcus Aurelius in the imperial power, was blamed by his wife for associating with other women. His answer was that she must remember that the name of wife was a title of dignity, not of pleasure.

So, in Greece an extraordinary situation arose. The Temple of Aphrodite at Corinth had 1,000 priestesses, who were sacred courtesans; they came down to the streets of Corinth at evening time, so that it became a proverb: 'Not every man can afford a journey to Corinth.' This amazing alliance of religion with prostitution can be seen in an almost incredible way in the fact that the reformer, Solon, was the first to allow the introduction of prostitutes into Athens and the building of brothels, and with the profits of the brothels a new temple was built to Aphrodite the goddess of love. The Greeks saw nothing wrong in the building of a temple with the proceeds of prostitution.

But apart altogether from the practice of common prostitution, there arose in Greece an amazing class of women called the *hetairai*. They were the mistresses of famous men; they were easily the most cultured and socially accomplished women of their day; their homes were nothing less than salons; and many of their names go down in history with as much fame as the great men with whom they associated. Thais was the *hetaira* of Alexander the Great; on Alexander's death she married Ptolemy and became the mother of the Egyptian royal family. Aspasia was the *hetaira* of Pericles, perhaps the greatest ruler and orator Athens ever had; and it is said that she taught Pericles his oratory and wrote his speeches for him. Epicurus, the famous philosopher, had his equally famous Leontinium. Socrates had his Diotima. The way in which these women were regarded can be seen from the visit that Socrates paid to Theodota, as the historian Xenophon tells of it. He went to see if she was as beautiful as she was said to be. He talked kindly to her; he told her that she must shut the door against the insolent, that she must care for her lovers in their sicknesses, and rejoice with them when honour came to them, and that she must tenderly love those who gave their love to her.

Here, then, in Greece we see a whole social system based on relationships outside marriage; we see that these relationships were accepted as natural and normal, and not in the least blameworthy; and we see that these relationships could, in fact, become the dominant thing in a man's life. We see an amazing situation in which Greek men kept their wives absolutely secluded in a compulsory purity, while they themselves found their real pleasure and their real life in relationships outside marriage.

The second thing which impaired the situation in Greece was that divorce required no legal process whatsoever. All that a man had to do was to dismiss his wife in the presence of two witnesses. The one saving clause was that he must return her dowry intact.

It is easy to see what an incredible novelty the Christian teaching regarding chastity and fidelity in marriage was in a civilization like that.

THE BOND THAT CANNOT BE BROKEN

3. *Marriage among the Romans*

Matthew 5:31-2 (*contd*)

THE history of the development of the marriage situation among the Romans is the history of tragedy. The whole of

Roman religion and society was originally founded on the home. The basis of the Roman commonwealth was the *patria potestas*, the father's power; the father had literally the power of life and death over his family. A Roman son never came of age as long as his father was alive. He might be a consul; he might have reached the highest honour and office the state could offer, but as long as his father was alive he was still within his father's power.

To the Roman, the home was everything. The Roman matron was not secluded like her Greek counterpart. She took her full part in life. 'Marriage', said Modestinus, the Latin jurist, 'is a life-long fellowship of all divine and human rights.' Prostitutes, of course, there were, but they were held in contempt, and to associate with them was dishonourable. There was, for instance, a Roman magistrate who was assaulted in a house of ill-repute, and who refused to prosecute or go to law about the case, because to do so would have been to admit that he had been in such a place. So high was the standard of Roman morality that for the first 500 years of the Roman commonwealth there was not one single recorded case of divorce. The first man to divorce his wife was Spurius Carvilius Ruga in the year 234 BC, and he did so because she was childless and he desired a child.

Then there came the Greeks. In the military and the imperial sense, Rome conquered Greece; but in the moral and the social sense, Greece conquered Rome. By the second century BC, Greek morals had begun to infiltrate into Rome, and the descent was catastrophic. Divorce became as common as marriage. The philosopher Seneca speaks of women who were married to be divorced and who were divorced to be married. He tells of women who identified the years, not by the names of the consuls, but by the names of their husbands. The satirist Juvenal writes: 'Is one husband enough for Iberina? Sooner will you prevail upon her to be content with one eye.' He cites the case of a woman who had eight husbands in five years. The Roman poet Martial cites the case of a woman who had ten husbands. A Roman orator, Metillus Numidicus, made an extraordinary speech: 'If, Romans, it were possible to love without wives, we would be free from trouble; but since it is the law of nature that we can neither live pleasantly with them, nor at all without them, we must take thought for the continuance of the race rather than for our own brief pleasure.' Marriage had become nothing more than an unfortunate necessity. There was a cynical Roman jest: 'Marriage brings only two happy days – the day when the husband first clasps his wife to his breast, and the day when he lays her in the tomb.'

To such a pass did things come that special taxes were levied on the unmarried, and the unmarried were prohibited from entering into inheritances. Special privileges were given to those who had children, for children were regarded as a disaster. The very law was manipulated in an attempt to rescue the necessary institution of marriage.

There lay the Roman tragedy, what the nineteenth-century historian William Lecky called 'that outburst of ungovernable and almost frantic depravity which followed upon the contact with Greece'. Again it is easy to see with what a shock the ancient world must have heard the demands of Christian chastity.

We shall leave the discussion of the ideal of Christian marriage until we come to Matthew 19:3–9. For now, we must simply note that with Christianity there had come into the world an ideal of chastity of which men and women did not dream.

A WORD IS A PLEDGE

Matthew 5:33-7

> 'You have heard that it was said by the people of the
> old days, "You shall not take an oath falsely, but you
> shall pay your oath in full to the Lord." But I say to
> you: Do not swear at all, neither by heaven, for it is the
> throne of God, nor by the earth, for it is the footstool of
> his feet, nor by Jerusalem, for it is the city of the Great
> King, nor by your head, for you cannot make one hair
> black or white. When you say, "Yes," let it be yes; and
> when you say, "No," let it be no. Anything which goes
> beyond that has its source in evil.'

ONE of the strange things about the Sermon on the Mount is
the number of occasions when Jesus was recalling to the Jews
that which they already knew. The Jewish teachers had always
insisted on the paramount obligation of telling the truth. 'The
world stands fast on three things, on justice, on truth, and on
peace.' 'Four persons are shut out from the presence of God
– the scoffer, the hypocrite, the liar, and the retailer of slander.'
'One who has given his word and who changes it is as bad as
an idolater.' The school of Shammai was so wedded to the
truth that they forbade the ordinary courteous politenesses of
society, as, for instance, when a bride was complimented for
her charming appearance when in fact she was not particularly
attractive.

Still more did the Jewish teachers insist on the truth, if the
truth had been guaranteed by an oath. Repeatedly, that
principle is laid down in the New Testament. The commandment has it: 'You shall not make wrongful use of the name of
the Lord your God, for the Lord will not acquit anyone who
misuses his name' (Exodus 20:7). That commandment has
nothing to do with swearing in the sense of using bad

language; it condemns the person who swears that something is true, or who makes some promise, in the name of God, and who has taken the oath falsely. 'When a man makes a vow to the Lord, or swears an oath to bind himself by a pledge, he shall not break his word' (Numbers 30:2). 'If you make a vow to the Lord your God, do not postpone fulfilling it; for the Lord your God will surely require it of you, and you would incur guilt' (Deuteronomy 23:21-2).

But in the time of Jesus there were two unsatisfactory things about taking oaths.

The first was what might be called *frivolous swearing*, taking an oath where no oath was necessary or proper. It had become far too common a custom to introduce a statement by saying 'By thy life', or 'By my head', or 'May I never see the comfort of Israel if . . .'. The Rabbis laid it down that to use any form of oath in a simple statement like 'That is an olive tree' was sinful and wrong. 'The yes of the righteous is yes,' they said, 'and their no is no.'

There is still need of warning here. Far too often, people use the most sacred language in the most meaningless way. They take the sacred names upon their lips in the most thoughtless and irreverent way. The sacred names should be kept for sacred things.

The second Jewish custom was in some ways even worse than that; it might be called *evasive swearing*. The Jews divided oaths into two classes, those which were absolutely binding and those which were not. Any oath which contained the name of God was absolutely binding; any oath which succeeded in evading the name of God was held not to be binding. The result was that if a man swore by the name of God in any form, he would rigidly keep that oath; but if he swore by heaven, or by earth, or by Jerusalem, or by his head, he felt quite free to break that oath. The result was that evasion had been brought to a fine art.

The idea behind this was that if God's name was used, God became a partner in the transaction; whereas if God's name was not used, God had nothing to do with the transaction. The principle which Jesus lays down is quite clear. In effect, Jesus is saying that, far from having to make God a partner in any transaction, no one can keep God out of any transaction. God is already there. Heaven is the throne of God; the earth is the footstool of God; Jerusalem is the city of God; our own heads do not belong to us; we cannot even make a hair white or black; our lives are God's; there is nothing in the world which does not belong to God; and therefore it does not matter whether God is actually named in so many words or not. God is there already.

Here is a great eternal truth. Life cannot be divided into compartments in some of which God is involved and in others of which he is not involved; there cannot be one kind of language in the church and another kind of language in the shipyard or the factory or the office; there cannot be one kind of standard of conduct in the church and another kind of standard in the business world. The fact is that God does not need to be invited into certain departments of life and kept out of others. He is everywhere, all through life and every activity of life. He hears not only the words which are spoken in his name; he hears all words; and there cannot be any such thing as a form of words which evades bringing God into a transaction. We will regard all promises as sacred, if we remember that all promises are made in the presence of God.

THE END OF OATHS

Matthew 5:33–7 (*contd*)

THIS passage concludes with the commandment that when people have to say yes, they should say yes, and nothing more; and when they have to say no, they should say no, and nothing more.

The ideal is that people should never need an oath to buttress or guarantee the truth of anything they may say. The character of an individual should make an oath completely unnecessary. The guarantee and the witness should lie in what that person is. Isocrates, the great Greek teacher and orator, said: 'A man must lead a life which will gain more confidence in him than ever an oath can do.' The second-century Christian theologian Clement of Alexandria insisted that Christians must lead such a life and demonstrate such a character that no one will ever dream of asking an oath from them. The ideal society is one in which no one's word will ever need an oath to guarantee its truth, and no one's promise will ever need an oath to guarantee its fulfilling.

Does this saying of Jesus then forbid the taking of an oath anywhere – for instance, in the witness box? There have been two sets of people who completely refused all oaths. There were the Essenes, an ancient sect of the Jews. The Jewish historian Josephus writes of them: 'They are eminent for fidelity and are ministers of peace. Whatsoever they say also is firmer than an oath. Swearing is avoided by them and they esteem it worse than perjury. For they say that he who cannot be believed without swearing is already condemned' (*The Jewish Wars*, 2:8:6).

There were, and still are, the Quakers. The Quakers will not in any situation submit to taking an oath. The utmost length to which their founder George Fox would go was to use the word *Verily*. He writes: 'I never wronged man or woman in all that time [the time that he worked in business]. While I was in that service, I used in my dealings the word *Verily*, and it was a common saying, "If George Fox says *Verily*, there is no altering him."'

In the ancient days, the Essenes would not in any circumstances take an oath, and to this day neither will the Quakers.

Are they correct in taking this line in this matter? There were occasions when Paul, as it were, put himself upon oath. '*I call on God as witness against me*,' he writes to the Corinthians, 'it was to spare you that I did not come again to Corinth' (2 Corinthians 1:23). And he wrote to the Galatians: 'In what I am writing to you, *before God*, I do not lie!' (Galatians 1:20). On these occasions, Paul is putting himself on oath. Jesus himself did not protest at being put on oath. At his trial before the high priest, the high priest said to him: 'I put you under oath before the living God, tell us if you are the Messiah, the Son of God' (Matthew 26:63). What then is the situation?

Let us look at the last part of this verse. The Revised Standard Version has it that the answer given must simply be yes or no; 'anything more than this comes from evil'. What does that mean? It can mean one of two things.

(a) If it is necessary to take an oath from someone, that necessity arises from the evil that is the individual. If there was no evil in that person, no oath would be necessary. That is to say, the fact that it is sometimes necessary to make someone take an oath is a demonstration of the evil in Christless human nature.

(b) The fact that it is necessary to put people on oath on certain occasions arises from the fact that this is an evil world. In a perfect world, in a world which was the kingdom of

God, no taking of oaths would ever be necessary. It is necessary only because of the evil of the world.

What Jesus is saying is this – the truly good person will never need to take an oath; the truth of the sayings and the reality of the promises of that person need no such guarantee. But the fact that oaths are still sometimes necessary is the proof that people are not good and that this is not a good world.

So, this saying of Jesus leaves two obligations upon us. It leaves upon us the obligation to make ourselves such that others will so see our transparent goodness that they will never ask an oath from us; and it leaves upon us the obligation to seek to make this world such a world that falsehood and infidelity will be so eliminated from it that the necessity for oaths will be abolished.

THE ANCIENT LAW

Matthew 5:38-42

> 'You have heard that it has been said, "An eye for an eye, and a tooth for a tooth." But I tell you not to resist evil; but if anyone strikes you on the right cheek, turn the other to him also; and if anyone wishes to obtain judgment against you for your tunic, give him your cloak also; and if anyone impresses you into the public service to go a mile, go with him two miles. Give to him who asks you, and do not turn away from him who wishes to borrow from you.'

FEW passages of the New Testament have more of the essence of the Christian ethic in them than this one. Here is the characteristic ethic of the Christian life, and the conduct which should distinguish the Christian from others.

Jesus begins by citing the oldest law in the world – an eye for an eye, and a tooth for a tooth. That law is known as the *lex talionis*, and it may be described as the law of tit for tat. It appears in the earliest known code of laws, the Code of Hammurabi, who reigned in Babylon from 2285 to 2242 BC. The Code of Hammurabi makes a curious distinction between the gentleman and the workman. 'If a man has caused the loss of a gentleman's eye, his eye one shall cause to be lost. If he has shattered a gentleman's limb, one shall shatter his limb. If he has caused a poor man to lose his eye, or shattered a poor man's limb, he shall pay one mina of silver . . . If he has made the tooth of a man who is his equal fall out, one shall make his tooth fall out. If he has made the tooth of a poor man fall out, he shall pay one third of a mina of silver.' The principle is clear and apparently simple – if a man has inflicted an injury on any person, an equivalent injury shall be inflicted upon him.

That law became part and parcel of the ethic of the Old Testament, where we find it laid down no fewer than three times. 'If any harm follows, then you shall give life for life, eye for eye, tooth for tooth, hand for hand, foot for foot, burn for burn, wound for wound, stripe for stripe' (Exodus 21:23–5). 'Anyone who maims another shall suffer the same injury in return: fracture for fracture, eye for eye, tooth for tooth; the injury inflicted is the injury to be suffered' (Leviticus 24:19–20). 'Show no pity: life for life, eye for eye, tooth for tooth, hand for hand, foot for foot' (Deuteronomy 19:21). These laws are often quoted as among the bloodthirsty, savage and merciless laws of the Old Testament; but before we begin to criticize, certain things must be noted.

(1) The *lex talionis*, the law of tit for tat, so far from being a savage and bloodthirsty law, is in fact *the beginning of mercy*. Its original aim was definitely *the limitation of*

vengeance. In the very earliest days, the vendetta and the blood feud were characteristic of tribal society. If a man of one tribe injured a man of another tribe, then at once *all* the members of the tribe of the injured man were out to take vengeance on *all* the members of the tribe of the man who committed the injury; and the vengeance desired was nothing less than death. *This law deliberately limits vengeance.* It lays it down that only those who committed the injury must be punished, and their punishment must be no more than the equivalent of the injury they have inflicted and the damage they have done. Seen against its historical setting, this is not a savage law but a law of mercy.

(2) Further, this was never a law which gave a *private individual* the right to extract vengeance; it was always a law which laid down how a *judge* in the law court must assess punishment and penalty (cf. Deuteronomy 19:18). This law was never intended to give the individual person the right to indulge even in the vengeance of tit for tat. It was always intended as a guide for a judge in the assessment of the penalty which any violent or unjust deed must receive.

(3) Still further, this law was never, at least in any even semi-civilized society, carried out literally. The Jewish jurists argued rightly that to carry it out literally might in fact be the reverse of justice, because it obviously might involve the displacement of a good eye or a good tooth for a bad eye or a bad tooth. And very soon the injury done was assessed at a money value; and the Jewish law in the tractate *Baba Kamma* carefully lays down how the damage is to be assessed. If a man has injured another, he is liable on five counts – for injury, for pain, for healing, for loss of time and for indignity suffered. In regard to *injury*, the injured man is looked on as a slave to be sold in the market place. His value *before* and *after* the injury was assessed, and the man responsible for the

injury had to pay the difference. He was responsible for the loss in value of the man injured. In regard to *pain*, it was estimated how much money a man would accept to be willing to undergo the pain of the injury inflicted, and the man responsible for the injury had to pay that sum. In regard to *healing*, the injurer had to pay all the expenses of the necessary medical attention, until a complete cure had been effected. In regard to *loss of time*, the injurer had to pay compensation for the wages lost while the injured man was unable to work, and he had also to pay compensation if the injured man had held a well-paid position and was now, in consequence of the injury, fit for less well-rewarded work. In regard to *indignity*, the injurer had to pay damages for the humiliation and indignity which the injury had inflicted. In actual practice, the type of compensation which the *lex talionis* laid down is strangely modern.

(4) And most important of all, it must be remembered that the *lex talionis* is by no means the whole of Old Testament ethics. There are glimpses and even splendours of mercy in the Old Testament. 'You shall not take vengeance or bear a grudge against any of your people' (Leviticus 19:18). 'If your enemies are hungry, give them bread to eat; and if they are thirsty, give them water to drink' (Proverbs 25:21). 'Do not say, "I will do to others as they have done to me"' (Proverbs 24:29). 'It is good to give one's cheek to the smiter, and be filled with insults' (Lamentations 3:30). There is abundant mercy in the Old Testament too.

So, we see that ancient ethics were based on the law of tit for tat. It is true that that law was a law of mercy; it is true that it was a law for a judge and not for a private individual; it is true that it was never literally carried out; it is true that there were accents of mercy speaking at the same time. But Jesus obliterated the very principle of that law, because retaliation, however controlled and restricted, has no place in the Christian life.

THE END OF RESENTMENT
AND OF RETALIATION

Matthew 5:38-42 (*contd*)

So, for the Christian, Jesus abolishes the old law of limited vengeance and introduces the new spirit of non-resentment and of non-retaliation. He goes on to take three examples of the Christian spirit in operation. To take these examples with a crude literalism is completely to miss their point. It is therefore very necessary to understand what Jesus is saying.

(1) He says that if anyone smites us on the right cheek, we must turn to him the other cheek also. There is far more here than meets the eye, far more than a mere matter of blows on the face.

Suppose a right-handed man is standing in front of another man, and suppose he wants to slap the other man on the right cheek, how must he do it? Unless he goes through the most complicated contortions, and unless he empties the blow of all force, he can hit the other man's cheek only in one way – *with the back of his hand*. Now according to Jewish Rabbinic law, to hit a man with the *back* of the hand was twice as insulting as to hit him with the *flat* of the hand. So, what Jesus is saying is this: 'Even if someone should direct at you the most deadly and calculated insult, you must on no account retaliate, and you must on no account resent it.'

It will not happen very often, if at all, that anyone will slap us on the face, but time and time again life brings to us insults either great or small; and Jesus is here saying that the true Christian has learned to resent no insult and to seek retaliation for no slight. Jesus himself was called a glutton and a drunkard (cf. Matthew 11:19). He was called the friend of tax-gatherers and prostitutes, with the implication that he was like the company he kept. The early Christians were called cannibals and fire-raisers, and were accused of immorality, gross and shameless, because their service included the Love Feast. When the nineteenth-century social reformer Lord Shaftesbury undertook the cause of the poor and the oppressed, he was warned that it would mean that 'he would become unpopular with his friends and people of his own class' and that 'he would have to give up all hope of ever being a cabinet minister'. When William Wilberforce began his crusade to free the slaves of the British Empire, some people deliberately spread slanderous rumours that he was a cruel husband and a wife-beater, and that his wife was black.

Time and time again in a church, people are 'insulted' because they are not invited to a platform party, because they are omitted from a vote of thanks, or because in some way they do not get the places due to them. True Christians have forgotten what it is to be insulted; they have learned from their Master to accept any insult and never to resent it, and never to seek to retaliate.

(2) Jesus goes on to say that if anyone tries to take away our tunic in a lawsuit, we must not only let that go, but must offer our cloak also. Again there is much more than meets the eye.

The tunic, *chitōn*, was the long, sack-like inner garment made of cotton or of linen. Even the poorest man would have a change of tunics. The cloak was the great, blanket-like outer garment which a man wore as a robe by day and used as a blanket at night. Of such garments, a Jew would have only one. Now it was actually the Jewish law that a man's tunic might be taken as a pledge, but not his cloak. 'If you take your neighbour's cloak in pawn, you shall restore it before the sun goes down; for it may be your neighbour's only clothing to use as cover; in what else shall that person sleep?' (Exodus 22:26–7). The point is that by right a man's cloak could not be taken permanently from him.

What Jesus is saying is this: 'Christians never demand rights; they never dispute about their legal rights; they do not consider themselves to have any legal rights at all.' There are people who are forever demanding their rights, who clutch their privileges to them and who will not be separated from them, who will militantly go to law rather than suffer what they regard as the slightest infringement of them. Churches are tragically full of people like that, officials whose territory has been invaded, office-bearers who have not been accorded their proper place, courts which do business with a manual of practice and procedure on the table all the time, lest anyone's rights should be invaded. People like that have not even begun to see what Christianity is. Christians think not of their rights, but of their duties; not of their privileges, but of their responsibilities. Christians are people who have forgotten that they have any rights at all; and those who will fight to the legal death for their rights, inside or outside the Church, are far from the Christian way.

(3) Jesus then goes on to speak of being compelled to go one mile, and says that in such a case the Christian must willingly go two miles.

There is here a picture of which we know little, for it is a picture from an occupied country. The word used for *to compel* is the verb *aggareuein*, and *aggareuein* is a word with a history. It comes from the noun *aggareus*, which is a Persian word meaning a *courier*. The Persians had an amazing postal system. Each road was divided into stages lasting one day. At each stage there was food for the courier, and water and fodder for the horses, and fresh horses for the road. But, if by any chance there was anything lacking, any private person could be pressed, that is, compelled into giving food, lodging, horses and assistance, and even into carrying the message himself for a stage. The word for such compulsion was *aggareuein*.

In the end, the word came to signify any kind of forced or pressured call to the service of the occupying power. In an occupied country, citizens could be compelled to supply food, to provide lodging, to carry baggage. Sometimes the occupying power exercised this right of compulsion in the most tyrannical and unsympathetic way. Always this threat of compulsion hung over the citizens. Palestine was an occupied country. At any moment, a man might feel the touch of the flat of a Roman spear on his shoulder, and know that he was compelled to serve the Romans, probably in the most menial way. That, in fact, is what happened to Simon of Cyrene, when he was compelled (*aggareuein*) to bear the cross of Jesus.

So, what Jesus is saying is: 'Suppose your masters come to you and compel you to be a guide or a porter for a mile, don't do a mile with bitter and obvious resentment; go two miles with cheerfulness and with a good grace.' What Jesus is saying is: 'Don't be always thinking of your liberty to do as you like; be always thinking of your duty and your privilege to be of service to others. When a task is laid on you, even if the task is unreasonable and hateful, don't do it as a grim duty to be resented; do it as a service to be gladly rendered.'

There are always two ways of doing things. We can do the irreducible minimum and not a stroke more; we can do it in such a way as to make it clear that we hate the whole thing; we can do it with the barest minimum of efficiency and no more; or we can do it with a smile, with a gracious courtesy, with a determination not only to do this thing, but to do it well and graciously. We can do it not simply as well as we have to, but far better than anyone has any right to expect us to. The inefficient worker, the resentful employee and the ungracious helper have not even begun to have the right idea of the Christian life. Christians are not concerned to do as they like; they are concerned only to help, even when the demand for help is discourteous, unreasonable and tyrannical.

So, in this passage, under the guise of vivid contemporary illustrations, Jesus is laying down three great rules – Christians will never resent or seek retaliation for any insult, however calculated and however deadly; Christians will never stand upon their legal rights or on any other rights they may believe themselves to possess; Christians will never think of their right to do as they like, but always of their duty to be of help. The question is: how do we measure up to that?

GRACIOUS GIVING

Matthew 5:38–42 (*contd*)

FINALLY, it is Jesus' demand that we should give to all who ask and never turn away from anyone who wishes to borrow. At its highest, the Jewish law of giving was a lovely thing. It was based on Deuteronomy 15:7–11:

> If there is among you anyone in need, a member of your community in any of your towns within the land that the Lord your God is giving you, do not be hard-hearted or tight-fisted towards your needy neighbour. You should rather open your hand, willingly lending enough to meet the need, whatever it may be. Be careful that you do not entertain a mean thought, thinking, 'The seventh year, the year of remission, is near,' and therefore view your needy neighbour with hostility and give

> nothing; your neighbour might cry to the Lord against
> you, and you would incur guilt. Give liberally and be
> ungrudging when you do so, for on this account the
> Lord your God will bless you in all your work and in
> all that you undertake. Since there will never cease to
> be some in need on the earth, I therefore command you,
> 'Open your hand to the poor and needy neighbour in
> your land.'

The point about the *seventh year* is that in every seventh year
there was a cancellation of debts; and grudging and calculating people might refuse to lend anything when the seventh
year was near, for fear that the debt would be cancelled and
they would lose what they had given.

It was on that passage that the Jewish law of giving was
founded. The Rabbis laid down five principles which ought
to govern giving.

(1) Giving must not be refused. 'Be careful not to refuse
charity, for everyone who refuses charity is put in the same
category with idolators.' If people refuse to give, the day may
well come when they have to beg – perhaps from the very
people to whom they refused to give.

(2) Giving must befit the person to whom the gift is given.
The law of Deuteronomy had said that people must be given
whatever they lack. That is to say, they must not be given that
bare sufficiency which will keep body and soul together; they
must be given enough to enable them to retain at least
something of the standard and the comfort which they once
knew. So, it is said, Hillel arranged that the poverty-stricken
son of a noble family should be given not simply enough to
keep him from starvation, but a horse to ride and a slave to
run before him; and once, when no slave was available, Hillel
himself acted as his slave and ran before him. There is something gracious and lovely in the idea that giving must not

only remove actual poverty; it must do something also to remove the humiliation which poverty brings.

(3) Giving must be carried out privately and secretly. There must be no one else there. In fact, the Rabbis went to the lengths of saying that in the highest kind of giving, givers must not know to whom they were giving, and the recipients must not know from whom they were receiving. There was a certain place in the Temple to which people came in secret and gave their gifts; and these gifts were used in secrecy to help the impoverished members of once noble families, and to give the daughters of such impoverished people the dowries without which they could not be married. Jews would have regarded with abhorrence the gift which was given for the sake of prestige, publicity or self-glorification.

(4) The manner of giving must befit the character and the temperament of the recipient. The rule was that if a man had means, but was too miserly to use them, a gift must be given as a gift but afterwards reclaimed from his estate as a loan. But if a man was too proud to ask for help, Rabbi Ishmael suggested that the giver should go to him and say: 'My son, perhaps you need a loan.' His self-respect was thus saved, but the loan was never to be asked back, and it was in fact not a loan but a gift. It was even laid down that if a man was unable to respond to an appeal for help, his very refusal must be such as to show that, if he could give nothing else, he at least gave sympathy. Even a refusal was to be such that it helped and did not hurt. Giving was to be carried out in such a way that the manner of the giving was to help as much as the gift.

(5) Giving was at once a privilege and an obligation, for in reality all giving is nothing less than giving to God. To give to some needy person was not something which people might *choose* to do; it was something they *must* do; for, if they refused, the refusal was to God. 'He who befriends the

poor lends to the Lord, and he will repay him for his good deed.' 'To everyone who shows mercy to other men, mercy is shown from heaven; but to him who shows no mercy to other men, no mercy is shown from heaven.' The Rabbis loved to point out that loving kindness was one of the very few things to which the law appointed no limit at all.

Are we then to say that Jesus urged upon us what can only be called indiscriminate giving? The answer cannot be given without qualification. It is clear that the effect of the giving on the receiver must be taken into account. Giving must never be such as to encourage the recipient in laziness and in shiftlessness, for such giving can only hurt. But at the same time it must be remembered that many people who say that they will give only through official channels, and who refuse to help personal cases, are frequently merely producing an excuse for not giving at all, and are removing the personal element from giving altogether. And it must also be remembered that it is better to help twenty fraudulent beggars than to risk turning away the one person in real need.

CHRISTIAN LOVE

I. *The meaning of it*

Matthew 5:43–8

> 'You have heard that it has been said, "You shall love your neighbour, and you shall hate your enemy"; but I say to you: Love your enemies, and pray for those who persecute you, so that you may become the sons of your Father who is in heaven; for he makes his sun to rise on the evil and the good, and sends rain on the righteous and the unrighteous. If you love those who love you, what reward can you expect? Do not even the tax-

gatherers do that? If you greet only your brothers, where is there anything extra about that? Do not even the Gentiles do that? So, then, you must be perfect even as your heavenly Father is perfect.'

C. G. MONTEFIORE, the Jewish scholar, calls this 'the central and most famous section' of the Sermon on the Mount. It is certainly true that there is no other passage of the New Testament which contains such a concentrated expression of the Christian ethic of personal relations. To the ordinary person, this passage describes essential Christianity in action, and even the person who never darkens the door of the church knows that Jesus said this, and very often condemns the professing Christian for falling so far short of its demands.

When we study this passage, we must first try to find out what Jesus was really saying and what he was demanding of his followers. If we are to try to live this out, we must obviously first of all be quite clear as to what it is asking. What does Jesus mean by *loving our enemies*?

Greek is a language which is rich in synonyms; its words often have shades of meaning which English does not possess. In Greek, there are four different words for *love*.

(1) There is the noun *storgē* with its accompanying verb *stergein*. These words are the characteristic words of *family love*. They are the words which describe the love of a parent for a child and a child for a parent. 'A child', said Plato, '*loves* [*stergein*] and is loved by those who brought him into the world.' 'Sweet is a father to his children,' said Philemon, 'if he has *love* [*storgē*].' These words describe family affection.

(2) There is the noun *erōs* and the accompanying verb *eran*. These words describe the love between the sexes; there is always passion there; and there is always sexual love. Sophocles described *erōs* as 'the terrible longing'. In these words, there is nothing essentially bad; they simply describe

the passion of human love; but as time went on, they began to be tinged with the idea of lust rather than love, and they never occur in the New Testament at all.

(3) There is *philia* with its accompanying verb *philein*. These are the warmest and the best Greek words for love. They describe real love, real affection. *Ho philountes*, the present participle, is the word which describes a person's closest and nearest and truest friends. It is the word which is used in the famous saying of the Greek poet Menander: 'Whom the gods *love*, dies young.' *Philein* can mean to *caress* or to *kiss*. It is the word of warm, tender affection, the highest kind of love.

(4) There is *agapē* with its accompanying verb *agapan*. These words indicate *unconquerable benevolence*, *invincible goodwill*. (*Agapē* is the word which is used here.) If we regard people with *agapē*, it means that no matter what they do to us, no matter how they treat us, no matter if they insult us or injure us or grieve us, we will never allow any bitterness against them to invade our hearts, but will regard them with that unconquerable benevolence and goodwill which will seek nothing but their highest good. From this, certain things emerge.

(1) Jesus never asked us to love our enemies in the same way as we love our nearest and dearest. The very word is different; to love our enemies in the same way as we love our nearest and dearest would be neither possible nor right. This is a different kind of love.

(2) Wherein does the main difference lie? In the case of our nearest and dearest, we cannot help loving them; we speak of *falling in love*; it is something which comes to us quite unsought; it is something which is born of the emotions of the heart. But in the case of our enemies, love is not only something of the *heart*; it is also something of the *will*. It is not something which we cannot help; it is something which

we have to will ourselves into doing. It is in fact a victory over that which comes instinctively to us by our very nature.

Agapē does not mean a feeling of the heart, which we cannot help, and which comes unbidden and unsought; it means a determination of the mind, whereby we achieve this unconquerable goodwill even to those who hurt and injure us. *Agapē*, someone has said, is the power to love those whom we do not like and who may not like us. In point of fact, we can only have *agapē* when Jesus Christ enables us to conquer our natural tendency to anger and to bitterness, and to achieve this invincible goodwill to all people.

(3) It is then quite obvious that the last thing *agapē*, Christian love, means is that we allow people to do absolutely as they like, and that we leave them quite unchecked. No one would say that parents really love their children if they let them do as they like. If we regard people with invincible goodwill, it will often mean that we must punish them, that we must restrain them, that we must discipline them, that we must protect them against themselves. But it will also mean that we do not punish them to satisfy our desire for revenge, but in order to make them better people. It will always mean that all Christian discipline and all Christian punishment must be aimed not at vengeance but at cure. Punishment will never be merely retributive; it will always be remedial.

(4) It must be noted that Jesus laid this love down as a basis for *personal relationships*. People use this passage as a basis for pacifism and as a text on which to speak about international relationships. Of course, it includes that, but first and foremost it deals with our personal relationships with our family and our neighbours and the people we meet with every day in life. It is very much easier to go about declaring that there should be no such thing as war between nation and nation, than to live a life in which we personally never allow

any such thing as bitterness to invade our relationships with those we meet with every day. First and foremost, this commandment of Jesus deals with personal relationships. It is a commandment of which we should say first and foremost: 'This means me.'

(5) We must note that this commandment is possible only for a Christian. Only the grace of Jesus Christ can enable us to have this unconquerable benevolence and this invincible goodwill in our personal relationships with other people. It is only when Christ lives in our hearts that bitterness will die and this love will spring to life. It is often said that this world would be perfect if only people would live according to the principles of the Sermon on the Mount; but the plain fact is that no one can even begin to live according to these principles without the help of Jesus Christ. We need Christ to enable us to obey Christ's command.

(6) Last – and it may be most important of all – we must note that this commandment does not only involve allowing people to do as they like to us; it also involves us doing something for them. *We are bidden to pray for them.* No one can pray for others and still hate them. When we take ourselves and those whom we are tempted to hate to God, something happens. We cannot go on hating others in the presence of God. The surest way of killing bitterness is to pray for those whom we are tempted to hate.

CHRISTIAN LOVE

2. *The reason for it*

Matthew 5:43–8 (*contd*)

WE have seen what Jesus meant when he commanded us to have this Christian love; and now we must go on to see why he demanded that we should have it. Why, then, does Jesus demand that people should have this love, this unconquerable benevolence, this invincible goodwill? The reason is very simple and tremendous – it is that such a love makes men and women like God.

Jesus pointed to the action of God in the world, and that is the action of unconquerable benevolence. God makes his sun to rise on the good and the evil; he sends his rain on the just and the unjust. Rabbi Joshua ben Nehemiah used to say: 'Have you ever noticed that the rain fell on the field of *A*, who was righteous, and not on the field of *B*, who was wicked? Or that the sun rose and shone on Israel, who was righteous, and not upon the Gentiles, who were wicked? God causes the sun to shine both on Israel and on the nations, for the Lord is good to all.' Even the Jewish Rabbi was moved and impressed with the sheer benevolence of God to saint and sinner alike.

There is a Rabbinic tale which tells of the destruction of the Egyptians in the Red Sea. When the Egyptians were drowned, so the tale runs, the angels began a hymn of praise, but God said sorrowfully: 'The work of my hands are sunk in the sea, and you would sing before me!' The love of God is such that he can never take pleasure in the destruction of any of the creatures whom his hands have made. The psalmist had it: 'The eyes of *all* look to you, and you give them their food in due season. You open your hand, satisfying the desire of *every living thing*' (Psalm 145:15–16). In God there is this universal benevolence even towards those who have broken his law and broken his heart.

Jesus says that we must have this love in order that we may become children of our Father who is in heaven. The word used is literally translated 'sons'. As was noted in the discussion of the beatitudes, Hebrew is not rich in adjectives; and for that reason Hebrew often uses *son of* . . . with an abstract noun, where we would use an adjective. For instance, *a son of peace* is *a peaceful man*; *a son of consolation* is *a consoling man*. So, *a son of God* is *a Godlike man*. The reason why we must have this unconquerable benevolence and goodwill is that God has it; and, if we have it, we become nothing less than *children of God, Godlike men and women*.

Here we have the key to one of the most difficult sentences in the New Testament, the sentence with which this passage finishes. Jesus said: 'You, therefore, must be perfect as your heavenly Father is perfect.' On the face of it, that sounds like a commandment which cannot possibly have anything to do with us. There is not one of us who would even faintly connect ourselves with perfection.

The Greek word for *perfect* is *teleios*. This word is often used in Greek in a very special way. It has nothing to do with what we might call abstract, philosophical, metaphysical perfection. A victim which is fit for a sacrifice to God, that is a victim which is without blemish, is *teleios*. A man who has reached his full-grown stature is *teleios* as distinct from a half-grown youth. A student who has reached a mature knowledge of a subject is *teleios* as opposed to a learner who is just beginning, and who as yet has no grasp of things.

To put it in another way, the Greek idea of perfection is *functional*. A thing is perfect if it fully realizes the purpose for which it was planned, designed and made. In point of fact, that meaning is involved in the derivation of the word. *Teleios* is the adjective formed from the noun *telos*. *Telos* means an *end*, a *purpose*, an *aim*, a *goal*. A thing is *teleios* if it achieves the purpose for which it is planned; human beings are perfect if they achieve the purpose for which they were created and sent into the world.

Let us take a very simple analogy. Suppose in my house there is a loose screw, and I want to tighten and adjust this screw. I go out and I buy a screwdriver. I find that the screwdriver exactly fits the grip of my hand; it is neither too large nor too small, too rough nor too smooth. I lay the screwdriver on the slot of the screw, and I find that it exactly fits. I then turn the screw and the screw is fixed. In the Greek sense, and especially in the New Testament sense, that screwdriver is *teleios*, because it exactly fulfilled the purpose for which I desired and bought it.

So, people will be *teleios* if they fulfil the purpose for which they were created. For what purpose were human beings created? The Bible leaves us in no doubt as to that. In the old creation story in the Revised Standard Version translation, we find God saying: 'Let us make man in our image after our likeness' (Genesis 1:26). *Human beings were created to be like God.* The characteristic of God is this universal benevolence, this unconquerable goodwill, this constant seeking of the highest good of every individual. The great characteristic of God is love to saint and to sinner alike. No matter what we do to him, God seeks nothing but our highest good.

Edward Denny's hymn has it of Jesus:

> Thy foes might hate, despise, revile,
> Thy friends unfaithful prove;
> Unwearied in forgiveness still,
> Thy heart could only love.

It is when we reproduce in our lives the unwearied, forgiving, sacrificial benevolence of God that we become like God, and are therefore *perfect* in the New Testament sense of the word. To put it at its simplest, those men and women who care most for others are the most perfect.

It is the whole teaching of the Bible that we attain our humanity only by becoming Godlike. The one thing which makes us like God is the love which never ceases to care for others, no matter what they do to it. We fulfil our humanity, we enter upon Christian perfection, when we learn to forgive as God forgives, and to love as God loves.

THE REWARD MOTIVE IN THE CHRISTIAN LIFE

Matthew 6:1–18

WHEN we study the opening verses of Matthew 6, we are immediately confronted with one most important question – what is the place of the reward motive in the Christian life? Three times in this section, Jesus speaks of God rewarding those who have given to him the kind of service which he desires (Matthew 6:4, 6, 18). This question is so important that we will do well to pause to examine it before we go on to study the chapter in detail.

It is very often stated that the reward motive has no place whatsoever in the Christian life. It is held that we must be good for the sake of being good, that virtue is its own reward, and that the whole conception of reward must be banished from the Christian life. There was an old saint who used to say that he would wish to quench all the fires of hell with water, and to burn up all the joys of heaven with fire, in order that men and women seek for goodness for nothing but goodness' sake, and in order that the idea of reward and punishment might be totally eliminated from life.

On the face of it, that point of view is very fine and noble; but it is not the point of view which Jesus held. We have already seen that three times in this passage Jesus speaks about reward. The right kind of almsgiving, the right kind of prayer and the right kind of fasting will all have their reward.

Nor is this an isolated instance of the idea of reward in the teaching of Jesus. He says of those who loyally bear persecution, who suffer insult without bitterness, that their reward will be great in heaven (Matthew 5:12). He says that those who give to one of these little ones a cup of cold water in the name of a disciple will not lose their reward (Matthew 10:42). At least part of the teaching of the parable of the talents is that faithful service will receive its reward (Matthew 25:14–30). In the parable of the last judgment, the plain teaching is that there is reward and punishment in accordance with our reaction to the needs of others (Matthew 25:31–46). It is abundantly clear that Jesus did not hesitate to speak in terms of rewards and punishments. And it may well be that we ought to be careful that we do not try to be more spiritual than Jesus was in our thinking about this matter of reward. There are certain obvious facts which we must note.

(1) It is an obvious rule of life that any action which achieves nothing is futile and meaningless. A goodness which achieves no end would be a meaningless goodness. As has been very truly said, 'Unless a thing is good for something, it is good for nothing.' Unless the Christian life has an aim and a goal which it is a joy to obtain, it becomes largely without meaning. Anyone who believes in the Christian way and the Christian promise cannot believe that goodness can have no result beyond itself.

(2) To banish all rewards and punishments from the idea of religion is in effect to say that injustice has the last word. It cannot reasonably be held that the end of the good person and the end of the bad person are one and the same. That would simply mean that God does not care whether we are good or not. It would mean, to put it crudely and bluntly, that there is no point in being good, and no special reason why we should live one kind of life instead of another. To eliminate

all rewards and punishments is really to say that in God there is neither justice nor love.

Rewards and punishments are necessary in order to make sense of life. In his collection called *Last Poems*, A. E. Housman wrote:

> Yonder, see the morning blink,
> The sun is up, and so must I,
> To wash and dress and eat and drink
> And look at things and talk and think
> And work, and God knows why.
>
> And often have I washed and dressed,
> And what's to show for all my pain?
> Let me lie abed and rest;
> Ten thousand times I've done my best,
> And all's to do again.

If there are no rewards and no punishments, then that poem's view of life is true. Action is meaningless, and all effort goes unavailingly whistling down the wind.

1. *The Christian idea of reward*

BUT having reached this point with the idea of reward in the Christian life, there are certain things about which we must be clear.

(1) When Jesus spoke of reward, he was very definitely *not* thinking in terms of material reward. It is quite true that in the Old Testament the ideas of goodness and prosperity are closely connected. If a man prospered, if his fields were fertile and his harvest great, if his children were many and his fortune large, it was taken as a proof that he was a good man.

That is precisely the problem at the back of the Book of Job. Job is in misfortune; his friends come to him to argue

that that misfortune must be the result of his own sin; and
Job most vehemently denies that charge. 'Think now,' said
Eliphaz, 'who that was innocent ever perished?' (Job 4:7).
'If you are pure and upright,' said Bildad, 'surely then he
will rouse himself for you and restore you your rightful place'
(Job 8:6). 'For you say, "My conduct is pure, and I am clean
in God's sight," said Zophar. 'But O that God would speak,
and open his lips to you' (Job 11:4–5). The very idea that the
Book of Job was written to contradict is that goodness and
material prosperity go hand in hand.

'I have been young, and now am old,' said the psalmist,
'yet I have not seen the righteous forsaken or their children
begging bread' (Psalm 37:25). 'A thousand may fall at your
side,' said the psalmist, 'ten thousand at your right hand, but
it will not come near you. You will only look with your eyes
and see the punishment of the wicked. Because you have
made the Lord your refuge, the Most High your dwelling-
place, no evil shall befall you, no scourge come near your
tent' (Psalm 91:7–10). These are things that Jesus could never
have said. It was certainly not material prosperity which Jesus
promised his disciples. He in fact promised them trial and
tribulation, suffering, persecution and death. Quite certainly,
Jesus did not think in terms of material rewards.

(2) The second thing which it is necessary to remember is
that the highest reward never comes to those who are seeking
it. If people are always looking for a reward, always reckoning
up that which they believe themselves to be earning, then
they will in fact miss the reward for which they are seeking.
And they will miss it because they are looking at God and
looking at life in the wrong way. People who are always
calculating their reward are thinking of God in terms of a
judge or an accountant, and above all they are thinking of
life in terms of *law*. They are thinking of doing so much and

earning so much. They are thinking of life in terms of a credit and debit balance sheet. They are thinking of presenting an account to God and of saying: 'I have done so much. Now I claim my reward.'

The basic mistake of this point of view is that it thinks of life in terms of law, instead of *love*. If we love a person deeply and passionately, humbly and selflessly, we will be quite sure that if we give that person all we have to give, we will still be in default; that if we give that person the sun, the moon and the stars, we will still be in debt. People who are in love are always in debt; the last thing that enters their minds is that they have earned a reward. If people have a *legal* view of life, they may think constantly in terms of reward that they have won; if they have a *loving* view of life, the idea of reward will never enter their minds.

The great paradox of Christian reward is this – those who look for reward, and who calculate that it is due to them, do not receive it; those whose only motive is love, and who never think that they have deserved any reward, do in fact receive it. The strange fact is that reward is at one and the same time the by-product and the ultimate end of the Christian life.

2. *The Christian reward*

WE must now go on to ask: what are the rewards of the Christian life?

(1) We begin by noting one basic and general truth. We have already seen that Jesus Christ does not think in terms of material reward at all. *The rewards of the Christian life are rewards only to a spiritually minded person.* To the materially minded person they would not be rewards at all. The Christian rewards are rewards only to a Christian.

(2) The first of the Christian rewards is *satisfaction*. Doing the right thing, obedience to Jesus Christ, taking his way – whatever else it may or may not bring, it always brings satisfaction. It may well be that, if people do the right thing, and obey Jesus Christ, they may lose their prosperity and their position; they may end in prison or in some cases may be killed, they may finish up in unpopularity, loneliness and disrepute – but they will still possess that inner satisfaction, which is greater than all the rest put together. No price ticket can be put upon this; this is not to be evaluated in terms of earthly currency, but there is nothing like it in all the world. It brings that contentment which is the crown of life.

The poet George Herbert was a member of a group of friends who used to meet to play their musical instruments together like a little orchestra. Once he was on his way to a meeting of this group, when he passed a man whose cart was stuck in the mud of the ditch. George Herbert laid aside his instrument and went to the help of the man. It was a long job to get the cart out, and he finished covered with mud. When he arrived at the house of his friends, it was too late for music. He told them what had detained him on the way. One said: 'You have missed all the music.' George Herbert smiled. 'Yes,' he said, 'but I will have songs at midnight.' He had the satisfaction of having done the Christ-like thing.

The novelist Godfrey Winn tells of a man who was the greatest plastic surgeon in Britain. During the Second World War, he gave up a private practice, which brought him in £10,000 a year (a not inconsiderable sum for that time), to devote all his time to remoulding the faces and the bodies of airmen who had been burned and mutilated in battle. Godfrey Winn said to him: ' What's your ambition, Mac?' Back came the answer: 'I want to be a good craftsman.' The £10,000 a year was nothing compared with the satisfaction of a selfless job well done.

Once a woman stopped the Congregationalist preacher Robert Dale of Birmingham on the street. 'God bless you, Dr Dale,' she said. She absolutely refused to give her name. She only thanked him and blessed him and passed on. Dale at that moment had been much depressed. 'But', he said, 'the mist broke, the sunlight came; I breathed the free air of the mountains of God.' In material things he was not one penny the richer, but in the deep satisfaction that comes to all preachers who discover they have helped someone, he had gained untold wealth.

The first Christian reward is the satisfaction which no money on earth can buy.

(3) The second reward of the Christian life is *still more work to do*. It is the paradox of the Christian idea of reward that a task well done does not bring rest and comfort and ease; it brings still greater demands and still more strenuous endeavours. In the parable of the talents, the reward of the faithful servants was still greater responsibility (Matthew 25:14–30). A really brilliant and able scholar is not exempted from work but is given harder work than that given to anyone else. The brilliant young musician is given not easier music to work on, but the challenge of more difficult pieces. The youth who has played well in the second eleven is not put into the third eleven, where he could walk through the game without breaking sweat; he is put into the first eleven, where he has to play his heart out. The Jews had a curious saying. They said that a wise teacher will treat the pupil 'like a young heifer whose burden is increased daily'. The Christian reward is the reverse of the world's reward. The world's reward would be an easier time; the reward of Christians is that God lays still more and more upon us to do for him and

for others. The harder the work we are given to do, the greater the reward.

(4) The third, and the final, Christian reward is what men and women all through the ages have called *the vision of God*. For worldly people, who have never given a thought to God, to be confronted with God will be a terror and not a joy. If people go their own way, they drift further and further from God; the gulf between them and God becomes ever wider, until in the end God becomes a grim stranger, whom they only wish to avoid. But, if men and women all their lives have sought to walk with God, if they have sought to obey their Lord, if goodness has been their quest through all their days, then throughout their lives they have been growing closer and closer to God, until in the end they pass into God's nearer presence, without fear and with radiant joy – and that is the greatest reward of all.

RIGHT THINGS FROM THE WRONG MOTIVE

Matthew 6:1

> 'Take care not to try to demonstrate how good you are in the presence of men, in order to be seen by them. If you do, you have no reward with your Father in heaven.'

To the Jews, there were above all three great works of the religious life, three great pillars on which the good life was based – *almsgiving*, *prayer* and *fasting*. Jesus would not for a moment have disputed that; what troubled him was that so often in human life the finest things were done from the wrong motives.

It is a strange fact that these three principal good works readily lend themselves to wrong motives. It was Jesus' warning that when these things were done with the sole intention of bringing glory to the doer, they lost by far the most important part of their value. People may make charitable donations, not really to help the people to whom they give, but simply to demonstrate their own generosity, and to bask in the warmth of the recipients' gratitude and the praise of society. Some people may pray in such a way that their prayer is not really addressed to God, but to those around them. Their praying may simply be an attempt to demonstrate their exceptional piety in such a way that no one can fail to see it. Some people may fast, not really for the good of their own souls, not really to humble themselves in the sight of God, but simply to show the world how splendidly self-disciplined they are. Some people may practise good works simply to win praise from others, to increase their own prestige, and to show the world how good they are.

As Jesus saw it, there is no doubt at all that that kind of thing does receive a certain kind of reward. Three times Jesus uses the phrase, as the Revised Standard Version has it: 'Truly I say to you, they have their reward' (Matthew 6:2, 5, 16). It would be better to translate it: 'They have received payment in full.' The word that is used in the Greek is the verb *apechein*, which was the technical business and commercial word for receiving payment in full. It was the word which was used on receipted accounts. For instance, one man signs a receipt given to another man: 'I have received [*apechō*] from you the rent of the olive press which you have on hire.' A tax-collector gives a receipt, saying: 'I have received [*apechō*] from you the tax which is due.' A man sells a slave and gives a receipt, saying: 'I have received [*apechō*] the whole price due to me.'

What Jesus is saying is this: 'If you make charitable gifts to demonstrate your own generosity, you will get the

admiration of the world – but that is all you will ever get.
That is your payment in full. If you pray in such a way as to
flaunt your piety in the face of others, you will gain the
reputation of being an extremely devout person – but that
is all you will ever get. That is your payment in full. If you
fast in such a way that everyone knows that you are fasting,
you will become known as an extremely abstemious and
ascetic person – but that is all you will ever get. That is your
payment in full.' Jesus is saying: 'If your one aim is to get
yourself the world's rewards, no doubt you will get them –
but you must not look for the rewards which God alone can
give.' And we would be sadly short-sighted creatures if we
grasped the rewards of time and let the rewards of eternity
go.

HOW NOT TO GIVE

Matthew 6:2-4

> 'So, when you give alms, do not sound a trumpet before
> you, as the hypocrites do in the synagogues and in the
> streets, that they may be praised by men. This is the
> truth I tell you – they are paid in full. But when you
> give alms, your left hand must not know what your right
> hand is doing, so that your almsgiving may be in secret,
> and your Father who sees what happens in secret will
> give you your reward in full.'

To the Jews, almsgiving was the most sacred of all religious
duties. How sacred it was may be seen from the fact that the
Jews used the same word – *tzedakah* – for both *righteousness*
and *almsgiving*. To give alms and to be righteous were one
and the same thing. To give alms was to gain merit in the
sight of God, and was even to win atonement and forgiveness

for past sins. 'It is better to give alms than to lay up gold. For almsgiving saves from death, and purges away every sin' (Tobit 12:8–9).

> For kindness to a father will not be forgotten,
>   and will be credited to you against your sins;
> in the day of your distress it will be remembered in
>   your favour;
>   like frost in fair weather, your sins will melt away.
>
> (Ecclesiasticus 3:14–15)

There was a Rabbinic saying: 'Greater is he who gives alms than he who offers all sacrifices.' Almsgiving stood first in the catalogue of good works.

It was then natural and inevitable that those who desired to be good should concentrate on almsgiving. The highest teaching of the Rabbis was exactly the same as the teaching of Jesus. They too forbade ostentatious almsgiving. 'He who gives alms in secret', they said, 'is greater than Moses.' The almsgiving which saves from death is that 'when the recipient does not know from whom he gets it, and when the giver does not know to whom he gives it'. There was a Rabbi who, when he wished to give alms, dropped money behind him, so that he would not see who picked it up. 'It would be better', they said, 'to give a man nothing, than to give him something, and to put him to shame.'

There was one particularly lovely custom connected with the Temple. In the Temple, there was a room called the Chamber of the Silent. People who wished to make atonement for some sin placed money there; and poor people from good families who had come down in the world were secretly helped by these contributions.

But, as in so many other things, practice fell far short of principle. Too often, the giver gave in such a way that everyone might see the gift, and gave in order to bring personal glory rather than to bring help to someone else. During the synagogue services, offerings were taken for the poor, and there were those who took good care that others should see how much they gave. J. J. Wettstein, the eighteenth-century Swiss New Testament scholar, describes an ancient custom: 'In the east water is so scarce that sometimes it had to be bought. When a man wanted to do a good act, and to bring blessing on his family, he went to a water-carrier with a good voice, and instructed him: "Give the thirsty a drink." The water-carrier filled his skin and went to the market place. "O thirsty ones," he cried, "come to drink the offering." And the giver stood by him and said, "Bless me, who gave you this drink."' That is precisely the kind of thing that Jesus condemns. He talks about the *hypocrites* who do things like that. The word *hupokritēs* is the Greek word for an actor. People like that put on an act of giving which is designed only to glorify themselves.

THE MOTIVES OF GIVING

Matthew 6:2–4 (*contd*)

LET us now look at some of the motives which lie behind the act of giving.

(1) People may give from *a sense of duty*. They may give not because they wish to give, but because they feel that giving is a duty which they cannot easily escape. It may even be that such people can come – perhaps without realizing it – to regard the poor as being in the world to allow them to carry out this duty, and thus to acquire merit in the sight of God.

It was said of a great but superior man: 'With all his giving he never gives himself.' When someone gives, as it were, from a sense of superiority, when the giving is done always with a certain calculation, when it comes from a sense of duty, even a sense of Christian duty, that person may give generously of things, but it is not enough. The one thing such people never give is themselves, and therefore the giving is incomplete.

(2) People may give from *motives of prestige*. They may give to take for themselves the glory of giving. The chances are that, if no one is to know about it, or if there is no publicity attached to it, they would not give at all. Unless they are duly thanked and praised and honoured, they are sadly disgruntled and discontented. They give, not to the glory of God, but to the glory of themselves. They give, not primarily to help those in need, but to gratify their own vanity and their own sense of power.

(3) People may give simply *because they have to*. They may give simply because the overflowing love and kindliness in their hearts will not allow them to do anything else. They may give because, try as they may, they cannot rid themselves of a sense of responsibility for those in need.

There was a kind of vast kindliness about the great eighteenth-century man of letters Dr Johnson. There was a poverty-stricken man called Robert Levett who had been a waiter in Paris and a doctor in the poorer parts of London. He had an appearance and manners, as Johnson said himself, such as to disgust the rich and to terrify the poor. Somehow or other he became a member of Johnson's household. Johnson's friend and biographer James Boswell was amazed at the whole business, but the playwright Oliver Goldsmith knew Johnson better. He said of Levett: 'He is poor and honest which is recommendation enough for Johnson. He is now become miserable, and that insures the protection of Johnson.' Misfortune was a passport to Johnson's heart.

Boswell tells this story of Johnson. 'Coming home late one night he found a poor woman lying on the street, so much exhausted that she could not walk: he took her upon his back and carried her to his house, where he discovered that she was one of these wretched females, who had fallen into the lowest state of vice, poverty and disease. Instead of harshly upbraiding her, he had her taken care of with all tenderness for a long time, at considerable expense, till she was restored to health, and endeavoured to put her in a virtuous way of living.' All that Johnson got out of that was unworthy suspicions about his own character, but the heart of the man demanded that he should give.

Surely one of the loveliest pictures in literary history is the picture of Johnson, in his own days of poverty, coming home in the small hours of the morning, and, as he walked along the Strand, slipping pennies into the hands of the waifs and strays, who were sleeping in the doorways because they had nowhere else to go. His literary executor Sir John Hawkins tells that someone asked him how he could bear to have his house filled with 'necessitous and undeserving people'. Johnson answered: 'If I did not assist them no one else would, and they must not be lost for want.' There you have real giving, the giving which is the upsurge of love in the heart of a man, the giving which is a kind of overflow of the love of God.

We have the pattern of this perfect giving in Jesus Christ himself. Paul wrote to his friends at Corinth: 'For you know the generous act of our Lord Jesus Christ, that though he was rich, yet for your sakes he became poor, so that by his poverty you might become rich' (2 Corinthians 8:9). Our giving must never be the grim and self-righteous outcome of a sense of duty. Still less must it be done to enhance our own glory and prestige in society; it must be the instinctive outflow of the loving heart; we must give to others as Jesus Christ gave himself to us.

HOW NOT TO PRAY

Matthew 6:5–8

> 'And when you pray, you must not be like the hypocrites, for they are fond of praying standing in the synagogues and at the corners of the streets, so that they may be seen by people. This is the truth I tell you – they are paid in full. But when you pray, go into your private room, and shut the door, and pray to your Father who is in secret; and your Father who sees what happens in secret will give you your reward in full.
>
> 'When you pray, do not pile up meaningless phrases, as the Gentiles do, for their idea is that they will be heard because of the length of their words. So, then, do not be like them, for your Father knows the things you need before you ask him.'

No nation ever had a higher ideal of prayer than the Jews had; and no religion ever ranked prayer higher in the scale of priorities than the Jews did. 'Great is prayer,' said the Rabbis, 'greater than all good works.' One of the loveliest things that was ever said about family worship is the Rabbinic saying: 'He who prays within his house surrounds it with a wall that is stronger than iron.' The only regret of the Rabbis was that it was not possible to pray all day long.

But certain faults had crept into the Jewish habits of prayer. It is to be noted that these faults are by no means peculiar to Jewish ideas of prayer; they can and do occur anywhere. And it is to be noted that they could only occur in a community where prayer was taken with the greatest seriousness. They are not the faults of neglect; they are the faults of misguided devotion.

(1) Prayer tended to become formalized. There were two things the daily use of which was prescribed for every Jew.

The first was the *Shema*, which consists of three short passages of Scripture – Deuteronomy 6:4–9, 11:13–21; Numbers 15:37–41. *Shema* is the imperative of the Hebrew word for *to hear*, and the *Shema* takes its name from the verse which was the essence and centre of the whole matter: 'Hear, O Israel, the Lord our God is one Lord.'

The full *Shema* had to be recited by every Jew every morning and every evening. It had to be said as early as possible. It had to be said as soon as the light was strong enough to distinguish between blue and white, or, as Rabbi Eliezer said, between blue and green. In any event, it had to be said before the third hour, that is, 9 am; and in the evening it had to be said before 9 pm. If the last possible moment for the saying of the *Shema* had come, no matter where a man found himself, at home, in the street, at work or in the synagogue, he must stop and say it.

There were many who loved the *Shema*, and who repeated it with reverence and adoration and love; but inevitably there were still more who gabbled their way through it and went their way. The *Shema* had every chance of becoming a vain repetition, which was mumbled like some incantation. We Christians are but ill-qualified to criticize, for everything that has been said about formally gabbling through the *Shema* can be said about grace before meals in many families.

The second thing which every Jew had to repeat daily was called the *Shemonēh 'esreh*, which means *the Eighteen*. It consisted of eighteen prayers, and was, and still is, an essential part of the synagogue service. In time the prayers became nineteen, but the old name remains. Most of these prayers are quite short, and nearly all of them are very lovely.

The twelfth runs:

> Let Thy mercy, O Lord, be showed upon the upright, the humble, the elders of thy people Israel, and the rest of its teachers; be favourable to the pious strangers among us, and to us all. Give thou a good reward to those who sincerely trust in thy name, that our lot may be cast among them in the world to come, that our hope be not deceived. Praised be thou, O Lord, who art the hope and confidence of the faithful.

The fifth runs:

> Bring us back to thy law, O our Father; bring us back, O King, to thy service; bring us back to thee by true repentance. Praised be thou, O Lord, who dost accept our repentance.

No church possesses a more beautiful liturgy than the *Shemonēh 'esreh*. The law was that Jews must recite it three times a day – once in the morning, once in the afternoon and once in the evening. The same thing happened again. Devout Jews prayed it with loving devotion; but there were many to whom this series of lovely prayers became a gabbled formula. There was even a summary supplied which might be prayed, if there was not the time to repeat the whole eighteen or they could not all be remembered. The repetition of the *Shemonēh 'esreh* became nothing more than a superstitious incantation. Again, we Christians are ill-qualified to criticize, for there are many occasions when we do precisely the same with the prayer which Christ taught us to pray.

HOW NOT TO PRAY

Matthew 6:5–8 (*contd*)

(2) FURTHER, the Jewish liturgy supplied stated prayers for all occasions. There was hardly an event or a sight in life which had not its stated formula of prayer. There was prayer before and after each meal; there were prayers in connection with the light, the fire and the lightning, on seeing the new moon, on comets, rain or tempest, at the sight of the sea, lakes or rivers, on receiving good news, on using new furniture, on entering or leaving a city. Everything had its prayer. Clearly, there is something infinitely lovely here. It was the intention that every happening in life should be brought into the presence of God.

But just because the prayers were so meticulously pre-scribed and stated, the whole system lent itself to formalism, and the danger was for the prayers to slip off the tongue with very little meaning. The tendency was glibly to repeat the right prayer at the right time. The great Rabbis knew that and tried to guard against it. 'If a man', they said, 'says his prayers, as if to get through a set task, that is no prayer.' 'Do not look on prayer as a formal duty, but as an act of humility by which to obtain the mercy of God.' Rabbi Eliezer was so impressed with the danger of formalism that it was his custom to compose one new prayer every day, that his prayer might be always fresh. It is quite clear that this kind of danger is not confined to Jewish religion. Even quiet times which began in devotion can end in the formalism of a rigid and ritualistic timetable.

(3) Still further, devout Jews prayed at regular times, always in the morning and the evening, and sometimes also at noon. Wherever they found themselves, they were bound

to pray. Clearly, they might be genuinely remembering God, or they might be carrying out a habitual formality.

Muslims have the same custom. It is a lovely thing that three times a day people should remember God; but there is a real danger that it may come to no more than this – that three times a day the prayers are gabbled without a thought of God.

(4) There was a tendency to connect prayer with certain places, and especially with the synagogue. It is undeniably true that there are certain places where God seems very near; but there were certain Rabbis who went to the lengths of saying that prayer was efficacious only if it was offered in the Temple or in the synagogue. So there grew up the custom of going to the Temple at the hours of prayer. In the first days of the Christian Church, even the disciples of Jesus thought in terms like these, for we read of Peter and John going up to the Temple at the hour of prayer (Acts 3:1).

There was a danger here, the danger that people might come to think of God as being confined to certain holy places and that they might forget that the whole earth is the temple of God. The wisest of the Rabbis saw this danger. They said: 'God says to Israel, pray in the synagogue of your city; if you cannot, pray in the field; if you cannot, pray in your house; if you cannot, pray on your bed; if you cannot, commune with your own heart upon your bed, and be still.'

The trouble about any system lies not in the system, but in those who use it. It is possible to make any system of prayer an instrument of devotion or a formality, glibly and unthinkingly to be gone through.

(5) There was among the Jews an undoubted tendency towards long prayers. That was a tendency by no means confined to the Jews. In eighteenth-century worship in

Scotland, length meant devotion. In such a Scottish service, there was a verse-by-verse lecture on Scripture which lasted for an hour, and a sermon which lasted for another hour. Prayers were lengthy and spontaneous. The liturgist Dr W. D. Maxwell writes: 'The efficacy of prayer was measured by its ardour and its fluency, and not least by its fervid lengthiness.' Rabbi Levi said: 'Whoever is long in prayer is heard.' Another saying has it: 'Whenever the righteous make their prayer long, their prayer is heard.'

There was – and still is – a kind of subconscious idea that if we batter long enough at God's door, he will answer; that God can be talked, and even pestered, into condescension. The wisest Rabbis were well aware of this danger. One of them said: 'It is forbidden to lengthen out the praise of the Holy One. It says in the Psalms: "*Who can* utter the mighty doings of the Lord, or show forth all his praise?" [Psalm 106:2]. There only *he who can* may lengthen out and tell his praise – *but no one can*.' 'Let a man's words before God always be few, as it is said, "Be not rash with your mouth, and let not your heart be hasty to utter a word before God; for God is in heaven, and you upon earth, therefore let your words be few" [Ecclesiastes 5:2].' 'The best adoration consists in keeping silence.' It is easy to confound verbosity with piety, and fluency with devotion – and into that mistake many of the Jews fell.

HOW NOT TO PRAY

Matthew 6:5–8 (*contd*)

(6) THERE were certain other forms of repetition, which the Jews, like all people of the middle east, were apt to use

and to overuse. People had a habit of hypnotizing themselves by the endless repetition of one phrase or even of one word. In 1 Kings 18:26, we read how the prophets of Baal cried out: 'O Baal answer us', for the space of half a day. In Acts 19:34, we read how the Ephesian mob, for two hours, kept shouting: 'Great is Artemis of the Ephesians.' Muslims will go on repeating the sacred syllable *HE* for hours on end. The Jews did that with the *Shema*. It is a kind of substitution of self-hypnotism for prayer.

There was another way in which Jewish prayer used repetition. There was an attempt to pile up every possible title and adjective in the address of the prayer to God. One famous prayer begins:

> Blessed, praised, and glorified, exalted, extolled and honoured, magnified and lauded be the name of the Holy One.

There is one Jewish prayer which actually begins with sixteen different adjectives attached to the name of God. There was a kind of intoxication with words. When people begin to think more of how they are praying than of what they are praying, their prayers die upon their lips.

(7) The final fault which Jesus found with certain of the Jews was that they prayed in order to be seen. The Jewish system of prayer made ostentation very easy. Jews prayed standing, with hands stretched out, palms upwards, and with heads bowed. Prayer had to be said in the morning and in the evening. It had to be said wherever they might be, and it was easy for people to make sure that at these hours they were at a busy street corner, or in a crowded city square, so that all the world might see with what devotion they prayed. It was easy to halt on the top step of the entrance to the synagogue, and there pray lengthily and demonstratively, so that all might

admire such exceptional piety. It was easy to put on an act of prayer which all the world might see.

The wisest of the Jewish Rabbis fully understood and unsparingly condemned this attitude. 'A man in whom is hypocrisy brings wrath upon the world, and his prayer is not heard.' 'Four classes of men do not receive the face of the glory of God – the mockers, the hypocrites, the liars and the slanderers.' The Rabbis said that no man could pray at all unless his heart was attuned to pray. They laid it down that for perfect prayer there were necessary an hour of private preparation beforehand and an hour of meditation afterwards. But the Jewish system of prayer did lend itself to ostentation, if in a person's heart there was pride.

In effect, Jesus lays down two great rules for prayer.

(1) He insists that all true prayer must be offered to God. The real fault of the people whom Jesus was criticizing was that they were praying to others and not to God. A certain great preacher once described an ornate and elaborate prayer offered in a Boston church as 'the most eloquent prayer ever offered to a Boston audience'. The preacher was much more concerned with impressing the congregation than with making contact with God. Whether in public or in private prayer, we should have no thought in our minds and no desire in our hearts but God.

(2) He insists that we must always remember that the God to whom we pray is a God of love who is more ready to answer than we are to pray. His gifts and his grace have not to be unwillingly extracted from him. We do not come to a God who has to be coaxed, or pestered, or battered into answering our prayers. We come to one whose one wish is to give. When we remember that, it is surely sufficient to go to God with the sigh of desire in our hearts, and on our lips the words 'Your will be done.'

THE DISCIPLE'S PRAYER

Matthew 6:9–15

> 'So, then, pray in this way:
> Our Father in heaven, let your name be held holy:
> Let your kingdom come:
> Let your will be done, as in heaven, so also on earth:
> Give us today bread for the coming day:
> Forgive us our debts as we forgive our debtors:
> And lead us not into temptation, but deliver us from the
>   evil one.
> For, if you forgive men their trespasses, your heavenly
>   Father will forgive you too; but if you do not forgive
>   men their trespasses, neither will your Father forgive
>   your trespasses.'

BEFORE we begin to think about the Lord's Prayer in detail, there are certain general facts which we will do well to remember about it.

We must note, first of all, that this is a prayer which Jesus taught his *disciples* to pray. Both Matthew and Luke are clear about that. Matthew sets the whole Sermon on the Mount in the context of the disciples (Matthew 5:1); and Luke tells us that Jesus taught this prayer in response to the request of one of his disciples (Luke 11:1). The Lord's Prayer is a prayer which only a disciple can pray; it is a prayer which only those who are committed to Jesus Christ can take upon their lips with any meaning.

The Lord's Prayer is not a child's prayer, as it is so often regarded; it is, in fact, not meaningful for a child. The Lord's Prayer is not the Family Prayer as it is sometimes called, unless by the word *family* we mean *the family of the Church*. The Lord's Prayer is specifically and definitely stated to be the *disciple's* prayer; and only on the lips of a disciple has the prayer its full meaning. To put it in another way, the Lord's Prayer can only really be prayed when those who pray it know what they are saying, and they cannot know that until they have entered into discipleship.

We must note the *order* of the petitions in the Lord's Prayer. The first three petitions have to do with God and with the glory of God; the second three petitions have to do with our needs and our necessities. That is to say, God is first given his supreme place – and then, and only then, do we turn to ourselves and our needs and desires. It is only when God is given his proper place that all other things fall into their proper places. Prayer must never be an attempt to bend the will of God to our desires; prayer ought always to be an attempt to submit our wills to the will of God.

The second part of the prayer, the part which deals with our needs and our necessities, is a marvellously created unity. It deals with the three essential human needs and the three spheres of time within which we all move. First, it asks for *bread*, for that which is necessary for the *maintenance of life*, and thereby brings the needs of the *present* to the throne of God. Second, it asks for *forgiveness* and thereby brings the *past* into the presence of God. Third, it asks for *help in temptation* and thereby commits all the future into the hands of God. In these three brief petitions, we are taught to lay the present, the past and the future before the footstool of the grace of God.

But not only is this a prayer which brings the whole of life to the presence of God; it is also a prayer which brings the whole of God to our lives. When we ask for *bread* to sustain our earthly lives, that request immediately directs our thoughts to *God the Father*, the Creator and the Sustainer of all life. When we ask for *forgiveness*, that request immediately directs our thoughts to *God the Son*, Jesus Christ our Saviour and

Redeemer. When we ask for help for future temptation, that request immediately directs our thoughts to *God the Holy Spirit*, the Comforter, the Strengthener, the Illuminator, the Guide and the Guardian of our way.

In the most amazing way, this brief second part of the Lord's Prayer takes the present, the past and the future, the whole of human life, and presents them to God the Father, God the Son and God the Holy Spirit, to God in all his fullness. In the Lord's Prayer, Jesus teaches us to bring the whole of life to the whole of God, and to bring the whole of God to the whole of life.

THE FATHER IN HEAVEN

Matthew 6:9

> Our Father in heaven.

It might well be said that the word *Father* used of God is a compact summary of the Christian faith. The great value of this word *Father* is that it settles all the relationships of this life.

(1) *It settles our relationship to the unseen world.* Missionaries tell us that one of the greatest reliefs which Christianity brings to the minds and hearts of those who hold a primitive religious belief is the certainty that there is only one God. For those who hold such beliefs, there are hordes of gods; every stream and river, and tree and valley, and hill and wood, and every natural force has its own god. Their world is crowded with gods. Still further, all these gods are jealous, grudging and hostile. They must all be placated, and people can never be sure that they have not omitted the honour due to some of these gods. The consequence is that the people

live in terror of the gods; they are haunted and not helped by their religion.

The most significant Greek legend of the gods is the legend of Prometheus. Prometheus was a god. It was in the days before people possessed fire; and life without fire was a cheerless and a comfortless thing. In pity, Prometheus took fire from heaven and gave it as a gift to human beings. Zeus, the king of the gods, was mightily angry that they should receive this gift. So he took Prometheus and chained him to a rock in the middle of the Adriatic Sea, where he was tortured with the heat and the thirst of the day and with the cold of the night. Even more, Zeus prepared a vulture to tear out Prometheus' liver, which always grew again, only to be torn out again.

That is what happened to the god who tried to help men and women. The whole conception is that the gods are jealous, vengeful and grudging; and the last thing the gods wish to do is to help the human race. That is the pagan idea of the attitude of the unseen world to human beings, and it means that people are haunted by the fear of a horde of jealous and grudging gods. So, when we discover that the God to whom we pray has the name and the heart of a *father*, it makes literally all the difference in the world. We need no longer shiver before a horde of jealous gods; we can rest in a father's love.

(2) *It settles our relationship to the seen world*, to this world of space and time in which we live. It is easy to think of this world as a hostile world. There are the chances and the changes of life; there are the iron laws of the universe which we break at our peril; there is suffering and death; but if we can be sure that behind this world there is not a capricious, jealous, mocking god, but a God whose name is Father, then although much may still remain dark, all is now bearable because behind all is love. It will always help us if

we regard this world as organized not for our comfort but for our training.

Take, for instance, *pain*. Pain might seem a bad thing, but pain has its place in the order of God. It sometimes happens that people are constituted in such a way that they are incapable of feeling pain. Such people are a danger to themselves and a problem to everyone else. If there were no such thing as pain, we would never know that we were ill, and often we would die before steps could be taken to deal with any disease or illness. That is not to say that pain cannot *become* a bad thing, but it is to say that more often than not pain is God's red light to tell us that there is danger ahead.

The eighteenth-century German scholar G. E. Lessing used to say that if he had one question to ask the Sphinx, it would be: 'Is this a friendly universe?' If we can be certain that the name of the God who created this world is *Father*, then we can also be certain that fundamentally this is a friendly universe. To call God *Father* is to settle our relationship to the world in which we live.

THE FATHER IN HEAVEN

Matthew 6:9 (*contd*)

(3) IF we believe that God is Father, *it settles our relationship to one another*. If God is Father, he is Father of all people. The Lord's Prayer does not teach us to pray *My Father*; it teaches us to pray *Our Father*. It is very significant that in the Lord's Prayer the words *I*, *me* and *mine* never occur; it is true to say that Jesus came to take these words out of life and to put in their place *we*, *us* and *ours*. God is no one's exclusive possession. The very phrase *Our Father*

involves *the elimination of self*. The fatherhood of God is the only possible basis of human relationships.

(4) If we believe that God is Father, *it settles our relationship to ourselves*. There are times for each and every one of us when we despise and hate ourselves. We know that we are lower than the lowest thing that crawls upon the earth. The heart knows its own bitterness, and no one knows our unworthiness better than we do ourselves.

The writer Mark Rutherford wished to add a new beatitude: 'Blessed are those who heal us of our self-despisings.' Blessed are those who give us back our self-respect. That is precisely what God does. In these grim, bleak, terrible moments, we can still remind ourselves that, even if we matter to no one else, we matter to God; that in the infinite mercy of God we are of royal lineage, children of the King of Kings.

(5) If we believe that God is Father, *it settles our relationship to God*. It is not that it removes the might, majesty and power of God. It is not that it makes God any the less God; but it makes that might, and majesty, and power approachable for us.

There is an old Roman story which tells how a Roman emperor was enjoying a triumph. He had the privilege, which Rome gave to her great victors, of marching his troops through the streets of Rome, with all his captured trophies and his prisoners in his train. So the emperor was on the march with his troops. The streets were lined with cheering people. The tall legionaries lined the streets' edges to keep the people in their places. At one point on the triumphal route, there was a little platform where the empress and her family were sitting to watch the emperor go by in all the pride of his triumph. On the platform with his mother, there was the emperor's youngest son, a little boy. As the emperor came near, the little boy jumped off the platform, burrowed through the crowd and tried to dodge between the legs of a legionary and to run out on to the road to meet his father's chariot. The legionary stooped down and stopped him. He swung him up in his arms: 'You can't do that, boy,' he said. 'Don't you know who that is in the chariot? That's the emperor. You can't run out to his chariot.' And the little boy laughed down. 'He may be your emperor,' he said, 'but he's my father.' That is exactly the way the Christian feels towards God. The might, and the majesty, and the power are the might, and the majesty, and the power of one whom Jesus taught us to call *Our Father*.

THE FATHER IN HEAVEN

Matthew 6:9 (*contd*)

So far, we have been thinking of the first two words of this address to God – *Our Father*; but God is not only *Our Father*, he is Our Father *who is in heaven*. The last words are of primary importance. They conserve two great truths.

(1) They remind us of the *holiness* of God. It is very easy to cheapen and to sentimentalize the whole idea of the fatherhood of God, and to make it an excuse for an easy-going, comfortable religion. 'He's a good fellow and all will be well.' As the German poet Heinrich Heine said of God: 'God will forgive. It is his trade.' If we were to say *Our Father*, and stop there, there might be some excuse for that; but it is Our Father *in heaven* to whom we pray. The love is there, but the holiness is there, too.

It is extraordinary how seldom Jesus used the word Father in regard to God. Mark's gospel is the earliest gospel, and is therefore the nearest thing we will ever have to an actual report of all that Jesus said and did; and in Mark's gospel Jesus calls God *Father* only six times, and never outside the circle of the disciples. To Jesus, the word *Father* was so sacred that he could hardly bear to use it; and he could never use it except among those who had grasped something of what it meant.

We must never use the word *Father* in regard to God cheaply, easily and sentimentally. God is not an easy-going parent who tolerantly shuts his eyes to all sins and faults and mistakes. This God, whom we can call Father, is the God whom we must still approach with reverence and adoration, and awe and wonder. God is our Father in heaven, and in God there is *love* and *holiness* combined.

(2) They remind us of the *power* of God. In human love, there is so often the tragedy of frustration. We may love people and yet be unable to help them achieve something, or to stop them doing something. Human love can be intense – and quite helpless. Any parent with an erring child, or any lover with a wandering loved one, knows that. But when we say *Our Father – in heaven*, we place two things side by side. We place side by side the *love* of God and the *power* of God. We tell ourselves that the power of God is always motivated by the love of God, and can never be exercised for anything but our good; we tell ourselves that the love of God is backed by the power of God, and that therefore its purposes can never be ultimately frustrated or defeated. It is love of which we think, but it is the love of God. When we pray *Our Father in heaven*, we must always remember the holiness of God, and we must always remember the power which moves in love, and the love which has behind it the undefeatable power of God.

THE HALLOWING OF THE NAME

Matthew 6:9 (*contd*)

Let your name be held holy.

'HALLOWED be your name' – it is probably true that of all the petitions of the Lord's Prayer this is the one whose meaning we would find it most difficult to express. First, then, let us concentrate on the actual meaning of the words.

The word which is translated as *hallowed* is a part of the Greek verb *hagiazesthai*. The Greek verb *hagiazesthai* is connected with the adjective *hagios*, and means *to treat a person or a thing as hagios*. *Hagios* is the word which is usually translated as *holy*; but the basic meaning of *hagios* is *different* or *separate*. A thing which is *hagios* is *different* from other things. A person who is *hagios* is *separate* from other people. So, a temple is *hagios* because it is *different* from other buildings. An altar is *hagios* because it exists for a purpose *different* from the purpose of ordinary things. God's day is *hagios* because it is *different* from other days. Priests are *hagios* because they are *separate* from other people. So, this petition means: 'Let God's name be treated differently from all other names; let God's name be given a position which is absolutely unique.'

But there is something to add to this. In Hebrew, the *name* does not mean simply the name by which a person is called – John or James, or whatever the name may be. In Hebrew, the *name* means the *nature*, the *character*, the *personality* of the person in so far as it is known or revealed to us. That becomes clear when we see how the Bible writers use the expression.

The psalmist says: 'Those who know your *name* put their trust in you' (Psalm 9:10). Quite clearly, that does not mean that those who know that God is called Yahweh will trust in him. It means that those who know what God is like, those who know the nature and the character of God, will put their trust in him. The psalmist says: 'Some take pride in chariots, and some in horses, but our pride is in the *name* of the Lord our God' (Psalm 20:7). Quite clearly, that does not mean that in a time of difficulty the psalmist will remember that God is called Yahweh. It means that at such a time some will put their trust in human and material aids and defences, but the psalmist will remember the nature and the character of God; he will remember what God is like, and that memory will give him confidence.

So, let us take these two things and put them together. *Hagiazesthai*, which is translated as *to hallow*, means *to regard as different*, to give a unique and special place to. The *name* is the *nature*, the *character*, the *personality* of the person in so far as it is known and revealed to us. Therefore, when we pray 'Hallowed be your name,' it means: 'Enable us to give to you the unique place which your nature and character deserve and demand.'

THE PRAYER FOR REVERENCE

Matthew 6:9 (*contd*)

Is there, then, one word in English for giving to God the unique place which his nature and character demand? There is such a word, and the word is *reverence*. This petition is a prayer that we should be enabled to show reverence for God as God deserves to be reverenced. In all true reverence of God, there are four essentials.

(1) In order to show reverence for God, we must believe that God exists. We cannot show reverence for someone who does not exist; we must begin by being sure of the existence of God.

To the modern mind, it is strange that the Bible nowhere attempts to prove the existence of God. For the Bible, God is an axiom. An axiom is a self-evident fact which is not itself proved, but which is the basis of all other proofs. For instance, 'A straight line is the shortest distance between two points' and 'Parallel lines, however far produced, will never meet' are axioms.

The Bible writers would have said that it was superfluous to prove the existence of God, because they *experienced* the presence of God every moment of their lives. They would have said that there was no more need to prove that God exists than the need for a husband to prove that his wife exists, or a wife her husband. The husband and wife meet every day, and they meet God every day.

But suppose we did need to try to prove that God exists, using our own minds to do so, how would we begin? We might begin from *the world in which we live*. William Paley's old argument, produced at the beginning of the nineteenth century, is not yet completely outdated. Suppose there is a man walking along the road. He strikes his foot against a watch lying in the dust. He has never in his life seen a watch before; he does not know what it is. He picks it up; he sees that it consists of a metal case, and inside the case a complicated arrangement of wheels, levers, springs and jewels. He sees that the whole thing is moving and working in the most orderly way. He sees further that the hands are moving round the dial in an obviously predetermined routine. What then does he say? Does he say: 'All these metals and jewels came together from the ends of the earth by chance, by chance made themselves into wheels and levers and springs, by chance assembled themselves into this mechanism, by chance wound themselves up and set themselves going, by chance acquired their obvious orderly working'? No. He says: 'I have found a watch; somewhere there must be a watchmaker.'

Order presupposes mind. We look at the world; we see a vast machine which is working in order. Suns rise and set in an unvarying succession. Tides ebb and flow to a timetable. Seasons follow each other in an order. We look at the world, and we are bound to say: 'Somewhere there must be a worldmaker.' The fact of the world drives us to God. As the astronomer Sir James Jeans has said, 'No astronomer can be an atheist.' The order of the world demands the mind of God behind it.

We might begin from *ourselves*. The one thing human beings have never created is life. We can alter and rearrange and change things; but we cannot create a living thing. Where then did we get our life? From our parents. Yes, but where did they get theirs? From their parents. But where did all this begin? At some time, life must have come into the world; and it must have come from outside the world, for human beings cannot create life; and once again we are driven back to God.

When we look in upon ourselves and out upon the world, we are driven to God. As the German philosopher Immanuel Kant said long ago, 'the moral law within us, and the starry heavens above us', drive us to God.

(2) Before we can show reverence for God, we must not only believe that God is, we must also know the kind of God he is. No one could show reverence for the Greek gods with their loves and wars, their hates and their adulteries, their trickeries and their mischief. No one can have reverence for capricious, immoral, impure gods. But, in God as we know him, there are three great qualities. There is *holiness*; there is *justice*; and there is *love*. We must show reverence for God not only because he exists, but because he is the God whom we know him to be.

(3) But people might believe that God is; they might be intellectually convinced that God is holy, just and loving; and still they might not have reverence. For reverence, there

is necessary *a constant awareness of God*. To show reverence for God means to live in a God-filled world, to live a life in which we never forget God. This awareness is not confined to the Church or to so-called holy places; it must be an awareness which exists everywhere and at all times.

Wordsworth spoke of it in 'Lines composed above Tintern Abbey':

> And I have felt
> A presence that disturbs me with the joy
> Of elevated thoughts; a sense sublime
> Of something far more deeply interfused,
> Whose dwelling is the light of setting suns,
> And the round ocean, and the living air,
> And the blue sky, and in the mind of man:
> A motion and a spirit, that impels
> All thinking things, all objects of all thought,
> And rolls through all things.

One of the finest of modern devotional poets is Henry Ernest Hardy, who wrote under the name of Father Andrew. In 'The Mystic Beauty', he writes:

> O London town has many moods,
> And mingled 'mongst its many broods
> A leavening of saints,
>
> And ever up and down its streets,
> If one has eyes to see one meets
> Stuff that an artist paints.
>
> I've seen a back street bathed in blue,
> Such as the soul of Whistler knew:
> A smudge of amber light,
>
> Where some fried fish-shop plied its trade,
> A perfect note of colour made –
> Oh, it was exquisite!

I once came through St James' Park
Betwixt the sunset and the dark,
And oh the mystery

Of grey and green and violet!
I would I never might forget
That evening harmony.

I hold it true that God is there
If beauty breaks through anywhere;
And his most blessed feet,

Who once life's roughest roadway trod,
Who came as man to show us God,
Still pass along the street.

God in the back street, God in St James' Park, God in the
fried fish shop – that is reverence. The trouble with most
people is that their awareness of God is spasmodic, acute at
certain times and places, totally absent at others. Reverence
means the constant awareness of God.

(4) There remains one further ingredient in reverence.
We must believe that God exists; we must know what kind
of a God he is; we must be constantly aware of God. But
people might have all these things and still not have reverence. To all these things must be added obedience and
submission to God. Reverence is knowledge plus submission.
In his catechism, Martin Luther asks: 'How is God's name
hallowed among us?' and his answer is: 'When both our life
and doctrine are truly Christian', that is to say, when our
intellectual convictions, and our practical actions, are in full
submission to the will of God.

To know that God is, to know what kind of a God he is,
to be constantly aware of God, and to be constantly obedient
to him – that is reverence, and that is what we pray for when
we pray: 'Hallowed be your name.' Let God be given the
reverence which his nature and character deserve.

GOD'S KINGDOM AND GOD'S WILL

Matthew 6:10

> Let your kingdom come:
> Let your will be done, as in heaven, so also on earth.

THE phrase *the kingdom of God* is characteristic of the whole New Testament. No phrase is used more often in prayer and in preaching and in Christian literature. It is, therefore, of primary importance that we should be clear as to what it means.

It is evident that the kingdom of God was central to the message of Jesus. The first emergence of Jesus on the scene of history was when he came into Galilee preaching the good news of the kingdom of God (Mark 1:14). Jesus himself described the preaching of the kingdom as an obligation laid upon him: 'I must proclaim the good news of the kingdom of God to the other cities also; for I was sent for this purpose' (Luke 4:43; Mark 1:38). Luke's description of Jesus' activity is that he went through every city and village preaching and showing the good news of the kingdom of God (Luke 8:1). Clearly the meaning of the kingdom of God is something which we are bound to try to understand.

When we do try to understand the meaning of this phrase, we meet with certain puzzling facts. We find that Jesus spoke of the kingdom in three different ways. He spoke of the kingdom as existing in the *past*. He said that Abraham, Isaac and Jacob and all the prophets were in the kingdom (Luke 13:28; Matthew 8:11). Clearly, therefore, the kingdom goes far back into history. He spoke of the kingdom as *present*. 'The kingdom of God', he said, 'is among you' (Luke 17:21). The kingdom of God is therefore a present reality here and now. He spoke of the kingdom of God as *future*, for he taught the disciples to pray for the coming of the kingdom in this his own prayer. How then can the kingdom be past, present and future all at the one time? How can the kingdom be at one and the same time something which existed, which exists, and for whose coming it is our duty to pray?

We find the key in this double petition of the Lord's Prayer. One of the most common characteristics of Hebrew style is what is technically known as *parallelism*. The Hebrew language tends to say everything twice. A thing is said in one way, and then in another way which repeats or amplifies or explains the first way. Almost any verse of the Psalms will show this parallelism in action. Almost every verse of the Psalms divides in two in the middle, and the second half repeats or amplifies or explains the first half.

Let us take some examples, and the point will become clear:

> God is our refuge and strength,
>> a very present help in trouble.
>>> (Psalm 46:1)

> The Lord of hosts is with us;
>> the God of Jacob is our refuge.
>>> (Psalm 46:7)

> The Lord is my shepherd;
>> I shall not want.
> He makes me lie down in green pastures;
>> he leads me beside still waters.
>>> (Psalm 23:1–2)

Let us apply this principle to these two petitions of the Lord's Prayer. Let us set them down side by side:

Your kingdom come,
Your will be done in earth as it is in heaven.

Let us assume that the second petition explains and amplifies and defines the first. We then have the perfect definition of the kingdom of God – *The kingdom of God is a society upon earth where God's will is as perfectly done as it is in heaven*. Here we have the explanation of how the kingdom can be past, present and future all at the one time. Anyone who at any time in history perfectly did God's will was within the kingdom; anyone who perfectly does God's will is within the kingdom; but since the world is very far from being a place where God's will is perfectly and universally done, the consummation of the kingdom is still in the future and is still something for which we must pray.

To be in the kingdom is to obey the will of God. Immediately we see that the kingdom is not something which primarily has to do with nations and peoples and countries. It is something which has to do with each one of us. The kingdom is in fact the most personal thing in the world. The kingdom demands the submission of *my* will, *my* heart, *my* life. It is only when each one of us makes a personal decision and submission that the kingdom comes.

The Chinese Christian prayed the well-known prayer: 'Lord, revive your Church, beginning with me' – and we might well paraphrase that and say: 'Lord, bring in your kingdom, beginning with me.' To pray for the kingdom of heaven is to pray that *we* may submit our wills entirely to the will of God.

GOD'S KINGDOM AND GOD'S WILL

Matthew 6:10 (*contd*)

FROM what we have already seen, it becomes clear that the most important thing in the world is to obey the will of God; the most important words in the world are 'Your will be done.' But it is equally clear that the frame of mind and the tone of voice in which these words are spoken will make a world of difference.

(1) Some people may say: 'Your will be done' in a tone of defeated resignation. They may say it not because they wish to say it, but because they have accepted the fact that they cannot possibly say anything else; they may say it because they have accepted the fact that God is too strong for them, and that it is useless to batter their heads against the walls of the universe. They may say it thinking only of the inescapable power of God which has them in its grip. As Edward Fitzgerald's *The Rubaiyat of Omar Khayyam* had it:

> But helpless Pieces of the Game He plays
> Upon this Chequer-board of Nights and Days;
>   Hither and thither moves, and checks, and slays,
> And one by one back in the closet lays.
>
> The Ball no question makes of Ayes and Noes.
> But Here or There as strikes the Player goes;
>   And He that Toss'd you down into the Field,
> He knows about it all – He knows – HE knows!

Some people may accept the will of God for no other reason than that they have realized that they cannot do anything else.

(2) Some people may say: 'Your will be done' in a tone of bitter resentment. The poet Walter Swinburne spoke of feeling

the trampling of the iron feet of God. In *Atalanta in Calydon*, he speaks of the supreme evil, God. Beethoven died all alone; and it is said that when they found his body his lips were drawn back in a snarl and his fists were clenched as if he were shaking his fists in the very face of God and of high heaven. Some may feel that God is their enemy, and yet an enemy so strong that they cannot resist. They may therefore accept God's will, but they may accept it with bitter resentment and smouldering anger.

(3) Some people may say: 'Your will be done' in perfect love and trust. They may say it gladly and willingly, no matter what that will may be. It should be easy for Christians to say: 'Your will be done' like that; for Christians can be very sure of two things about God.

(a) They can be sure of the *wisdom* of God. Sometimes when we want something built or constructed, or altered or repaired, we take it to the craftsman and consult him about it. He makes some suggestion, and we often end up by saying: 'Well, do what you think best. You are the expert.' God is the expert in life, and his guidance can never lead anyone astray.

When Richard Cameron, the Scottish Covenanter, was killed, his head and his hands were cut off by one Murray and taken to Edinburgh. 'His father being in prison for the same cause, the enemy carried them to him, to add grief unto his former sorrow, and inquired at him if he knew them. Taking his son's head and hands, which were very fair (being a man of fair complexion like himself), he kissed them and said, "I know them – I know them. They are my son's – my own dear son's. It is the Lord. Good is the will of the Lord, who cannot wrong me or mine, but hath made goodness and mercy to follow us all our days."' When a man can speak like that, when he is quite sure that his times are in the hands of the infinite wisdom of God, it is easy to say: 'Your will be done.'

(b) He can be sure of the *love* of God. We do not believe in a mocking and a capricious God, or in a blind and iron determinism. Thomas Hardy finishes his novel *Tess of the D'Urbervilles* with the grim words: 'The President of the Immortals had ended his sport with Tess.' We believe in a God whose name is love. As J. G. Whittier's hymn has it:

> I know not where His islands lift
> > Their fronded palms in air.
> I only know I cannot drift
> > Beyond His love and care.

As Robert Browning triumphantly declared his faith in lines from 'Paracelsus':

> God, Thou art love! I build my faith on that ...
> I know thee who has kept my path and made
> Light for me in the darkness, tempering sorrow
> So that it reached me like a solemn joy.
> It were too strange that I should doubt thy love.

And as Paul had it: 'He who did not withhold his own Son, but gave him up for all of us, will he not with him also give us everything else?' (Romans 8:32). No one can look at the cross and doubt the love of God; and when we are sure of the love of God, it is easy to say: 'Your will be done.'

OUR DAILY BREAD

Matthew 6:11

Give us today bread for the coming day.

ONE would have thought that this is the one petition of the Lord's Prayer about the meaning of which there could have been no possible doubt. It seems on the face of it to be the simplest and the most direct of them all. But it is a fact that many interpreters have offered many interpretations of it. Before we think of its simple and obvious meaning, let us look at some of the other explanations which have been offered.

(1) The bread has been identified with the bread of the Lord's Supper. From the very beginning, the Lord's Prayer has been closely connected with the Lord's table. In the very first orders of service which we possess, it is always laid down that the Lord's Prayer should be prayed at the Lord's table, and some have taken this petition as a prayer to be granted the daily privilege of sitting at the table of our Lord, and of eating the spiritual food which men and women receive there.

(2) The bread has been identified with the spiritual food of the word of God. We sometimes sing the hymn:

> Break thou the bread of life,
> Dear Lord, to me,
> As thou didst break the loaves
> Beside the sea.
> Beyond the sacred page
> I seek thee, Lord.
> My spirit pants for thee,
> O living word.

So this petition has been taken to be a prayer for the true teaching, the true doctrine, the essential truth, which are in the Scriptures and the word of God, and which are indeed food for the mind and heart and soul.

(3) The bread has been taken to stand for Jesus himself. Jesus called himself *the bread of life* (John 6:33–5), and this has been taken to be a prayer that daily we may be fed on him who is the living bread. It was in that way that Matthew

Arnold used the phrase, when he wrote his poem 'East London' about the saint of God he met in the East End of London one suffocating day:

'Twas August, and the fierce sun overhead
Smote on the squalid streets of Bethnal Green,
And the pale weaver, through his windows seen,
In Spitalfields, look'd thrice dispirited.

I met a preacher there I knew and said:
'Ill and o'er worked, how fare you in this scene?'
'Bravely!' said he, 'for I of late have been
Much cheer'd with thoughts of Christ, the living bread.'

So, this petition has been taken as a prayer that we too might be cheered and strengthened with Christ the living bread.

(4) This petition has been taken in a purely Jewish sense. The bread has been taken to be the bread of the heavenly kingdom. Luke tells how one of the bystanders said to Jesus: 'Blessed is anyone who will eat bread in the kingdom of God' (Luke 14:15). The Jews had a strange yet vivid idea. They held that when the Messiah came, and when the golden age dawned, there would be what they called the messianic banquet, at which the chosen ones of God would sit down. The slain bodies of the monsters Behemoth and Leviathan would provide the meat and the fish courses of the banquet. It would be a kind of reception feast given by God to his own people. So, this has been taken to be a petition for a place at the final messianic banquet of the people of God.

Although we need not agree that any one of these explanations is the main meaning of this petition, we need not reject any of them as false. They all have their own truth and their own relevance.

The difficulty of interpreting this petition was increased by the fact that there was very considerable doubt as to the meaning of the word *epiousios*, which is the word translated in the Revised Standard Version as *daily*. The extraordinary fact was that, until a short time ago, there was no other known occurrence of this word in the whole of Greek literature. The third-century Christian scholar Origen knew this, and indeed held that Matthew had invented the word. It was therefore not possible to be sure what it precisely meant. But not very long ago a papyrus fragment turned up with this word on it; and the papyrus fragment was actually a woman's shopping list! And against an item on it was the word *epiousios*. It was a note to remind her to buy supplies of a certain food for the coming day. So, very simply, what this petition means is: 'Give me the things we need to eat for this coming day. Help me to get the things I've got on my shopping list when I go out this morning. Give me the things we need to eat when the children come in from school, and the family come in from work. Grant that the table is not bare when we sit down together today.' This is a simple prayer that God will supply us with the things we need for the coming day.

OUR DAILY BREAD

Matthew 6:11 (*contd*)

WHEN we see that this is a simple petition for our everyday needs, certain tremendous truths emerge from it.

(1) It tells us that God cares for our bodies. Jesus showed us that; he spent so much time healing people's diseases and satisfying physical hunger. He was anxious when he thought that the crowd who had followed him out into the lonely places had a long journey home, and no food to eat before

they set out upon it. We do well to remember that God is interested in our bodies. Any teaching which belittles, despises and slanders the body is wrong. We can see what God thinks of our human bodies, when we remember that he himself in Jesus Christ took a human body upon him. It is not simply *soul* salvation, it is *whole* salvation, the salvation of body, mind and spirit, at which Christianity aims.

(2) This petition teaches us to pray for our *daily* bread, for bread *for the coming day*. It teaches us to live one day at a time, and not to worry and be anxious about the distant and the unknown future. When Jesus taught his disciples to pray this petition, there is little doubt that his mind was going back to the story of the manna in the wilderness (Exodus 16:1–21). The children of Israel were starving in the wilderness, and God sent them the manna, the food from heaven; but there was one condition – they must gather only enough for their immediate needs. If they tried to gather too much, and to store it up, it went bad. They had to be satisfied with enough for the day. As one Rabbi put it: 'The portion of a day in its day, because he who created the day created sustenance for the day.' And as another Rabbi had it: 'He who possesses what he can eat today, and says, "What shall I eat tomorrow?" is a man of little faith.' This petition tells us to live one day at a time. It forbids the anxious worry which is so characteristic of the life which has not learned to trust God.

(3) By implication, this petition gives God his proper place. It admits that it is from God we receive the food which is necessary to support life. No one has ever created a seed which will grow. The scientist can analyse a seed into its constituent elements, but no synthetic seed would ever grow. All living things come from God. Our food, therefore, is the direct gift of God.

(4) This petition very wisely reminds us of how prayer works. If people prayed this prayer, and then sat back and waited for bread to fall into their hands, they would certainly starve. It reminds us that prayer and work go hand in hand and that when we pray we must go on to work to make our prayers come true. It is true that the living seed comes from God, but it is equally true that it is our task to grow and to cultivate that seed. Dick Sheppard, the famous pacifist and preacher, used to love a certain story. There was a man who had an allotment; he had with great toil reclaimed a piece of ground, clearing away the stones, eradicating the rank growth of weeds, enriching and feeding the ground, until it produced the loveliest flowers and vegetables. One evening he was showing a pious friend around his allotment. The pious friend said: 'It's wonderful what God can do with a bit of ground like this, isn't it?' 'Yes,' said the man who had put in such toil, 'but you should have seen this bit of ground when God had it to himself!' God's bounty and human toil must combine. Prayer, like faith, without works is dead. When we pray this petition, we are recognizing two basic truths – that without God we can do nothing, and that without our effort and co-operation God can do nothing for us.

(5) We must note that Jesus did not teach us to pray: 'Give *me my* daily bread.' He taught us to pray: 'Give *us our* daily bread.' The problem of the world is not that there is not enough to go round; there is enough and to spare. The problem is not the *supply* of life's essentials; it is the *distribution* of them. This prayer teaches us never to be selfish in our prayers. It is a prayer which we can help God to answer by giving to others who are less fortunate than we are. This prayer is not only a prayer that we may *receive* our daily bread; it is also a prayer that we may *share* our daily bread with others.

FORGIVENESS HUMAN AND DIVINE

Matthew 6:12, 14–15

> Forgive us our debts as we forgive our debtors . . . For,
> if you forgive men their trespasses, your heavenly
> Father will forgive you too; but if you do not forgive
> men their trespasses, neither will your Father forgive
> your trespasses.

BEFORE we can honestly pray this petition of the Lord's Prayer,
we must realize that we need to pray it. That is to say, before
we can pray this petition we must have a sense of sin. Sin is
not nowadays a popular word. Men and women rather resent
being called, or treated as, hell-deserving sinners.

The trouble is that most people have a wrong conception
of sin. They would readily agree that the burglar, the drunkard,
the murderer, the adulterer and the foul-mouthed person are
sinners. But they themselves are guilty of none of these sins;
they live decent, ordinary, respectable lives, and have never
even been in danger of appearing in court, or going to prison,
or achieving some notoriety in the newspapers. They therefore
feel that sin has nothing to do with them.

The New Testament uses five different words for *sin*.

(1) The most common word is *hamartia*. This was
originally a shooting word and means *a missing of the target*.
To fail to hit the target was *hamartia*. Therefore *sin is the
failure to be what we might have been and could have been*.

The nineteenth-century writer Charles Lamb has a picture
of a man named Samuel le Grice. Le Grice was a brilliant
youth who never fulfilled his promise. Lamb says that
there were three stages in his career. There was a time when
people said: 'He will do something.' There was a time
when people said: 'He could do something if he would.' There

was a time when people said: 'He might have done something, if he had liked.' The poet Edwin Muir writes in his *Autobiography*: 'After a certain age all of us, good and bad, are grief-stricken because of powers within us which have never been realized: because, in other words, we are not what we should be.'

That precisely is *hamartia*; and that is precisely the situation in which we are all involved. Are we as good husbands or wives as we could be? Are we as good sons or daughters as we could be? Are we as good workers or employers as we could be? Can any one of us dare to claim that we are all we might have been, and have done all we could have done? When we realize that sin means the failure to hit the target, the failure to be all that we might have been and could have been, then it is clear that every one of us is a sinner.

(2) The second word for sin is *parabasis*, which literally means *a stepping across. Sin is the stepping across the line which is drawn between right and wrong.*

Do we always stay on the right side of the line which divides honesty and dishonesty? Is there never any such thing as a petty dishonesty in our lives?

Do we always stay on the right side of the line which divides truth and falsehood? Do we never, by word or by silence, twist or evade or distort the truth?

Do we always stay on the right side of the line which divides kindness and courtesy from selfishness and harshness? Is there never an unkind action or a discourteous word in our lives?

When we think of it in this way, there can be none who can claim always to have remained on the right side of the dividing line.

(3) The third word for sin is *paraptōma*, which means *a slipping across*. It is the kind of slip which someone might

make on a slippery or an icy road. It is not so deliberate as *parabasis*. Again and again, we speak of words 'slipping out'; again and again, we are swept away by some impulse or passion which has momentarily gained control of us and which has made us lose our self-control. The best of us can slip into sin when for the moment we are off our guard.

(4) The fourth word for sin is *anomia*, which means *lawlessness*. *Anomia* is the sin of the person who knows the right, and who yet does the wrong; the sin of the one who knows the law, and who yet breaks the law. The first of all the human instincts is the instinct to do what we like; and therefore there come into many people's lives times when they wish to kick over the traces and to defy the law, and to do or to take the forbidden thing. In 'Mandalay', Rudyard Kipling makes the old soldier say:

> Ship me somewheres east of Suez, where the best is
> like the worst,
> Where there aren't no Ten Commandments, an' a man
> can raise a thirst.

Even if there are some who can say that they have never broken any of the Ten Commandments, there are none who can say that they have never wished to break any of them.

(5) The fifth word for sin is the word *opheilēma*, which is the word used in the body of the Lord's Prayer; and *opheilēma* means *a debt*. It means *a failure to pay that which is due*, a failure in duty. None of us could ever dare to claim that we have perfectly fulfilled our duty to other people and to God: such perfection does not exist in this world.

So, when we come to see what sin really is, we come to see that it is a universal disease in which we are all involved. Outward respectability in the sight of others and inward sinfulness in the sight of God may well go hand in hand.

This, in fact, is a petition of the Lord's Prayer which we all need to pray.

FORGIVENESS HUMAN AND DIVINE

Matthew 6:12, 14–15 (*contd*)

NOT only do we need to realize that we need to pray this petition of the Lord's Prayer; we also need to realize what we are doing when we pray it. Of all the petitions of the Lord's Prayer, this is the most frightening.

'Forgive us our debts as we forgive our debtors.' The literal meaning is: 'Forgive us our sins *in proportion as* we forgive those who have sinned against us.' In verses 14 and 15, Jesus says in the plainest possible language that if we forgive others, God will forgive us; but if we refuse to forgive others, God will refuse to forgive us. It is, therefore, quite clear that if we pray this petition with an unhealed breach, an unsettled quarrel in our lives, we are asking God *not* to forgive us.

If we say: 'I will never forgive so-and-so for what he or she has done to me,' if we say: 'I will never forget what so-and-so did to me,' and then go and take this petition on our lips, we are quite deliberately asking God not to forgive us. As someone has put it: 'Forgiveness, like peace, is one and indivisible.' Human forgiveness and divine forgiveness are inextricably intertwined. Our forgiveness of one another and God's forgiveness of us cannot be separated; they are inter-linked and interdependent. If we remembered what we are doing when we take this petition on our lips, there would be times when we would not dare to pray it.

When Robert Louis Stevenson lived in the South Sea Islands, he always used to conduct family worship in the mornings for his household. It always concluded with the

Lord's Prayer. One morning, in the middle of the Lord's Prayer, he rose from his knees and left the room. His health was always precarious, and his wife followed him thinking that he was ill. 'Is there anything wrong?' she said. 'Only this,' said Stevenson. 'I am not fit to pray the Lord's Prayer today.' None of us is fit to pray the Lord's Prayer so long as the unforgiving spirit holds sway within our hearts. If we have not put things right with our neighbours, we cannot put things right with God.

If we are to have this Christian forgiveness in our lives, three things are necessary.

(1) We must learn *to understand*. There is always a reason why people do things. If they are boorish and impolite and bad-tempered, maybe they are worried or in pain. If they treat us with suspicion and dislike, maybe they have misunderstood, or have been misinformed about something we have said or done. Maybe they are victims of their own environment or their own heredity. Maybe they find life difficult, and human relations are a problem for them. Forgiveness would be very much easier for us if we tried to understand before we allowed ourselves to condemn.

(2) We must learn *to forget*. As long as we brood upon a snub or an insult, there is no hope that we will forgive. We so often say: 'I can't forget what so-and-so did to me,' or: 'I will never forget how I was treated by such-and-such a person or in such-and-such a place.' These are dangerous sayings, because we can in the end make it humanly impossible for us to forget. We can print the memory indelibly upon our minds.

The famous Scottish man of letters, Andrew Lang, once wrote and published a very kind review of a book by a young man. The young man repaid him with a bitter and insulting attack. About three years later, Andrew Lang was staying with

Robert Bridges, the Poet Laureate. Bridges saw Lang reading a certain book. 'Why,' he said, 'that's another book by that ungrateful young cub who behaved so shamefully to you.' To his astonishment, he found that Andrew Lang's mind was a blank on the whole affair. He had completely forgotten the bitter and insulting attack. To forgive, said Bridges, was the sign of greatness, but to forget was sublime. Nothing but the cleansing spirit of Christ can take from these memories of ours the old bitterness that we must forget.

(3) We must learn *to love*. We have already seen that Christian love, *agapē*, is that unconquerable benevolence, that undefeatable goodwill, which will never seek anything but the highest good of others, no matter what they do to us, and no matter how they treat us. That love can come to us only when Christ, who is that love, comes to dwell within our hearts – and he cannot come unless we invite him.

To be forgiven we must forgive, and that is a condition of forgiveness which only the power of Christ can enable us to fulfil.

THE ORDEAL OF TEMPTATION

Matthew 6:13

> And lead us not into temptation, but deliver us from the evil one.

THERE are two matters of meaning at which we must look before we begin to study this petition in detail.

(1) To modern ears, the word *tempt* is always a bad word; it always means *to seek to seduce into evil*. But in the Bible the verb *peirazein* is often better translated by the word *test* than by the word *tempt*. In its New Testament usage, to *tempt* people is not so much to seek to seduce them into sin as it is

to test their strength and their loyalty and their ability for service.

In the Old Testament, we read the story of how God tested the loyalty of Abraham by seeming to demand the sacrifice of his only son Isaac. In the Authorized Version, the story begins: 'And it came to pass that God did *tempt* Abraham' (Genesis 22:1). Obviously the word *tempt* cannot there mean to seek to seduce into sin, for that is something that God would never do. It means rather to submit to a test of loyalty and obedience. When we read the story of the temptations of Jesus, it begins: 'Then Jesus was led up by the Spirit into the wilderness to be *tempted* by the devil' (Matthew 4:1). If we take the word *tempt* there in the sense of to seduce into sin, it makes the Holy Spirit a partner in an attempt to compel Jesus to sin. Time and again in the Bible, we will find that the word *tempt* has the idea of *testing* in it, at least as much as the idea of seeking to lead into sin.

Here, then, is one of the great and precious truths about temptation. Temptation is not designed to make us fall. Temptation is designed to make us stronger and better men and women. Temptation is not designed to make us sinners. It is designed to make us good. We may fail in the test, but we are not meant to. We are meant to emerge stronger and finer. In one sense, temptation is not so much the *penalty* of being human; it is the glory of being human. If metal is to be used in a great engineering project, it is tested at stresses and strains far beyond those which it is ever likely to have to bear. So we have to be tested before God can use us greatly in his service.

All that is true; but it is also true that the Bible is never in any doubt that there is a power of evil in this world. The Bible is not a speculative book, and it does not discuss the origin of that power of evil, but it knows that it is there. Quite certainly, this petition of the Lord's Prayer should be translated not as 'Deliver us from evil' but as 'Deliver us from the evil one.' The Bible thinks of evil not as an abstract principle or force, but as an active, personal power in opposition to God.

The development of the idea of Satan in the Bible is of the greatest interest. In Hebrew, the word *Satan* simply means an *adversary*. It can often be used of human beings. A person's adversary is called *Satan*. In the Authorized Version, the Philistines are afraid that David may turn out to be their *Satan* (1 Samuel 29:4); Solomon declares that God has given him such peace and prosperity that there is no *Satan* left to oppose him (1 Kings 5:4); David regards Abishai as his *Satan* (2 Samuel 19:22). In all these cases, *Satan* means an *adversary* or *opponent*. From that, the word *Satan* goes on to mean *one who pleads a case against someone*. Then the word leaves earth and, as it were, enters heaven. The Jews had the idea that in heaven there was an angel whose charge it was to state the case against an individual, a kind of prosecuting angel; and that became the function of *Satan*. At that stage, Satan is not an evil power: he is part of the judgment apparatus of heaven. In Job 1:6, Satan is numbered among the sons of God: 'One day the heavenly beings came to present themselves before the Lord, and Satan also came among them.' At this stage, Satan is the divine prosecutor of human beings.

But it is not so very great a step from *stating* a case against an individual to *making up a case* against that person. And that is the next step. The other name of Satan is the devil; and *devil* comes from the Greek word *diabolos*, which is the regular word for a *slanderer*. So *Satan* becomes the *devil*, the slanderer *par excellence*, the adversary of men and women, the power who is out to frustrate the purposes of God and to ruin the human race. Satan comes to stand for everything which is anti-human and anti-God. It is from that ruining power that Jesus teaches us to pray to be delivered. The origin of that power is not discussed; there are no speculations. As someone has put it – if we wake up and find the house on fire, we do not sit down in a chair and write or read a treatise on the origin of fires in private houses; we set out to try to extinguish the fire and to save the house. So the Bible wastes no time in speculations about the origin of evil. It equips people to fight the battle against the evil which is unquestionably there.

THE ATTACK OF TEMPTATION

Matthew 6:13 (*contd*)

LIFE is always under attack from temptation, but no enemy can launch an invasion until a bridgehead has been found. Where then does temptation find its bridgehead? Where do our temptations come from? To be forewarned is to be fore-armed, and if we know where the attack is likely to come from, we will have a better chance to overcome it.

(1) Sometimes the attack of temptation comes from outside us. There are people whose influence is bad. There are people in whose company it would be very difficult even to suggest doing a dishonourable thing, and there are people in whose company it is easy to do the wrong things. When Robert Burns was a young man, he went to Irvine to learn flax-dressing. There he fell in with a certain Robert Brown, who was a man who had seen much of the world, and who had a fascinating and a dominating personality. Burns tells us that he admired him and strove to imitate him. Burns goes on: 'He was the only man I ever saw who was a greater fool than myself when Woman was the guiding star . . . He spoke

of a certain fashionable failing with levity, which hitherto I had regarded with horror . . . Here his friendship did me a mischief.' There are friendships and associations which can do us a mischief. In a tempting world, we should be very careful in our choice of friends and of the society in which we will move. We should give the temptations which come from outside as little chance as possible.

(2) It is one of the tragic facts of life that temptations can come to us from those who love us; and of all kinds of temptation, this is the hardest to fight. It comes from people who love us and who have not the slightest intention of harming us.

The kind of thing that happens is this. We may know that we ought to take a certain course of action; we may feel divinely drawn to a certain career; but to follow that course of action may involve unpopularity and risk; to accept that career may be to give up all that the world calls success. It may well be that in such circumstances those who love us will seek to dissuade us from acting as we know we ought, and they will do so because they love us. They counsel caution, prudence, worldly wisdom; they want to see those they love do well in a worldly sense; they do not wish to see us throw our chances away; and so they seek to stop us doing what we know to be right for us.

In 'Gareth and Lynette', Tennyson tells the story of Gareth, the youngest son of Lot and Bellicent. Gareth wishes to join his brothers in the service of King Arthur. Bellicent, his mother, does not wish him to go. 'Hast thou no pity on my loneliness?' she asks. His father Lot is old and lies 'like a log all but smouldered out'. Both his brothers have gone to Arthur's court. Must he go too? If he will stay at home, she will arrange the hunt, and find him a princess for his bride, and make him happy. It was because she

loved him that she wished to keep him; the tempter was
speaking with the very voice of love. But Gareth answers:

> O mother,
> How can you keep me tethered to you – shame.
> Man am I grown, and man's work must I do.
> Follow the deer? Follow Christ the King.
> Live pure, speak true, right wrong, follow the King –
> Else, wherefore born?

The youth went out, but the voice of love tempted him to
stay.

That was what happened to Jesus. 'One's foes', said Jesus,
'will be members of one's own household' (Matthew 10:36).
They came and tried to take him home, because they said
that he was mad (Mark 3:21). To them he seemed to be
throwing his life and his career away; to them he seemed to
be making a fool of himself; and they tried to stop him.
Sometimes the bitterest of all temptations come to us from
the voice of love.

(3) There is one very odd way in which temptation can
come, especially to younger people. There is in most of us a
peculiar streak which, at least in certain company, makes us
wish to appear worse than we are. We do not wish to appear
soft and pious, namby-pamby and holy. We would rather be
thought daredevil, bold adventurers, men and women of the
world and not innocents. St Augustine has a famous passage
in his confessions: 'Among my equals I was ashamed of being
less shameless than others, when I heard them boast of their
wickedness . . . And I took pleasure not only in the pleasure
of the deed but in the praise . . . I made myself worse than I
was, that I might not be reproached, and when in anything I
had not sinned as the most abandoned ones, I would say that
I had done what I had not done, that I might not seem

contemptible.' Many people have begun on some addiction, or introduced themselves to some habit, because they did not wish to appear less experienced in worldliness than the company in which they happened to be. One of the great defences against temptation is simply the courage to be good.

THE ATTACK OF TEMPTATION

Matthew 6:13 (*contd*)

(4) BUT temptation comes not only from outside us; it comes from inside us too. If there was nothing in us to which temptation could appeal, then it would be helpless to defeat us. In every one of us, there is some weak spot; and at that weak spot, temptation launches its attack.

The point of vulnerability differs in all of us. What is a violent temptation to one person leaves another quite unmoved; and what leaves one person quite unmoved may be an irresistible temptation to another. J. M. Barrie wrote a play called *The Will*. Mr Devizes, the lawyer, noticed that an old clerk, who had been in his service for many years, was looking very ill. He asked him if anything was the matter. The old man told him that his doctor had informed him that he was suffering from an incurable and ultimately fatal disease.

> Mr DEVIZES [*uncomfortably*]: I'm sure it's not – what you fear. Any specialist would tell you so.
> SURTEES [*without looking up*]: I've been to one, sir – yesterday.
> Mr DEVIZES: Well?
> SURTEES: It's – that, sir.
> Mr DEVIZES: He couldn't be sure.

SURTEES: Yes, sir.

Mr DEVIZES: An operation –

SURTEES: Too late for that, he said. If I had been
operated on long ago, I might have had a chance.

Mr DEVIZES: But you didn't have it long ago.

SURTEES: Not to my knowledge, sir; but he says it was
there all the same, always in me, a black spot, not
as big as a pin's head, but waiting to spread and
destroy me in the fullness of time.

Mr DEVIZES [*helpless*]: It seems damnably unfair.

SURTEES [*humbly*]: I don't know, sir. He says there is a
spot of that kind in pretty nigh all of us, and, if we
don't look out, it does for us in the end.

Mr DEVIZES: No. No. No.

SURTEES: He called it the accursed thing. I think he
meant we should know of it, and be on the watch.

In each one of us there is the weak spot, which, if we are
not on the watch, can ruin us. Somewhere within us there is
the flaw, some fault of temperament which can ruin life, some
instinct or passion so strong that it may at any time snap the
leash, some quirk in our make-up that makes what is a
pleasure to someone else a menace to us. We should realize
it, and be on the watch.

(5) But, strangely enough, temptation comes sometimes
not from our weakest point, but from our strongest point. If
there is one thing of which we are in the habit of saying:
'That is one thing anyway which I would never do,' it is just
there that we should be upon the watch. History is full of the
stories of fortresses which were taken just at the point where
the defenders thought them so strong that no guard was
necessary. Nothing gives temptation its chance like over-
confidence. At our weakest and at our strongest points, we
must be on our guard.

THE DEFENCE AGAINST TEMPTATION

Matthew 6:13 (*contd*)

WE have thought of the attack of temptation; let us now assemble our defences against temptation.

(1) There is the simple defence of *self-respect*. When Nehemiah's life was in danger, it was suggested that he should quit his work and shut himself in the Temple until the danger was past. His answer was: 'Should a man like me run away? Would a man like me go into the temple to save his life? I will not go in!' (Nehemiah 6:11). People may escape many things, but they cannot escape themselves. They must live with their memories; and if they have lost their self-respect, life becomes intolerable. Once the American President James Garfield was urged to take a profitable, but dishonourable, course of action. It was said: 'No one will ever know.' His answer was: 'President Garfield will know – and I've got to sleep with him.' When we are tempted, we may well defend ourselves by saying: 'Is someone like me going to do a thing like that?'

(2) There is the defence of *tradition*. None of us can lightly fail the traditions and the heritage into which we have entered, and which have taken generations to build up. When Pericles, the greatest of the statesmen of Athens, was going to address the Athenian Assembly, he always whispered to himself: 'Pericles, remember that you are an Athenian and that you go to speak to Athenians.'

One of the epics of the Second World War was the defence of Tobruk. The Coldstream Guards cut their way out of Tobruk, but only a handful of them survived, and even these were just shadows of men. The Royal Air Force (RAF) was caring for 200 survivors out of two battalions. A Coldstream

Guards officer was in the mess. Another officer said to him: 'After all, as Foot Guards, you had no option but to have a go.' And an RAF man standing there said: 'It must be pretty tough to be in the Brigade of Guards, because tradition compels you to carry on irrespective of circumstances.'

The power of a tradition is one of the greatest things in life. We belong to a country, a school, a family, a church. What we do affects that to which we belong. We cannot lightly betray the traditions into which we have entered.

(3) There is the defence of *those whom we love and those who love us*. Many people would sin if the only penalty they had to bear was the penalty they would have to bear themselves; but they are saved from sin because they could not meet the pain that would appear in someone's eyes, if they made shipwreck of their lives.

The American novelist Laura E. Richards has a parable like this:

> A man sat by the door of his house smoking his pipe, and his neighbour sat beside him and tempted him. 'You are poor,' said the neighbour, 'and you are out of work and here is a way of bettering yourself. It will be an easy job and it will bring in money, and it is no more dishonest than things that are done every day by respectable people. You will be a fool to throw away such a chance as this. Come with me and we will settle the matter at once.' And the man listened. Just then his young wife came to the door of the cottage and she had her baby in her arms. 'Will you hold the baby for a minute,' she said. 'He is fretful and I must hang out the clothes to dry.' The man took the baby and held him on his knees. And as he held him, the child looked up, and the eyes of the child spoke: 'I am flesh of your flesh,' said the child's eyes. 'I am soul of your soul. Where you

> lead I shall follow. Lead the way, father. My feet come
> after yours.' Then said the man to his neighbour: 'Go,
> and come here no more.'

Some people might be perfectly willing to pay the price
of sin if that price affected only themselves. But if they
remember that their sin will break someone else's heart, they
will have a strong defence against temptation.

(4) There is the defence of *the presence of Jesus Christ*.
Jesus is not a figure in a book; he is a living presence. Sometimes we ask: 'What would you do, if you suddenly found
Christ standing beside you? How would you live, if Jesus
Christ was a guest in your house?' But the whole point of the
Christian faith is that Jesus Christ *is* beside us, and he *is* a
guest in every home. His is the inescapable presence, and,
therefore, we must make all life fit for him to see. We have a
strong defence against temptation in the memory of the
continual presence of Jesus Christ.

HOW NOT TO FAST

Matthew 6:16–18

> 'When you fast, don't put on a sad face, as the hypo-
> crites do, for they disfigure their faces, so that all men
> may see that they are fasting. This is the truth I tell you
> – they are paid in full. But when you fast, anoint your
> head and wash your face, so that to men you may not
> look as if you were fasting, but to your Father who is in
> secret; and your Father, who sees what happens in
> secret, will give you your reward in full.'

To this day, fasting is an essential part of religious life in the
middle east. Muslims strictly keep the fast of Ramadan,
which falls in the ninth month of the Muslim year, and

which commemorates the first revelation which came to Muhammad. The fast lasts from dawn – when it is light enough to distinguish a white thread from a black thread – until sunset. Bathing, drinking, smoking, smelling perfumes, eating and all unnecessary indulgences are forbidden. Nurses and pregnant women are exempt. Soldiers and those on a journey are excused, but must at some other time fast for an equivalent number of days. If for health's sake a person must have food, the breach of the law of fasting must be made good by giving to the poor.

The Jewish fasting customs were exactly the same. It is to be noted that, as we have said, fasting lasted from dawn to sunset; outside that time, normal meals could be eaten. For Jews, in the time of Jesus, there was only one compulsory fast, the fast on the Day of Atonement. On that day from morning to evening, people had 'to deny themselves' (Leviticus 16:31). The Jewish scribal law lays it down: 'On the Day of Atonement it is forbidden to eat, or to drink, or to bathe, or to anoint oneself, or to wear sandals, or to indulge in conjugal intercourse.' Even young children had to be trained to some measure of fasting on the Day of Atonement so that, when they grew up, they would be prepared to accept the national fast.

But, although there was only the one compulsory, universal day of fasting, the Jews made great use of private fasting.

There was *the fasting which was connected with mourning*. Between the time of death and burial, mourners must abstain from all meat and wine. There was fasting *to make amends for some sin*. It was said, for instance, that Reuben fasted for seven years for his share in the selling of Joseph: 'He drank no wine or other liquor; no flesh passed his lips, and he ate no appetising food' (The Testament of Reuben, 1:10). For the same reason, 'Simeon afflicted his soul with fasting for two years, because he had hated Joseph' (The Testament of Simeon, 3:4). In repentance of his sin with Tamar, it was said that Judah to his old age 'took neither wine nor flesh, and saw no pleasure' (The Testament of Judah, 15:4). It is fair to say that Jewish thought saw no value in fasting apart from repentance. The fast was only designed to be the outer expression of an inward sorrow. The writer of Ecclesiasticus (34:31) says: 'So if one fasts for his sins, and goes again and does the same things, who will listen to his prayer? And what has he gained by humbling himself?'

In many cases, fasting was an act of *national penitence*. So the whole nation fasted after the disaster of the civil war with Benjamin (Judges 20:26). Samuel made the people fast because they had strayed away after Baal (1 Samuel 7:6). Nehemiah made the people fast and confess their sins (Nehemiah 9:1). Again and again, the nation fasted as a sign of national penitence before God.

Sometimes fasting was *a preparation for revelation*. Moses in the mountain fasted for forty days and forty nights (Exodus 24:15). Daniel fasted as he awaited God's word (Daniel 9:3). Jesus himself fasted as he awaited the ordeal of temptation (Matthew 4:2). This was a sound principle, for when the body is most disciplined, the mental and the spiritual faculties are most alert. Sometimes fasting was *an appeal to God*. If, for instance, the rains failed and the harvest was in jeopardy, a national fast would be called as an appeal to God.

In Jewish fasting, there were really three main ideas in people's minds.

(1) Fasting was a deliberate attempt *to draw the attention of God* to the person who fasted. This was a very primitive idea. The fasting was designed to attract God's attention, and to make him notice those who thus denied themselves.

(2) Fasting was a deliberate attempt *to prove that penitence was real*. Fasting was a guarantee of the sincerity of words and prayers. It is easy to see that there was a danger here, for that which was meant to be a *proof* of repentance could very easily come to be regarded as a *substitute* for repentance.

(3) A great deal of fasting was *vicarious*, done on behalf of others. It was not designed to save an individual's own soul so much as to move God to liberate the nation from its distresses. It was as if specially devoted people said: 'Ordinary people cannot do this. They are too involved in work and in the world. We will do this extra thing to counterbalance the necessary deficiency of piety in others.'

Such then was the Jewish theory and practice of fasting.

HOW NOT TO FAST

Matthew 6:16–18 (*contd*)

HIGH as the ideal of fasting might be, the practice of it involved certain inevitable dangers. The great danger was that some people might fast as a sign of superior piety, that their fasting might be a deliberate demonstration, not to God, but to others, of how devoted and disciplined they were. That is precisely what Jesus was condemning. He was condemning fasting when it was used as an ostentatious parade of piety. The Jewish days of fasting were Monday and Thursday. These were market days, and into the towns and villages, and especially into Jerusalem, there crowded the people from the country. The result was that those who were ostentatiously fasting would on those days have a bigger audience to see and admire their piety. There were many who took deliberate steps to see that others could not miss the fact that they were fasting. They walked through the streets with hair deliberately unkempt and dishevelled, with clothes deliberately soiled and disarrayed. They even went to the lengths of deliberately whitening their faces to accentuate their paleness. This was no act of humility; it was a deliberate act of spiritual pride and ostentation.

The wisest of the Rabbis would have condemned this as unsparingly as Jesus did. They were quite clear that fasting for its own sake was valueless. They said that a vow of abstinence was like an iron collar which prisoners had to wear; and those who imposed on themselves such a vow were said to be like people who, finding such a collar lying about, misguidedly put it on, thereby voluntarily undertaking a useless slavery. One of the finest things ever said is the Rabbinic saying: 'A man will have to give an account on the judgment day for every good thing which he might have enjoyed, and did not.'

The New Zealand minister, Dr F. W. Boreham, has a story which is a commentary on the wrong idea of fasting. A traveller in the Rocky Mountains fell in with an old Roman Catholic priest; he was amazed to find so aged a man struggling amid the rocks and the precipices and the steep passes. The traveller asked the priest: 'What are you doing here?' The old man answered: 'I am seeking the beauty of the world.' 'But', said the traveller, 'surely you have left it very late in life!' 'So the old man told his story. He had spent nearly all his life in a monastery; he had never been further outside it than the cloisters. He fell seriously ill, and in his illness he had a vision. He saw an angel standing beside his bed. 'What have you come for?' he asked the angel. 'To lead you home,' the angel said. 'And is it a very beautiful world to which I am going?' asked the old man. 'It is a very beautiful world you are leaving,' said the angel. 'And then,' said the old man, 'I remembered that I had seen nothing of it except

the fields and the trees around the monastery.' So he said to
the angel: 'But I have seen very little of the world which I am
leaving.' 'Then,' said the angel, ' I fear you will see very
little beauty in the world to which you are going.' 'I was in
trouble,' said the old man, 'and I begged that I might stay for
just two more years. My prayer was granted, and I am
spending all my little hoard of gold, and all the time I have,
in exploring the world's loveliness – and I find it very
wonderful!'

It is our duty to accept and enjoy the world's loveliness,
and not to reject it. There is no religious value in fasting
undertaken for its own sake, or as an ostentatious demonstration of superior piety.

THE TRUE FASTING

Matthew 6:16–18 (*contd*)

ALTHOUGH Jesus condemned the wrong kind of fasting, his
words imply that there is a wise fasting, in which he expected
that the Christian would take part. This is a thing of which
few of us ever think. There are very few ordinary people in
whose lives fasting plays any part at all. And yet there are
many reasons why a wise fasting is an excellent thing.

(1) Fasting is *good for health.* Many of us live a life in
which it is easy to get soft and flabby. It is even possible for
people to reach the stage when they live to eat instead of
eating to live. It would do a great many people a great deal of
physical good to practise fasting far more than they do.

(2) Fasting is *good for self-discipline.* It is easy to become
almost completely self-indulgent. It is easy to come to a stage
when we deny ourselves nothing which it is in our power to
have or to pay for. It would do most of us a great deal of good

if for some time each week we set aside our wishes and our desires, and exercised a stringent and an antiseptic self-discipline.

(3) Fasting preserves us from becoming *the slaves of a habit*. There are not a few of us who indulge in certain habits because we find it impossible to stop them. They have become so essential that we cannot break them; we develop such a craving for certain things that what ought to be a pleasure has become a necessity; and to be cut off from the thing which we have learned to desire so much can be a purgatory. If we practised a wise fasting, no pleasure would become a chain, and no habit would come to rule our lives. We would have control over our pleasures, and not our pleasures over us.

(4) Fasting preserves *the ability to do without things*. One of the great tests in life is the number of things which we have come to regard as essential. Clearly, the fewer things we regard as essentials, the more independent we will be. When all kinds of things become essentials, we are at the mercy of the luxuries of life. It is no bad thing to walk down a street of shop windows, and to look in at them and remind ourselves of all the things that we can do without. Some kind of fasting preserves the ability to do without the things which should never be allowed to become essentials.

(5) Fasting makes us *appreciate things all the more*. It may be that there was a time in life when some pleasure came so seldom that we really enjoyed it when it did come. It may be that nowadays the appetite is blunted; the palate is dulled; the edge has gone off it. What was once a sharp pleasure has become simply a drug which we cannot do without. Fasting keeps the thrill in pleasure by keeping pleasure always fresh and new.

Fasting has gone almost completely out of the lives of ordinary people. Jesus condemned the wrong kind of fasting, but he never meant that fasting should be completely eliminated from life and living. We would do well to practise it in our own way and according to our own need. And the reason for practising it is:

> So that earth's bliss may be our guide,
> And not our chain.

THE TRUE TREASURE

Matthew 6:19–21

> 'Do not lay up for yourselves treasures upon earth, where moth and rust destroy them, and where thieves dig through and steal. Lay up for yourselves treasures in heaven, where moth and rust do not destroy them, and where thieves do not dig through and steal. For where your treasure is, there will your heart be also.'

In the ordinary, everyday management of life, it is simple wisdom to acquire for oneself only those things which will last. Whether we are buying clothes, or a car, or a carpet for the floor, or furniture, it is common sense to avoid shoddy goods and to buy the things which have solidity and permanence and craftsmanship built into them. That is exactly what Jesus is saying here; he is telling us to concentrate on the things which will last.

Jesus calls up three pictures from the three great sources of wealth in Palestine.

(1) He tells people to avoid the things that *the moth can destroy*.

In the middle east, part of an individual's wealth often consisted in fine and elaborate clothes. When Gehazi, the servant of Elisha, wished to make some forbidden profit out of Naaman, after his master had cured him, he asked him for a talent of silver and *changes of clothing* (2 Kings 5:22). One of the things which tempted Achan to sin was a beautiful mantle from Shinar (Joshua 7:21).

But such things were foolish things to set the heart upon, for the moths might get at them, when they were stored away, and all their beauty and their value would be destroyed. There was no permanence about possessions like that.

(2) He tells people to avoid the things that *rust can destroy*.

The word translated as *rust* is *brōsis*. It literally means an *eating away*, but it is nowhere else used to mean *rust*. Most likely, the picture is this. In the middle east, many individuals' wealth consisted in the corn and the grain that was stored away in great barns. But into that corn and grain there could come worms, rats and mice, until the store was polluted and destroyed. In all probability, the reference is to the way in which those and other vermin could get into a granary and eat away the grain.

There was no permanence about possessions like that.

(3) He tells people to avoid the treasures *which thieves can steal by digging through*.

The word which is used for *to dig through* – the Revised Standard Version has *break in* – is *diorussein*. In Palestine, the walls of many of the houses were made of nothing stronger than baked clay; and burglars did effect an entry by literally digging through the wall. The reference here is to someone who has hoarded in the house a little store of gold, only to find, on returning home one day, that burglars have dug through the flimsy walls and that the treasure is gone.

There is no permanence about a treasure which is at the mercy of any enterprising thief.

So Jesus warns people against three kinds of pleasures and possessions.

(1) He warns them against the pleasures which will wear out like an old suit of clothes. The finest garment in the world, moths or no moths, will in the end disintegrate. All purely physical pleasures have a way of wearing out. At each successive enjoyment of them, the thrill becomes less thrilling. It requires more of them to produce the same effect. They are like a drug which loses its initial potency and which becomes increasingly less effective. It is foolish to look for pleasure in things which are bound to offer diminishing returns.

(2) He warns against the pleasures which can be eroded away. The grain store is the inevitable prey of the marauding rats and mice which nibble and gnaw away the grain. There are certain pleasures which inevitably lose their attraction as we grow older. It may be that we become physically less able to enjoy them; it may be that as our minds mature they cease in any sense to satisfy us. In life, we should never give our hearts to the joys the years can take away; we should find our delight in the things whose thrill time is powerless to erode.

(3) He warns against the pleasures which can be stolen away. All material things are like that; not one of them is secure; and if people build their happiness on them, they are building on a most insecure basis. Suppose a person's life is so arranged that happiness depends on the possession of money; suppose a recession and economic crash comes and that person wakes up to find the money gone; then, with the wealth, happiness has also gone.

If we are wise, we will build our happiness on things which we cannot lose, things which are independent of the chances and the changes of this life.

Robert Burns wrote in 'Tam o' Shanter' of the fleeting things:

> But pleasures are like poppies spread:
> You seize the flower, its bloom is shed;
> Or like the snow falls in the river,
> A moment white – then melts for ever.

Anyone whose happiness depends on things like that is doomed to disappointment. Anyone whose treasure is in *things* is bound to lose that treasure, for in things there is no permanence, and no thing lasts forever.

TREASURE IN HEAVEN

Matthew 6:19-21 (*contd*)

THE Jews were very familiar with the phrase *treasure in heaven*. They identified such treasure with two things in particular.

(1) They said that the deeds of kindness which people did upon earth became their treasure in heaven.

The Jews had a famous story about a certain King Monobaz of Adiabēne who became a convert to Judaism. 'Monobaz distributed all his treasures to the poor in the year of famine. His brothers sent to him and said, "Thy fathers gathered treasures, and added to those of their fathers, but thou hast dispersed yours and theirs." He said to them, "My fathers gathered treasures for below, I have gathered treasures for above; they stored treasures in a place over which the hand of man can rule, but I have stored treasures in a place over which the hand of man cannot rule; my fathers collected treasures which bear no interest, I have gathered treasures which bear interest; my fathers gathered treasures of money, I have gathered treasures in souls; my fathers gathered treasures for others, I have gathered treasures for myself; my fathers gathered treasures in this world, I have gathered treasures for the world to come."'

Both Jesus and the Jewish Rabbis were sure that what is selfishly hoarded is lost, but that what is generously given away brings treasure in heaven.

That was also the principle of the Christian Church in the days to come. The early Church always lovingly cared for the poor, the sick, the distressed, the helpless and those for whom no one else cared. In the days of the terrible Decian persecution in Rome, the Roman authorities broke into a Christian church. They were out to loot the treasures which they believed the church to possess. The Roman prefect demanded from Laurentius, the deacon: 'Show me your treasures at once.' Laurentius pointed at the widows and orphans who were being fed, the sick who were being nursed, the poor whose needs were being supplied. 'These', he said, 'are the treasures of the Church.'

The Church has always believed that 'what we keep, we lose, and what we spend, we have'.

(2) The Jews always connected the phrase *treasure in heaven* with *character*. When Rabbi Yose ben Kisma was asked if he would dwell in a pagan city on condition of receiving very high pay for his services, he replied that he would not dwell anywhere except in a home of the law, 'for', he said, 'in the hour of a man's departure neither silver, nor gold, nor precious stones accompany him, but only his knowledge of the law, and his good works'. As the grim Spanish proverb has it, 'There are no pockets in a shroud.'

The only thing which we can take out of this world into the world beyond is ourselves; and the finer the self we bring, the greater our treasure in heaven will be.

(3) Jesus ends this section by stating that where a person's treasure is, that person's heart is there also. If everything that

people value and set their hearts upon is on earth, then they will have no interest in any world beyond this world; if all through their lives their eyes are on eternity, then they will evaluate lightly the things of this world. If everything which people count valuable is on this earth, then they will leave this earth reluctantly and grudgingly; if their thoughts have been directed to the world beyond, they will leave this world with gladness, because they go at last to God. Once Dr Johnson was shown round a noble castle and its grounds; when he had seen round it, he turned to his companions and said: 'These are the things which make it difficult to die.'

Jesus never said that this world was unimportant; but he said and implied over and over again that its importance is not in itself, but in that to which it leads. This world is not the end of life, it is a stage on the way; and therefore we should never lose our hearts to this world and to the things of this world. Our eyes ought to be forever fixed on the goal beyond.

THE DISTORTED VISION

Matthew 6:22–3

> 'The light of the body is the eye. So then, if your eye is generous, the whole body will be full of light; but if your eye is grudging, your whole body will be in the dark. If, then, the light which is in you is darkness, how great is that darkness!'

THE idea behind this passage is one of childlike simplicity. The eye is regarded as the window by which the light gets into the whole body. The state of a window decides what light gets into a room. If the window is clear, clean and undistorted, the light will come flooding into the room and will illuminate every corner of it. If the glass of the window is coloured or frosted, distorted, dirty or obscure, the light will be hindered and the room will not be lit up.

The amount of light which gets into any room depends on the state of the window through which it has to pass. So, says Jesus, the light which gets into any individual's heart and soul and being depends on the spiritual state of the eye through which it has to pass, for the eye is the window of the whole body.

The view we take of people depends on the kind of eye we have. There are certain obvious things which can blind our eyes and distort our vision.

(1) *Prejudice* can distort our vision. There is nothing which so destroys people's judgment as prejudice does. It prevents them from forming the clear, reasonable and logical judgment which it is everyone's duty to form. It blinds them alike to the facts and to the significance of the facts.

Almost all new discoveries have had to fight their way against unreasonable prejudice. When Sir James Simpson discovered the virtues of chloroform, and in particular its benefits to relieve the pain of childbirth, he had to fight against the prejudice of the medical and religious world of his day. One of his biographers writes: 'Prejudice, the crippling determination to walk only in time-worn paths, and to eschew new ways, rose up against it, and did their best to smother the new-found blessing.' 'Many of the clergy held that to try to remove the primal curse on women was to fight against divine law.'

One of the most necessary things in life is the fearless self-examination which will enable us to see when we are acting on principle and when we are the victims of our own unreasonable and unreasoning prejudices. In anyone who is swayed by prejudice, the eye is darkened and the vision distorted.

(2) *Jealousy* can distort our vision. Shakespeare gave us the classic example of that in the tragedy of *Othello*. Othello, the Moor, won fame by his heroic exploits and married Desdemona, who loved him with utter devotion and complete fidelity. As general of the army of Venice, Othello promoted Cassio and passed over Iago. Iago was consumed with jealousy. By careful plotting and the manipulation of facts, Iago sowed in Othello's mind the suspicion that Cassio and Desdemona were having an affair. He manufactured evidence to prove it, and moved Othello to such a passion of jealousy that he finally murdered Desdemona by smothering her with a pillow. The literary critic A. C. Bradley writes: 'Such jealousy as Othello's converts human nature into chaos, and liberates the beast in man.'

Many a marriage and many a friendship have been wrecked on the rock of a jealousy which distorted perfectly innocent incidents into guilty actions, and which blinded the eye to truth and fact.

(3) *Self-conceit* can distort our vision. In her biography of the novelist Mark Rutherford, Catherine Macdonald Maclean has a curiously caustic sentence about John Chapman, the bookseller and publisher, who was at one time Mark Rutherford's employer: 'Handsome in the Byronic fashion and pleasant-mannered, he was exceedingly attractive to women, and he thought himself even more attractive to them than he actually was.'

Self-conceit can doubly affect our vision, for it renders us incapable of seeing ourselves as we really are, and incapable of seeing others as they really are. If people are convinced of their own surpassing wisdom, they will never be able to realize their own foolishness; and if they are blind to everything except their own virtues, they will never be aware of their own faults. Whenever they compare themselves with others, they will do so to their own advantage, and to the disadvantage of other people. They will be forever incapable of self-criticism, and therefore forever incapable of self-improvement. The light in which they should see themselves and see others will be darkness.

THE NECESSITY OF THE GENEROUS EYE

Matthew 6:22-3 (*contd*)

HERE, Jesus speaks of one special virtue which fills the eye with light, and one special fault which fills the eye with darkness. The Authorized Version speaks here about the eye being *single* and the eye being *evil*. Certainly that is the literal meaning of the Greek, but the words *single* and *evil* are here used in a special way which is common enough in the Greek in which Scripture is written.

The word for *single* is *haplous*, and its corresponding noun is *haplotēs*. Regularly in the Greek of the Bible, these words mean *generous* and *generosity*. James speaks of God who gives *generously* (James 1:5), and the adverb he uses is *haplōs*.

Similarly in Romans 12:8, Paul urges his friends to give generously (*haplōs*). Paul reminds the Corinthian church of the generosity (*haplotēs*) of the churches in Macedonia, and talks about their own generosity to all (2 Corinthians 9:11). It is *the generous eye* which Jesus is commending.

The word which is translated in the Authorized Version as *evil* is *ponēros*. Certainly that is the normal meaning of the word; but both in the New Testament and in the Septuagint, *ponēros* regularly means *niggardly* or *grudging*. Deuteronomy speaks of the duty of lending to a neighbour who is in need. But the matter was complicated by the fact that every seventh year was a year of release when debts were cancelled.

It might, therefore, very well happen that, if the seventh year was near, a cautious person might refuse to help, in case the person helped took advantage of the seventh year never to repay the debt. So the law lays it down: 'Be careful that you do not entertain a mean thought, thinking, "The seventh year, the year of remission, is near"', and therefore view your needy neighbour with hostility and give nothing' (Deuteronomy 15:9). Clearly *ponēros* there means *niggardly*, *grudging* and *ungenerous*. It is the advice of the proverb: 'Do not eat the bread of the stingy' (Proverbs 23:6). That is to say, 'Don't be a guest in the house of someone who grudges you every bite you eat.' Another proverb has it: 'The miser is in a hurry to get rich' (Proverbs 28:22).

So Jesus is saying: 'There is nothing like generosity for giving you a clear and undistorted view of life and of people; and there is nothing like the grudging and ungenerous spirit for distorting your view of life and of people.'

(1) We must be generous in our *judgments of others*. It is characteristic of human nature to think the worst, and to find a malignant delight in repeating the worst. Every day in life, the reputations of perfectly innocent people are destroyed by gossiping groups whose judgments are dipped in poison. The world would be saved a great deal of heartbreak if we would put the best, and not the worst, construction on the actions of other people.

(2) We must be generous in our *actions*. In her biography of Mark Rutherford, Catherine Macdonald Maclean speaks of the days when Mark Rutherford came to work in London: 'It was about this time that there can be noted in him the beginning of that "cherishing pity for the souls of men" which was to become habitual with him . . . The burning question with him, haunted as he was at times by the fate of many in the district in which he lived, was, "What can *I* do? Wherein

can *I* help them?" It seemed to him then, as always, that any kind of action was of more value than the most vehement indignation that spent itself in talk.' In the nineteenth century when Mark Rutherford was with Chapman the publisher, the novelist George Eliot, or Marian Evans as her real name was, lived and worked in the same place. One thing impressed him about her: 'She was poor. She had only a small income of her own; and, although she hoped to earn a livelihood as a woman of letters, her future was very uncertain. But she was fantastically generous. She was always helping lame dogs over stiles, and the poverty of others pressed on her more than her own. She wept more bitterly because she could not adequately relieve a sister's poverty than because of any of her own privations.'

It is when we begin to feel like that that we begin to see people and things clearly. It is then that our eye becomes full of light.

There are three great evils of the ungenerous spirit, of the eye that is grudging.

(1) It makes it *impossible to live with ourselves*. If people are forever envying others their success, grudging others their happiness and shutting their hearts against the needs of others, they become the most pitiable of creatures – people who bear a grudge. There grows within them a bitterness and a resentment which robs them of their happiness, steals away their peace and destroys their contentment.

(2) It makes it *impossible to live with other people*. Mean people are abhorred by all; the people whom everyone despises are those who are miserly of heart. Charity covers a multitude of sins, but the grudging spirit makes useless a multitude of virtues. However bad generous people may be, there are those who will love them; and however good mean people may be, everyone will detest them.

(3) It makes it *impossible to live with God*. There is no one so generous as God; and, in the last analysis, there can be no fellowship between two people who guide their lives by diametrically opposite principles. There can be no fellowship between the God whose heart is afire with love, and the man or woman whose heart is frozen with meanness.

The grudging eye distorts our vision; the generous eye alone sees clearly, for it alone sees as God sees.

THE EXCLUSIVE SERVICE

Matthew 6:24

> 'No man can be a slave to two owners; for either he
> will hate the one and love the other, or he will cleave to
> the one and despise the other. You cannot be a slave to
> God and to material things.'

To one brought up in the ancient world, this is an even more vivid saying than it is to us. The Revised Standard Version translates it: 'No one can serve two masters.' But that is not nearly strong enough. The word which the RSV translates as *serve* is *douleuein*; *doulos* is a slave, and *douleuein* means *to be a slave to*. The word that the RSV translates as *master* is *kurios*, and *kurios* is the word which denotes *absolute ownership*. We get the meaning far better if we translate it: 'No man can be a slave to two owners.'

To understand all that this means and implies, we must remember two things about the slave in the ancient world. First, the slave in the eyes of the law was not a person but a thing. Slaves had absolutely no rights of their own; their master could do with them absolutely as he liked. In the eyes of the law, slaves were *living tools*. Their master could sell them, beat them, throw them out and even kill them. Their

master possessed them as completely as he possessed any of
his material possessions. Second, in the ancient world, slaves
had literally no time which was their own. Every moment of
their lives belonged to their master. Under modern conditions,
people have certain hours of work, and outside these hours
of work their time is their own. It is indeed often possible for
people nowadays to find their real interest in life outside
working hours. It is possible for someone to work in an office
during the day and play the violin in an orchestra at night;
and it may be that it is in the music that that person finds
real life. Another person may work on a building site or in
a factory during the day and run a youth club at night,
and it may be that it is in the youth club that the real
delight and the real expression of personality is found. But
it was very different for those who were slaves. Slaves had
literally no moment of time which belonged to them. Every
moment belonged to their owner and was at their owner's
disposal.

Here, then, is our relationship to God. In regard to God,
we have no rights of our own; God must be undisputed master
of our lives. We can never ask: 'What do I wish to do?' We
must always ask: 'What does God wish me to do?' We have
no time which is our own. We cannot sometimes say: 'I will
do what God wishes me to do' and at other times say: 'I will
do what I like.' As Christians, we have no time off from being
Christians; there is no time when we can relax our Christian
standards, as if we were off duty. A partial or a spasmodic
service of God is not enough. Being a Christian is a full-time
job. Nowhere in the Bible is the exclusive service which God
demands more clearly set forth.

Jesus goes on to say: 'You cannot serve God and mamon.'
The correct spelling is with one *m*. *Mamon* was a Hebrew
word for *material possessions*. Originally, it was not a bad

word at all. The Rabbis, for instance, had a saying: 'Let the *mamon* of thy neighbour be as dear to thee as thine own.' That is to say, people should regard their neighbours' material possessions as being as sacrosanct as their own. But the word *mamon* had a most curious and a most revealing history. It comes from a root which means *to entrust*; and *mamon* was that which was entrusted to a banker or to a safe deposit of some kind. *Mamon* was the wealth which was entrusted to another person for safe-keeping. But as the years went on, *mamon* came to mean not *that which is entrusted*, but *that in which people put their trust*. The end of the process was that *mamon* came to be spelled with a capital M and came to be regarded as nothing less than a god.

The history of that word shows vividly how material possessions can usurp a place in life which they were never meant to have. Originally, another person's material possessions were the things which people entrusted to others for safe-keeping; in the end, they came to be the things in which they put their trust. Surely there is no better description of a person's god than to say that it is the power in whom he or she trusts; and when people put their trust in material things, then material things have become not their support but their god.

THE PLACE OF MATERIAL POSSESSIONS

Matthew 6:24 (*contd*)

THIS saying of Jesus is bound to turn our thoughts to the place which material possessions should have in life. At the basis of Jesus' teaching about possessions, there are three great principles.

(1) In the last analysis, *all things belong to God*. Scripture makes that abundantly clear. 'The earth is the Lord's and all that is in it, the world and those who live in it' (Psalm 24:1). 'For every wild animal of the forest is mine, the cattle on a thousand hills . . . If I were hungry, I would not tell you, for the world and all that is in it is mine' (Psalm 50:10, 12).

In Jesus' teaching, it is the master who gives his servants the talents (Matthew 25:15), and the owner who gives the tenants the vineyard (Matthew 21:33). This principle has far-reaching consequences. Men and women can buy and sell things; they can to some extent alter and rearrange things; but they cannot create things. The ultimate ownership of all things belongs to God. There is nothing in this world of which we can say: 'This is mine.' Of all things, we can only say: 'This belongs to God, and God has given me the use of it.'

Therefore this basic principle of life emerges. There is nothing in this world of which anyone can say: 'This is mine, and I will therefore do what I like with it.' Of everything, we *must* say: 'This is God's, and I must use it as its owner would have it to be used.' There is a story of a city child who was taken for a day in the country. For the first time in her life, she saw a drift of bluebells. She turned to her teacher and said: 'Do you think God would mind if I picked one of his flowers?' That is the correct attitude to life and all things in the world.

(2) The second basic principle is that *people are always more important than things*. If possessions have to be acquired, if money has to be amassed, if wealth has to be accumulated at the expense of treating people as things, then all such riches are wrong. Whenever and wherever that principle is forgotten, or neglected, or defied, far-reaching disaster is certain to follow.

In Britain, we are to this day suffering in the world of industrial relationships from the fact that in the days of the Industrial Revolution people were treated as things. Sir Arthur Bryant in *English Saga* tells of some of the things which happened in those days. Children of seven and eight years of age – there is actually a case of a child of three – were employed in the mines. Some of them dragged trucks along galleries on all fours; some of them pumped out water standing knee-deep in the water for twelve hours a day; some of them, called trappers, opened and shut the ventilating doors of the shafts, and were shut into little ventilating chambers for as much as sixteen hours a day. In 1815, children were working in the mills from 5 am to 8 pm without even a Saturday half-holiday, and with half an hour off for breakfast and half an hour off for dinner. In 1833, there were 84,000 children under fourteen years of age in the factories. There is actually a case recorded in which the children whose labour was no longer required were taken to a common and turned adrift. The owners objected to the expression 'turned adrift'. They said that the children had been set at liberty. They agreed that the children might find things hard. 'They would have to beg their way or something of that sort.' In 1842, the weavers of Burnley and the miners of Staffordshire were being paid barely enough to live on. There were those who saw the criminal folly of all this. Thomas Carlyle thundered: 'If the cotton industry is founded on the bodies of rickety children, it must go; if the devil gets in your cotton mill, shut the mill.' It was pleaded that cheap labour was necessary to keep costs down. The poet Samuel Taylor Coleridge answered: 'You talk about making this article cheaper by reducing its price in the market from 8d to 6d. But suppose in so doing you have rendered your country weaker against a foreign foe; suppose you have demoralized thousands of your fellow-countrymen, and have sown discontent between one class of society and another, your article is tolerably dear, I take it, after all.'

It is perfectly true that things are very different nowadays. But there is such a thing as collective memory. Deep in the subconscious memory of people, the impression of these bad days is indelibly impressed. Whenever people are treated as things, as machines, as instruments for producing so much labour and for enriching those who employ them, then as certainly as the night follows the day, disaster follows. A nation forgets at its peril the principle that people are always more important than things.

(3) The third principle is that *wealth is always a subordinate good*. The Bible does not say that 'Money is the root of all evil'; it says that '*The love of money* is a root of all kinds of evil' (1 Timothy 6:10). It is quite possible to find in material things what someone has called 'a rival salvation'. Some people may think that, because they are wealthy, they can buy anything – that they can buy their way out of any situation. Wealth can become their measuring rod; wealth can become their one desire; wealth can become the one weapon with which they face life. If people desire material things for an honourable independence, to help their families and to do something for others, that is good; but if they desire it simply to heap pleasure upon pleasure, and to add luxury, if wealth has become the thing they live for and live by, then wealth has ceased to be a subordinate good, and has usurped the place in life which only God should occupy.

One thing emerges from all this – the possession of wealth, money and material things is not a sin, but it is a grave *responsibility*. If people own many material things, it is not so much a matter for congratulation as it is a matter for prayer, that they may use them as God would want them to.

THE TWO GREAT QUESTIONS
ABOUT POSSESSIONS

Matthew 6:24 (*contd*)

THERE are two great questions about possessions, and on the answer to these questions everything depends.

(1) *How did people gain their possessions?* Did they gain them in a way that they would be glad that Jesus Christ should see, or did they gain them in a way that they would wish to hide from Jesus Christ?

Possessions may be gained at the expense of honesty and honour. The poet and novelist George Macdonald tells of a village shopkeeper who grew very rich. Whenever he was measuring cloth, he measured it with his two thumbs inside the measure so that he always gave short measure. George Macdonald says of him: 'He took from his soul, and he put it in his siller-bag.' People can enrich their bank accounts at the expense of impoverishing their souls.

Possessions may be gained by the deliberate smashing of some weaker rival. Many people's success is founded on someone else's failure. Many have gained advancement by pushing someone else out of the way. It is hard to see how those who prosper in such a way can sleep at nights.

Possessions may be gained at the expense of still higher duties. Robertson Nicoll, the great editor, was born in a manse in the north-east of Scotland. His father had one passion, to buy and to read books. He was a minister and he never had more than £200 a year. But he amassed the greatest private library in Scotland, amounting to 17,000 books. He did not use them in his sermons; he was simply consumed to own and to read them. When he was forty, he married a girl of twenty-four. In eight years she was dead of tuberculosis; of a

family of five, only two lived to be over twenty. That can-
cerous growth of books filled every room and every passage
in the manse. It may have delighted the owner of the books,
but it killed his wife and family.

There are possessions which can be acquired at too great a
cost. The question we must always ask is: 'How do I acquire
the things which I possess?'

(2) *How do people use their possessions?* There are
various ways in which people may use the things they have
acquired.

They may not use them at all. They may have the miser's
acquisitiveness which delights simply in possession. Their
possessions may be quite useless – and uselessness always
invites disaster.

They may use them completely selfishly. It is possible to
want a larger salary for no other reason than to purchase a
bigger car, a new television set or a more expensive holiday.
People may think of possessions simply and solely in terms
of what they can do for them.

They may use them malignantly. People can use their
possessions to persuade someone else to do things they have
no right to do, or to sell things they have no right to sell.
Many young people have been bribed or dazzled into sin by
someone else's money. Wealth gives power, and corrupt
people can use their possessions to corrupt others – and that
in the sight of God is a very terrible sin.

*People may use their possessions for their own independ-
ence and for the happiness of others.* It does not need great
wealth to do that, for it is possible to be just as generous with
£1 as with £1,000. We will not go far wrong if we use our
possessions to see how much happiness we can bring to
others. Paul remembered a saying of Jesus which everyone
else had forgotten: 'It is more blessed to give than to receive'

(Acts 20:35). It is characteristic of God to give; and if in our lives giving always ranks above receiving, we will use aright what we possess, however much or however little it may be.

THE FORBIDDEN WORRY

Matthew 6:25–34

> 'I tell you, therefore, do not worry about your life, about what you are to eat, or what you are to drink; and do not worry about your body, about what you are to wear. Is not your life more than food, and your body more than clothes? Look at the birds of the air, and see that they do not sow, or reap, or gather things into storehouses, and yet your heavenly Father feeds them. Are you not better than they? Who of you can add one span to his life by worrying about it? And why do you worry about clothes? Learn a lesson from the lilies of the field, from the way in which they grow. They do not toil or spin; but I tell you that not even Solomon in all his glory was clothed like one of these. If God so clothes the grass of the field, which exists today, and which is thrown into the oven tomorrow, shall he not much more clothe you, O you of little faith? So then do not worry, saying, What are we to eat? or, What are we to drink? or, What are we to wear? The Gentiles seek after all these things. But seek first his kingdom and his righteousness and all these things will come to you in addition. So, then, do not worry about tomorrow; tomorrow will worry about itself. Its own troubles are quite enough for the day.'

WE must begin our study of this passage by making sure that we understand what Jesus is forbidding and what he is demanding. The Authorized Version translates Jesus' commandment: 'Take no thought for the morrow.' Strange to say, the Authorized Version was the first translation to translate it in that way. John Wyclif's translation had it: 'Be not busy to your life.' The translations of Tyndale, Cranmer and the Geneva Version all had: 'Be not careful for your life.' They used the word *careful* in the literal sense of *full of care*. The older versions were in fact more accurate. It is not ordinary, prudent foresight, such as becomes any individual, that Jesus forbids; it is *worry*. Jesus is not advocating a shiftless, thriftless, reckless, thoughtless, improvident attitude to life; he is forbidding a careworn, worried fear, which takes all the joy out of life.

The word which is used is the word *merimnan*, which means *to worry anxiously*. Its corresponding noun is *merimna*, which means *worry*. In a papyrus letter, a wife writes to her absent husband: 'I cannot sleep at night or by day, because of the *worry* [*merimna*] I have about your welfare.' A mother, on hearing of her son's good health and prosperity, writes back: 'That is all my prayer and all my *anxiety* [*merimna*].' Anacreon, the poet from ancient Greece, writes: 'When I drink wine, my worries [*merimna*] go to sleep.' In Greek, the word is the characteristic word for anxiety, worry and care.

The Jews themselves were very familiar with this attitude to life. It was the teaching of the great Rabbis that life ought to be met with a combination of prudence and serenity. They insisted, for instance, that every man must teach his son a trade; for, they said, not to teach him a trade was to teach him to steal. That is to say, they believed in taking all the necessary steps for the prudent handling of life. But at the same time, they said: 'He who has a loaf in his basket, and who says, "What will I eat tomorrow?" is a man of little faith.'

Jesus is here teaching a lesson which the people knew well – the lesson of prudence and forethought and serenity and trust combined.

WORRY AND ITS CURE

Matthew 6:25–34 (*contd*)

In these ten verses, Jesus sets out seven different arguments and defences against worry.

(1) He begins by pointing out (verse 25) that God gave us life, and if he gave us life, surely we can trust him for the lesser things. If God gave us life, surely we can trust him to give us food to sustain that life. If God gave us bodies, surely we can trust him for garments to clothe these bodies. If anyone gives us a gift which is beyond price, surely we can be certain that such a giver will not be mean, stingy, niggardly, careless and forgetful about much less costly gifts. So, the first argument is that if God gave us life, we can trust him for the things which are necessary to support life.

(2) Jesus goes on to speak about the birds (verse 26). There is no worry in their lives, no attempt to pile up goods for an unforeseen and unforeseeable future; and yet their lives go on. More than one Jewish Rabbi was fascinated by the way in which the animals live. 'In my life,' said Rabbi Simeon, 'I have never seen a stag as a dryer of figs, or a lion as a porter, or a fox as a merchant, yet they are all nourished without worry. If they, who are created to serve me, are nourished without worry, how much more ought I, who am created to serve my Maker, to be nourished without worry; but I have corrupted my ways, and so I have impaired my substance.' The point that Jesus is making is not that the birds do not work; it has been said that no one works harder than the average sparrow to make a living; the point that he is making is that they do not worry. There is not to be found in them the human weakness of straining to see a future which cannot be seen, and of seeking to find

security in things stored up and accumulated against the future.

(3) In verse 27, Jesus goes on to prove that worry is in any event useless. The verse can bear two meanings. It can mean that none of us by worrying can add a cubit to our height; but a cubit is eighteen inches, and we surely would never contemplate adding eighteen inches to our height! It can mean that by worrying we cannot add the shortest space to our lives; and that meaning is more likely. It is Jesus' argument that worry is pointless anyway.

(4) Jesus goes on to speak about the flowers (verses 28–30), and he speaks about them as one who loved them. The lilies of the field were the scarlet poppies and anemones. They bloomed one day on the hillsides of Palestine; and yet in their brief life they were clothed with a beauty which surpassed the beauty of the robes of kings. When they died, they were used for nothing better than for burning. The point is this. The Palestinian oven was made of clay. It was like a clay box set on bricks over the fire. When it was desired to raise the temperature of it especially quickly, some handfuls of dried grasses and wild flowers were flung *inside* the oven and set alight. The flowers had but one day of life; and then they were set alight to help a woman to heat an oven when she was baking in a hurry; and yet God clothes them with a beauty which is beyond human power to imitate. If God gives such beauty to a short-lived flower, how much more will he care for us? Surely the generosity which is so lavish to the flower of a day will not be forgetful of human life, the crown of creation.

(5) Jesus goes on to advance a very fundamental argument against worry. Worry, he says, is characteristic of pagans, and not of those who know what God is like (verse 32). Worry is essentially distrust of God. Such a distrust may be

understandable in pagans who believe in a jealous, capricious, unpredictable god; but it is beyond comprehension in anyone who has learned to call God by the name of Father. Christians cannot worry because they believe in the love of God.

(6) Jesus goes on to advance two ways in which to defeat worry. The first is to seek first, to concentrate upon, the kingdom of God. We have seen that to be in the kingdom and to do the will of God is one and the same thing (Matthew 6:10). To concentrate on the doing of, and the acceptance of, God's will is the way to defeat worry. We know how in our own lives a great love can drive out every other concern. Such a love can inspire our work, intensify our study, purify our lives, dominate our whole being. It was Jesus' conviction that worry is banished when God becomes the dominating power of our lives.

(7) Last, Jesus says that worry can be defeated when we acquire the art of living one day at a time (verse 34). The Jews had a saying: 'Do not worry over tomorrow's evils, for you know not what today will bring forth. Perhaps tomorrow you will not be alive, and you will have worried for a world which will not be yours.' If each day is lived as it comes, if each task is done as it appears, then the sum of all the days is bound to be good. It is Jesus' advice that we should handle the demands of each day as it comes, without worrying about the unknown future and the things which may never happen.

THE FOLLY OF WORRY

Matthew 6:25–34 (*contd*)

LET us now see if we can gather up Jesus' arguments against worry.

(1) *Worry is needless, useless and even actively injurious.*
Worry cannot affect the past, for the past is past. The words
of *The Rubaiyat of Omar Khayyam* are grimly right:

> The moving finger writes, and, having writ,
> Moves on; nor all thy piety nor wit
>   Shall lure it back to cancel half a line,
> Nor all thy tears wash out a word of it.

The past is past. It is not that we can or ought to dissociate
ourselves from our past; but we ought to use our past as a
spur and a guide for better action in the future, and not as
something about which we brood until we have worried
ourselves into a paralysis of action.

Equally, worry about the future is useless. Alistair
MacLean in one of his sermons tells of a story which he had
read. A London doctor was the hero. 'He was paralysed and
bedridden, but almost outrageously cheerful, and his smile
so brave and radiant that everyone forgot to be sorry for him.
His children adored him, and when one of his boys was
leaving the nest and starting forth upon life's adventure, Dr
Greatheart gave him good advice: "Johnny," he said, "the
thing to do, my lad, is to hold your own end up, and to do it
like a gentleman, and please remember the biggest troubles
you have got to face are those that never come."' Worry about
the future is wasted effort, and the future of reality is seldom
as bad as the future of our fears.

But worry is worse than useless; it is often actively injurious. The two typical diseases of modern life are the
stomach ulcer and the coronary thrombosis, and in many cases
both are the result of worry. It is a medical fact that those
who laugh most live longest. The worry which wears out the
mind wears out the body along with it. Worry affects our
judgment, lessens our powers of decision and renders us

progressively incapable of dealing with life. Let each of us give our best to every situation – we cannot give more – and let us leave the rest to God.

(2) *Worry is blind*. Worry refuses to learn the lesson of *nature*. Jesus bids men and women look at the birds, and see the bounty which is behind nature, and trust the love that lies behind that bounty. Worry refuses to learn the lesson of *history*. There was a psalmist who cheered himself with the memory of history. 'My God,' he cries. 'My soul is cast down within me.' And then he goes on: '*Therefore* I remember you from the land of Jordan and of Hermon, from Mount Mizar' (Psalm 42:6; cf. Deuteronomy 3:8). When he was up against it, he comforted himself with the memory of what God had done. Those who feed their hearts on the record of what God has done in the past will never worry about the future. Worry refuses to learn the lesson of *life*. We are still alive and our heads are still above water; and yet if someone had told us that we would have to go through what we have actually gone through, we would have said that it was impossible. The lesson of life is that somehow we have been enabled to bear the unbearable and to do the undoable and to pass the breaking point and not to break. The lesson of life is that worry is unnecessary.

(3) *Worry is essentially irreligious*. Worry is not caused by external circumstances. In the same circumstances, one person can be absolutely serene and another can be worried to death. Both worry and serenity come not from circumstances but from the heart. Alistair MacLean quotes a story from Johann Tauler, the fourteenth-century German mystic. One day, Tauler met a beggar. 'God give you a good day, my friend,' he said. The beggar answered: 'I thank God I never had a bad one.' Then Tauler said: 'God give you a happy life, my friend.' 'I thank God', said the beggar, 'I am never

unhappy.' Tauler in amazement said: 'What do you mean?' 'Well,' said the beggar, 'when it is fine, I thank God, when it rains, I thank God; when I have plenty, I thank God; when I am hungry, I thank God; and since God's will is my will, and whatever pleases him pleases me, why should I say I am unhappy when I am not?' Tauler looked at the man in astonishment. 'Who are you?' he asked. 'I am a king,' said the beggar. 'Where then is your kingdom?' asked Tauler. And the beggar answered quietly: '*In my heart.*'

Isaiah said it long ago: 'Those of steadfast mind you keep in peace – in peace because they trust in you' (Isaiah 26:3). As the north-country woman had it: 'I am always happy, and my secret is always to sail the seas, and ever to keep the heart in port.'

There may be greater sins than worry, but very certainly there is no more disabling sin. 'Take no anxious thought for the morrow' – that is the commandment of Jesus, and it is the way not only to peace but also to power.

THE ERROR OF JUDGMENT

Matthew 7:1-5

'Do not judge others, in order that you may not be judged; for with the standard of judgment with which you judge you will be judged; and with the measure you measure to others it will be measured to you. Why do you look for the speck of dust in your brother's eye, and never notice the plank that is in your own eye? Or, how will you say to your brother: "Let me remove the speck of dust from your eye," and, see, there is a plank in your own eye? Hypocrite! first remove the plank from your own eye; then you will see clearly to remove the speck of dust from your brother's eye.'

WHEN Jesus spoke like this, as so often in the Sermon on the Mount, he was using words and ideas which were quite familiar to the highest thoughts of the Jews. Many a time, the Rabbis warned people against judging others. 'He who judges his neighbour favourably', they said, 'will be judged favourably by God.' They laid it down that there were six great works which brought credit in this world and profit in the world to come – study, visiting the sick, hospitality, devotion in prayer, the education of children in the law, and *thinking the best of other people*. The Jews knew that kindliness in judgment is nothing less than a sacred duty.

One would have thought that this would have been a commandment easy to obey, for history is strewn with the record of the most amazing misjudgments. There have been so many that one would have thought it would be a warning to everyone not to judge at all.

It has been so in literature. In the *Edinburgh Review* of November 1814, Lord Jeffrey wrote a review of Wordsworth's newly published poem 'The Excursion', in which he delivered the now famous, or infamous, verdict: 'This will never do.' In a review of Keats' 'Endymion', *The Quarterly* patronizingly noted 'a certain amount of talent which deserves to be put in the right way'.

Again and again, men and women who became famous have been dismissed as nonentities. In his autobiography, the novelist Gilbert Frankau tells how in the Victorian days his mother's house was a salon where the most brilliant people met. His mother arranged for the entertainment of her guests. Once she engaged a young Australian soprano to sing. After she had sung, Gilbert Frankau's mother said: 'What an appalling voice! She ought to be muzzled and allowed to sing no more!' The young singer's name was Nellie Melba, who became one of the most famous sopranos of all time.

Gilbert Frankau himself was producing a play. He sent to a theatrical agency for a young male actor to play the leading male part. The young man was interviewed and tested. After the test, Gilbert Frankau telephoned the agent. 'This man', he said, 'will never do. He cannot act, and he never will be able to act, and you had better tell him to look for some other profession before he starves. By the way, tell me his name again so that I can cross him off my list.' The actor was Ronald Colman, who was to become one of the most famous the screen has ever known.

Again and again, people have been guilty of the most notorious moral misjudgments. Collie Knox tells of what happened to himself and a friend. He himself had been badly injured in a flying accident while serving in the Royal Flying Corps. The friend had that very day been decorated for gallantry at Buckingham Palace. They had changed from service dress into civilian clothes and were lunching together at a famous London restaurant, when a girl came up and handed to each of them a white feather – the badge of cowardice.

There is hardly anyone who has not been guilty of some grave misjudgment; there is hardly anyone who has not suffered from someone else's misjudgment. And yet the strange fact is that there is hardly any commandment of Jesus which is more consistently broken and neglected.

NO ONE SHOULD JUDGE

Matthew 7:1–5 (*contd*)

THERE are three great reasons why no one should judge another person.

(1) *We never know the whole facts or the whole person.* Long ago, Hillel, the famous Rabbi, said: 'Do not judge a man until you yourself have come into his circumstances or situation.' No one knows the strength of another person's temptations. People who have a placid and equable temperament know nothing of the temptations of hot-blooded people whose emotions are quickly aroused. People brought up in good homes and in Christian surroundings know nothing of the temptation of those brought up in a slum, or in a place pervaded by evil. Those of us who are blessed with fine parents know nothing of the temptations of people who bear the burden of a difficult upbringing. The fact is that if we realized what some people have to go through, so far from condemning them, we would be amazed that they have succeeded in being as good as they are.

No more do we know the whole person. In one set of circumstances, a person may be unlovely and graceless; in another, that same person may be a tower of strength and beauty. In one of his novels, Mark Rutherford tells of a man who married for the second time. His wife had also been married before, and she had a daughter in her teens. The daughter seemed a sullen and unlovely creature, without a grain of attractiveness in her. The man could make nothing of her. Then, unexpectedly, the mother fell ill. At once the daughter was transformed. She became the perfect nurse, the embodiment of service and tireless devotion. Her sullenness was lit by a sudden radiance, and there appeared in her a person no one would ever have dreamt was there.

There is a kind of crystal called Labrador spar. At first sight it is dull and without lustre; but if it is turned round and round, and here and there, it will suddenly come into a position where the light strikes it in a certain way and it will sparkle with flashing beauty. People are like that. They may seem unlovely simply because we do not know the whole person. Everyone has something good in him or her. Our task is not to condemn, and to judge by, the superficial unloveliness, but to look for the underlying beauty. That is what we would have others do to us, and that is what we must do to them.

(2) *It is almost impossible for any of us to be strictly impartial in our judgment.* Again and again, we are swayed by instinctive and unreasoning reactions to people.

It is told that sometimes, when the Greeks held a particularly important and difficult trial, they held it in the dark so that judge and jury would not even see the man on trial, and so would be influenced by nothing but the facts of the case.

The sixteenth-century essayist Montaigne tells a grim tale. There was a Persian judge who had given a biased verdict, and he had given it under the influence of bribery. When Cambysses, the king, discovered what had happened, he ordered the judge to be executed. Then he had the skin flayed from the dead body and preserved; and with the skin he covered the seat of the chair on which judges sat in judgment, that it might be a grim reminder to them never to allow prejudice to affect their verdicts.

Only a completely impartial person has a right to judge. It is not in human nature to be completely impartial. Only God can judge.

(3) But it was Jesus who stated the supreme reason why we should not judge others. *No one is good enough to judge another person.* Jesus drew a vivid picture showing the difficulty in trying to extract a speck of dust from someone else's eye when all the time there is a plank in our own eye. The humour of the picture would raise a laugh which would drive the lesson home.

Only the faultless have a right to look for faults in others. None of us has a right to criticize another person unless we are prepared at least to try to do the thing we criticize better. Every Saturday, the football grounds are full of people who are violent critics, and who would yet make a pretty poor show if they themselves were to descend to the arena. Every association and every church is full of people who are prepared to criticize from the body of the hall, or even from an armchair, but who would never even dream of taking office themselves. The world is full of people who claim the right to be extremely vocal in criticism and totally exempt from action.

No one has a right to criticize others without being prepared to venture in the same situation. No one is good enough to criticize others.

We have quite enough to do to rectify our own lives without seeking censoriously to rectify the lives of others. We would do well to concentrate on our own faults, and to leave the faults of others to God.

THE TRUTH AND THE HEARER

Matthew 7:6

> 'Do not give that which is holy to the dogs, and do not cast your pearls before pigs, lest they trample upon them with their feet, and turn and rend you.'

THIS is a very difficult saying of Jesus, for, on the face of it, it seems to demand an exclusiveness which is the very reverse of the Christian message. It was, in fact, a saying which was used in two ways in the early Church.

(1) It was used by the Jews, who believed that God's gifts and God's grace were for Jews alone. It was used by those

Jews who were the enemies of Paul, and who argued that a Gentile must become circumcised and accept the law and become a Jew before he could become a Christian. It was indeed a text which could be used – or misused – in the interests of Jewish exclusiveness.

(2) The early Church used this text in a special way. The early Church was under a double threat. It was under the threat which came from *outside*. The early Church was an island of Christian purity in a surrounding sea of Gentile immorality; and it was always supremely liable to be infected with the taint of the world. It was also under the threat which came from *inside*. In those early days, Christian men and women were thinking things out, and it was inevitable that there would be those whose speculations would wander into the pathways of heresy; there were those who tried to effect a compromise between Christian and pagan thought, and to arrive at some synthesis of belief which would satisfy both. If the Christian Church was to survive, it had to defend itself alike from the threat from outside and the threat from inside, or it would have become simply another of the many religions which competed within the Roman Empire.

In particular the early Church was very careful about whom it admitted to the Lord's table, and this text became associated with the Lord's table. The Lord's Supper began with the announcement: 'Holy things for holy people.' The fifth-century church historian Theodoret quotes what he says is an unwritten saying of Jesus: 'My mysteries are for myself and for my people.' *The Apostolic Constitutions* lay it down that at the beginning of the Lord's Supper the deacon shall say: 'Let none of the catechumens [that is, those still under instruction], let none of the hearers [that is, those who had come to the service because they were interested in Christianity], let none of the unbelievers, let none of the heretics, stay here.' There was a fencing of the table against all but pledged Christians. The *Didachē*, or, to give it its full name, *The Teaching of the Twelve Apostles*, which dates back to AD 100 and which is the first service order book of the Christian Church, lays it down: 'Let no one eat or drink of your Eucharist except those baptized into the name of the Lord; for, as regards this, the Lord has said, "Give not that which is holy unto dogs."' It is Tertullian's complaint that the heretics allow all kinds of people, even the pagan, into the Lord's Supper, and by so doing, 'That which is holy they will cast to the dogs, and pearls (although, to be sure, they are not real ones) to swine' (*De Praescriptione*, 41).

In all these instances, this text is used as a basis of exclusiveness. It was not that the Church was not missionary-minded; the Church in the early days was consumed with the desire to win everyone: but the Church was desperately aware of the utter necessity of maintaining the purity of the faith, lest Christianity should be gradually assimilated to, and ultimately swallowed up in, the surrounding sea of paganism.

It is easy to see the *temporary* meaning of this text; but we must try to see its *permanent* meaning as well.

REACHING THOSE WHO ARE UNFIT TO HEAR

Matthew 7:6 (*contd*)

IT is just possible that this saying of Jesus has become altered accidentally in its transmission. It is a good example of the Hebrew habit of parallelism, which we have already met (Matthew 6:10). Let us set it down in its parallel clauses:

> Do not give what is holy to dogs;
> And do not throw your pearls before swine.

With the exception of one word, the parallelism is complete. *Give* is paralleled by *throw*; *dogs* by *swine*; but *holy* is not really balanced by *pearls*. There the parallelism breaks down. It so happens that there are two Hebrew words which are very like each other, especially when we remember that Hebrew has no written vowels. The word for *holy* is *kadosh* (*K D SH*); and the Aramaic word for an *earring* is *kadasha* (*K D SH*). The consonants are exactly the same, and in primitive written Hebrew the words would look exactly the same. Still further, in the *Talmud*, 'an earring in a swine's snout' is a proverbial phrase for something which is entirely incongruous and out of place. It is by no means impossible that the original phrase ran:

> Do not give an earring to dogs;
> And do not throw your pearls before swine,

in which case the parallelism would be perfect.

If that is the real meaning of the phrase, it would simply mean that there are certain people who are not fit, not able, to receive the message which the Church is so willing to give. It would not then be a statement of exclusiveness; it would be the statement of a practical difficulty of communication which meets the preacher in every age. It is quite true that there are certain people to whom it is impossible to impart truth. Something has to happen to them before they can be taught. There is actually a Rabbinic saying: 'Even as a treasure must not be shown to everyone, so with the words of the law; one must not go deeply into them, except in the presence of suitable people.'

This is in fact a universal truth. It is not to everyone that we can talk of everything. Within a group of friends, we may sit and talk about our faith; we may allow our minds to question and adventure; we may talk about the things which puzzle and perplex; and we may allow our minds to go out on the roads of speculation. But if people with more orthodox views join the group, they might well brand us as a set of dangerous heretics; or if others joined who had a simple and unquestioning faith, that faith might well be disturbed and shaken. A medical film might well be to one person an eye-opening, valuable and salutary experience, while to another it might equally produce a reaction of offence or, worse still, of titillation.

So, there are some people who cannot receive Christian truth. It may be that their minds are shut; it may be that their minds are brutalized and that they see everything through a film of filth; it may be that they have lived a life which has obscured their ability to see the truth; it may be that it is in their nature to mock all things holy; it may be, as sometimes happens, that we and they have absolutely no common ground on which we can argue.

People can only understand what they are prepared to understand. It is not to everyone that we can lay bare the secrets of our hearts. There are always those to whom the preaching of Christ will be foolishness, and in whose minds the truth, when expressed in words, will meet an insuperable barrier.

What is to be done with these people? Are they to be abandoned as hopeless? Is the Christian message simply to be withdrawn from them? What Christian words cannot do, a Christian life can often do. People may be blind and impervious to any Christian argument in words; but they can have no answer to the demonstration of a Christian life.

Cecil Northcott in *A Modern Epiphany* tells of a discussion in a camp of young people where representatives of many nations were living together. 'One wet night the campers were discussing various ways of telling people about Christ. They turned to the girl from Africa. "Maria," they asked, "what do you do in your country?" "Oh," said Maria, "we don't have missions or give pamphlets away. We just *send* one or two Christian families to live and work in a village, and when people see what Christians are like, then they want to be Christians too."' In the end, the only all-conquering argument is the argument of a Christian life.

It is often impossible to talk to some people about Jesus Christ. Their insensitiveness, their moral blindness, their intellectual pride, their cynical mockery and the distorted view make them impervious to words about Christ. But it is always possible to show Christ to others; and the weakness of the Church lies not in the lack of Christian arguments but in the lack of Christian lives.

THE CHARTER OF PRAYER

Matthew 7:7-11

> 'Keep on asking, and it will be given you;
> Keep on seeking, and you will find;
> Keep on knocking, and it will be opened to you.
> For everyone that asks receives;
> And he who seeks finds;
> And to him who knocks it will be opened.
> What man is there, who, if his son will ask him for bread, will give him a stone? Or, if he will ask for a fish, will he give him a serpent? If, then, you, who are grudging, know how to give good gifts to your children, how much more will your Father in heaven give good things to them that ask him?'

EVERYONE who prays is bound to want to know to what kind of God they are praying. So we want to know in what kind of atmosphere our prayers will be heard. Are we praying to a grudging God out of whom every gift has to be squeezed and coerced? Are we praying to a mocking God whose gifts may well be double-edged? Are we praying to a God whose heart is so kind that he is more ready to give than we are to ask?

Jesus came from a nation which loved prayer. The Jewish Rabbis said the loveliest things about prayer. 'God is as near to his creatures as the ear to the mouth.' 'Human beings can hardly hear two people talking at once, but God, if all the world calls to him at the one time, hears their cry.' 'A man is annoyed by being worried by the requests of his friends, but with God, all the time a man puts his needs and requests before him, God loves him all the more.' Jesus had been brought up to love prayer; and in this passage he gives us the Christian charter of prayer.

Jesus' argument is very simple. One of the Jewish Rabbis asked: 'Is there a man who ever hates his son?' Jesus' argument is that no father ever refused the request of his son; and God the great Father will never refuse the requests of his children.

Jesus' examples are carefully chosen. He takes three examples, for Luke adds a third to the two Matthew gives. If a son asks for bread, will his father give him a stone? If a son asks for a fish, will his father give him a serpent? If a son asks for an egg, will his father give him a scorpion? (Luke 11:12). The point is that in each case the two things cited bear a close resemblance.

The little, round, limestone stones on the seashore were exactly the shape and the colour of little loaves. If a child asks for bread, will a parent mock that child by offering a stone, which looks like bread but which is impossible to eat?

If a child asks for a fish, will a parent give that child a serpent? Almost certainly, the *serpent* is an *eel*. According to the Jewish food laws, an eel could not be eaten, because an eel was an unclean fish. 'Everything in the waters that does not have fins and scales is detestable to you' (Leviticus 11:12). That regulation ruled out the eel as an article of diet. If a child asks for a fish, will a parent indeed give that child a fish, but a fish which it is forbidden to eat, and which is useless to eat? Would a parent mock a child's hunger like that?

If the child asks for an egg, will the parent give that child a scorpion? The scorpion is a dangerous little animal. In action it is rather like a small lobster, with claws with which it clutches its victim. Its sting is in its tail, and it brings its tail up over its back to strike its victim. The sting can be exceedingly painful, and sometimes even fatal. When the scorpion is at rest, its claws and tail are folded in; and there is a pale kind of scorpion, which, when folded up, would look exactly like an egg. If a child asks for an egg, will a parent mock that child by offering that child a stinging scorpion?

God will never refuse our prayers; and God will never mock our prayers. The Greeks had their stories about the gods who answered people's prayers, but the answer was an answer with a barb in it, a double-edged gift. Aurora, the goddess of the dawn, fell in love with Tithonus, a mortal youth, so the Greek story ran. Zeus, the king of the gods, offered her any gift that she might choose for her mortal lover. Aurora very naturally chose that Tithonus might live forever, but she had forgotten to ask that Tithonus might remain forever young; and so Tithonus grew older and older and older, and could never die, and the gift became a curse.

There is a lesson here: God will always answer our prayers; *but he will answer them in his way*, and his way will be the way of perfect wisdom and of perfect love. Often, if he answered our prayers as we at the moment desired, it would be the worst thing possible for us, for in our ignorance we often ask for gifts which would be our ruin. This saying of Jesus tells us not only that God will answer, but also that God will answer in wisdom and in love.

Although this is the charter of prayer, it lays certain obligations upon us. In Greek, there are two kinds of imperative: there is the *aorist* imperative, which issues one definite command. 'Shut the door behind you' would be an *aorist* imperative. There is the *present* imperative, which issues a command that a person should always do something or should go on doing something. 'Always shut doors behind you' would be a present imperative. The imperatives here are *present* imperatives; therefore Jesus is saying: 'Go on asking; go on seeking; go on knocking.' He is telling us to persist in prayer; he is telling us never to be discouraged in prayer. Clearly, therein lies the test of our sincerity. Do we really want a thing? Is a thing such that we can bring it repeatedly into the presence of God, for the biggest test of any desire is: can I pray about it?

Jesus here lays down the twin facts that God will always answer our prayers *in his way*, in wisdom and in love; and that we must bring to God an undiscouraged life of prayer, which tests the rightness of the things we pray for, and which tests our own sincerity in asking for them.

THE EVEREST OF ETHICS

Matthew 7:12

> 'So, then, all the things which you wish that men should do to you, so do you too do to them; for this is the law and the prophets.'

THIS is probably the most universally famous thing that Jesus ever said. With this commandment, the Sermon on the Mount reaches its summit. This saying of Jesus has been called 'the capstone of the whole discourse'. It is the topmost peak of social ethics, and the Everest of all ethical teaching.

It is possible to quote Rabbinic parallels for almost everything that Jesus said in the Sermon on the Mount; but there is no real parallel to this saying. This is something which had never been said before. It is new teaching, and a new view of life and of life's obligations.

It is not difficult to find many parallels to this saying in its negative form. As we have seen, there were two most famous Jewish teachers. There was Shammai, who was famous for his stern and rigid austerity; and there was Hillel, who was famous for his sweet graciousness. The Jews had a story like this: 'A pagan came to Shammai and said, "I am prepared to be received as a proselyte [convert] on the condition that you teach me the whole law while I am standing on one leg." Shammai drove him away with a foot-rule which he had in his hand. He went to Hillel, who received him as a proselyte. He said to him, "*What is hateful to yourself, do to no other*; that is the whole law, and the rest is commentary. Go and learn."' There is the Golden Rule in its negative form.

In the Book of Tobit, there is a passage in which the aged Tobias teaches his son all that is necessary for life. One of his maxims is: 'What you hate, do not do to anyone' (Tobit 4:15).

There is a Jewish work called *The Letter of Aristeas*, which purports to be an account of the Jewish scholars who went to Alexandria to translate the Hebrew Scriptures into Greek, and who produced the Septuagint. The Egyptian king gave them a banquet at which he asked them certain difficult questions. 'What is the teaching of wisdom?' he asked. A Jewish scholar answered: 'As you wish that no evil should befall you, but to be a partaker of all good things, so you should act on the same principle towards your subjects and offenders, and you should mildly admonish the noble and the good. For God draws all men unto himself by his benignity' (*The Letter of Aristeas*, 207).

Rabbi Eliezer came nearer to Jesus' way of putting it when he said: 'Let the honour of thy friend be as dear unto thee as thine own.' The psalmist again had the negative form when he said that only those who do no evil to their friends can approach God (Psalm 15:3).

It is not difficult to find this rule in Jewish teaching in its *negative* form, but there is no parallel to the *positive* form in which Jesus put it.

The same is true of the teaching of other religions. The negative form is one of the basic principles of Confucius. Tsze-Kung asked him: 'Is there one word which may serve as a rule of practice for all one's life?' Confucius said: 'Is not *reciprocity* such a word? What you do not want done to yourself, do not do to others.'

There are certain beautiful lines in the Buddhist *Hymns of the Faith* which come very near the Christian teaching:

> All men tremble at the rod, all men fear death;
> Putting oneself in the place of others, kill not, nor cause
>   to kill.
> All men tremble at the rod, unto all men life is dear;
> Doing as one would be done by, kill not nor cause to
>   kill.

With the Greeks and the Romans, it is the same. The orator Isocrates tells how King Nicocles advised his subordinate officials: 'Do not do to others the things which make you angry when you experience them at the hands of other people.' The philosopher Epictetus condemned slavery on the principle: 'What you avoid suffering yourselves, seek not to inflict upon others.' The Stoics had as one of their basic maxims: 'What you do not wish to be done to you, do not do to anyone else.' And it is told that the emperor Alexander Severus had that sentence engraved upon the walls of his palace so that he might never forget it as a rule of life.

In its negative form, this rule is in fact the basis of all ethical teaching; but no one but Jesus ever put it in its positive form. Many voices had said: 'Do not do to others what you would not have them do to you,' but no voice had ever said: 'Do to others what you would have them do to you.'

THE GOLDEN RULE OF JESUS

Matthew 7:12 (*contd*)

LET us see just how the positive form of the Golden Rule differs from the negative form; and let us see just how much more Jesus was demanding than any teacher had ever demanded before.

When this rule is put in its negative form, when we are told that we must refrain from doing to others that which we would not wish them to do to us, it is not an essentially religious rule at all. It is simply a common-sense statement without which no social intercourse at all would be possible. Sir Thomas Browne, the seventeenth-century author and physician, once said: 'We are beholden to every man we meet that he doth not kill us.' In a sense that is true, but if we could not assume that the conduct and the behaviour of other people to us would conform to the accepted standards of civilized life, then life would be intolerable. The negative form of the Golden Rule is not in any sense an extra; it is something without which life could not go on at all.

Further, the negative form of the rule involves nothing more than *not* doing certain things; it means refraining from certain actions. It is never very difficult *not* to do things. That we must not do injury to other people is not a specially religious principle; it is, rather, a legal principle. It is the kind of principle that could well be kept by those who have no belief and no interest in religion at all. Such people might always refrain from doing any injury to anyone else, and yet be quite useless citizens to their neighbours. They could satisfy the negative form of the rule by simple inaction; if they consistently did nothing, they would never break the rule. And a goodness which consists in doing nothing would be a contradiction of everything that Christian goodness means.

When this rule is put positively, when we are told that we must actively do to others what we would have them do to us, a new principle enters into life, and a new attitude to others. It is one thing to say: 'I must not injure people; I must not do to them what I would object to their doing to me.' That, the law can compel us to do. It is quite another thing to say: 'I must go out of my way to help other people and to be kind to them, as I would wish them to help and to be kind to me.' That, only love can compel us to do. The attitude which says: 'I must do no harm to people' is quite different from the attitude which says: 'I must do my best to help people.'

To take a very simple analogy – if we own a car, the law can compel us to drive it in such a way that we do not injure anyone else on the road, but no law can compel us to stop and give a lift to someone who is obviously in need of help. It is quite a simple thing to refrain from hurting and injuring people; it is not so very difficult to respect their principles and their feelings; it is a far harder thing to make it the chosen and deliberate policy of life to go out of our way to be as kind to them as we would wish them to be to us.

And yet it is just that new attitude which makes life beautiful. Jane Stoddart quotes an incident from the life of the nineteenth-century statesman W. H. Smith. 'When Smith was at the War Office, his private secretary, Mr Fleetwood Wilson, noticed that at the end of a week's work, when his chief was preparing to leave for Greenlands on a Saturday afternoon, he used to pack a despatch-box with the papers he required to take with him, and carry it himself on his journey. Mr Wilson remarked that Mr Smith would save himself much trouble if he did as was the practice of other ministers – leave the papers to be put in an office "pouch" and sent by post. Mr Smith looked rather ashamed for a moment, and then, looking up at his secretary, said: "Well, my dear Wilson, the fact is this: our postman who brings the letters from Henley has plenty to carry. I watched him one morning coming up the approach with my heavy pouch in addition to his usual load, and I determined to save him as much as I could."' An action like that shows a certain attitude to others. It is the attitude which believes that we should treat one another not as the law allows, but as love demands.

It is perfectly possible for people to observe the negative form of the Golden Rule. They could without very serious difficulty so discipline their lives that they would not do to others what they did not wish others to do to them; but the only people who can even begin to satisfy the positive form of the rule are those men and women who have the love of Christ within their hearts. They will try to forgive as they would wish to be forgiven, to help as they would wish to be helped, to praise as they would wish to be praised, to understand as they would wish to be understood. They will never seek to avoid doing things; they will always look for things to do. Clearly this will make life much more complicated; clearly they will have much less time to spend on their own desires and their own activities, for time and time again they will have to stop what they are doing to help someone else. It will be a principle which will dominate their lives at home, in the factory, on the bus, in the office, in the street, on the train, in their leisure activities – everywhere. They can never do it until self withers and dies within their hearts. To obey this commandment, we must become new men and women with a new centre to our lives; and if the world was composed of people who sought to obey this rule, it would be a new world.

LIFE AT THE CROSSROADS

Matthew 7:13–14

> 'Go in through the narrow gate; for wide is the gate and broad is the road which leads to ruin, and there are many who go in through it. Narrow is the gate and hard is the way that leads to life, and those who find it are few.'

THERE is always a certain dramatic quality about life, for it has been said that all life is focused on our position at the crossroads. In every action of life, we are confronted with a choice; and we can never evade the choice, because we can never stand still. We must always take one way or the other. Because of that, it has always been one of the supreme functions of the great men and women of history that they should confront people with that inevitable choice. As the end drew near, Moses spoke to the people: 'See, I have set before you today life and prosperity, and death and adversity . . . Choose life so that you and your descendants may live' (Deuteronomy 30:15, 19). When Joshua was laying down the leadership of the nation at the end of his life, he presented them with the same choice: 'Choose this day whom you will serve' (Joshua 24:15). Jeremiah heard the voice of God saying to him: 'And to this people you shall say: Thus says the Lord: See, I am setting before you the way of life and the way of death' (Jeremiah 21:8). In 'The Ways', John Oxenham wrote:

> To every man there openeth
> A way and ways and a way;
> And the high soul climbs the high way,
> And the low soul gropes the low;
> And in between on the misty flats
> The rest drift to and fro;
> But to every man there openeth
> A high way and a low;
> And every man decideth
> The way his soul shall go.

That is the choice with which Jesus is confronting us in this passage. There is a broad and an easy way, and there are many who take it; but the end of it is ruin. There is a narrow and a hard way, and there are few who take it; but the end of it is life. Cebes, the disciple of Socrates, writes in the *Tabula*: 'Dost thou see a little door, and a way in front of the door, which is not much crowded, but the travellers are few? That is the way that leadeth to true instruction.' Let us examine the difference between the two ways.

(1) It is the difference between *the hard and the easy way*. There is never any easy way to greatness; greatness is always the product of toil. Hesiod, the old Greek poet, writes: 'Wickedness can be had in abundance easily; smooth is the road, and very nigh she dwells; but in front of virtue the gods immortal have put sweat.' Epicharmus said: 'The gods demand of us toil as the price of all good things.' 'Knave,' he warns, 'yearn not for the soft things, lest thou earn the hard.'

Once the eighteenth-century Irish statesman Edmund Burke made a great speech in the House of Commons. Afterwards, his brother Richard Burke was observed deep in thought. He was asked what he was thinking about, and answered: 'I have been wondering how it has come about that Ned has contrived to monopolize all the talents of our family; but then again I remember that, when we were at play, he was always at work.' Even when a thing is done with an appearance of ease, that ease is the product of unremitting toil. The skill of the concert pianist or the champion golfer did not come without sweat. There has never been any other way to greatness than the way of toil, and anything else which promises such a way is a delusion and a snare.

(2) It is the difference between *the long and the short way*. Very rarely, something may emerge complete and perfect in a flash, but far oftener greatness is the result of long labour and constant attention to detail. Horace, the Latin poet, in *The Art of Poetry*, advises Piso, when he has written something, to keep it beside him for nine years before he publishes it. He tells how a pupil used to take exercises to Quintilius, the famous critic. Quintilius would say: 'Scratch it out; the work has been badly turned, send it back to the fire and the anvil.' Virgil's *Aeneid* occupied the last ten years of the poet's life; and as he was dying, he would have destroyed it because he thought it so imperfect, if his friends had not stopped him. Plato's *Republic* begins with a simple sentence: 'I went down to the Piraeus yesterday with Glaucon, the son of Ariston, that I might offer up prayer to the goddess.' On Plato's own manuscript, in his own handwriting, there were no fewer than thirteen different versions of that opening sentence. The master writer had laboured at arrangement after arrangement that he might get the cadences exactly right. Thomas Gray's 'Elegy written in a Country Churchyard' is one of the immortal poems. It was begun in the summer of 1742; it was finally privately circulated on 12th June 1750.

Its dignified and precise perfection of style had taken eight years to produce. No one ever arrived at a masterpiece by a short cut. In this world, we are constantly faced with the short way, which promises immediate results, and the long way, of which the results are in the far distance. But the lasting things never come quickly; the long way is the best way in the end.

(3) It is the difference between *the disciplined and the undisciplined way*. Nothing was ever achieved without discipline; and many athletes and many men and women in other fields have been ruined because they abandoned discipline and let themselves go. The poet Samuel Taylor Coleridge is the supreme tragedy of indiscipline. Never did so great a mind produce so little. He left Cambridge University to join the army; he left the army because, in spite of all his erudition, he could not rub down a horse; he returned to Oxford and left without a degree. He began a paper called *The Watchman*, which lived for ten issues and then died. It has been said of him: 'He lost himself in visions of work to be done, that always remained to be done. Coleridge had every poetic gift but one – the gift of sustained and concentrated effort.' In his head and in his mind he had all kinds of books, as he said himself, 'completed save for transcription'. 'I am on the eve', he says, 'of sending to the press two octavo [the book's form] volumes.' But the books were never composed outside Coleridge's mind, because he would not face the discipline of sitting down to write them out. No one ever reached any eminence, and no one having reached it ever maintained it, without discipline.

(4) It is the difference between *the thoughtful and the thoughtless way*. Here we come to the heart of the matter. None of us would ever take the easy, the short, the undisciplined way, if we only thought. Everything in this world has two

aspects – how it looks at the moment, and how it will look in the time to come. The easy way may look very inviting at the moment, and the hard way may look very daunting. The only way to get our values right is to see not the beginning but the end of the way, to see things not in the light of time but in the light of eternity.

THE FALSE PROPHETS

Matthew 7:15–20

> 'Beware of false prophets, who come to you in sheep's clothing, but who within are rapacious wolves. You will recognize them from their fruits. Surely men do not gather grapes from thorns, and figs from thistles? So every good tree produces fine fruit; but every rotten tree produces bad fruit. A good tree cannot produce bad fruit, nor can a rotten tree produce fine fruit. Every tree which does not produce fine fruit is cut down and thrown into the fire. So then you will recognize them from their fruits.'

ALMOST every phrase and word in this section would ring an answering bell in the minds of the Jews who heard it for the first time.

The Jews knew all about *false prophets*. Jeremiah, for instance, had his conflict with the prophets who said: '"Peace, peace", when there is no peace' (Jeremiah 6:14, 8:11). *Wolves* was the very name by which false rulers and false prophets were called. In the bad days, Ezekiel had said: 'Its officials within it are like wolves tearing the prey, shedding blood, destroying lives to get dishonest gain' (Ezekiel 22:27). Zephaniah drew a grim picture of the state of things in Israel, when 'The officials within it are roaring lions; its judges are evening wolves that leave nothing until the morning. Its prophets are reckless, faithless persons' (Zephaniah 3:3–4). When Paul was warning the elders of Ephesus of dangers to come, as he took a last farewell of them, he said: 'Savage wolves will come in among you, not sparing the flock' (Acts 20:29). Jesus said that he was sending out his disciples as sheep in the midst of wolves (Matthew 10:16); and he told of the good shepherd who protected the flock from the wolves with his life (John 10:12). Here indeed was a picture which everyone could recognize and understand.

He said that the false prophets were like wolves in *sheep's clothing*. When the shepherd watched his flocks upon the hillside, his garment was a sheepskin, worn with the skin outside and the fleece inside. But a man might wear a shepherd's dress and still not be a shepherd. The prophets had acquired a conventional dress. Elijah had a mantle (1 Kings 19:13, 19), and that mantle had been a hairy cloak (2 Kings 1:8). That sheepskin mantle had become the uniform of the prophets, just as the Greek philosophers had worn the philosopher's robe. It was by that mantle that the prophet could be distinguished from other men. But sometimes that form of dress was worn by those who had no right to it, for Zechariah in his picture of the great days to come says: 'They will not put on a hairy mantle in order to deceive' (Zechariah 13:4). There were those who wore a prophet's cloak but who lived anything but a prophet's life.

There were false prophets in the ancient days, but there were also false prophets in New Testament times. Matthew was written about AD 85, and at that time prophets were still an institution in the Church. They had no fixed abode, and had given up everything to wander throughout the country, bringing to the churches a message which they believed to come directly from God.

At their best, the prophets were the inspiration of the Church, for they had abandoned everything to serve God and the Church of God. But the office of prophet was singularly liable to abuse. There were some who used it to gain prestige and to impose on the generosity of local congregations, and so live a life of comfortable and even pampered idleness. The *Didachē* is the first order book of the Christian Church; it dates to about AD 100; and its regulations concerning these wandering prophets are very illuminating. A true prophet was to be held in the highest honour; he was to be welcomed; his word must never be disregarded, and his freedom must never be curtailed; but 'He shall remain one day, and, if necessary, another day also; but if he remain three days, he is a false prophet.' He must never ask for anything but bread. 'If he asks for money, he is a false prophet.' Prophets all claim to speak in the Spirit, but there is one acid test: 'By their characters a true and a false prophet shall be known.' 'Every prophet that teacheth the truth, if he do not what he teacheth, is a false prophet.' If a prophet, claiming to speak in the Spirit, orders a table and a meal to be set before him, he is a false prophet. 'Whosoever shall say in the Spirit: Give me money or any other things, ye shall not hear him; but if he tell you to give in the matter of others who have need, let no one judge him.' If a wanderer comes to a congregation, and wishes to settle there, if he has a trade, 'let him work and eat'. If he has no trade, 'consider in your wisdom how he may not live with you as a Christian in idleness . . . But if he will not do this, he is a trafficker in Christ. Beware of such' (*Didachē*, chapters 11–12).

Past history and present events made the words of Jesus meaningful to those who heard them for the first time, and to those to whom Matthew transmitted them.

KNOWN BY THEIR FRUITS

Matthew 7:15–20 (*contd*)

THE Jews, the Greeks and the Romans all used the idea that a tree is to be judged by its fruits. 'Like root, like fruit,' ran the proverb. Epictetus was later to say: 'How can a vine grow not like a vine but like an olive, or, how can an olive grow not like an olive but like a vine?' (Epictetus, *Discourses*, 2:20). Seneca declared that good cannot grow from evil any more than a fig tree can from an olive.

But there is more in this than meets the eye. 'Are grapes gathered from thorns?' asked Jesus. There was a certain thorn, the buckthorn, which had little black berries which closely resembled little grapes. 'Or figs from thistles?' There was a certain thistle which had a flower which, at least at a distance, might well be taken for a fig.

The point is real, and relevant, and salutary. There may be a superficial resemblance between the true and the false prophet. The false prophet may wear the right clothes and use the right language; but you cannot sustain life with the berries of a buckthorn or the flowers of a thistle; and the life of the soul can never be sustained with the food which a false prophet offers. The real test of any teaching is: does it strengthen people to bear the burdens of life, and to walk in the way wherein they ought to go?

Let us then look at the false prophets and see their characteristics. If the way is difficult and the gate is so narrow that it is hard to find, then we must be very careful to get ourselves teachers who will help us to find it, and not teachers who will lure us away from it.

The basic fault of false prophets is *self-interest*. True shepherds care for the flock more than they care for their own lives; wolves care for nothing but to satisfy their own gluttony and their own greed. False prophets are in the business of teaching not for what they can give to others, but for what they can get out of it for themselves.

The Jews were alive to this danger. The Rabbis were the Jewish teachers, but it was one of the most important principles of Jewish law that a Rabbi must have a trade by which he earned his living, and must on no account accept any payment for teaching. Rabbi Zadok said: 'Make the knowledge of the law neither a crown wherewith to make a show, nor a spade wherewith to dig.' Rabbi Hillel said: 'He who uses the crown of the law for external aims fades away.' The Jews knew all about teachers who used their teaching self-interestedly for no other reason than to make a profit for themselves. There are three ways in which teachers can be dominated by self-interest.

(1) They may teach solely for *gain*. It is told that there was trouble in the Church in the Scottish town of Ecclefechan, where Thomas Carlyle's father was an elder. It was a dispute between the congregation and the minister on a matter of money and of salary. When much had been said on both sides, Carlyle's father rose and uttered one devastating sentence: 'Give the hireling his wages, and let him go.' No one can live on nothing, and few can do their best work when the pressure of material things is too fiercely on them; but the great privilege of teaching is not the pay it offers but the thrill of opening the minds of children, and young people, and men and women to the truth.

(2) They may teach solely for *prestige*. They may teach in order to help others, or they may teach to show how clever they are. The theologian James Denney once said a savage thing: 'No man can at one and the same time prove that he is clever and that Christ is wonderful.' Prestige is the last thing that the great teachers desire. J. P. Struthers was a saint of God.

He spent all his life in the service of the little Reformed Presbyterian Church when he could have occupied any pulpit in Britain. People loved him, and the better they knew him the more they loved him. Two men were talking of him. One man knew all that Struthers had done, but did not know Struthers personally. Remembering Struthers' saintly ministry, he said: 'Struthers will have a front seat in the kingdom of heaven.' The other had known Struthers personally, and his answer was: 'Struthers would be miserable in a front seat anywhere.' There are some teachers and preachers who use their message as a setting for themselves. False prophets are interested in self-display; true prophets desire self-obliteration.

(3) They may teach solely *to transmit their own ideas*. False prophets are out to disseminate their own versions of the truth; true prophets are out to proclaim God's truth. It is quite true that we must think all things out for ourselves; but it was said of John Brown, the eighteenth-century minister of the Scottish town of Haddington, that when he preached, repeatedly he used to pause 'as if listening for a voice'. True prophets listen to God before they speak. They never forget that they are nothing more than voices to speak for God and channels through which God's grace can come to men and women. It is the duty of every teacher and preacher to bring to men and women not their private ideas of the truth, but the truth as it is in Jesus Christ.

THE FRUITS OF FALSENESS

Matthew 7:15-20 (*contd*)

THIS passage has much to say about the evil fruits of the false prophets. What are the false effects, the evil fruits, which a false prophet may produce?

(1) Teaching is false if it produces *a religion which consists solely or mainly in the observance of externals*. That is what was wrong with the scribes and Pharisees. To them, religion consisted in the observance of the ceremonial law. If people went through the correct procedure of handwashing, if on the Sabbath they never carried anything weighing more than two figs, if they never walked on the Sabbath further than the prescribed distance, if they were meticulous in giving tithes of everything down to the herbs of the kitchen garden, then they were considered to be good.

It is easy to confuse religion with religious practices. It is possible – and indeed not uncommon – to teach that religion consists in going to church, observing the Lord's Day, fulfilling one's financial obligations to the church and reading one's Bible. A person might do all these things and be far from being a Christian, for Christianity is an attitude of the heart to God and to one another.

(2) Teaching is false if it produces *a religion which consists in prohibitions*. Any religion which is based on a series of 'you shall nots' is a false religion. There have been some teachers who have said to those who have set out on the Christian way: 'From now on you will no longer go to the cinema; from now on you will no longer dance; from now on you will no longer smoke or use make-up; from now on you will no longer read a novel or a Sunday newspaper; from now on you will never enter a theatre.'

If we could become Christians simply by abstaining from doing things, Christianity would be a much easier religion than it is. But the whole essence of Christianity is that it does not consist in *not* doing things; it consists in doing things. A negative Christianity on our part can never answer the positive love of God.

(3) Teaching is false if it produces *an easy religion*. There were false teachers in the days of Paul, an echo of whose teaching we can hear in Romans 6. They said to Paul: 'You believe that God's grace is the biggest thing in the universe?' 'Yes.' 'You believe that God's grace is wide enough to cover every sin?' 'Yes.' 'Well then, if that is so, let us go on sinning to our hearts' content. God will forgive. And, after all, our sin is simply giving God's wonderful grace an opportunity to operate.' A religion like that is a travesty of religion because it is an insult to the love of God.

Any teaching which takes the iron out of religion, any teaching which takes the cross out of Christianity, any teaching which eliminates the threat from the voice of Christ, any teaching which pushes judgment into the background and makes people think lightly of sin, is false teaching.

(4) Teaching is false if it *divorces religion and life*. Any teaching which removes the Christian from the life and activity of the world is false. That was the mistake the monks and the hermits made. It was their belief that to live the Christian life they must retire to a desert or to a monastery, that they must cut themselves off from the engrossing and tempting life of the world, that they could only be truly Christian by ceasing to live in the world. Jesus said, as he prayed for his disciples: 'I am not asking you to take them out of the world, but I ask you to protect them from the evil one' (John 17:15). There was one particular instance of a journalist who found it hard to maintain her Christian principles in the life of a daily newspaper, and who left it to take up work on a purely religious journal.

No one can be a good soldier by running away, and the Christian is the soldier of Christ. How shall the leaven ever work if the leaven refuses to be inserted into the mass? What is witness worth unless it is witness to those who do not believe? Any teaching which encourages people to take what the President of Princeton Theological Seminary, John Mackay, called 'the balcony view of life' is wrong. Christians are not spectators from the balcony; they are involved in the warfare of life.

(5) Teaching is false if it produces *a religion which is arrogant and separatist*. Any teaching which encourages people to withdraw into a narrow sect, and to regard the rest of the world as sinners, is false teaching. The function of religion is not to erect middle walls of partition but to tear them down. It is the dream of Jesus Christ that there shall be one flock and one shepherd (John 10:16). Exclusiveness is not a religious quality; it is an irreligious quality. Harry Emerson Fosdick, the American Baptist minister, quotes four lines of doggerel:

> We are God's chosen few,
>> All others will be damned;
> There is no room in heaven for you;
>> We can't have heaven crammed.

Religion is meant to bring people closer together, not to drive them apart. Religion is meant to gather people into one family, not to split them up into hostile groups. The teaching which declares that any church or any sect has a monopoly of the grace of God is false teaching, for Christ is not the Christ who divides, he is the Christ who unites.

ON FALSE PRETENCES

Matthew 7:21–3

'Not everyone that says to me: "Lord, Lord" will enter into the kingdom of heaven, but he who does the will of

> my father who is in heaven. Many will say to me on
> that day: "Lord, Lord, did we not prophesy in your
> name, and in your name did we not cast out devils, and
> in your name did we not do many deeds of power?"
> Then will I publicly announce to them: "I never knew
> you. Depart from me you doers of iniquity."'

THERE is an apparently surprising feature about this passage. Jesus is quite ready to concede that many of the false prophets will do and say wonderful and impressive things.

We must remember what the ancient world was like. Miracles were common events. The frequency of miracles came from the ancient idea of illness. In the ancient world, all illness was held to be the work of demons. People became ill because a demon had succeeded in exercising some malign influence over them or in winning a way into some part of their bodies. Cures were therefore brought about by exorcism. The result of all this was that a great deal of illness was what we would call psychological, as were a great many cures. If people succeeded in convincing – or deluding – themselves into a belief that demons were in them or had them in their power, they would undoubtedly be ill. And if someone could convince them that the hold of the demons was broken, then quite certainly they would be cured.

The leaders of the Church never denied pagan miracles. In answer to the miracles of Christ, the Roman philosopher Celsus quoted the miracles attributed to Aesculapius and Apollo. Writing in the third century, the biblical scholar Origen, who met his arguments, did not for a moment deny these miracles. He simply answered: 'Such curative power is of itself neither good nor bad, but within the reach of godless as well as of honest people' (Origen, *Against Celsus*, 3:22). Even in the New Testament, we read of Jewish exorcists who added the name of Jesus to their repertoire and who banished devils by its aid (Acts 19:13). There was many an impostor who rendered lip-service to Jesus Christ and who used his name to produce wonderful effects on demon-possessed people. What Jesus is saying is that if anyone uses his name under false pretences, the day of reckoning will come. The real motives will be exposed, and that person will be banished from the presence of God.

There are two great permanent truths within this passage. There is only one way in which people's sincerity can be proved, and that is by their practice. Fine words can never be a substitute for fine deeds. There is only one proof of love, and that proof is obedience. There is no point in saying that we love a person and then doing things which break that person's heart. When we were young, maybe we used sometimes to say to our mothers: 'Mother, I love you.' And maybe our mothers sometimes smiled a little wistfully and said: 'I wish you would show it a little more in the way you behave.' So often we confess God with our lips and deny him with our lives. It is not difficult to recite a creed, but it is difficult to live the Christian life. Faith without practice is a contradiction in terms, and love without obedience is an impossibility.

At the back of this passage is the idea of judgment. All through it there runs the certainty that the day of reckoning comes. Some people may succeed over a period in maintaining the pretences and the disguises, but there comes a day when the pretences are shown for what they are, and the disguises are stripped away. We may deceive others with our words, but we cannot deceive God. 'You discern my thoughts from far away,' said the psalmist (Psalm 139:2). No one can ultimately deceive the God who sees the heart.

THE ONLY TRUE FOUNDATION

Matthew 7:24-7

'So, then, everyone who hears these words of mine and does them will be likened to a wise man who built his house upon the rock. And the rain came down, and the rivers swelled, and the wind blew, and fell upon that house, and it did not fall, for it was founded upon the rock. And everyone who hears these words of mine and does not do them will be likened to a foolish man who built his house upon the sand. And the rain came down, and the rivers swelled, and the winds blew and beat upon that house, and it fell; and its fall was great.'

And when Jesus had ended these words, the people were astonished at his teaching, for he was teaching them as one who had authority, and not as their scribes.

JESUS was in a double sense an expert. He was an expert in Scripture. The writer of Proverbs gave him the hint for his picture: 'When the tempest passes, the wicked are no more, but the righteous are established for ever' (Proverbs 10:25). Here is the germ of the picture which Jesus drew of the two houses and the two builders. But Jesus was also an expert in life. He was the craftsman who knew all about the building of houses, and when he spoke about the foundations of a house he knew what he was talking about. This is no illustration formed by a scholar in his study; this is the illustration of a practical man.

Nor is this a far-fetched illustration; it is a story of the kind of thing which could well happen. In Palestine, the builder must think ahead. There were many gullies which in summer were pleasant sandy hollows, but in winter became raging torrents of rushing water. A man might be looking for a house; he might find a pleasantly sheltered sandy hollow;

and he might think this a very suitable place. But, if he was a short-sighted man, he might well have built his house in the dried-up bed of a river, and when the winter came, his house would disintegrate. Even on an ordinary site, it was tempting to begin building on the smoothed-over sand and not to bother digging down to the shelf of rock below; but that way disaster lay ahead.

Only a house whose foundations are firm can withstand the storm; and only a life whose foundations are sure can stand the test. Jesus demanded two things.

(1) He demanded that men and women should *listen*. One of the great difficulties which face us today is the simple fact that people often do not know what Jesus said or what the Church teaches. In fact, the matter is worse. They often have a quite mistaken notion of what Jesus said and of what the Church teaches. It is never a matter for pride or self-congratulation to condemn either a person, or an institution, unheard – and that today is precisely what so many do. The first step to the Christian life is simply to give Jesus Christ a chance to be heard.

(2) He demanded that men and women should *do*. Knowledge only becomes relevant when it is translated into action. It would be perfectly possible to pass an examination in Christian ethics with the highest distinction, and yet not to be a Christian. Knowledge must become action; theory must become practice; theology must become life. There is little point in consulting a doctor about our health unless we are prepared to act upon the things we are told. There is little point in going to an expert unless we are prepared to act upon the advice given to us. And yet there are thousands of people who listen to the teaching of Jesus Christ every Sunday, and who have a very good knowledge of what Jesus taught, and who yet make little or no deliberate attempt to

put it into practice. If we are to be in any sense followers of Jesus, we must *hear* and *do*.

Is there any word in which *hearing* and *doing* are summed up? There is such a word, and that word is *obedience*. Jesus demands our implicit obedience. To learn to obey is the most important thing in life.

Some time ago, there was a report of the case of a sailor in the Royal Navy who was very severely punished for a breach of discipline. So severe was the punishment that in certain civilian quarters it was thought to be far too severe. A newspaper asked its readers to express their opinions about the severity of the punishment.

One who answered was a man who himself had served for years in the Royal Navy. In his view, the punishment was not too severe. He held that discipline was absolutely essential, for the purpose of discipline was to condition those in service automatically and unquestioningly to obey orders, and on such obedience their lives might well depend. He cited a case from his own experience. He was in a launch which was towing a much heavier vessel in a rough sea. The vessel was attached to the launch by a wire cable. Suddenly in the midst of the wind and the spray there came a single, insistent word of command from the officer in charge of the launch. 'Down!' he shouted. On the spot, the crew of the launch flung themselves down. Just at that moment, the wire towing-cable snapped, and the broken parts of it whipped about like a maddened steel snake. If any man had been struck by it, he would have been instantly killed. But the whole crew automatically obeyed, and no one was injured. If anyone had stopped to argue or to ask why, he would have been a dead man. Obedience saved lives.

It is such obedience that Jesus demands. It is Jesus' claim that obedience to him is the only sure foundation for life; and it is his promise that the life which is founded on obedience to him is safe, no matter what storms may come.

LOVE IN ACTION

OF all the gospel writers, Matthew is the most orderly. He never sets out his material haphazardly. If in Matthew one thing follows another in a certain sequence, there is always a reason for that sequence; and it is so here. In chapters 5–7, Matthew has given us the Sermon on the Mount. That is to say, in these chapters he has given us his account of the *words* of Jesus; and now in chapter 8 he gives us an account of the *deeds* of Jesus. Chapters 5–7 show us the divine wisdom in speech; chapter 8 shows us the divine love in action.

Chapter 8 is a chapter of miracles. Let us look at these miracles as a whole, before we proceed to deal with them in detail. In the chapter, there are seven miraculous happenings.

(1) There is the healing of the leper (verses 1–4). Here we see Jesus touching the untouchable. Lepers were banished from human society; to touch them, and even to approach them, was to break the law. Here we see the man who was kept at arm's length by everyone else wrapped around with pity and the compassion of the love of God.

(2) There is the healing of the centurion's servant (verses 5–13). The centurion was a Gentile, and therefore strict orthodox Jews would have said that he was merely fuel for the fires of hell; he was the servant of a foreign government and of an occupying power, and therefore nationalistic Jews would have said that he was a candidate for assassination and not for assistance; the servant was a slave, and a slave was no more than a living tool. Here we see the love of God

going out to help the man whom everyone hated and the slave whom everyone despised.

(3) There is the healing of Peter's wife's mother (verses 14–15). This miracle took place in a humble cottage in a humble home in Palestine. There was no publicity; there was no admiring audience; there was only Jesus and the family circle. Here we see the infinite love of the God of all the universe displaying all its power when there was none but the circle of the family to see.

(4) There was the healing of all the sick who were brought to the doors at evening time (verses 16–17). Here we see the sheer universality of the love of God in action. To Jesus, no one was ever a nuisance; he had no hours when he was on duty and hours when he was off duty. Anyone could come to him at any time and receive the willing, gracious help of the love of God.

(5) There was the reaction of the scribe (verses 18–22). On the face of it, this little section appears to be out of place in a chapter on miracles; but this is the miracle of personality. That any scribe should be moved to follow Jesus is nothing less than a miracle. Somehow this scribe had forgotten his devotion to the scribal law; somehow, although Jesus contradicted all the things to which he had dedicated his life, he saw in Jesus not an enemy but a friend, not an opponent but a master.

It must have been an instinctive reaction. The American author Negley Farson writes of his old grandfather. When Farson was a boy, he did not know his grandfather's history and all that he had done; but, he says: 'All I knew was that he made other men around him look like mongrel dogs.' That scribe saw in Jesus a splendour and a magnificence he had never encountered before. The miracle happened, and the scribe's heart ran out to Jesus Christ.

(6) There is the miracle of the calming of the storm (verses 23–7). Here we see Jesus dealing with the waves and the billows which can threaten to engulf us. As the theologian E. B. Pusey had it when his wife died, 'All through that time it was as if there was a hand beneath my chin to bear me up.' Here is the love of God bringing peace and serenity into tumult and confusion.

(7) There is the healing of the two demon-possessed men (verses 28–34). In the ancient world, people believed that all illness was due to the action of devils. Here we see the power of God dealing with the power of the devil; here we see God's goodness invading earth's evil, God's love going out against evil's malignancy and malevolence. Here we see the goodness and the love which save us triumphantly overcoming the evil and the hatred which ruin us.

THE LIVING DEATH

Matthew 8:1–4

> When Jesus had come down from the mountain, great crowds followed him; and, look you, a leper came to him, and remained kneeling before him. 'Lord,' he said, 'you can cleanse me, if you are willing to do so.' Jesus stretched out his hand and touched him. 'I am willing,' he said, 'be cleansed.' And immediately his leprosy was cleansed. And Jesus said to him: 'See that you tell no one; but go, show yourself to the priest, and bring the gift which Moses ordered, so that they will be convinced that you are cured.'

IN the ancient world, leprosy was the most terrible of all diseases. In an article on disease in Palestine, E. W. Masterman writes: 'No other disease reduces a human being for so many years to so hideous a wreck.'

It might begin with little nodules which go on to ulcerate. The ulcers develop a foul discharge; the eyebrows fall out; the eyes become staring; the vocal chords become ulcerated, the voice becomes hoarse and the breath wheezes. The hands and feet always ulcerate. Slowly, the sufferer becomes a mass of ulcerated growths. The average course of that kind of leprosy is nine years, and it ends in mental decay, coma and ultimately death.

Leprosy might begin with the loss of all sensation in some part of the body; the nerve trunks are affected; the muscles waste away; the tendons contract until the hands are like claws. There follows ulceration of the hands and feet. Then comes the progressive loss of fingers and toes, until in the end a whole hand or a whole foot may drop off. The duration of that kind of leprosy is anything from twenty to thirty years. It is a kind of terrible progressive death in which the sufferer dies by inches.

The physical condition of the leper was terrible; but there was something which made it worse. The Jewish historian Josephus tells us that lepers were treated 'as if they were, in effect, dead men'. Immediately leprosy was diagnosed, the leper was absolutely and completely banished from human society. 'He shall remain unclean as long as he has the disease; he is unclean. He shall live alone; his dwelling shall be outside the camp' (Leviticus 13:46). Lepers had to go with torn clothes and dishevelled hair, with a covering upon the upper lip, and, as they went, they had to cry: 'Unclean, unclean' (Leviticus 13:45). In the middle ages, if anyone contracted leprosy, the priest donned his stole and took his crucifix, and brought the leper into the church. He then read the burial service over the person, who for all human purposes was dead.

In Palestine in the time of Jesus, lepers were barred from Jerusalem and from all walled towns. In the synagogue, there was provided for them a little isolated chamber, ten feet high and six feet wide, called the *Mechitsah*. The law enumerated sixty-one different contacts which could defile, and the defilement involved in contact with a leper was second only to the defilement involved in contact with a dead body. A leper did not even have to enter a house, but need only look in across the threshold for that house to become unclean even to the roof beams. Even in an open place it was illegal to greet a leper. No one might come nearer to a leper than four cubits – a cubit is eighteen inches. If the wind was blowing towards a person from a leper, the leper must stand at least 100 cubits away. One Rabbi would not even eat an egg bought in a street where a leper had passed by. Another Rabbi actually boasted that he flung stones at lepers to keep them away. Other Rabbis hid themselves, or took to their heels, at the sight of a leper even in the distance.

There never has been any disease which so separated one human being from another as leprosy did. And it was just such a man whom Jesus touched. To a Jew, there would be no more amazing sentence in the New Testament than the simple statement: 'And Jesus stretched out his hand and touched the leper.'

COMPASSION BEYOND THE LAW

Matthew 8:1–4 (*contd*)

IN this story, we must note two things – the leper's *approach* and Jesus' *response*. In the leper's approach, there were three elements.

(1) The leper came with *confidence*. He had no doubt that, if Jesus willed, Jesus could make him clean.

Lepers would never have come near an orthodox scribe or Rabbi; they knew too well that they would be stoned away; but this man came to Jesus. He had perfect confidence in Jesus' willingness to welcome him though anyone else would have driven him away. No one need ever feel too unclean to come to Jesus Christ.

He had perfect confidence in Jesus' power. Leprosy was the one disease for which there was no prescribed Rabbinic remedy. But this man was sure that Jesus could do what no one else could do. No one need ever feel incurable in body or unforgivable in soul while Jesus Christ exists.

(2) The leper came with *humility*. He did not demand healing; he only said: '*If you will*, you can cleanse me.' It was as if he said: 'I know I don't matter; I know that others will flee from me and will have nothing to do with me; I know that I have no claim on you; but perhaps in your divine condescension you will give your power even to such as I am.' It is the humble heart which is conscious of nothing but its need that finds its way to Christ.

(3) The leper came with *reverence*. The Authorized Version says that he *worshipped* Jesus. The Greek verb is *proskunein*, and that word is never used of anything but *worship of the gods*; it always describes a person's feeling and action in the presence of the divine. That leper could never have told anyone what he thought Jesus was; but he knew that in the presence of Jesus he was in the presence of God. We do not need to put this into theological or philosophical terms; it is enough to be convinced that when we are confronted with Jesus Christ, we are confronted with the love and the power of Almighty God.

So, to this approach of the leper there came the reaction of Jesus. First and foremost, that reaction was *compassion*. The law said that Jesus must avoid contact with that man and threatened him with terrible uncleanness if he allowed the leper to come within six feet of him; but Jesus stretched out his hand and touched him. The medical knowledge of the day would have said that Jesus was running a desperate risk of a ghastly infection; but Jesus stretched out his hand and touched him.

For Jesus, there was only one obligation in life – and that was to help. There was only one law – and that law was love. The obligation of love took precedence over all other rules and laws and regulations; it made him defy all physical risks. To good doctors, anyone stricken with some terrible disease is not a disgusting spectacle but a human being who needs their skill. They see a child sick with an infectious disease not as a menace but as a child who needs to be helped. Jesus was like that; God is like that; we must be like that. The true Christian will break any convention and will take any risk to help those who are in need.

TRUE PRUDENCE

Matthew 8:1–4 (*contd*)

But there remain two things in this incident which show that, while Jesus would defy the law and risk any infection to help, he was not senselessly reckless, nor did he forget the demands of true prudence.

(1) He ordered the man to keep silent, and not to broadcast what he had done for him. This injunction to silence is common on Jesus' lips (Matthew 9:30, 12:16, 17:9; Mark 1:34, 5:43, 7:36, 8:26). Why should Jesus command this silence?

Palestine was an occupied country, and the Jews were a proud race. They never forgot that they were God's chosen people. They dreamed of the day when their divine deliverer would come. But for the most part, they dreamed of that day in terms of military conquest and political power. For that reason, Palestine was the most inflammable country in the world. It lived amid revolutions. Leader after leader arose, had his moment of glory and was then eliminated by the might of Rome. Now, if this leper had gone out and told everyone what Jesus had done for him, there would have been a rush to install a man with powers such as Jesus possessed as a political leader and a military commander.

Jesus had to educate the minds of men and women; he had to change their ideas; he had somehow to enable them to see that his power was love and not force of arms. He had to work almost in secrecy until they knew him for what he was, the lover and not the destroyer of human lives. Jesus commanded those he helped to keep silent in case they should use him to make their own dreams come true instead of waiting on the dream of God. They had to be silent until they had learned the right things to say about him.

(2) Jesus sent the leper to the priests to make the correct offering and to receive a certificate that he was clean. The Jews were so terrified of the infection of leprosy that there was a prescribed ritual in the very unlikely event of a cure.

The ritual is described in Leviticus 14. The leper was examined by a priest. Two birds were taken, and one was killed over running water. In addition, there were taken cedar wood, crimson yarn and hyssop. These things were taken, together with the living bird, and dipped in the blood of the dead bird, and then the living bird was allowed to go free. The man washed himself and his clothes, and shaved himself. Seven days were allowed to pass, and then he was re-examined. He must then shave his hair, his head and his eyebrows. Certain sacrifices were then made consisting of

345

two male lambs without blemish, and one ewe-lamb; three-tenths of a measure of fine flour mingled with oil; and one log (a liquid measure) of oil. The restored leper was touched on the tip of the right ear, the right thumb and the right big toe with blood and oil. He was examined for one last time, and, if the cure was real, he was allowed to go with a certificate that he was cleansed.

Jesus told this man to go through that process. There is guidance here. Jesus was telling that man not to neglect the treatment that was available for him in those days. We do not receive miracles by neglecting the medical and scientific treatment open to us. We must do all we can do before God's power may co-operate with our efforts. A miracle does not come by a lazy waiting upon God to do it all; it comes from the co-operation of our faith-filled efforts with the limitless grace of God.

A GOOD MAN'S PLEA

Matthew 8:5–13

> When Jesus had come into Capernaum, a centurion came to him. 'Lord,' he appealed to him, 'my servant lies at home, paralysed, suffering terribly.' He said to him: 'Am I to come and cure him?' 'Lord,' answered the centurion, 'I am not worthy that you should enter my house; but, only speak a word, and my servant will be cured. For even I am a man under authority, and I have soldiers under me. I say to one soldier, "Go!" and he goes, and to another, "Do this!" and he does it.' Jesus was amazed when he heard this, and said to those who were following him, 'This is the truth I tell you – not even in Israel have I found so great a faith. I tell you that many will come from the east and west and will sit

down at table with Abraham and Isaac and Jacob in the kingdom of heaven; but the sons of the kingdom will be cast into outer darkness. There will be weeping and gnashing of teeth there.' And Jesus said to the centurion, 'Go; let it be done for you as you have believed.' And his servant was healed at that hour.

EVEN in the brief appearance that he makes on the stage of the New Testament story, this centurion is one of the most attractive characters in the gospels. The centurions were the backbone of the Roman army. In a Roman legion there were 6,000 men; the legion was divided into 60 centuries, each containing 100 men, and in command of each century there was a centurion. These centurions were the long-service, regular soldiers of the Roman army. They were responsible for the discipline of the regiment, and they were the cement which held the army together. In peace and in war alike, the morale of the Roman army depended on them. In his description of the Roman army, the Greek historian Polybius describes what a centurion should be: 'They must not be so much venturesome seekers after danger as men who can command, steady in action, and reliable; they ought not to be over-anxious to rush into the fight, but when hard pressed, they must be ready to hold their ground, and die at their posts.' The centurions were the finest men in the Roman army.

It is interesting to note that every centurion mentioned in the New Testament is mentioned with honour. There was the centurion who recognized Jesus on the cross as the Son of God; there was Cornelius, the first Gentile convert to the Christian Church; there was the centurion who suddenly discovered that Paul was a Roman citizen, and who rescued him from the fury of the rioting mob; there was the centurion who was informed that the Jews had planned to murder Paul between Jerusalem and Caesarea, and who took steps to foil their plans; there was the centurion whom Felix ordered to look after Paul; and there was the centurion accompanying Paul on his last journey to Rome, who treated him with every courtesy and accepted him as leader when the storm struck the ship (Matthew 27:54; Acts 10:22, 10:26, 22:26, 23:17, 23:23, 24:23, 27:3, 27:43).

But there was something very special about this centurion at Capernaum, and that was his attitude to his servant. This servant would be a slave, but the centurion was grieved that his servant was ill and was determined to do everything in his power to save him.

That was the reverse of the normal attitude of master to slave. In the Roman Empire, slaves did not matter. It was of no importance to anyone if they suffered and whether they lived or died. Aristotle, talking about the friendships which are possible in life, writes: 'There can be no friendship nor justice towards inanimate things; indeed, not even towards a horse or an ox, nor yet towards a slave as a slave. For master and slave have nothing in common: a slave is a living tool, just as a tool is an inanimate slave.'

A slave was no better than a thing. A slave had no legal rights whatsoever; his master was free to treat him, or maltreat him, as he liked. Gaius, the Roman legal expert, lays it down in his *Institutes*: 'We may note that it is universally accepted that the master possesses the power of life and death over the slave.' Varro, the Roman writer on agriculture, has a grim passage in which he divides the instruments of agriculture into three classes – the articulate, the inarticulate and the mute, 'the articulate comprising the slaves, the inarticulate comprising the cattle, and the mute comprising the vehicles'. The only difference between a slave and an animal or a cart was that the slave could speak.

Cato, another Roman writer on agriculture, has a passage which shows how unusual the attitude of this centurion was. He is giving advice to a man taking over a farm: 'Look over the livestock, and hold a sale. Sell your oil, if the price is satisfactory, and sell the surplus of your wine and grain. Sell worn-out oxen, blemished cattle, blemished sheep, wool, hides, an old wagon, old tools, an old slave, a sickly slave, and whatever else is superfluous.' Cato's blunt advice is to throw out the slave who is sick. The fifth-century archbishop of Ravenna, Peter Chrysologus, sums the matter up: 'Whatever a master does to a slave, undeservedly, in anger, willingly, unwillingly, in forgetfulness, after careful thought, knowingly, unknowingly, is judgment, justice and law.'

It is quite clear that this centurion was an extraordinary man, for he loved his slave. It may well be that it was his totally unusual and unexpected gentleness and love which so moved Jesus when the centurion first came to him. Love always covers a multitude of sins; those who care for others are always near to Jesus Christ.

THE PASSPORT OF FAITH

Matthew 8:5–13 (*contd*)

NOT only was this centurion quite extraordinary in his attitude to his servant; he was also a man of a most extraordinary faith. He wished for Jesus' power to help and to heal his servant, but there was one problem. He was a Gentile and Jesus was a Jew; and, according to the Jewish law, a Jew could not enter the house of a Gentile, for all Gentile dwelling places were unclean. The *Mishnah* lays it down: 'The dwelling places of Gentiles are unclean.' It is to that ruling that Jesus refers when he puts the question: 'Am I to come and heal him?'

It was not that this law of uncleanness meant anything to Jesus; it was not that he would have refused to enter anyone's house; it was simply that he was testing the other's faith. It was then that the centurion's faith reached its peak. As a soldier, he knew well what it was to give a command and to have that command instantly and unquestioningly carried out; so he said to Jesus: 'You don't need to come to my house; I am not fit for you to enter my house; all you have to do is to speak the word of command, and that command will be obeyed.' There spoke the voice of faith, and Jesus laid it down that faith is the only passport to the blessedness of God.

Here, Jesus uses a famous and vivid Jewish picture. The Jews believed that when the Messiah came there would be a great banquet at which all Jews would sit down to feast. Behemoth, the greatest of the land animals, and Leviathan, the greatest of the inhabitants of the sea, would provide the fare for the banqueters. 'And you have kept them to be eaten by whom you wish, and when you wish' (4 Ezra [2 Esdras] 6:52). 'And behemoth shall be revealed from his place, and leviathan shall ascend from the sea, those two great monsters which I created on the fifth day of creation, and shall have kept until that time; and then shall they be food for all that are left' (2 Baruch 29:4).

The Jews looked forward with all their hearts to this messianic banquet, but it never for a moment crossed their minds that any Gentile would ever sit down at it. By that time, the Gentiles would have been destroyed. 'The nation and kingdom that will not serve you shall perish; those nations shall be utterly laid waste' (Isaiah 60:12). Yet here is Jesus saying that many shall come from the east and from the west, and sit down at table at that banquet.

Still worse, he says that many of the heirs of the kingdom will be shut out. The word used literally means 'sons'. A son is an heir; therefore the sons of the kingdom are those who are to inherit the kingdom, for the son is always heir; but the Jews are to lose their inheritance. Always in Jewish thought 'the inheritance of sinners is darkness' (Psalms of Solomon 15:10). The Rabbis had a saying: 'The sinners in Gehenna will be covered with darkness.' To the Jews, the extraordinary and the shattering thing about all this was that Gentiles, whom they expected to be absolutely shut out, were to be guests at the messianic banquet, and the Jews, who they expected to be welcomed with open arms, were to be shut out in the outer darkness. The tables were to be turned, and all expectations were to be reversed.

The Jews had to learn that the passport to God's presence is not membership of any nation; it is faith. The Jews believed that they belonged to the chosen people and that because they were Jews they were therefore dear to God. They belonged to God's people, and that was enough automatically to gain them salvation. Jesus taught that the only aristocracy in the kingdom of God is the aristocracy of faith. Jesus Christ is not the possession of any one race; Jesus Christ is the possession of every man and every woman in every race in whose heart there is faith.

THE POWER WHICH ANNIHILATES DISTANCE

Matthew 8:5–13 (*contd*)

So Jesus spoke the word, and the servant of the centurion was healed. Not so very long ago, this would have been a miracle at which the minds of most people would have staggered. It is not so very difficult to think of Jesus healing when he and the sufferer were in actual contact; but to think of Jesus healing at a distance, healing with a word a man he had never seen and never touched, seemed a thing almost, if not completely, beyond belief. But the strange thing is that science itself has come to see that there are forces which are working in a way which is still mysterious, but which is undeniable.

Again and again, people have been confronted by a power which does not travel by the ordinary contacts and the ordinary routes and the ordinary channels.

One of the classic instances of this comes from the life of the Swedish theologian and scientist Emanuel Swedenborg. In 1759, Swedenborg was in Gothenburg. He described a fire occurring in Stockholm 300 miles away. He gave an account of the fire to the city authorities. He told them when it began, where it began, the name of the owner of the house, and when it was put out – and subsequent research proved him correct in every detail. Knowledge had come to him by a route which was not any of the routes known in everyday human experience.

W. B. Yeats, the famous Irish poet, had experiences like this. He had certain symbols for certain things, and he experimented, not so much scientifically, but in everyday life, in the transmission of these symbols to other people by what might be called the sheer power of thought. He had an uncle in Sligo, who was by no means a mystical or devotional or spiritual man. He used to visit him each summer. 'There are some high sandhills and low cliffs, and I adopted the practice of walking by the seashore while he walked on the cliffs of sandhills; I, without speaking, would imagine the symbol, and he would notice what passed before his mind's eye, and in a short time he would practically never fail of the appropriate vision.' Yeats tells of an incident at a London dinner party, where all the guests were intimate friends: 'I had written upon a piece of paper: "In five minutes York Powell will talk of a burning house," thrust the paper under my neighbour's plate, and imagined my fire symbol, and waited in silence. Powell shifted the conversation from topic to topic, and within the five minutes was describing a fire he had seen as a young man.'

People have always quoted things like that. In the 1930s, the American psychologist Dr J. B. Rhine began definite scientific experiments in what he called Extra-Sensory Perception, a phenomenon which was commonly called by its initial letters, ESP. Dr Rhine carried out, in Duke University, thousands of experiments which go to show that people can become aware of things by other means than the ordinary senses. In one such experiment, a pack of twenty-five cards marked with certain symbols is used. A person is asked to name the cards as they are dealt, without seeing them. One of the students who participated in these experiments was called Hubert Pearce. On the first 5,000 trials – a trial is a run through the whole pack of cards – he averaged ten correct out of twenty-five, when the laws of chance would say that four correct could be expected. On one occasion, in conditions of special concentration, he named the whole twenty-five cards correctly. The mathematical odds against this feat being pure chance are 298,023,223,876,953,125 to 1.

Another experimenter called Brugman carried out a different experiment. He selected two subjects. He put the sender of the messages in an upstairs room and the receiver below. Between the rooms, there was an opening covered by two layers of glass with an air space between, so that the sending of any message based on sound was quite impossible. Through the glass panel, the sender looked at the hands of the receiver. In front of the receiver was a table with forty-eight squares. The receiver was blindfolded. Between him and the squared table was a thick curtain. He held a pointer which passed through the curtain on to the table. The experiment was that the sender had to will the receiver to move the pointer to a certain square. According to the laws of chance, the receiver should have been right in four out of 180 results. In point of fact, he was right in sixty. It is difficult to avoid the conclusion that the mind of the sender was influencing the mind of the receiver.

It is a definitely proven fact that a certain Dr Pierre Janet in eighteen out of twenty-five cases was able to hypnotize subjects at a distance, and he was partially successful in four other cases.

There is no doubt that mind can act on mind across the distances in a way which we are beginning to see, although as yet we are far from understanding. If human minds can get to this length, how much more can the mind of Jesus? The strange thing about this miracle is that as thinking has changed, instead of making it harder, the development of new ideas has made it easier to believe it.

A MIRACLE IN A COTTAGE

Matthew 8:14–15

> And when Jesus had come into Peter's house, he saw Peter's mother-in-law lying in bed, ill with a fever. So he touched her hand and the fever left her. And she rose, and busied herself serving them.

WHEN we compare Mark's narrative of events with that of Matthew, we see that this incident happened in Capernaum, on the Sabbath day, after Jesus had worshipped in the synagogue. When Jesus was in Capernaum, his headquarters

354

were in the house of Peter, for Jesus never had any home of his own. Peter was married, and legend has it that later on Peter's wife was his helper in the work of the gospel. Clement of Alexandria (*Stromateis*, 7:6) tells us that Peter and his wife were martyred together. Peter, so the story runs, had the grim ordeal of seeing his wife suffer before he suffered himself. 'On seeing his wife led to death, Peter rejoiced on account of her call and her conveyance home, and called very encouragingly and comfortingly, addressing her by name, "Remember thou the Lord."'

On this occasion, Peter's wife's mother was ill with a fever. There were three kinds of fever which were common in Palestine. There was a fever which was called Malta fever, and which was marked by weakness, anaemia and wasting away, and which lasted for months, and often ended in a decline which finished in death. There was what was called intermittent fever, which may well have been very like typhoid fever. And above all there was malaria. In the regions where the Jordan River entered and left the Sea of Galilee, there was marshy ground; there the malarial mosquitoes bred and flourished, and both Capernaum and Tiberias were areas where malaria was very prevalent. It was often accompanied by jaundice and shivering, and was a most wretched and miserable experience for the sufferer from it. It was most likely malaria from which Peter's wife's mother was suffering.

This miracle tells us much about Jesus, and not a little about the woman whom he cured.

(1) Jesus had come from the synagogue; there he had dealt with and had cured the demon-possessed man (Mark 1:21–8). As Matthew has it, he had healed the centurion's servant on the way home. Miracles did not cost Jesus nothing; virtue went out of him with every healing, and beyond a doubt he

would be tired. It would be for rest that he came into Peter's house, and yet no sooner was he in it than there came still another demand on him for help and healing.

Here there was no publicity, here there was no crowd to look and to admire and to be astonished. Here there was only a simple cottage and a poor woman suffering from a common fever. And yet in those circumstances Jesus put forth all his power.

Jesus was never too tired to help; the demands of human need never came to him as an intolerable nuisance. Jesus was not one of these people who are at their best in public and at their worst in private. No situation was too humble for him to help. He did not need an admiring audience to be at his best. In a crowd or in a cottage, his love and his power were at the disposal of anyone who needed him.

(2) But this miracle also tells us something about the woman whom Jesus healed. No sooner had he healed her than she busied herself in attending to his needs and to the needs of the other guests. She clearly regarded herself as 'saved to serve'. He had healed her; and her one desire was to use her new-found health to be of use and of service to him and to others.

How do we use the gifts of Christ? Once Oscar Wilde wrote what he himself called 'the best short story in the world'. W. B. Yeats quotes it in his autobiography in all of what he calls 'its terrible beauty'. Yeats quotes it in its original simplicity before it had been decorated and spoiled by the literary devices of its final form:

> Christ came from a white plain to a purple city, and, as he passed through the first street, he heard voices overhead, and saw a young man lying drunk upon a window-sill. 'Why do you waste your soul in drunkenness?' he said. The man said, 'Lord, I was a leper, and

you healed me, what else can I do?' A little farther
through the town he saw a young man following a
harlot, and said, 'Why do you dissolve your soul in
debauchery?' And the young man answered, 'Lord, I
was blind and you healed me, what else can I do?' At
last, in the middle of the city, he saw an old man
crouching, weeping on the ground, and, when he asked
why he wept, the old man answered, 'Lord, I was dead,
and you raised me into life, what else can I do but weep?'

That is a terrible parable of how the gifts of Christ and the
mercy of God are used. Peter's wife's mother used the gift of
her restored health to serve Jesus and to serve others. That is
the way in which we should use every gift of God.

MIRACLES IN A CROWD

Matthew 8:16–17

And, when it was late in the day, they brought to him
many who were in the power of evil spirits, and he cast
out the spirits with a word, and healed all those who
were ill. This happened that the saying spoken through
the prophet Isaiah might be fulfilled: 'He took our
weaknesses and carried our sins.'

As we have already seen, Mark's account of this series of
incidents makes it clear that they happened on the Sabbath
day (Mark 1:21–34). That explains why this scene happened
late in the day, at the evening time. According to the Sabbath
law, which forbade all work on the Sabbath day, it was illegal
to heal on the Sabbath. Steps could be taken to prevent a
person from getting any worse, but no steps might be taken to
make that person any better. The general law was that
on the Sabbath medical attention might only be given to

those whose lives were actually in danger. Further, it was illegal to carry a burden on the Sabbath day, and a burden was anything which weighed more than two dried figs. It was, therefore, illegal to carry a sick person from place to place on a stretcher or in one's arms or on one's shoulders, for to do so would have been to carry a burden. Officially the Sabbath ended when two stars could be seen in the sky, for there were no clocks to tell the time in those days. That is why the crowd in Capernaum waited until the evening time to come to Jesus for the healing which they knew he could give.

But we must think of what Jesus had been doing on that Sabbath day. He had been in the synagogue and had healed the demon-possessed man. He had sent healing to the centurion's servant. He had healed Peter's wife's mother. No doubt he had preached and taught all day; and no doubt he had encountered those who were bitter in their opposition to him. Now it was evening. God gave the day for work, and the evening for rest. The evening is the time of quiet when work is laid aside. But it was not so for Jesus. At the time when he might have expected rest, he was surrounded by the insistent demands of human need – and selflessly and un-complainingly and with a divine generosity he met them all. As long as there was someone in need, there was no rest for Jesus Christ.

That scene called to Matthew's mind the saying of Isaiah (Isaiah 53:4), where it is said of the servant of the Lord that he bore our weaknesses and carried our sins.

As followers of Christ, we cannot seek for rest while there are others to be helped and healed; and the strange thing is that we will find our own weariness refreshed and our own weakness strengthened in the service of others. Somehow we will find that as the demands come, strength also comes; and somehow we will find that we are able to go on for the sake of others when we feel that we cannot take another step for ourselves.

THE SUMMONS TO COUNT THE COST

Matthew 8:18–22

> When Jesus saw the great crowds surrounding him, he gave orders to go away, across to the other side. A scribe came to him. 'Teacher,' he said, 'I will follow you wherever you may be going.' Jesus said to him: 'The foxes have lairs, and the birds of the sky have places where they may lodge, but the Son of Man has nowhere where he may lay his head.' Another of his disciples said: 'Lord, let me first go away and bury my father.' Jesus said to him: 'Follow me, and let the dead bury their dead.'

AT first sight, this section seems out of place in this chapter. The chapter is a chapter of miracles, and at first sight these verses do not seem to fit into a chapter which tells of a series of miraculous events. Why then does Matthew put it here?

It has been suggested that Matthew inserted this passage here because his thoughts were running on Jesus as the Suffering Servant. He has just quoted Isaiah 53:4: 'He has borne our infirmities and carried our diseases' (Matthew 8:17), and very naturally, it is said, that picture led on in Matthew's thoughts to the picture of the one who had nowhere to lay his head. In his commentary on Matthew, A. Plummer has it: 'Jesus' life began in a borrowed stable and ended in a borrowed tomb.' So it is suggested that Matthew inserted this passage here because both it and the immediately preceding verses show Jesus as the Suffering Servant of God.

It may be so, but it is even more likely that Matthew inserted this passage in this chapter of miracles because he saw a miracle in it. It was a scribe who wished to follow Jesus. He gave Jesus the highest title of honour that he knew. 'Teacher', he called him; the Greek is *didaskalos*, which is the normal translation of the Hebrew word *Rabbi*. To him, Jesus was the greatest teacher to whom he had ever listened and whom he had ever seen.

It was indeed a miracle that any scribe should give to Jesus that title and should wish to follow him. Jesus stood for the destruction and the end of all that narrow legalism on which scribal religion was built; and it was indeed a miracle that a scribe should come to see anything lovely or anything desirable in Jesus. This is the miracle of the impact of the personality of Jesus Christ on men and women.

The impact of one personality on another can indeed produce the most wonderful effects. Very often, people are launched on careers of scholarship by the impact of the personality of a great teacher upon them; many have been moved to the Christian way and to a life of Christian service by the impact of a great Christian personality on their lives. Preaching itself has been described and defined as 'truth through personality'.

The broadcaster W. H. Elliott, in his autobiography *Undiscovered Ends*, tells a story about Edith Evans, the great actress: 'When her husband died, she came to us, full of grief . . . In our drawing room at Chester Square she poured out her feelings about it for an hour or so, and they were feelings that came from springs that were very deep. Her personality filled the room. The room was not big enough! . . . For days that room of ours was "electric," as I expressed it then. The strong vibrations had not gone.'

This story is the story of the impact of the personality of Jesus on the life of a Jewish scribe. It remains true that to this day what is needed most of all is not so much to talk to people about Jesus as to confront them with Jesus, and to allow the personality of Jesus to do the rest.

But there is more than that. No sooner had the scribe undergone this reaction than Jesus told him that the foxes have their lairs and the birds of the sky have a place in the trees to rest, but the Son of Man has no place on earth to lay his head. It is as if Jesus said to this man: 'Before you follow me – *think what you are doing*. Before you follow me – *count the cost*.'

Jesus did not want followers who were swept away by a moment of emotion, which quickly blazed and just as quickly died. He did not want those who were carried away by a tide of mere feeling, which quickly flowed and just as quickly ebbed. He wanted disciples who knew what they were doing. He talked about taking up a cross (Matthew 10:38). He talked about setting himself above the dearest relationships in life (Luke 14:26); he talked about giving away everything to the poor (Matthew 19:21). He was always saying: 'Yes, I know that your heart is running out to me, but – *do you love me enough for that?*'

In any sphere of life, people must be confronted with the facts. If young men and women express a desire for scholarship, we must say to them: 'Good, but are you prepared to scorn pleasures and spend days in serious work?' When an explorer is building up a team, there will be vast numbers of people offering their services; but the leader must weed out the romantics from the realists by saying: 'Good, but are you prepared for the snow and the ice, for the swamps and the heat, for the exhaustion and the weariness of it all?' When a young person wishes to become an athlete, the trainer must say: 'Good, but are you prepared for the self-denial and self-discipline that alone will bring you the achievement and fame of which you dream?' This is not to discourage enthusiasm, but it is to say that enthusiasm which has not faced the facts will soon be dead ashes instead of a flame.

No one could ever say that the decision to follow Jesus was made under false pretences. Jesus was uncompromisingly honest. We do Jesus a grave disservice if ever we lead people to believe that the Christian way is an easy way. There is no thrill like the way of Christ, and there is no glory like the end of that way; but Jesus never said it was an easy way. The way to glory always involved a cross.

THE TRAGEDY OF THE UNSEIZED MOMENT

Matthew 8:18–22 (*contd*)

BUT there was another man who wished to follow Jesus. He said he would follow Jesus, if he was first allowed to go and bury his father. Jesus' answer was: 'Follow me and leave the dead to bury their own dead.' At first sight, that seems a hard saying. To the Jews, it was a sacred duty to ensure decent burial for a dead parent. When Jacob died, Joseph asked permission from Pharaoh to go and bury his father: 'My father made me swear an oath; he said, "I am about to die. In the tomb that I hewed out for myself in the land of Canaan, there you shall bury me." Now therefore let me go up, so that I may bury my father; then I will return' (Genesis 50:5). Because of the apparently stern and unsympathetic character of this saying, different explanations have been given of it.

It has been suggested that in the translation into Greek of the Aramaic which Jesus used, there has been a mistake; and that Jesus is saying that the man can well leave the burying of his father to the official buriers. There is a strange verse in Ezekiel 39:15: 'As the searchers pass through the land, anyone who sees a human bone shall set up a sign by it, until the buriers have buried it in the Valley of Hamon-gog.' That seems to imply a kind of official called a *burier*; and it has been suggested that Jesus is saying that the man can leave the burial to these officials. That does not seem a very likely explanation.

It has been suggested that this is indeed a hard saying, and that Jesus is saying bluntly that the society in which this man is living is dead in sin, and he must get out of it as quickly as possible, even if it means leaving his father still unburied; that nothing, not even the most sacred duty, must delay his embarkation on the Christian way.

But the true explanation undoubtedly lies in the way in which the Jews used this phrase – 'I must bury my father' – and in the way in which it is still used in this part of the world.

The German theologian Hans Wendt quotes an incident related by a Syrian missionary, M. Waldmeier. This missionary was friendly with an intelligent and rich young Turk. He advised him to make a tour of Europe at the close of his education, so that his education would be completed and his mind broadened. The Turk answered: 'I must first of all bury my father.' The missionary expressed his sympathy and sorrow that the young man's father had died. But the young Turk explained that his father was still very much alive, and that what he meant was that he must fulfil all his duties to his parents and to his relatives before he could leave them to go on the suggested tour; that, in fact, he could not leave home until after his father's death, which might not happen for many years.

That is undoubtedly what the man in this gospel incident meant. He meant: 'I will follow you some day, when my father is dead, and when I am free to go.' He was in fact putting off his following of Jesus for many years to come.

Jesus was wise: Jesus knew the human heart; and Jesus knew well that if the man did not follow him at that precise moment, he never would. Again and again, there come to us moments of impulse when we are moved to the higher things; and again and again, we let them pass without acting upon them.

The tragedy of life is so often the tragedy of the unseized moment. We are moved to some fine action, we are moved to the abandoning of some weakness or habit, we are moved to say something to someone, some word of sympathy, or warning, or encouragement; but the moment passes, and the thing is never done, the evil thing is never conquered, the word is never spoken. In the best of us, there is a certain lethargy and inertia; there is a certain habit of procrastination, there is a certain fear and indecision; and often the moment of fine impulse is never turned into action and into fact.

Jesus was saying to this man: 'You are feeling at the moment that you must get out of that dead society in which you move; you say you will get out when the years have passed and your father has died; get out now – or you will never get out at all.'

In his autobiography, the writer H. G. Wells told of a crucial moment in his life. He was apprenticed to a draper, and there seemed to be little or no future for him. There came to him one day what he called 'an inward and prophetic voice: "Get out of this trade before it is too late; at any cost get out of it."' He did not wait; he got out; and that is why he became H. G. Wells.

May God give to us that strength of decision which will save us from the tragedy of the unseized moment.

THE PEACE OF THE PRESENCE

Matthew 8:23–7

> When he embarked on the boat, his disciples followed him. And, look you, a great upheaval arose on the sea, so that the boat was hidden by the waves; and he was sleeping. They came and wakened him. 'Lord,' they said, 'save us; we are perishing.' He said to them, 'Why are you such cowards, you whose faith is little?' Then, when he had been roused from sleep, he rebuked the winds and the sea, and there was a great calm. The men were amazed. 'What kind of man is this,' they said, 'for the winds and the sea obey him?'

IN one sense, this was a very ordinary scene on the Sea of Galilee. The Sea of Galilee is small; it is only thirteen miles from north to south and eight miles from east to west at its widest. The Jordan valley makes a deep cleft in the surface of the earth, and the Sea of Galilee is part of that cleft. It is 680 feet below sea level. That gives it a climate which is warm and gracious, but it also creates dangers. On the west side, there are hills with valleys and gullies; and, when a cold wind comes from the west, these valleys and gullies act like gigantic funnels. The wind, as it were, becomes compressed in them, and rushes down upon the lake with savage violence and with startling suddenness, so that the calm of one moment can become the raging storm of the next. The storms on the Sea of Galilee combine suddenness and violence in a unique way.

W. M. Thomson in *The Land and the Book* describes his experience on the shores of the Sea of Galilee:

On the occasion referred to, we subsequently pitched
our tents at the shore, and remained for three days and
nights exposed to this tremendous wind. We had to
double-pin all the tent-ropes, and frequently were
obliged to hang with our whole weight upon them to
keep the quivering tabernacle from being carried up
bodily into the air . . . The whole lake, as we had it, was
lashed into fury; the waves repeatedly rolled up to our
tent door, tumbling over the ropes with such violence
as to carry away the tent-pins. And, moreover, these
winds are not only violent, but they come down
suddenly, and often when the sky is perfectly clear. I
once went to swim near the hot baths, and, before I was
aware, a wind came rushing over the cliffs with such
force that it was with great difficulty that I could regain
the shore.

Dr W. M. Christie, who spent many years in Galilee, says
that during these storms the winds seem to blow from all the
directions at the same time, for they rush down the narrow
gorges in the hills and strike the water at an angle. He tells of
one occasion:

A company of visitors were standing on the shore at
Tiberias, and, noting the glassy surface of the water
and the smallness of the lake, they expressed doubts as
to the possibility of such storms as those described in
the gospels. Almost immediately the wind sprang up.
In twenty minutes the sea was white with foam-crested
waves. Great billows broke over the towers at the
corners of the city walls, and the visitors were compelled
to seek shelter from the blinding spray, though now 200
yards from the lakeside.

In less than half an hour, the placid sunshine had become a
raging storm.

That is what happened to Jesus and his disciples. The words in the Greek are very vivid. The storm is called a *seismos*, which is the word for an *earthquake*. The waves were so high that the boat was hidden (*kaluptesthai*) in the trough as the crest of the waves towered over them. Jesus was asleep. (If we read the narrative in Mark 4:1, 35, we see that before they had set out he had been using the boat as a pulpit to address the people, and no doubt he was exhausted.) In their moment of terror the disciples awoke him, and the storm became a calm.

CALM AMID THE STORM

Matthew 8:23–7 (*contd*)

In this story, there is something very much more than the calming of a storm at sea. Suppose that Jesus did in actual physical fact still a raging storm on the Sea of Galilee somewhere round about AD 28, that would in truth be a very wonderful thing; but it would have very little to do with us. It would be the story of an isolated wonder, which had no relevance for us in the twenty-first century. If that is all the story means, we may well ask: 'Why does he not do it now? Why does he allow those who love him nowadays to be drowned in the raging of the sea without intervening to save them?' If we take the story simply as the stilling of a weather storm, it actually produces problems which for some of us are heartbreaking.

But the meaning of this story is far greater than that – the meaning of this story is not that Jesus stopped a storm in Galilee; the meaning is that *wherever Jesus is, the storms of life become a calm*. It means that in the presence of Jesus the most terrible of tempests turns to peace.

When the cold, bleak wind of sorrow blows, there is calm and comfort in the presence of Jesus Christ. When the hot blast of passion blows, there is peace and security in the presence of Jesus Christ. When the storms of doubt seek to uproot the very foundations of the faith, there is a steady safety in the presence of Jesus Christ. In every storm that shakes the human heart, there is peace with Jesus Christ.

Margaret Avery tells a wonderful story. In a little village school in the hill country, a teacher had been telling the children of the stilling of the storm at sea. Shortly afterwards, there came a terrible blizzard. When school closed for the day, the teacher had almost to drag the children bodily through the tempest. They were in very real danger. In the midst of it all, she heard a little boy say as if to himself: 'We could be doing with that chap Jesus here now.' The child had got it right; that teacher must have been a wonderful teacher. The lesson of this story is that when the storms of life shake our souls, Jesus Christ is there, and in his presence the raging of the storm turns to the peace that no storm can ever take away.

THE DEMON-HAUNTED UNIVERSE

Matthew 8:28–34

> And, when he had come to the other side, to the territory of the Gadarenes, two demon-possessed men met him, as they emerged from the tombs. They were very fierce, so that no one was able to pass by that road. And, look you, they shouted: 'What have we to do with you, you Son of God? Have you come to torture us before the proper time?' A good distance away from them a herd of many pigs was grazing. The devils urged Jesus: 'If you cast us out, send us into the herd of pigs.' He said to them: 'Begone.' They came out and went into the

herd of pigs. And, look you, the whole herd rushed down the cliff into the sea, and died in the waters. Those who were herding them fled, and went away into the town and related the whole story, and told of the things which had happened to the demon-possessed men. And, look you, the whole town came out to meet Jesus: and when they saw him, they urged him to depart from their districts.

BEFORE we begin to study this passage in detail, we may try to clear up one difficulty which meets the student of the gospels. There was clearly some uncertainty in the mind of the gospel writers as to where this incident actually happened. That uncertainty is reflected in the differences between the three gospels. In the Authorized Version, Matthew says that this happened in the country of the *Gergesenes* (Matthew 8:28); Mark and Luke say that it happened in the country of the *Gadarenes* (Mark 5:1; Luke 8:26). There are even very considerable differences between the different manuscripts of each gospel. In the Revised Standard Version (so also the New Revised Standard Version), which follows the best manuscripts, and which makes use of the most up-to-date scholarship, Matthew places the incident in the country of the *Gadarenes*; Mark and Luke in the country of the *Gerasenes*.

The difficulty is that no one has ever really succeeded in identifying this place beyond doubt. *Gerasa* can hardly be right, for the only Gerasa of which we have any information was thirty-six miles inland, south-east of the lake, in Gilead; and it is certain that Jesus did not travel thirty-six miles inland. *Gadara* is almost certainly right, because Gadara was a town six miles inland from the shores of the lake, and it would be very natural for the town burying place and the town grazing place to be some distance outside the town. *Gergesa* is very likely due to the conjecture of Origen, the great third-century Alexandrian scholar. He knew that Gerasa was impossible; he doubted that Gadara was possible; and he actually knew of a village called Gergesa which was on the eastern shores of the lake, and so he conjectured that Gergesa must be the place. The differences are simply due to the fact that those who copied the manuscripts did not know Palestine well enough to be sure where this incident actually happened.

This miracle confronts us with the idea of demon-possession which is so common in the gospels. The ancient world believed unquestioningly and intensely in evil spirits. The air was so full of these spirits that it was not even possible to insert into it the point of a needle without coming against one. Some said that there were 7,500,000 of them; there were 10,000 of them on a person's right hand and 10,000 on the left; and all were waiting to do harm. They lived in unclean places such as tombs, and places where no cleansing water was to be found. They lived in the deserts where their howling could be heard. (We still speak of a *howling* desert.) They were specially dangerous to the lonely traveller, to the woman in childbirth, to the newly married bride and bridegroom, to children who were out after dark, and to travellers by night. They were specially dangerous in the midday heat, and between sunset and sunrise. The male demons were called *shedim*, and the female *lilin* after Lilith. The female demons had long hair, and were specially dangerous to children; that was why children had their guardian angels (cf. Matthew 18:10).

As to the origin of the demons, different views were held. Some held that they had been there since the beginning of the world. Some held that they were the spirits of wicked, malignant people who had died, and who even after their death still carried on their evil work. Most commonly of all, they were connected with the strange old story in Genesis 6:1–8. That story tells how the sinning angels came to earth and seduced mortal women. The demons were held to be the descendants of the children produced by that evil union.

To these demons, all illness was ascribed. They were held to be responsible not only for diseases like epilepsy and mental illness, but also for physical illness. The Egyptians held that the body had thirty-six different parts, and that every one could be occupied by a demon. One of their favourite ways of gaining an entry into people's bodies was to lurk beside them while they ate, and so to settle on their food.

It may seem fantastic to us; but the ancient peoples believed implicitly in demons. If people gained the idea that they were possessed by demons, they would easily go on to produce all the symptoms of demon-possession. They could genuinely convince themselves that there were demons inside them. To this day, people can think themselves into having a pain or into the idea that they are ill; that could happen even more easily in days when there was much of what we would call superstition, and when people's knowledge was much more primitive than it is now. Even if there are no such things as demons, people could be cured only by the assumption that, for them at least, the demons were very real indeed.

THE DEFEAT OF THE DEMONS

Matthew 8:28–34 (*contd*)

WHEN Jesus came to the other side of the lake, he was confronted by two demon-possessed men, who dwelt in the tombs, for the tombs were the natural place for the demons to inhabit. These men were so fierce that they were a danger to passers-by, and the prudent traveller would give them a very wide berth indeed.

W. M. Thomson in *The Land and the Book* tells us that he himself, in the nineteenth century, saw men who were exactly like these two demon-possessed men in the tombs at Gadara:

> There are some very similar cases at the present day – furious and dangerous maniacs, who wander about the mountains and sleep in caves and tombs. In their worst paroxysms they are quite unmanageable, and prodigiously strong ... And it is one of the most common traits of this madness that the victims refuse to wear clothes. I have often seen them absolutely naked in the crowded streets of Beirut and Sidon. There are also cases in which they run wildly about the country and frighten the whole neighbourhood.

Apart from anything else, Jesus showed a most unusual courage in stopping to speak to these two men at all.

If we really want the details of this story, we have to go to Mark. Mark's narrative (Mark 5:1–19) is much longer, and what Matthew gives us is only a summary. This is a miracle story which has caused much discussion, and the discussion has centred round the destruction of the herd of pigs. Many have found it strange and have considered it heartless that Jesus should destroy a herd of animals like this. But it is almost certain that Jesus did not in fact deliberately destroy the pigs.

We must try to visualize what happened. The men were shouting and shrieking (Mark 5:7; Luke 8:28). We must remember that they were completely convinced that they were occupied by demons. Now it was normal and orthodox belief, shared by everyone, that when the Messiah and the time of judgment came, the demons would be destroyed. That is what the men meant when they asked Jesus why he had come to torture them before the proper time. They were so convinced that they were possessed by demons that nothing could have rid them of that conviction other than visible demonstration that the demons had gone out of them.

Something had to be done which to them would be un-answerable proof. Almost certainly what happened was that their shouting and shrieking alarmed the herd of pigs; and in their terror the pigs took flight and plunged into the lake. Water was fatal to demons. Thereupon Jesus seized the chance which had come to him. 'Look,' he said. 'Look at these swine; they are gone into the depths of the lake and your demons are gone with them forever.' Jesus knew that in no other way could he ever convince these two men that they were in fact cured. If that is so, Jesus did not deliberately destroy the herd of swine. He used their stampede to help two poor sufferers believe in their cure.

Even if Jesus did deliberately work the destruction of this herd of pigs, it could surely never be held against him. There is such a thing as being over-fastidious. The New Testament scholar T. R. Glover spoke of people who think they are being religious when in fact they are being fastidious.

We could never compare the value of a herd of swine with the value of someone's immortal soul. Most of us do not refuse to eat bacon for breakfast or pork for dinner. Our sympathy with pigs does not extend far enough to prevent our eating them; are we then to complain if Jesus restored sanity to two men's minds at the cost of a herd of pigs? This is not to say that we encourage or even condone cruelty to animals. It is simply to say that we must preserve a sense of proportion in life.

The supreme tragedy of this story lies in its conclusion. Those who were herding the pigs ran back to the town and told what had happened; and the result was that the people of the town begged Jesus to leave their territory at once.

Here is human selfishness at its worst. It did not matter to these people that two men had been given back their reason; all that mattered to them was that their pigs had perished. It is so often the case that people in effect say: 'I don't care what happens to anyone else, if my profits and my comfort and my case are preserved.' We may be amazed at the callousness of these people of Gadara, but we must take care that we too do not resent any helping of others which reduces our own privileges.

THE GROWTH OF OPPOSITION

WE have repeatedly seen that in Matthew's gospel there is nothing haphazard. It is carefully planned and carefully designed.

In chapter 9 we see another example of this careful planning, for here we see the first shadows of the gathering storm. We see the opposition beginning to grow; we hear the first hint of the charges which are going to be levelled against Jesus, and which are finally going to bring about his death. In this chapter, four charges are made against Jesus.

(1) He is accused of *blasphemy*. In Matthew 9:1–8, we see Jesus curing the paralytic by forgiving his sins; and we hear the scribes accusing him of blasphemy because he claimed to do what only God can do. Jesus was accused of blasphemy because he spoke with the voice of God. *Blasphēmia* literally means *insult* or *slander*; and Jesus' enemies accused him of insulting God because he claimed for himself the very powers of God.

(2) He is accused of *immorality*. In Matthew 9:10–13, we see Jesus sitting at a feast with tax-gatherers and sinners. The

Pharisees demanded to know the reason why he ate with such people. The implication was that he was like the company he kept.

Jesus was in effect accused of being an immoral character because he kept company with immoral characters. Once people are disliked, it is the easiest thing in the world to misinterpret and to misrepresent everything they do.

The author and politician Harold Nicolson tells of a talk he had with the British Prime Minister, Stanley Baldwin. Nicolson was at the time starting out on a political career, and he went to ask Mr Baldwin, a political veteran, for any advice he might care to give. Baldwin said something like this: 'You are going to try to be a statesman, and to handle the affairs of the country. Well, I have had a long experience of such a life, and I will give you three rules which you would do well to follow. First, if you are a subscriber to a press-cutting agency, cancel your subscription at once. Second, never laugh at your opponents' mistakes. Third, *steel yourself to the attribution of false motives*.' One of the favourite weapons of any public figure's enemies is the attribution of false motives; that is what Jesus' enemies did to him.

(3) He is accused of *slackness in piety*. In Matthew 9:14–17, the disciples of John ask Jesus' disciples why their Master does not fast. He was not going through the orthodox motions of religion, and therefore the orthodox were suspicious of him. Anyone who breaks the conventions will suffer for it; and anyone who breaks the religious conventions will suffer especially. Jesus broke the orthodox conventions of religious piety, and he was criticized for it.

(4) He is accused of *being in league with the devil*. In Matthew 9:31–4 we see him curing a dumb man, and his enemies ascribe the cure to an association with the devil.

Whenever a new power comes into life – it has been said, for instance, of spiritual healing – there are those who will say: 'We must be cautious; this may well be the work of the devil and not of God.' It is a strange fact that when people meet something which they do not like, and which they do not understand, and which cuts across their preconceived notions, they very often ascribe it to the devil and not to God.

Here we see the beginning of the campaign against Jesus. The slanderers are at work. The whispering tongues are poisoning truth, and wrong motives are being ascribed. The drive to eliminate this disturbing Jesus has begun.

GET RIGHT WITH GOD

Matthew 9:1–8

> Jesus embarked on the boat, and crossed to the other side, and came to his own town. And, look you, they brought to him a paralysed man lying on a bed. When Jesus saw their faith, he said to the paralysed man, 'Courage, child, your sins are forgiven.' And, look you, some of the scribes said to themselves, 'This fellow is blaspheming.' Jesus knew their thoughts. 'Why,' he said, 'do you think evil thoughts in your hearts? Which is easier – to say, "Your sins are forgiven," or, to say, "Rise and walk"? But to let you understand that the Son of Man has authority on earth to forgive sins –' then he said to the paralysed man, 'Rise; lift your bed; and go to your house.' And he rose and went away to his house. When the crowds saw this, they were moved to awe, and glorified God because he had given such power to men.

FROM Mark 2:1, we learn that this incident took place in Capernaum; and it is interesting to note that by this time Jesus had become so identified with Capernaum that it could be called his own town. At this stage in his ministry, Capernaum was the centre of his work.

A paralysed man was brought to him, carried on a bed by some friends. Here is a wonderful picture of a man who was saved by the faith of his friends. Had it not been for them, he would never have reached the healing presence of Jesus at all. It may well be that he had become dully resigned and defeatedly hopeless, and that they had carried him almost against his will to Jesus. However that may be, he was certainly saved by the faith of his friends.

W. B. Yeats in his play *The Cat and the Moon* has a sentence: 'Did you ever know a holy man but has a wicked man for his comrade, and his heart's darling?' It is very characteristic of really holy men and women that they cling to a really bad or an entirely thoughtless friend, until they have brought that friend into the presence of Jesus. If any one of us has a friend who does not know Christ, or who does not care for Christ, or who is even hostile to Christ, it is our Christian duty not to let that friend go. We must bring our friends into Christ's presence.

We cannot force people against their wills to accept Christ. The nineteenth-century poet Coventry Patmore once said that we cannot teach another religious truth; we can only point out to others a way whereby they may find it for themselves. We cannot make people Christians, but we can do everything possible to bring them into Christ's presence.

Jesus' approach to this man might seem astonishing. He began by telling him that his sins were forgiven. There was a double reason for that. In Palestine, it was a universal belief that *all* sickness was the result of sin, and that no sickness could ever be cured until sin was forgiven. Rabbi Ami said: 'There is no death without sin, and no pains without some transgression.' Rabbi Alexander said: 'The sick arises not from his sickness, until his sins are forgiven.' Rabbi Chija ben Abba said: 'No sick person is cured from sickness, until all his sins are forgiven him.' This unbreakable connection between suffering and sin was part of the orthodox Jewish belief of the time of Jesus. For that reason, there is no doubt at all that this man could never have been cured until he was convinced that his sins had been forgiven. It is most probable that he had indeed been a sinner, and that he was convinced that his illness was the result of his sin, as it may very well have been; and without the assurance of forgiveness, healing could never have come to him.

In point of fact, modern medicine would agree wholeheartedly that the mind can and does influence the physical condition of the body, and that people cannot have healthy bodies when their minds are not in a healthy state.

Paul Tournier in *A Doctor's Case Book* quotes an actual example of that: 'There was, for example, the girl whom one of my friends had been treating for several months for anaemia, without much success. As a last resort my colleague decided to send her to the medical officer of the district in which she worked in order to get his permission to send her into a mountain sanatorium. A week later the patient brought word back from the medical officer. He proved to be a good fellow and he had granted the permit, but he added, "On analysing the blood, however, I do not arrive at anything like the figures you quote." My friend, somewhat put out, at once took a fresh sample of the blood, and rushed to his laboratory. Sure enough the blood count had suddenly changed. "If I had not been the kind of person who keeps carefully to laboratory routine," my friend's story goes on, "and if I had not previously checked my figures at each of my patient's visits, I might have thought that I had made a mistake." He returned to the patient and asked her, "Has anything out of the ordinary happened in your life since your last visit?" "Yes, something has happened," she replied. "I have suddenly been able to forgive someone against whom I bore a nasty grudge; and all at once I felt I could at last say, yes, to life!"' Her mental attitude was changed, and the very state of her blood was changed along with it. Her mind was cured, and her body was well on the way to being cured.

This man in the gospel story knew that he was a sinner; because he was a sinner, he was certain that God was his enemy; because he felt God was his enemy, he was paralysed and ill. Once Jesus brought to him the forgiveness of God, he knew that God was no longer his enemy but his friend, and therefore he was cured.

But it was the manner of the cure which scandalized the scribes. Jesus had dared to forgive sin; to forgive sin is the prerogative of God; therefore Jesus had insulted God. Jesus did not stop to argue. He took issue with them on their own ground. 'Which', he demanded, 'is easier – to say: "Your sins are forgiven," or to say: "Get up and walk"?' Now remember that these scribes believed that no one could get up and walk without forgiveness. If Jesus was able to make this man get up and walk, then that was unanswerable proof that the man's sins were forgiven, and that Jesus' claim was true.

So Jesus demonstrated that he was able to bring for-giveness to the soul and health to the body. And it remains eternally true that we can never be right physically until we are right spiritually, that health in body and peace with God go hand in hand.

THE MAN WHOM EVERYONE HATED

Matthew 9:9

> As Jesus passed on from there, he saw a man called
> Matthew seated at the tax-collector's table. 'Follow me,'
> he said to him; and he arose and followed him.

THERE was never a more unlikely candidate for the office of apostle than Matthew. Matthew was what the Authorized Version calls a *publican*; the *publicani* were tax-gatherers, and were so called because they dealt with public money and with public funds.

The problem for the Roman government was how to devise a system whereby the taxes could be collected as efficiently and as cheaply as possible. They did so by auctioning the right to collect taxes in a certain area. The man who bought that right was responsible to the Roman government for an agreed sum; anything he could raise over and above that, he was allowed to keep as commission.

Obviously, this system lent itself to grave abuses. People did not really know how much they ought to pay in the days before newspapers and radio and television, nor had they any right of appeal against the tax-collector. The consequence was that many tax-collectors became wealthy through illegal extortion. This system had led to so many abuses that in Palestine it had been brought to an end before the time of Jesus; but taxes still had to be paid, and there were still abuses.

There were three great stated taxes. There was a ground tax, by which a man had to pay one-tenth of his grain and one-fifth of his fruit and vine to the government either in cash or in kind. There was income tax, which was one per cent of a man's income. There was a poll tax which had to be paid by every male from the age of fourteen to the age of sixty-five, and by every female from the age of twelve to sixty-five. These were statutory taxes and could not well be used by tax-collectors for private profit.

But in addition to these taxes there were all sorts of other taxes. There was a duty of anything from 2·5 per cent to 12·5 per cent on all goods imported and exported. A tax had to be paid to travel on main roads, to cross bridges, to enter market places and towns or harbours. There was a tax on pack animals, and a tax on the wheels and axles of carts. There were purchase taxes on goods bought and sold. There were certain commodities which were government monopolies. For instance, in Egypt the trade in nitrate, beer and papyrus was entirely in government control.

Although the old method of auctioning the taxes had been stopped, all kinds of people were needed to collect these taxes. The people who collected them were drawn from the provincials themselves. Often they were volunteers. Usually, in any district one person was responsible for one tax, and it was not difficult for such a person to line his own pockets in addition to collecting the taxes which were legally due.

These tax-gatherers were universally hated. They had entered the service of their country's conquerors, and they amassed their fortunes at the expense of their country's misfortunes. They were notoriously dishonest. Not only did they fleece their own people, but they also did their best to swindle the government, and they made a flourishing income by taking bribes from rich people who wished to avoid taxes which they should have paid.

Every country dislikes its tax officials, sometimes to the point of hatred; but the hatred of the Jews for them was doubly violent. The Jews were fanatical nationalists. But what roused the Jews more than anything else was their religious conviction that God alone was king, and that to pay taxes to any mortal ruler was an infringement of God's rights and an insult to his majesty. By Jewish law, a tax-gatherer was debarred from the synagogue; he was included with things and animals unclean, and Leviticus 20:25 was applied to them; he was forbidden to be a witness in any case; 'robbers, murderers and tax-gatherers' were classed together.

When Jesus called Matthew, he called a man whom everyone hated. Here is one of the greatest instances in the New Testament of Jesus' power to see in a man not only what he was, but also what he could be. No one ever had such faith in the possibilities of human nature as Jesus had.

A CHALLENGE ISSUED AND RECEIVED

Matthew 9:9 (*contd*)

CAPERNAUM was in the territory of Herod Antipas, and in all probability Matthew was not directly in the service of the Romans but in the service of Herod. Capernaum was a great meeting place of roads. In particular the great road from Egypt to Damascus, the Way of the Sea, passed through Capernaum. It was there that it entered the dominion of Herod for business purposes; and no doubt Matthew was one of those customs officers who exacted duty on all goods and commodities as they entered and left the territory of Herod.

It is not to be thought that Matthew had never seen Jesus before. No doubt Matthew had heard about this young Galilaean who came with a message breathtakingly new, who spoke with an authority the like of which no one had ever heard before, and who numbered among his friends men and women from whom the orthodox good people of the day shrank in loathing. No doubt Matthew had listened on the outskirts of the crowd and had felt his heart stir within him. Perhaps Matthew had wondered wistfully if even yet it was not too late to set sail and to seek a newer world, to leave his old life and his old shame and to begin again. So he found Jesus standing before him; he heard Jesus issue his challenge; and Matthew accepted that challenge and rose up and left all and followed him.

We must note *what Matthew lost and what Matthew found*. He lost a comfortable job, but found a destiny. He lost a good income, but found honour. He lost a comfortable security, but found an adventure of the like of which he had never dreamed. It may be that if we accept the challenge of Christ, we shall find ourselves poorer in material things. It may be that the worldly ambitions will have to go. But beyond doubt we will find a peace and a joy and a thrill in life that we never knew before. In Jesus Christ, we will find a wealth surpassing anything we may have to abandon for the sake of Christ.

We must note *what Matthew left and what Matthew took*. He left his tax-collector's table, but from it took one thing – his pen. Here is a shining example of how Jesus can use whatever gifts people may bring to him. It is not likely that the others of the Twelve were handy with a pen. Galilaean fishermen would not have much skill in writing or in putting words together. But Matthew had; and this man, whose trade had taught him to use a pen, used that skill to compose the first handbook of the teaching of Jesus, which must rank as one of the most important books the world has ever read.

When Matthew left the tax-collector's table that day, he gave up much in the material sense, but in the spiritual sense he became heir to a fortune.

WHERE THE NEED IS GREATEST

Matthew 9:10–13

> He was sitting at table in the house, and, look you, many
> tax-gatherers and sinners came and sat at table with
> Jesus and his disciples. When the Pharisees saw this,
> they said to his disciples, 'Why does your teacher eat
> with tax-gatherers and sinners?' He heard this. 'Those
> who are well', he said, 'do not need a doctor, but those
> who are ill. Go and learn what the saying means: "It is
> mercy I wish, and not sacrifice." For I did not come to
> invite the righteous, but sinners.'

JESUS did not only call Matthew to follow him and be his
disciple; he actually sat at table with men and women like
Matthew, with tax-gatherers and sinners.

A very interesting question arises here – where was this
meal Jesus ate with tax-gatherers and sinners? It is only Luke
who definitely says that the meal was in the house of Matthew
or Levi (cf. Matthew 9:10–13; Mark 2:14–17; Luke 5:27–
32). As far as the narrative in Matthew and Mark goes, it
could well have been in Jesus' house, or in the house where
Jesus was staying. If the meal was in Jesus' house, Jesus'
saying becomes even more pointed. Jesus said: 'I came not
to call the righteous, but sinners.'

The word that is used for to *call* is the Greek word *kalein*,
which is in fact the technical Greek word for inviting a guest
to a house or to a meal. In the parable of the great feast
(Matthew 22:1–10; Luke 14:15–24), we remember well how
the invited guests refused their invitation and how the poor,
the lame, the disabled and the blind were gathered together
from the highways and the byways and the hedgerows to sit
at the table of the king. It may well be that Jesus is saying:

'When you make a feast, you invite the coldly orthodox and the piously self-righteous; when I make a feast, I invite those who are most conscious of their sin and those whose need of God is greatest.'

However that may be, whether this meal was in the house of Matthew or in the house where Jesus was staying, it was to the orthodox scribes and Pharisees a most shocking proceeding. Broadly speaking, in Palestine people were divided into two sections. There were the orthodox who rigidly kept the law in every small detail; and there were those who did not keep its minor regulations. The second were classed as *the people of the land*; and it was forbidden to the orthodox to go on a journey with them, to do any business with them, to give anything to them or to receive anything from them, to entertain them as guests or to be guests in their houses. By keeping company with people like this, Jesus was doing something which the pious people of his day would never have done.

Jesus' defence was perfectly simple; he merely said that he went where the need was greatest. It would be a poor doctor who visited only houses where people enjoyed good health. The doctor's place is where people are ill; it is a doctor's glory and task to go to those who need healing.

Diogenes was one of the great teachers of ancient Greece. He was a man who loved virtue, and was a man with a caustic tongue. He never tired of comparing the decadence of Athens, where he spent most of his time, with the strong simplicities of Sparta. One day, someone said to him: 'If you think so much of Sparta and so little of Athens, why don't you leave Athens and go and stay in Sparta?' His answer was: 'Whatever I may wish to do, I must stay where men need me most.' It was sinners who needed Jesus, and among sinners he would move.

When Jesus said: 'I came not to call the righteous, but sinners,' we must understand what he was saying. He was not saying that there were some people who were so good that they had no need of anything which he could give; still less was he saying that he was not interested in people who were good. This is a highly compressed saying. Jesus was saying: 'I did not come to invite people who are so self-satisfied that they are convinced they do not need anyone's help; I came to invite people who are very conscious of their sin and desperately aware of their need for a saviour.' He was saying: 'It is only those who know how much they need me who can accept my invitation.'

Those scribes and Pharisees had a view of religion which is by no means dead.

(1) They were more concerned with the preservation of their own holiness than with the helping of another's sin. They were like doctors who refused to visit the sick in case they themselves became infected. They shrank away in fastidious disgust from sinners; they did not want anything to do with people like that. Essentially, their religion was selfish; they were much more concerned to save their own souls than to save the souls of others. And they had forgotten that that was the surest way to lose their own souls.

(2) They were more concerned with criticism than with encouragement. They were far more concerned to point out the faults of other people than to help them conquer these faults. When doctors see some particularly unpleasant disease, which would turn the stomach of anyone else to look at, they are not filled with disgust; they are filled with the desire to help. Our first instinct should never be to condemn sinners; our first instinct should be to help them.

(3) They practised a goodness which issued in condemnation rather than in forgiveness and in sympathy. They would

rather leave people in the gutter than give them a hand to get out of it. They were like doctors who were very much concerned to diagnose disease but not in the least concerned to help cure it.

(4) They practised a religion which consisted in outward orthodoxy rather than in practical help. Jesus loved that saying from Hosea 6:6 which said that God desired mercy and not sacrifice, for he quoted it more than once (cf. Matthew 12:7). We may diligently go through all the motions of orthodox piety, but if our hands are never stretched out to help those in need, we are not really religious people.

PRESENT JOY AND FUTURE SORROW

Matthew 9:14–15

> Then the disciples of John came to him. 'Why', they said, 'do we and the Pharisees fast frequently, while your disciples do not fast?' Jesus said to them, 'Surely the bridegroom's closest friends cannot mourn while the bridegroom is with them? But the days will come when the bridegroom will be taken away from them, and then they will fast.'

To the Jews, almsgiving, prayer and fasting were the three great works of the religious life. We have already fully described Jewish fasting when we were dealing with Matthew 6:16–18. In his commentary on Matthew, A. H. McNeile suggests that this incident may have taken place when the autumn rains had not fallen, and a public fast had been ordained.

When Jesus was asked why he and his disciples did not practise fasting, he answered with a vivid picture. The Authorized Version speaks of the *children of the bridechamber*, which is a correct literal translation of the Greek. A Jewish wedding was a time of special festivity. The unique feature of it was that the couple who were married did not go away for a honeymoon; they spent their honeymoon at home.

For a week after the wedding, open house was kept; the bride and bridegroom were treated as, and even addressed as, king and queen. And during that week their closest friends shared all the joy and all the festivities with them; these closest friends were called *the children of the bridechamber*. On such an occasion, there came into the lives of poor and simple people a joy, a rejoicing, a festivity, a plenty that might come only once in a lifetime.

So Jesus compares himself to the bridegroom and his disciples to the bridegroom's closest friends. How could a company like that be sad and grim? This was no time for fasting, but for the rejoicing of a lifetime. There are great things in this passage.

(1) It tells us that to be with Jesus is a thing of joy; it tells us that in the presence of Jesus there is a sheer, thrilling effervescence of life; it tells us that a gloom-encompassed Christianity is an impossibility. Those who walk with Christ walk in radiance of joy.

(2) It also tells us that no joy lasts forever. For John's disciples, the time of sorrow had come because John was already in prison. For Jesus' disciples, that time of sorrow would most certainly come. It is one of the great inevitabilities of life that the dearest joy must come to an end.

Epictetus, the Greek philosopher, said grimly: 'When you are kissing your child, say to yourself: "One day you must die."' That is why we must know God and Jesus Christ. Jesus alone is the same yesterday, today and forever; God alone abides amid all the chances and the changes of life. The dearest human relationships must some day come to an end;

it is only the joy of heaven which lasts forever, and if we have it in our hearts, nothing can take it away.

(3) This also is a challenge. It may be that at the time the disciples did not see it, but Jesus is saying to them: 'You have experienced the joy that following me can bring; can you also go through the trouble, the hardship, the suffering of a Christian's cross?' The Christian way brings its joy; but the Christian way also brings its blood and sweat and tears, which cannot take the joy away but which nonetheless must be faced. So Jesus says: 'Are you ready for both – the Christian joy and the Christian cross?'

(4) Enshrined in this saying is the courage of Jesus. Jesus was never under any illusions; clearly at the end of the road he saw the cross awaiting him. Here the curtain is lifted, and there is a glimpse into the mind of Jesus. He knew that for him the way of life was the way of the cross, and yet he did not swerve one step aside from it. Here is the courage of the man who knows what God's way costs, and who yet goes on.

THE PROBLEM OF THE NEW IDEA

Matthew 9:16–17

> 'No one puts a patch of unshrunken cloth on an old garment, for, if he does, the patch which he uses to fill in the hole tears the garment apart, and the rent is worse than ever. No one puts new wine into old wine skins. If he does, the wine skins burst, and the wine is spilled, and the skins perish; but they put new wine into new skins, and both are preserved.'

JESUS was perfectly conscious that he came to men and women with new ideas and with a new conception of the truth, and he was well aware how difficult it is to get a new idea into people's minds. So he used two pictures which any Jew would understand.

(1) 'No one', he said, 'takes a piece of new and un-shrunken cloth to patch an old garment. If that happens, on the first occasion that the garment becomes wet, the new patch shrinks, and as it shrinks, it tears the cloth apart, and the rent in the garment gapes wider than ever.'

The Jews were passionately attached to things as they were. The law was to them God's last and final word; to add one word to it, or to subtract one word from it, was a deadly sin. It was the avowed object of the scribes and Pharisees 'to build a fence around the law'. To them, a new idea was not so much a mistake as a sin.

That spirit is by no means dead. Very often in a church, if a new idea or a new method or any change is suggested, the objection is promptly raised: 'We never did that before.'

I once heard two theologians talking together. One was a younger man who was intensely interested in all that the new thinkers have to say; the other was an older man of a rigid and conventional orthodoxy. The older man heard the younger man with a kind of half-contemptuous tolerance, and finally closed the conversation by saying: 'The old is better.'

Throughout all its history, the Church has clung to the old. What Jesus is saying is that there comes a time when patching is folly, and when the only thing to do is to scrap something entirely and to begin again. There are forms of church government, there are forms of church service, there are forms of words expressing our beliefs, which we so often try to adjust and tinker with in order to bring them up to date; we try to patch them. No one would willingly, or recklessly, or callously abandon what has stood the test of time and of the years and in which former generations have found their comfort and put their trust; but the fact remains that this is a growing and an expanding universe; and there comes a time when patches are useless, and when individuals and churches have to accept the adventure of the new, or withdraw into the backwater, where they worship not God but the past.

(2) No one, said Jesus, tries to put new wine into old wine skins. In the old days, wine was stored in skins and not in bottles. When new wine was put into a skin, the wine was still fermenting. The gases which it gave off exerted pressure on the skin. In a new skin there was a certain elasticity, and no harm was done because the skin gave with the pressure. But an old skin had grown hard and had lost all its elasticity, and, if new and fermenting wine was put into it, it could not give to the pressure of the gases; it could only burst.

To put this into contemporary terms: our minds must be elastic enough to receive and to contain new ideas. The history of progress is the history of the overcoming of the prejudices of the shut mind. Every new idea has had to battle for its existence against the instinctive opposition of the human mind. The car, the train and the aeroplane were in the beginning regarded with suspicion. Sir James Simpson had to fight to introduce chloroform, and Joseph Lister had to struggle to introduce antiseptics. Copernicus was compelled to retract his statement that the earth went round the sun, and not the sun round the earth. Even Jonas Hanway, who brought the umbrella to Britain, had to suffer a barrage of missiles and insults when he first walked down the street with it.

This dislike of the new enters into every sphere of life. Norman Marlow, an expert on railways, made many journeys on the footplates of locomotives. In his book *Footplate and Signal Cabin*, he tells of a journey he made not long after the amalgamation of the railways. Locomotives which had been used on one branch of the railways were being tested out on other lines. He was on the footplate of a Manchester-to-

Penzance express, a 'Jubilee' class 4–6–0. The driver was a
Great Western Railway driver who had been used to driving
locomotives of the 'Castle' class. 'The driver did nothing but
discourse with moody eloquence on the wretchedness of the
engine he was driving' as compared with the 'Castle' engines.
He refused to use the technique necessary for the new engine,
although he had been instructed in it and knew it perfectly
well. He insisted on driving his 'Jubilee' as if it had been a
'Castle' and grumbled all the way that he could not get better
speed than 50 miles per hour. He was used to 'Castles', and
with him nothing else had a chance. At Crewe a new driver
took over, a man who was quite prepared to adopt the necessary new technique, and soon he had the 'Jubilee' travelling
at 80 miles per hour. Even in engine-driving, people resented
new ideas.

Within the Church, this resentment of the new is chronic,
and the attempt to pour new things into old moulds is
almost universal. We attempt to pour the activities of a
modern congregation into an ancient church building which
was never meant for them. We attempt to pour the truth of
new discoveries into creeds which are based on Greek
metaphysics. We attempt to pour modern instruction into
outworn language which cannot express it. We read God's
word to men and women of the twenty-first century in
Elizabethan English, and seek to present the needs of modern
men and women to God in prayer language which is 400
years old.

It may be that we would do well to remember that when
any living thing stops growing, it starts dying. It may be that
we need to pray that God would deliver us from the shut
mind.

It so happens that we are living in an age of rapid and
tremendous changes. Viscount Samuel was born in 1870, and

he begins his autobiography with a description of the London of his childhood. 'We had no motor-cars, or motor-buses, or taxis, or tube railways; there were no bicycles – except the high "pennyfarthings"; there were no electric light or telephones, no cinemas or broadcasts.' That was just over a century ago. We are living in a changing and an expanding world. It is Jesus' warning that the Church dare not be the only institution which lives in the past.

THE IMPERFECT FAITH
AND THE PERFECT POWER

Matthew 9:18–31

BEFORE we deal with this passage in detail, we must look at it as a whole; for in it there is something wonderful.

It has three miracle stories in it: the healing of the ruler's daughter (verses 18–19, 23–6); the healing of the woman with the issue of blood (verses 20–2); and the healing of the two blind men (verses 27–31). Each of these stories has something in common. Let us look at them one by one.

(1) Beyond doubt, the ruler came to Jesus when everything else had failed. He was, as we shall see, a ruler of the synagogue; that is to say, he was a pillar of Jewish orthodoxy. He was one of the men who despised and hated Jesus, and who would have been glad to see him eliminated. No doubt he tried every kind of doctor, and every kind of cure; and only in sheer desperation, and as a last resort, did he come to Jesus at all.

That is to say, *the ruler came to Jesus from a very inadequate motive*. He did not come to Jesus as a result of an outflow of the love of his heart; he came to Jesus because he had tried everything and everyone else, and because there was nowhere else to go. The hymn-writer F. W. Faber makes God say of a straying child of God:

> If goodness lead him not,
> Then weariness may toss him to my breast.

This man came to Jesus simply because desperation drove him there.

(2) The woman with the issue of blood crept up behind Jesus in the crowd and touched the hem of his cloak. Suppose we were reading that story with a detached and critical awareness, what would we say that woman showed? We would say that she showed nothing other than superstition. To touch the edge of Jesus' cloak is the same kind of thing as to look for healing power in the relics and the handkerchiefs of saints.

This woman came to Jesus with what we would call a very inadequate faith. She came with what seems much more like superstition than faith.

(3) The two blind men came to Jesus, crying out: 'Have pity on us, you Son of David.' *Son of David* was not a title that Jesus desired; *Son of David* was the kind of title that a Jewish nationalist might use. So many of the Jews were waiting for a great leader of the line of David who would be the conquering general who would lead them to military and political triumph over their Roman masters. That is the idea which lies behind the title *Son of David*.

So *these blind men came to Jesus with a very inadequate conception of who he was*. They saw in him no more than the conquering hero of David's line.

Here is an astonishing thing. The ruler came to Jesus with an *inadequate motive*; the woman came to Jesus with an *inadequate faith*; the blind men came to Jesus with an *inadequate conception* of who he was, or, if we like to put it so, with an *inadequate theology*; and yet they found his love and power waiting for their needs. Here we see a tremendous thing. It does not matter how we come to Christ, if only we come. No matter how inadequately and how imperfectly we come, his love and his arms are open to receive us.

There is a double lesson here. It means that we do not wait to ask Christ's help until our motives, our faith and our theology are perfect; we may come to him exactly as we are. And it means that we have no right to criticize others whose motives we suspect, whose faith we question and whose theology we believe to be mistaken. It is not how we come to Christ that matters; it is that we should come at all, for he is willing to accept us as we are, and able to make us what we ought to be.

THE AWAKENING TOUCH

Matthew 9:18–19, 23–6

> While he was saying these things, look you, a ruler came and knelt before him in worship. 'My daughter', he said, 'has just died. But come and lay your hand upon her, and she will live.' Jesus rose and went with him, and his disciples came too . . . And Jesus came to the house of the ruler, and he saw the flute-players and the tumult of the crowd. 'Leave us,' he said, 'for the maid is not dead; she is asleep.' And they laughed at him. When the crowd had been put out, he went in and took her hand, and the maid arose. And the report of this went out to the whole country.

MATTHEW tells this story much more briefly than the other gospel writers do. If we want further details of it, we must read it in Mark 5:21–43 and in Luke 8:40–56. There we discover that the ruler's name was Jairus, and that he was a ruler of the synagogue (Mark 5:22; Luke 8:41).

The ruler of the synagogue was a very important person. He was elected from among the elders. He was not a teaching or a preaching official; he had 'the care of the external order in public worship, and the supervision of the concerns of the synagogue in general'. He appointed those who were to read and to pray in the service, and invited those who were to preach. It was his duty to see that nothing unfitting took place within the synagogue; and the care of the synagogue buildings was in his oversight. The whole practical administration of the synagogue was in his hands.

It is clear that such a man would come to Jesus only as a last resort. He would be one of those strictly orthodox Jews who regarded Jesus as a dangerous heretic; and it was only when everything else had failed that he turned in desperation to Jesus. Jesus might well have said to him: 'When things were going well with you, you wanted to kill me; now that things are going badly, you are appealing for my help.' And Jesus might well have refused help to a man who came like that. But he bore no grudge; here was a man who needed him, and Jesus' one desire was to help. Injured pride and the unforgiving spirit had no part in the mind of Jesus.

So Jesus went with the ruler of the synagogue to his house, and there he found a scene of pandemonium. The Jews set very high the obligation of mourning over the dead. 'Whoever is remiss', they said, 'in mourning over the death of a wise man deserves to be burned alive.' There were three mourning customs which characterized every Jewish household of grief.

There was the *rending of garments*. There were no fewer than thirty-nine different rules and regulations which laid down how garments should be rent. The rent was to be made standing. Clothes were to be rent to the heart so that the skin was exposed. For a father or mother, the rent was exactly over the heart; for others, it was on the right side. The rent must be big enough for a fist to be inserted into it. For seven days, the rent must be left gaping open; for the next thirty days, it must be loosely stitched so that it could still be seen; only then could it be permanently repaired. It would obviously have been improper for women to rend their garments in such a way that the breast was exposed. So it was laid down that a woman must rend her inner garment in private; she must then reverse the garment so that she wore it back to front; and then in public she must rend her outer garment.

There was *wailing for the dead*. In a house of grief, an incessant wailing was kept up. The wailing was done by professional wailing women. They still exist in the middle east, and W. M. Thomson in *The Land and the Book* describes them: 'There are in every city and community women exceedingly cunning in this business. They are always sent for and kept in readiness. When a fresh company of sympathisers comes in, these women make haste to take up a wailing, that the newly-come may the more easily unite their tears with the mourners. They know the domestic history of every person, and immediately strike up an impromptu lamentation, in which they introduce the names of their relatives who have recently died, touching some tender chord in every heart; and thus each one weeps for his own dead, and the performance, which would otherwise be difficult or impossible, comes easy and natural.'

There were *the flute-players*. The music of the flute was especially associated with death. The *Talmud* lays it down: 'The husband is bound to bury his dead wife, and to make lamentations and mourning for her, according to the custom of all countries. And also the very poorest among the Israelites will not allow her less than two flutes and one wailing woman;

but, if he be rich, let all things be done according to his qualities.' Even in Rome, the flute-players were a feature of days of grief. There were flute-players at the funeral of the Roman emperor Claudius, and Seneca tells us that they made such a shrilling that even Claudius himself, dead though he was, might have heard them. So insistent and so emotionally exciting was the wailing of the flute that Roman law limited the number of flute-players at any funeral to ten.

We can then picture the scene in the house of the ruler of the synagogue. The garments were being torn; the wailing women were uttering their shrieks in an abandonment of synthetic grief; the flutes were shrilling their eerie sound. In that house, there was all the pandemonium of middle-eastern grief.

Into that excited and hysterical atmosphere came Jesus. Authoritatively he sent them all out. Quietly he told them that the girl was not dead but only asleep, and they laughed at him. It is a strangely human touch, this. The mourners were so luxuriating in their grief that they even resented hope.

It is probable that when Jesus said the girl was asleep, he meant exactly what he said. In Greek as in English, a dead person was often said to be asleep. In fact, the word *cemetery* comes from the Greek word *koimētērion* and means *a place where people sleep*. In Greek there are two words for *to sleep*: the one is *koimasthai*, which is very commonly used both of natural sleep and of the sleep of death; the other is *katheudein*, which is not used nearly so frequently of the sleep of death, but which much more usually means natural sleep. It is *katheudein* which is used in this passage.

In this part of the world, cataleptic coma was by no means uncommon. Burial in the middle east follows death very quickly, because the climate makes it necessary. Henry Baker Tristram, who travelled extensively in the Bible lands, writes:

'Interments always take place at latest on the evening of the day of death, and frequently at night, if the deceased have lived till after sunset.' Because of the commonness of this state of coma, and because of the commonness of speedy burial, not infrequently people were buried alive, as the evidence of the tombs shows. It may well be that here we have an example not so much of divine healing as of divine diagnosis; and that Jesus saved this girl from a terrible end.

One thing is certain: Jesus that day in Capernaum rescued a young Jewish girl from the grasp of death.

ALL HEAVEN'S POWER FOR ONE

Matthew 9:20–2

> And, look you, a woman who had had a haemorrhage for twelve years came up behind him, and touched the tassel of his cloak. For she said to herself, 'If I only touch his cloak, I will be cured.' Jesus turned and saw her. 'Courage, daughter!' he said. 'Your faith has brought you healing.' And the woman was cured from that hour.

FROM the Jewish point of view, this woman could not have suffered from any more terrible or humiliating disease than an issue of blood. It was a trouble which was very common in Palestine. The *Talmud* sets out no fewer than eleven different cures for it. Some of them were tonics and astringents which may well have been effective; others were merely superstitious remedies. One was to carry the ashes of an ostrich egg in a linen bag in summer and in a cotton bag in winter; another was to carry about a barleycorn which had been found in the dung of a white she-ass. When Mark tells this story, he makes it clear that this woman had tried everything, and had gone to every available doctor, and was worse instead of better (Mark 5:26).

The horror of the disease was that it rendered the sufferer unclean. The law laid it down: 'If a woman has a discharge of blood for many days, not at the time of her impurity, or if she has a discharge beyond the time of her impurity, for all the days of the discharge she shall continue in uncleanness; as in the days of her impurity, she shall be unclean. Every bed on which she lies during all the days of her discharge shall be treated as the bed of her impurity; and everything on which she sits shall be unclean, as in the uncleanness of her impurity. Whoever touches these things shall be unclean, and shall wash his clothes, and bathe in water, and be unclean until the evening' (Leviticus 15:25–7).

That is to say, a woman with an issue of blood was unclean; everything and everyone she touched was infected with that uncleanness. She was absolutely shut off from the worship of God and from the fellowship of other men and women. She should not even have been in the crowd surrounding Jesus, for, if they had known it, she was infecting with her uncleanness everyone whom she touched. There is little wonder that she was desperately eager to try anything which might rescue her from her life of isolation and humiliation.

So she slipped up behind Jesus and touched what the Authorized Version calls the *hem* of his garment. The Greek word is *kraspedon*, the Hebrew is *zizith*, and the Revised Standard Version translates it as *fringe*.

These fringes were four tassels of hyacinth blue worn by a Jew on the corners of his outer garment. They were worn in obedience to the injunction of the law in Numbers 15:37–41 and Deuteronomy 22:12. Matthew again refers to them in 14:36 and 23:5. They consisted of four threads passing through the four corners of the garment and meeting in eight.

One of the threads was longer than the others. It was twisted seven times round the others, and a double knot formed; then eight times, then eleven times, then thirteen times. The thread and the knots stood for the five books of the law.

The idea of the fringe was twofold. It was meant to identify a Jew as a Jew, and as a member of the chosen people, no matter where he was; and it was meant to remind a Jew every time he put on and took off his clothes that he belonged to God. In later times, when the Jews were universally persecuted, the tassels were worn on the undergarment, and today they are worn on the prayer shawl which devout Jews wear when they pray.

It was the tassel on the robe of Jesus that this woman touched.

When she touched it, it was as if time stood still. It was as if we were watching a film and suddenly the picture stopped and left us looking at one scene. The extraordinary, and the movingly beautiful, thing about this scene is that all at once in the middle of that crowd Jesus halted; and for the moment it seemed that for him no one but that woman and nothing but her need existed. She was not simply a poor woman lost in the crowd; she was someone to whom Jesus gave the whole of himself.

For Jesus, no one is ever lost in the crowd, because Jesus is like God. The Irish poet W. B. Yeats once wrote in one of his moments of mystical beauty: 'The love of God is infinite for every human soul, because every human soul is unique; no other can satisfy the same need in God.' God gives all of himself to each individual person.

The world is not like that. The world is apt to divide people into those who are important and those who are unimportant.

In *A Night to Remember*, Walter Lord tells in detail the story of the sinking of the *Titanic* in April 1912. There was an appalling loss of life when that new and supposedly unsinkable liner hit an iceberg in the middle of the Atlantic. After the tragedy had been announced, the New York news-paper *The American* featured a leading article devoted entirely to the death of John Jacob Astor, the millionaire; and at the end of the leader, almost casually, it was mentioned that 1,800 others were also lost. The only one who really mattered, the only one with real news value, was the millionaire. The other losses were of no real importance.

Men and women can be like that, but God can never be like that. Alexander Bain, the psychologist, said in a very different connection that the sensual person has what he calls 'a voluminous tenderness'. In the highest and the best sense, there is a voluminous tenderness in God. James Agate said of the writer G. K. Chesterton: 'Unlike some thinkers, Chesterton understood his fellow-men; the woes of a jockey were as familiar to him as the worries of a judge . . . Chesterton, more than any man I have ever known, had the common touch . . . He had about him that bounty of heart which men call kindness, and which makes the whole world kin.' That is the reflection of the love of God which does not allow anyone to be lost in the crowd.

This is something to remember in a day and an age when the individual is in danger of getting lost. Men and women tend to become numbers in a system of social security; they tend as members of an association or union almost to lose their right to be individuals at all. W. B. Yeats said of Augustus John, the famous artist and portrait painter: 'He was supremely interested in the revolt from all that makes one man like another.' To God, one person is never like another; each person is his individual child, and each of us has all God's love and all God's power at our disposal.

To Jesus, this woman was not lost in the crowd; in her hour of need, to him she was all that mattered. Jesus is like that for every one of us.

FAITH'S TEST AND FAITH'S REWARD

Matthew 9:27–31

> And, as he passed on from there, two blind men followed him, shouting. 'Have pity on us,' they said, 'you Son of David.' When he came into the house, the blind men came to him. Jesus said to them, 'Do you believe that I am able to do this?' 'Yes, Lord,' they said. Then he touched their eyes. 'Be it to you,' he said, 'according to your faith.' And their eyes were opened. And Jesus sternly commanded them, 'See, let no one know of this.' But they went out and spread abroad the story of him all over the country.

BLINDNESS was a distressingly common disease in Palestine. It came partly from the glare of the sun on unprotected eyes, and partly because people knew nothing of the importance of cleanliness and hygiene. In particular, the clouds of unclean flies carried infections which led to loss of sight.

The name by which these two blind men addressed Jesus was *Son of David*. When we study the occurrences of that title within the gospels, we find that it is almost always used by crowds or by people who knew Jesus only, as it were, at a distance (Matthew 15:22, 20:30–1; Mark 10:47, 12:35–7). The term *Son of David* describes Jesus in the popular conception of the Messiah. For centuries, the Jews had awaited the promised deliverer of David's line, the leader who would not only restore their freedom, but who would lead them to power and glory and greatness. It was in that

403

way that these blind men thought of Jesus; they saw in him the wonder-worker who would lead the people to freedom and to conquest. They came to Jesus with a very inadequate idea of who and what he was, and yet he healed them. The way in which Jesus dealt with them is illuminating.

(1) Clearly, he did not answer their shouts at once. Jesus wished to be quite sure that they were sincere and earnest in their desire for what he could give them. It might well have been that they had taken up a popular cry just because everyone else was shouting, and that, as soon as Jesus had passed by, they would simply forget. He wanted first of all to be sure that their request was genuine and that their sense of need was real.

After all, there were advantages in being a beggar; a man was rid of all the responsibility of working and of making a living.

There are people who in actual fact do not wish their chains to be broken. W. B. Yeats tells of Lionel Johnson, the scholar and poet. Johnson was an alcoholic. He had, as he said himself, 'a craving that made every atom of his body cry out'. But, when it was suggested that he should undergo treatment to overcome this craving, his answer quite frankly was: 'I do not want to be cured.'

There are not a few people who in their heart of hearts do not dislike their weakness; and there are many people who, if they were honest, would have to say that they do not wish to lose their sins. Jesus had first of all to be sure that these men sincerely and earnestly desired the healing he could give.

(2) It is interesting to note that Jesus in effect compelled these people to see him alone. Because he did not answer them in the streets, they had to come to him in the house. It is the law of the spiritual life that sooner or later every individual must confront Jesus alone. It is all very well to take a decision

for Jesus on the flood tide of emotion at some great gathering, or in some little group which is charged with spiritual power. But after the crowd, people have to go home and be alone; after the fellowship, they must go back to the essential isolation of every human soul; and what really matters is not what people do in the crowd, but what they do when they are alone with Christ. Jesus compelled these men to face him alone.

(3) Jesus asked these men only one question: 'Do you believe that I am able to do this?' The one essential for a miracle is faith. There is nothing mysterious or theological about this. No doctor can cure a sick person who goes to him in a completely hopeless frame of mind. No medicine will do any good if those taking it think they might as well be drinking water. The way to a miracle is to place one's life in the hands of Jesus Christ and say: 'I know that you can make me what I ought to be.'

THE TWO REACTIONS

Matthew 9:32-4

> As they were going away, look you, they brought to
> him a dumb man who was demon-possessed; and, when
> the demon had been expelled from him, he spoke. And
> the crowds were amazed. 'Nothing like this', they said,
> 'was ever seen in Israel.' But the Pharisees said, 'He
> casts out the demons by the power of the prince of the
> demons.'

THERE are few passages which show better than this the impossibility of an attitude of neutrality towards Jesus. Here we have the picture of two reactions to him. The attitude of the crowds was amazed wonder; the attitude of the Pharisees was virulent hatred. It must always remain true that what the eye sees depends upon what the heart feels.

The crowds looked on Jesus with wonder, because they were simple people with a crying sense of need; and they saw that in Jesus their need could be supplied in the most astonishing way. Jesus will always appear wonderful to those with a sense of need; and the deeper the sense of need, the more wonderful Jesus will appear to be.

The Pharisees saw Jesus as one who was in league with all the powers of evil. They did not deny his wondrous powers; but they attributed them to his complicity with the prince of the devils. This verdict of the Pharisees was due to certain attitudes of mind.

(1) They were too set in their ways to change. As we have seen, as far as they were concerned not one word could be added to or subtracted from the law. To them, all the great things belonged to the past. To them, to change a tradition or a convention was a deadly sin. Anything that was new was wrong. And when Jesus came with a new interpretation of what real religion was, they hated him, as they had hated the prophets long ago.

(2) They were too proud in their self-satisfaction to submit. If Jesus was right, they were wrong. The Pharisees were so well satisfied with themselves that they saw no need to change; and they hated anyone who wished to change them. Repentance is the gate whereby we all must enter the kingdom; and repentance means the recognition of the error of our ways, the realization that in Christ alone there is life, and the surrender to him and to his will and power, whereby alone we can be changed.

(3) They were too prejudiced to see. Their eyes were so blinded by their own ideas that they could not see in Jesus Christ the truth and the power of God.

Those who have a sense of need will always see wonders in Jesus Christ. People who are so set in their ways that they will not change, people who are so proud in their self-righteousness that they cannot submit, people who are so blinded by their prejudices that they cannot see, will always resent and hate and seek to eliminate him.

THE THREEFOLD WORK

Matthew 9:35

> And Jesus made a tour of all the towns and villages, teaching in synagogues, and heralding forth the good news of the kingdom, and healing every disease and every illness.

HERE in one sentence we see the threefold activity which was the essence of the life of Jesus.

(1) Jesus was the *herald*. The herald is the one who brings a message from the king; Jesus was the one who brought a message from God. The duty of the herald is the proclamation of certainties; preaching must always be the proclamation of certainties. No church can ever be composed of people who are certain, as it were, by proxy. It is not only the preacher who must be certain. The people must be certain too.

There has never been a time when this certainty was more needed than it is today. Geoffrey Heawood, headmaster of a great English public school, has written that the great tragedy and problem of this age is that we are standing at the crossroads, and the signposts have fallen down.

Beverley Nichols, the novelist, once wrote a book composed of interviews with famous people. One of the interviews was with Hilaire Belloc, one of the most famous of English Roman Catholics. After the interview, Nichols wrote: 'I was sorry for Mr Belloc because I felt that he had nailed at least some of his colours to the wrong mast; but I was still sorrier for myself and for my own generation, because I knew that we had no colours of any kind to nail to any mast.'

We live in an age of uncertainty, an age when people have ceased to be sure of anything. Jesus was the herald of God, who came proclaiming the certainties by which men and women live; and we too must be able to say: 'I know whom I have believed.'

(2) Jesus was *teacher*. It is not enough to proclaim the Christian certainties and let it go at that; we must also be able to show the significance of these certainties for life and for living. The importance and the problem of this lie in the fact that we teach Christianity, not by talking about it, but by living it. It is not the Christian's duty to discuss Christianity with others, so much as it is to show them what Christianity is.

A writer who lived in India in the days before Partition writes like this: 'I remember a British battalion, which like most battalions came to parade service because they had to, sang hymns they liked, listened to the preacher if they thought him interesting, and left the Church alone for the rest of the week. But their rescue work at the time of the Quetta earthquake so impressed a Brahmin that he demanded immediate baptism, because only the Christian religion could make men behave like that.'

The thing which taught that Brahmin what Christianity was like was Christianity in action. To put this at its highest: our duty is not to talk to people about Jesus Christ, but to show him to them. A saint has been defined as someone in whom Christ lives again. All Christians must be teachers, and they must teach others what Christianity is, not by their words, but by their lives.

(3) Jesus was *healer*. The gospel which Jesus brought did not stop at words; it was translated into deeds. If we read through the gospels, we will see that Jesus spent far more time healing the sick, feeding the hungry and comforting the sorrowing than he did merely talking about God. He turned the words of Christian truth into the deeds of Christian love. We are not truly Christian until our Christian belief issues in Christian action. The priest would have said that religion consists of sacrifice; the scribe would have said that religion consists of law; but Jesus Christ said that religion consists of love.

THE DIVINE COMPASSION

Matthew 9:36

> When he saw the crowds, he was moved with compassion to the depths of his being, for they were bewildered and dejected, like sheep who have no shepherd.

WHEN Jesus saw the crowd of ordinary men and women, he was *moved with compassion*. The word which is used for *moved with compassion* (*splagchnistheis*) is the strongest word for pity in the Greek language. It is formed from the word *splagchna*, which means *the bowels*, and it describes the compassion which moves people to the deepest depths of their being. In the gospels, apart from its use in some of the parables, it is used only of Jesus (Matthew 9:36, 14:14, 15:32, 20:34; Mark 1:41; Luke 7:13). When we study these passages, we are able to see the things which moved Jesus most of all.

(1) He was moved to compassion by the world's *pain*. He was moved with compassion for the sick (Matthew 14:14), for the blind (Matthew 20:34) and for those in the grip of the

demons (Mark 9:22). In all our afflictions, he is afflicted. He could not see a sufferer without longing to ease the pain.

(2) He was moved to compassion by the world's *sorrow*. The sight of the widow at Nain, following the body of her son out to burial, moved his heart (Luke 7:13). He was filled with a great desire to wipe the tear from every eye.

(3) He was moved to compassion by the world's *hunger*. The sight of the tired and hungry crowds was a call upon his power (Matthew 15:32). No Christian can be content to have too much while others have too little.

(4) He was moved to compassion by the world's *loneliness*. The sight of a leper, banished from all human society, living a life which was a living death of loneliness and universal abandonment, called forth his pity and his power (Mark 1:41).

(5) He was moved to compassion by the world's *bewilderment*. That is what moved Jesus on this occasion. The common people were desperately longing for God; and the scribes and the Pharisees, the priests and the Sadducees, the pillars of orthodox religion of his day, had nothing to offer them. The orthodox teachers had neither guidance, nor comfort, nor strength to give. John Milton, in *Lycidas*, describes almost savagely the religious leaders who have nothing to offer:

> Blind mouths! that scarce themselves know how to hold
> A sheep-hook, or have learnt aught else the least
> That to the faithful herdsman's art belongs!
> . . . Their lean and flashy songs
> Grate on their scrannel pipes of wretched straw,
> The hungry sheep look up and are not fed.

The words that are used to describe the state of ordinary people are vivid words. The word that we have translated as *bewildered* is *eskulmenoi*. It can describe a corpse which is *flayed* and *mangled*; someone who is *robbed* through extortion, or *pestered* by those without pity, or treated with *wanton insolence*; someone who is utterly *wearied* by a journey which seems to know no end. The word that we have translated as *dejected* is *errimenoi*. It means *laid prostrate*. It can describe someone prostrated with drink or someone laid low with mortal wounds.

The Jewish leaders, who should have been giving men and women strength to live, were bewildering them with subtle arguments about the law which had no help and comfort in them. When they should have been helping men and women to stand upright, they were bowing them down under the intolerable weight of the scribal law. They were offering a religion which was a handicap instead of a support. We must always remember that Christianity exists not to discourage but to encourage; not to weigh people down with burdens but to lift them up with wings.

THE WAITING HARVEST

Matthew 9:37–8

> Then he said to his disciples, 'The harvest is great, but the workers are few. Therefore, pray to the Lord of the harvest to send out workers for his harvest.'

HERE is one of the most characteristic things Jesus ever said. When he and the orthodox religious leaders of his day looked on the crowd of ordinary men and women, they saw them in quite different ways. The Pharisees saw the masses as chaff to be destroyed and burned up; Jesus saw them as a harvest to be reaped and to be saved. The Pharisees in their pride looked for the destruction of sinners; Jesus in love died for the salvation of sinners.

But here also is one of the great Christian truths and one of the supreme Christian challenges. That harvest will never be reaped unless there are reapers to reap it. It is one of the blazing truths of Christian faith and life that *Jesus Christ needs us*. When he was upon this earth, his voice could reach so few. He was never outside Palestine, and there was a world which was waiting. He still wants the world to hear the good news of the gospel; but they will never hear unless others tell them. He wants all men and women to hear the good news; but they will never hear it unless there are those who are prepared to cross the seas and the mountains and bring the good news to them.

Nor is prayer enough. Some people might say: 'I will pray for the coming of Christ's kingdom every day in life.' But in this, as in so many things, prayer without works is dead. Martin Luther had a friend who felt about the Christian faith as he did. The friend was also a monk. They came to an agreement. Luther would go down into the dust and heat of the battle for the Reformation in the world; the friend would stay in the monastery and uphold Luther's hands in prayer. So they began that way. Then, one night, the friend had a dream. He saw a vast field of corn as big as the world; and one solitary man was seeking to reap it – an impossible and a heart-breaking task. Then he caught a glimpse of the reaper's face; and the reaper was Martin Luther; and Luther's friend saw the truth in a flash. 'I must leave my prayers', he said, 'and get to work.' And so he left his pious solitude and went down to the world to labour in the harvest.

It is the dream of Christ that we should all be missionaries and reapers. There are those who cannot do other than pray, because of physical limitations, and their prayers are indeed the strength of the labourers. But that is not the way for most of us, for those of us who have strength of body and health of mind. Not even the giving of our money is enough. If the harvest of men and women is ever to be reaped, then every one of us must be a reaper, for there is someone whom each one of us could – and must – bring to God.

THE MESSENGERS OF THE KING

Matthew 10:1-4

> And when he had summoned his twelve disciples, he gave them power over unclean spirits, so that they were able to cast them out, and so that they were able to heal every disease and every sickness. These are the names of the twelve apostles: first and foremost Simon, who is called Peter, and Andrew, his brother; James, the son of Zebedee, and John, his brother; Philip and Bartholomew; Thomas and Matthew, the tax-collector; James, the son of Alphaeus, and Thaddaeus; Simon the Cananaean and Judas Iscariot, who was also his betrayer.

METHODICALLY, and yet with a certain drama, Matthew unfolds his story of Jesus. In the story of the baptism, Matthew shows us Jesus accepting his task. In the story of the temptations, Matthew shows us Jesus deciding on the method which he will use to embark upon his task. In the Sermon on the Mount, we listen to Jesus' words of wisdom. In Matthew 8, we look on Jesus' deeds of power. In Matthew 9, we see the growing opposition gathering itself against Jesus. And now we see Jesus choosing his disciples.

If a leader is about to embark upon any great undertaking, the first thing that must be done is that staff must be chosen. On those selected, the present effect and the future success of the work both depend. Here Jesus is choosing his staff, his right-hand men, his helpers during his earthly life, and those who would carry on his work when he left this earth and returned to his glory.

There are two facts about the Twelve which are bound to strike us at once.

(1) They were very ordinary men. They had no wealth; they had no academic background; they had no social position. They were chosen from among ordinary people, men who did the ordinary things, men who had no special education, men who had no social advantages.

It has been said that Jesus is looking not so much for extraordinary people as for ordinary people who can do ordinary things extraordinarily well. Jesus sees in each one of us not only what we are, but also what he can make us. Jesus chose these men not only for what they were but also for what they were capable of becoming under his influence and in his power.

We need never think that we have nothing to offer Jesus, for Jesus can take what the most ordinary people can offer and use it for greatness.

(2) They were the most extraordinary mixture. There was, for instance, Matthew, the tax-gatherer. Everyone would regard Matthew as a collaborator, as one who had sold himself into the hands of his country's masters for gain, the very reverse of a patriot and a lover of his country. And with Matthew there was Simon the *Cananaean*. Luke (6:16) calls him Simon *Zelōtēs*, which means Simon the *Zealot*.

Josephus (*Antiquities*, 8:1:6) describes these Zealots; he calls them the fourth party of the Jews, the other three parties being the Pharisees, the Sadducees and the Essenes. He says that they had 'an inviolable attachment to liberty' and that they said that 'God is to be their ruler and Lord'. They were prepared to face any kind of death for their country, and did not shrink to see their loved ones die in the struggle for freedom. They refused to give to any earthly man the name and the title of king. They had an immovable resolution which would undergo any pain. They were prepared to go to the lengths of secret murder and stealthy assassination to seek to rid their country of foreign rule. They were the patriots *par excellence* among the Jews, the most nationalist of all the nationalists.

The plain fact is that if Simon the Zealot had met Matthew the tax-gatherer anywhere else than in the company of Jesus, he would have stuck a dagger in him. Here is the tremendous truth that people who hate each other can learn to love each other when they both love Jesus Christ. Too often, religion has been a means of creating divisions. It was meant to be – and in the presence of the living Jesus it was – a means of bringing together those who without Christ were separated from each other.

We may ask why Jesus chose *twelve* special apostles. The reason is very likely because there were *twelve* tribes; just as in the old dispensation there had been twelve tribes of Israel, so in the new dispensation there are twelve apostles of the new Israel. The New Testament itself does not tell us very much about these men. As the scholar A. Plummer has it, 'In the New Testament it is the work, and not the workers, that is glorified.' But, although we do not know much about them, the New Testament is very conscious of their greatness in the Church, for the Book of Revelation tells us that the twelve foundation stones of the holy city are inscribed with their names (Revelation 21:14). These men, simple men with no great background, men from many differing spheres of belief, were the very foundation stones on which the Church was built. It is on the stuff of ordinary men and women that the Church of Christ is founded.

THE MAKING OF THE MESSENGERS

Matthew 10:1–4 (*contd*)

WHEN we put together the three accounts of the calling of the Twelve (Matthew 10:1–4; Mark 3:13–19; Luke 6:13–16), certain illuminating facts emerge.

(1) He *chose* them. Luke 6:13 says that Jesus called his disciples, and *chose from them twelve*. It is as if Jesus' eyes moved over the crowds who followed him, and the smaller band who stayed with him when the crowds had departed, and as if all the time he was searching for the men to whom he could commit his work. As it has been said, 'God is always looking for hands to use.' God is always saying: 'Whom shall I send, and who will go for us?' (Isaiah 6:8).

There are many tasks in the kingdom – the task of those who must go out and the task of those who must stay at home, the task of those who must use their hands and the task of those who must use their minds, the task which will fasten the eyes of all upon the doer and the task which no one will ever see. And always Jesus' eyes are searching the crowds for those who will do his work.

(2) He *called* them. Jesus does not compel us to do his work; he offers us work to do. Jesus does not coerce; he invites. Jesus does not make conscripts; he seeks volunteers. As it has been put, we are free to be faithful and free to be faithless. But to each one of us there comes the summons which we can accept or refuse.

(3) He *appointed* them. The Authorized Version has it that he ordained them (Mark 3:14). The word which is translated as *ordain* is the simple Greek word *poiein*, which means *to make* or *to do* but which is often technically used for *appointing to some office*. Jesus was like a king appointing his men to be his ministers; he was like a general allocating their tasks to his commanders. It was not a case of drifting unconsciously into the service of Jesus Christ; it was a case of definitely being appointed to it. Those who are appointed to some earthly office by some earthly king might well be proud; how much greater their pride when they are appointed by the King of Kings?

(4) These men were appointed from *among the disciples*. The word disciple means *a learner*. The men and women whom Christ needs and desires are those who are willing to learn. The shut mind cannot serve him. Servants of Christ must be willing to learn more every day. Each day, we must be a step nearer Jesus and a little nearer God.

(5) The reasons why these men were chosen are equally significant. They were chosen *to be with him* (Mark 3:14). If they were to do his work in the world, they must live in his presence before they went out to the world; they must go from the presence of Jesus into the presence of men and women.

It is told that on one occasion Alexander Whyte, the Principal of New College, Edinburgh, preached a most powerful and most moving sermon. After the service, a friend said to him: 'You preached today as if you had come straight from the presence of Jesus Christ.' Whyte answered: 'Perhaps I did.'

No work of Christ can ever be done except by men and women who come from the presence of Christ. Sometimes in the complexity of the activities of the modern Church we are so busy with committees and courts and administration and making the wheels go round that we are in danger of forgetting that none of these things matters, if it is carried on by people who have not been with Christ before they have been with others.

(6) They were called to be *apostles* (Mark 3:14; Luke 6:13). The word *apostle* literally means *one who is sent out*; it is the word for an *envoy* or an *ambassador*. Christians are Jesus Christ's ambassadors. They go forth from the presence of Christ, bearing with them the word and the beauty of their Master.

(7) They were called to be the *heralds* of Christ. In Matthew 10:7, they are bidden *to preach*. The word is *kērussein*, which comes from the noun *kērux*, which means a *herald*. Christians are the heralds of Christ. That is why they must begin in the presence of Christ. Christians are not meant to bring to others their own opinions; they bring a message of divine certainties from Jesus Christ – and they cannot bring that message unless first in the presence they have received it.

THE COMMISSION OF THE KING'S MESSENGER

Matthew 10:5–8a

> Jesus sent out these twelve, and these were the orders he gave them: 'Do not', he said, 'go out on the road to the Gentiles, and do not enter into any city of the Samaritans; but go rather to the sheep of the house of Israel who have perished. As you go make this proclamation: The kingdom of heaven is near. Heal the sick, raise the dead, cleanse the leper, cast out demons.'

HERE we have the beginning of the King's commission to his messengers. The word which is used in the Greek for Jesus

commanding the Twelve or *giving them orders* is interesting
and illuminating. It is the word *paragellein*. This word in
Greek has four special usages. (1) It is the regular word of
military command; Jesus was like a general sending his
commanders out on a campaign and briefing them before they
went. (2) It is the word used of calling one's friends to one's
help. Jesus was like a man with a great ideal summoning his
friends to make that ideal come true. (3) It is the word which
is used of a teacher giving rules and principles to students.
Jesus was like a teacher sending his students out into the
world, equipped with his teaching and his message. (4) It is
the word which is regularly used for an imperial command.
Jesus was like a king despatching his ambassadors into the
world to carry out his orders and to speak for him.

This passage begins with what everyone must find a very
difficult instruction. It begins by forbidding the Twelve to go
to the Gentiles or to the Samaritans. There are many who
find it very difficult to believe that Jesus ever said this at all.
This apparent exclusiveness is very unlike him; and it has
been suggested that this saying was put into his mouth by
those who in the later days wished to keep the gospel for the
Jews, the very people who bitterly opposed Paul when he
wished to take the gospel to the Gentiles.

But there are certain things to be remembered. This saying
is so uncharacteristic of Jesus that no one could have invented
it; he must have said it, and so there must be some explanation.

We can be quite certain it was not a *permanent* command.
Within the gospel itself, we see Jesus talking graciously and
privately to a woman of Samaria and revealing his true
identity (John 4:4–42); we see him telling one of his immortal
stories (Luke 10:30); we see him healing the daughter of a
Syro-Phoenician woman (Matthew 15:28); and Matthew
himself tells us of Jesus' final commission of his disciples to

go out into all the world and to bring all nations into the gospel (Matthew 28:19–20). What then is the explanation?

The Twelve were forbidden to go to the Gentiles; that meant that they could not go north into Syria, nor could they even go east into the Decapolis, which was largely a Gentile region. They could not go south into Samaria, for that was forbidden. The effect of this order was in actual fact to limit the first journeys of the Twelve to Galilee. There were three good reasons for that.

(1) The Jews had in God's scheme of things a very special place; in the justice of God they had to be given the first offer of the gospel. It is true that they rejected it; but the whole of history was designed to give them the first opportunity to accept.

(2) The Twelve were not equipped to preach to the Gentiles. They had neither the background nor the knowledge nor the technique. Before the gospel could be effectively brought to the Gentiles, a man with Paul's life and background had to emerge. A message has little chance of success if the messenger is ill-equipped to deliver it. If preachers or teachers are wise, they will be aware of their own limitations and will see clearly what they are and are not fitted to do.

(3) But the great reason for this command is simply this – wise commanders know that they must limit their objectives. They must direct their attack at one chosen point. If they spread their forces here, there and everywhere, they dissipate their strength and invite failure. The smaller their forces, the more limited the immediate objective must be. To attempt to attack on too broad a front is simply to court disaster. Jesus knew that, and his aim was to concentrate his attack on Galilee; for Galilee, as we have seen, was the most open of all parts of Palestine to a new gospel and a new message (cf. the discussion of Matthew 4:12–17). This command of Jesus

was a *temporary* command. He was the wise commander who refused to diffuse and dissipate his forces; he skilfully concentrated his attack on one limited objective in order to achieve an ultimate and universal victory.

THE WORDS AND WORKS
OF THE KING'S MESSENGER

Matthew 10:5–8a (*contd*)

THE King's messengers had words to speak and deeds to do.

(1) They had to announce the imminence of the kingdom. As we have seen (cf. the discussion of Matthew 6:10–11), the kingdom of God is a society on earth where God's will is as perfectly done as it is in heaven. Of all persons who ever lived in the world, Jesus was, and is, the only person who ever perfectly did, and obeyed, and fulfilled God's will. Therefore in him the kingdom had come. It is as if the messengers of the King were to say: 'Look! You have dreamed of the kingdom, and you have longed for the kingdom. Here in the life of Jesus *is* the kingdom. Look at him, and see what being in the kingdom means.' In Jesus, the kingdom of God had come to men and women.

(2) But the task of the Twelve was not confined to speaking words; it involved doing deeds. They had to heal the sick, to raise the dead, to cleanse the lepers and to cast out demons. All these injunctions are to be taken in a double sense. They are to be taken *physically*, because Jesus Christ came to bring health and healing to human bodies. But they are also to be taken *spiritually*. They describe the change brought about by Jesus Christ in human souls.

(a) They were to *heal the sick*. The word used for *sick* is very suggestive. It is a part of the Greek verb *asthenein*, the primary meaning of which is *to be weak*; *asthenēs* is the standard Greek adjective for *weak*. When Christ comes to us, he strengthens the weak will, he buttresses the weak resistance, he nerves the feeble arm for fight, he confirms the weak resolution. Jesus Christ fills our human weakness with his divine power.

(b) They were to *raise the dead*. We can be dead in sin. Our will to resist can be broken; our vision of the good can be darkened until it does not exist; we may be helplessly and hopelessly in the grip of our sins, blind to goodness and deaf to God. When Jesus Christ comes into our lives, he resurrects us to goodness and revitalizes the goodness within us which our sinning has killed.

(c) They were to cleanse *the lepers*. As we have seen, the leper was regarded as polluted. Leviticus says of him: 'He shall remain unclean as long as he has the disease; he is unclean. He shall live alone; his dwelling shall be outside the camp' (Leviticus 13:46). Second Kings 7:3–4 shows us the lepers who only in the days of deadly famine dared to enter into the city. Second Kings 15:5 tells us how Azariah the king was smitten with leprosy, and to the day of his death he had to live in a lazar-house, separated from everyone. It is interesting to note that even in Persia this pollution of the leper was believed in. Herodotus (1:138) tells us that: 'if a man in Persia has the leprosy he is not allowed to enter into a city or to have any dealings with any other Persians; he must, they say, have sinned against the sun'.

So, the Twelve were to bring cleansing to the polluted. People can stain their lives with sin; they can pollute their minds, their hearts and their bodies with the consequences of their sin. Their words, their actions and their influence can become so polluted that they are an unclean influence on all with whom they come into contact. Jesus Christ can cleanse the soul that has stained itself with sin; he can bring to men and women the divine antiseptic against sin; he cleanses human sin with the divine purity.

(d) They were to *cast out demons*. A demon-possessed man or woman was in the grip of an evil power. Such people were no longer in control of themselves and of their actions; the evil power within had overcome them. People can be taken over by evil; they can be dominated by evil habits; evil can have a mesmeric fascination for them. Jesus comes not only to cancel sin but to break the power of cancelled sin. Jesus Christ brings to all who are enslaved by sin the liberating power of God.

THE EQUIPMENT OF THE KING'S MESSENGER

Matthew 10:8b–10

> 'Freely you have received; freely give. Do not set out to get gold or silver or bronze for your purses; do not take a bag for the journey, nor two tunics, nor shoes, nor a staff. The workman deserves his sustenance.'

THIS is a passage in which every sentence and every phrase would ring an answering bell in the minds of the Jews who heard it. In it, Jesus was giving to his disciples the instructions which the Rabbis at their best gave to their students and disciples.

'Freely you have received,' says Jesus; 'freely give.' A Rabbi was bound by law to give his teaching freely and for nothing; the Rabbi was absolutely forbidden to take money for teaching the law which Moses had freely received from God. In only one case could a Rabbi accept payment. He might accept payment for teaching a child, for to teach a child is the parent's task, and no one else should be expected to spend time and labour doing what is the parent's own duty to do; but higher teaching had to be given without money and without price.

In the *Mishnah*, the law lays it down that, if a man takes payment for acting as a judge, his judgments are invalid; that if he takes payment for giving evidence as a witness, his witness is void. Rabbi Zadok said: 'Make not the law a crown wherewith to aggrandize thyself, nor a spade wherewith to dig.' Rabbi Hillel said: 'He who makes a worldly use of the crown of the law shall waste away. Hence thou mayest infer that whosoever desires a profit for himself from the words of the law is helping on his own destruction.' It was laid down: 'As God taught Moses gratis – so do thou.'

There is a story of Rabbi Tarphon. At the end of the fig harvest, he was walking in a garden; and he ate some of the figs which had been left behind. The watchmen came upon him and beat him. He told them who he was, and because he was a famous Rabbi they let him go. All his life he regretted that he had used his status as a Rabbi to help himself. 'Yet all his days did he grieve, for he said, "Woe is me, for I have used the crown of the law for my own profit!"'

When Jesus told his disciples that they had freely received and must freely give, he was telling them what the teachers of his own people had been telling their students for a long time. Anyone who possesses a precious secret surely has a duty not to hold on to it expecting to be paid for it, but willingly to pass it on. It is a privilege to share with others the riches God has given us.

Jesus told the Twelve not to set out to acquire gold or silver or bronze for their *purses*; the Greek literally means for their *girdles*. The girdle, which the Jews wore round their waists, was rather broad, and at each end for part of its length it was double; money was carried in the double part of the girdle, so that the girdle was the usual purse of Jews. Jesus told the Twelve not to take a *bag* for the journey. The bag may be one of two things. It may simply be a bag like a haversack in which provisions would ordinarily have been carried. But there is another possibility. The word is *pēra*, which can mean a beggar's *collecting bag*; sometimes the wandering philosophers took a collection in such a bag after addressing the crowd.

In all these instructions, Jesus was not laying upon the Twelve a deliberate and calculated discomfort. He was once again speaking words which were very familiar to any Jew. The *Talmud* tells us that: 'No one is to go to the Temple Mount with staff, shoes, girdle of money, or dusty feet.' The idea was that when a man entered the Temple, he must make it quite clear that he had left behind everything which had to do with trade and business and worldly affairs. What Jesus is saying to his disciples is: 'You must treat the whole world as the Temple of God. If you are to serve God, you must never give the impression that you are out for what you can get.' Jesus' instructions mean that servants of God must show by their attitude to material things that their first interest is God.

Finally, Jesus says that workers deserve their sustenance. Once again, the Jews would recognize this. It is true that a Rabbi might not accept payment, but it is also true that it was considered at once a privilege and an obligation to support a Rabbi, if he was truly a man of God. Rabbi Eliezer ben Jacob said: 'He who receives a Rabbi in his house, or as his guest, and lets him have his enjoyment from his possessions, the Scripture ascribes it to him as if he had offered the continual offerings.' Rabbi Jochanan laid it down that it was the duty of every Jewish community to support a Rabbi, and the more so because a Rabbi naturally neglects his own affairs to concentrate on the affairs of God.

Here then is the double truth: the servant of God must never be over-concerned with material things, but the people of God must never fail in their duty to see that those who serve God receive reasonable support. This passage lays an obligation on teacher and on people alike.

THE CONDUCT OF THE KING'S MESSENGER

Matthew 10:11–15

> 'When you enter into any city or village, make inquiries as to who in it is worthy, and stay there until you go out of it. When you come into a household, give your greetings to it. If the house is worthy, let your peace come upon it; if it is not worthy, let your peace return to you. If anyone will not receive you, and will not listen to your words, when you leave that house or that city, shake off the dust of it from your feet. This is the truth I tell you – it will be easier for the land of Sodom and Gomorrah on the day of judgment than for that city.'

HERE is a passage full of the most practical advice for the King's messengers.

When they entered a city or a village, they were to seek a house that is worthy. The point is that if they took up their residence in a house which had an evil reputation for morals or for conduct or for fellowship, it would seriously hinder their usefulness. They were not to identify themselves with anyone who might prove to be a handicap. That is not for a moment to say that they were not to seek to win such people for Christ, but it is to say that the messengers of Christ must take care whom they make their closest friends.

When they entered a house, they were to stay there until they moved on to another place. This was a matter of courtesy. They might well be tempted, after they had won certain supporters and converts in a place, to move on to a house which could provide more luxury, more comfort and better entertainment. The messengers of Christ must never give the impression that they court people for the sake of material things, and that their movements are dictated by the demands of their own comfort.

The passage about giving a greeting, and, as it were, taking the greeting back again, is typical of this part of the world. In the middle east, a spoken word was thought to have a kind of active and independent existence. It went out from the mouth as independently as a bullet from a gun. This idea emerges regularly in the Old Testament, especially in connection with words spoken by God. Isaiah hears God say: 'By myself I have sworn, from my mouth has gone forth in righteousness a word that shall not return' (Isaiah 45:23). 'So shall my word be that goes out from my mouth; it shall not return to me empty, but it shall accomplish that which I purpose, and succeed in the thing for which I sent it' (Isaiah 55:11). Zechariah sees the flying scroll, and hears the voice: 'This is the curse that goes out over the face of the whole land' (Zechariah 5:3).

To this day in the middle east, if a man speaks his blessing to a passer-by, and then discovers that the passer-by is of another faith, he will come and take his blessing back again. The idea here is that the messengers of the King can send their blessing to rest upon a house, and, if the house is unworthy of it, can, as it were, recall it.

If in any place their message is refused, the messengers of the King were to shake the dust of that place off their feet and to move on. To the Jews, the dust of a Gentile place or road was polluting; therefore, when the Jews crossed the border of Palestine and entered into their own country after a journey in Gentile lands, they shook the dust of the Gentile roads off their feet that the last particle of pollution might be cleansed away. So Jesus said: 'If a city or a village will not receive you, you must treat it like a Gentile place.' Again, we must be clear as to what Jesus is saying. In this passage, there is both a temporary and an eternal truth.

(1) The temporary truth is this. Jesus was not saying that certain people had to be abandoned as being outside the message of the gospel and beyond the reach of grace. This was an instruction like the opening instruction not to go to the Gentiles and to the Samaritans. It came from the situation in which it was given. It was simply due to the time factor; time was short; as many as possible must hear the proclamation of the kingdom; there was not time then to argue with the disputatious and to seek to win the stubborn; that would come later. At the moment, the disciples had to tour the country as quickly as possible, and therefore they had to move on when there was no immediate welcome for the message which they brought.

(2) The permanent truth is this. It is one of the great basic facts of life that time and time again an opportunity comes to us – and does not come back. To those people in Palestine, there was coming the opportunity to receive the gospel; but if they did not take it, the opportunity might well never return. As the proverb has it, 'Three things come not back – the spoken word, the spent arrow and the lost opportunity.'

This happens in every sphere of life. In his autobiography, *Chiaroscuro*, the painter Augustus John tells of an incident and adds a laconic comment. He was in Barcelona: 'It was time to leave for Marseilles. I had sent forward my baggage and was walking to the station, when I encountered three

Gitanas engaged in buying flowers at a booth. I was so struck by their beauty and flashing elegance that I almost missed my train. Even when I reached Marseilles and met my friend, this vision still haunted me, and I positively had to return. But I did not find these gypsies again. *One never does.*' The artist was always looking for glimpses of beauty to transfer to his canvas – but he knew well that if he did not paint the beauty when he found it, all the chances were that he would never catch that glimpse again. The tragedy of life is so often the tragedy of the lost opportunity.

Finally, it is said that it will be easier for Sodom and Gomorrah in the day of judgment than for the town or the village which has refused the message of Christ and the kingdom. Sodom and Gomorrah are in the New Testament proverbial for wickedness (Matthew 11:23–4; Luke 10:12–13, 17:29; Romans 9:29; 2 Peter 2:6; Jude 7). It is interesting and relevant to note that just before their destruction, Sodom and Gomorrah had been guilty of a grave and vicious breach of the laws of hospitality (Genesis 19:1–11). They, too, had rejected the messengers of God. But, even at their worst, Sodom and Gomorrah had never had the opportunity to reject the message of Christ and his kingdom. That is why it would be easier for them at the last than for the towns and villages of Galilee; for it is always true that the greater the privilege has been, the greater the responsibility is.

THE CHALLENGE OF THE KING
TO HIS MESSENGERS

Matthew 10:16–22

'Look you, it is I who am sending you out as sheep in the midst of wolves. Show yourself as wise as serpents, and as pure as doves. Beware of men! For they will hand you over to the councils, and they will scourge you in their synagogues. You will be brought before rulers and kings for my sake, that you make your witness to them and to the Gentiles. But when they hand you over, do not worry how you are to speak, or what you are to say. What you are to speak will be given to you in that hour, for it is not you who speak, but the Spirit of your Father who speaks in you. Brother will hand over brother to death, and father will hand over child. Children will rise up against parents, and will murder them; and you will be hated by all for my name's sake. But he who endures to the end will be saved.'

BEFORE we deal with this passage in detail, we may note two things about it in general.

When we were studying the Sermon on the Mount (pp. 96–101), we saw that one of Matthew's great characteristics was his love of orderly arrangement (pp. 9–10). We saw that it was Matthew's custom to collect in one place all the material on any given subject, even if it was spoken by Jesus on different occasions. Matthew was the systematizer of his material. This passage is one of the instances where Matthew collects his material from different times. Here he collects the things which Jesus said on various occasions about persecution.

There is no doubt that even when Jesus sent out the Twelve for the first time, he told them what to expect. But at the very beginning, Matthew relates how Jesus told his disciples not to go at that time to the Gentiles or to the Samaritans; and yet in this passage Matthew shows us Jesus foretelling persecution and trial before rulers and kings, that is to say, far beyond Palestine. The explanation is that Matthew collects Jesus' references to persecution and puts together both what Jesus said when he sent his disciples out on their first expedition and what Jesus told them after his resurrection, when he was sending them out into all the world. Here we have the words, not only of Jesus of Galilee, but also of the risen Christ.

Further, we must note that in these words Jesus was making use of ideas and pictures which were part and parcel of Jewish thought. We have seen again and again how it was the custom of the Jews, in their pictures of the future, to divide time into two ages. There was the present age, which is wholly bad; there was the age to come, which would be the golden age of God; and in between there was the day of the Lord, which would be a terrible time of chaos and destruction and judgment. Now in Jewish thought, one of the ever-recurring features of the day of the Lord was that it would split friends and family into two, and that the dearest bonds of earth would be destroyed in bitter enmities.

'All friends shall conquer one another' (4 Ezra [2 Esdras] 5:9). 'At that time friends shall make war on friends like enemies' (4 Ezra [2 Esdras] 6:24). 'And they will strive with one another, the young with the old, and the old with the young, the poor with the rich, and the lowly with the great, and the beggar with the prince' (Jubilees 23:19). 'And they will hate one another, and provoke one another to fight; and the mean will rule over the honourable, and those of low degree shall be extolled above the famous' (Apocalypse of Baruch 70:3). 'And they shall begin to fight among themselves, and their right hand shall be strong against themselves, and a man shall not know his brother, nor a son his father or his mother, till there be no number of the corpses through their slaughter' (1 Enoch 56:7). 'And in those days the destitute shall go forth and carry off their children, and they shall abandon them, so that their children shall perish through them; yea they shall abandon their children that are still

431

sucklings, and not return to them; and shall have no pity on their loved ones' (1 Enoch 99:5). 'And in those days in one place the fathers together with their sons shall be smitten and brothers one with another shall fall in death till the streams flow with their blood. For a man shall not withhold his hand from slaying his sons and his sons' sons, and the sinner shall not withhold his hand from his honoured brother; from dawn to sunset they shall slay each other' (1 Enoch 100:1–2).

All these quotations are taken from the books which the Jews wrote and knew and loved, and on which they fed their hearts and their hopes, in the days between the Old and the New Testaments. Jesus knew these books; his disciples knew these books; and when Jesus spoke of the terrors to come, and of the divisions which would tear apart the closest ties of earth, he was in effect saying: '*The day of the Lord has come.*' And his disciples would know that he was saying this, and would go out in the knowledge that they were living in the greatest days of history.

THE KING'S HONESTY TO HIS MESSENGERS

Matthew 10:16–22 (*contd*)

No one can read this passage without being deeply impressed with the honesty of Jesus. He never hesitated to tell people what they might expect, if they followed him. It is as if he said: 'Here is my task for you – at its grimmest and at its worst – do you accept it?' In his commentary, Plummer comments: 'This is not the world's way to win adherents.' The world will offer people roses, roses all the way, comfort, ease, advancement and the fulfilment of their worldly ambitions. Jesus offered his followers hardship and death. And yet the proof of history is that Jesus was right. In their heart of hearts, people love a call to adventure.

After the siege of Rome, in 1849, the Italian statesman Garibaldi issued the following proclamation to his followers: 'Soldiers, all our efforts against superior forces have been unavailing. I have nothing to offer you but hunger and thirst, hardship and death; but I call on all who love their country to join with me' – and they came in their hundreds.

During the Second World War, after Dunkirk, the British Prime Minister Winston Churchill offered his country 'blood, toil, sweat and tears'.

The American historian William Prescott tells how in the sixteenth century Francisco Pizarro, that reckless adventurer, offered his little band the tremendous choice between the known safety of Panama and the as yet unknown splendour of Peru. He took his sword and traced a line with it on the sand from east to west: 'Friends and comrades!' he said. 'On that side are toil, hunger, nakedness, the drenching storm, desertion and death; on this side, ease and pleasure. There lies Peru with its riches; here, Panama and its poverty. Choose each man what best becomes a brave Castilian. For my part I go south' – and he stepped across the line. And thirteen men, whose names are immortal, chose adventure with him.

When Sir Ernest Shackleton proposed his march to the South Pole, he asked for volunteers for that trek through the blizzards across the polar ice. He expected to have difficulty, but he was inundated with letters from young and old, rich and poor, from every part of society, all desiring to share in that great adventure.

It may be that the Church must learn again that we will never attract men and women to an easy way; it is the call of the heroic which ultimately speaks to people's hearts.

433

Jesus offered his disciples three kinds of trial.

(1) The *state* would persecute them; they would be brought before councils and kings and governors. Long before this, Aristotle had wondered if a good man could ever really be a good citizen; for, he said, it was the duty of the citizen always to support and to obey the state, and there were times when the good man would find that impossible. When Christ's followers were brought to court and to judgment, they were not to worry about what they would say; for God would give them words. 'I will be with your mouth and teach you what you are to speak,' God had promised Moses (Exodus 4:12). It was not the humiliation which the early Christians dreaded, nor even the cruel pain and the agony. But many of them feared that their own lack of skill in words and defence might injure rather than commend the faith. It is the promise of God that when people are on trial for their faith, the words will come to them.

(2) The *Church* would persecute them; they would be scourged in the synagogues. The Church does not like to be upset, and has its own ways of dealing with disturbers of the peace. The Christians were, and are, those who turn the world upside down (Acts 17:6). It has often been true that those with a message from God have had to undergo the hatred and the enmity of a fossilized orthodoxy.

(3) The *family* would persecute them; their nearest and dearest would think them mad, and shut the door against them. Sometimes the Christian is confronted with the hardest choice of all – the choice between obedience to Christ and obedience to family and to friends.

Jesus warned his disciples that in the days to come they might well find state and Church and family joining forces against them.

THE REASONS FOR THE PERSECUTION
OF THE KING'S MESSENGERS

Matthew 10:16–22 (*contd*)

LOOKING at things from our own point of view, we find it hard to understand why any government should wish to persecute the Christians, whose only aim was to live in purity, in charity and in reverence. But in later days the Roman government had what it considered good reason for persecuting the Christians (see, on this subject, pp. 129–31).

(1) There were certain slanders current about the Christians. They were accused of being cannibals because of the words of the sacrament, which spoke of eating Christ's body and drinking his blood. They were accused of immorality because the title of their weekly feast was the *agapē*, the love feast. They were accused of fire-raising because of the pictures which the Christian preachers drew of the coming of the end of the world. They were accused of being disloyal and disaffected citizens because they would not take the oath to the godhead of the emperor.

(2) It is doubtful if even the pagans really believed these slanderous charges. But there were other charges which were more serious. The Christians were accused of 'tampering with family relationships'. It was the truth that Christianity often split families, as we have seen. And to pagans, Christianity appeared to be something which divided parents and children, and husbands and wives.

(3) A real difficulty was the position of slaves in the Christian Church. In the Roman Empire, there were 60,000,000 slaves. It was always one of the terrors of the empire that these slaves might rise in revolt. If the structure of the empire was to remain intact, they must be kept in their

place; nothing must be done by anyone to encourage them to rebel, or the consequences might be terrible beyond imagining.

Now the Christian Church made no attempt to free the slaves, or to condemn slavery; but it did, within the Church at least, treat the slaves as equals. Clement of Alexandria pleaded that 'slaves are like ourselves', and the Golden Rule applied to them. The fourth-century writer Lactantius wrote: 'Slaves are not slaves to us. We deem them brothers after the Spirit, in religion fellow-servants.' It is a notable fact that, although there were thousands of slaves in the Christian Church, the inscription *slave* is never encountered in the Roman Christian tombs.

Worse than that, it was perfectly possible for a slave to hold high office in the Christian Church. In the early second century, two bishops of Rome, Callistus and Pius, had been slaves. And it was not uncommon for elders and deacons to be slaves.

And still worse, in AD 220, the former slave Callistus declared that henceforth the Christian Church would sanction the marriage of a highborn girl to a freed man, a marriage which was in fact illegal under Roman law, and, therefore, not a marriage at all.

In its treatment of slaves, the Christian Church must necessarily have seemed to the Roman authorities a force which was disrupting the very basis of civilization and threatening the very existence of the empire by giving slaves a position which they should never have had, as Roman law saw it.

(4) There is no doubt that Christianity seriously affected certain vested interests connected with pagan religion. When Christianity came to Ephesus, the trade of the silversmiths was dealt a mortal blow, for far fewer desired to buy the

images which they fashioned (Acts 19:24–7). Pliny 'the Younger' was governor of Bithynia in the reign of Trajan, and in a letter to the emperor (Pliny, *Letters*, 10:96) he tells how he had taken steps to check the rapid growth of Christianity so that 'the temples which had been deserted now begin to be frequented; the sacred festivals, after a long intermission, are revived; while there is a general demand for sacrificial animals, which for some time past have met with few purchasers'. It is clear that the spread of Christianity meant the abolition of certain trades and activities; and those who lost their trade and lost their money not unnaturally resented it.

Christianity preaches a view of society which no totalitarian state can accept. Christianity deliberately aims to obliterate certain trades and professions and ways of making money. It still does – and therefore Christians are still liable to persecution for their faith.

THE PRUDENCE OF THE KING'S MESSENGER

Matthew 10:23

> 'When they persecute you in one city, flee into another. This is the truth I tell you – you will not complete your tour of the cities of Israel, until the Son of Man shall come.'

THIS passage counsels a wise and a Christian prudence. In the days of persecution, a certain danger always threatened the Christian witness. There were always those who actually courted martyrdom; they were wound up to such a pitch of hysterical and fanatical enthusiasm that they went out of their way to become martyrs for the faith. Jesus was wise. He told his followers that there must be no wanton waste of Christian lives; that they must not pointlessly and needlessly throw their lives away. As someone has put it, the life of every Christian witness is precious and must not be recklessly thrown away. 'Bravado is not martyrdom.' Often the Christians had to die for their faith, but they must not throw away their lives in a way that did not really help the faith. As it was later said, people must contend *lawfully* for the faith.

When Jesus spoke like this, he was speaking in a way which Jews would recognize and understand. No people were ever more persecuted than the Jews have always been; and no people were ever clearer as to where the duties of the martyr lay. The teaching of the great Rabbis was quite clear. When it was a question of *public sanctification* or *open profanation* of God's name, duty was plain – people must be prepared to lay down their lives. But when that public declaration was not in question, they might save their lives by breaking the law; but for no reason must they commit idolatry, unchastity or murder.

The case the Rabbis cited was this: suppose a Jew is seized by a Roman soldier, and the soldier says mockingly, and with no other intention than to humiliate and to make a fool of the Jew: 'Eat this pork.' Then the Jew may eat, for 'God's laws are given for life and not for death.' But suppose the Roman says: 'Eat this pork as a sign that you renounce Judaism; eat this pork as a sign that you are ready to worship Jupiter and the emperor,' the Jew must die rather than eat. In any time of official persecution, the Jew must die rather than abandon his faith. As the Rabbis said, 'The words of the law are only firm in that man who would die for their sake.'

The Jews were forbidden to throw away their lives in needless acts of pointless martyrdom; but when it came to a question of true witness, they must be prepared to die.

We do well to remember that, while we are bound to accept martyrdom for our faith, we are forbidden to court martyrdom. If suffering for the faith comes to us in the course of duty, it must be accepted; but it must not be needlessly invited; to invite it does more harm than good to the faith we bear. The self-constituted martyr is much too common in all human affairs.

It has been said that there is sometimes more heroism in daring to flee from danger than in stopping to meet it. There is real wisdom in recognizing when to escape. André Maurois in *Why France Fell* tells of a conversation he had with Winston Churchill. There was a time at the beginning of the Second World War when Great Britain seemed strangely inactive and unwilling to act. Churchill said to Maurois: 'Have you observed the habits of lobsters'? 'No,' answered Maurois to this somewhat surprising question. Churchill went on: 'Well, if you have the opportunity, study them. At certain periods in his life the lobster loses his protective shell. At this moment of moulting even the bravest crustacean retires into a crevice in the rock, and waits patiently until a new carapace has time to grow. As soon as this new armour has grown strong, he sallies out of the crevice, and becomes once more a fighter, lord of the seas. England, through the faults of imprudent ministers, has lost its carapace: we must wait in our crevice until the new one has time to grow strong.' This was a time when inaction was wiser than action, and when to escape was wiser than to attack.

If people are weak in the faith, they will do well to avoid arguments about doubtful things and not to plunge into them. If we know that we are susceptible to a certain temptation, we will do well to avoid the places where that temptation will speak to us and not to frequent them. If we know that there are people who anger and irritate us, and who bring the worst out of us, we will be wise to avoid their society and not to seek it. Courage is not recklessness; there is no virtue in running needless risks; God's grace is meant to protect not the foolhardy but the prudent.

THE COMING OF THE KING

Matthew 10:23 (*contd*)

THIS passage contains one strange saying which we cannot honestly neglect. Matthew depicts Jesus as sending out his disciples, and, as he does so, saying to them: 'You will not complete your tour of the cities of Israel until the Son of Man shall come.' On the face of it, that seems to mean that before his followers had completed their preaching tour, Jesus' day of glory and his return to power would have taken place. The difficulty is just this – that did not in fact happen, and if, at that moment, Jesus had that expectation, he was mistaken. If he said this in this way, he foretold something which actually did not happen. But there is a perfectly good and sufficient explanation of this apparent difficulty.

The people of the early Church believed intensely in the second coming of Jesus, and they believed it would happen soon, certainly within their own lifetime. There could be nothing more natural than that, because they were living in days of savage persecution, and they were longing for the day of their release and their glory. The result was that they fastened on every possible saying of Jesus which could be interpreted as foretelling his triumphant and glorious return; and sometimes they quite naturally used things which Jesus said, and read into them something more definite than was originally there.

We can see this process happening within the pages of the New Testament itself. There are three versions of the one saying of Jesus. Let us set them down one after another:

> Truly I tell you, there are some standing here who will not taste death before they see the Son of Man coming in his kingdom. (Matthew 16:28)

> Truly I tell you, there are some standing here who will not taste death until they see the kingdom of God has come with power. (Mark 9:1)

> But I truly tell you, there are some standing here who will not taste death before they see the kingdom of God. (Luke 9:27)

Now it is clear that these are three versions of the same saying. Mark is the earliest gospel, and therefore Mark's version is most likely to be strictly accurate. Mark says that there were some listening to Jesus who would not die until they saw the kingdom of God coming with power. That was gloriously true, for within thirty years of the cross the message of crucified and risen Christ had swept across the world and had reached Rome, the capital of the world. Indeed men and women were being swept into the kingdom; indeed the kingdom was coming with power. Luke transmits the saying in the same way as Mark.

Now look at Matthew. His version is slightly different; he says that there are some who will not die until they see the Son of Man coming in power. That, in fact, did not happen. The explanation is that Matthew was writing between AD 80 and 90, in days when terrible persecution was raging. People were clutching at everything which promised release from agony; and he took a saying which foretold the spread of the kingdom and turned it into a saying which foretold the return of Christ within a lifetime – and who shall blame him?

That is what Matthew has done here. Take this saying in our passage and write it as Mark or Luke would have written it: 'You will not complete your tour of the cities of Israel until the *kingdom of God* shall come.' That was blessedly true, for as the tour went on, the hearts of men and women opened to Jesus Christ, and they took him as Master and Lord.

In a passage like this, we must not think of Jesus as mistaken; we must rather think that Matthew read into a promise of the coming of the kingdom a promise of the second coming of Jesus Christ – because, in days of terror, people clutched at the hope of Christ; and Christ did come to them in the Spirit, for no one ever suffered alone for Christ.

THE KING'S MESSENGER
AND THE KING'S SUFFERINGS

Matthew 10:24–5

> 'The scholar is not above his teacher, nor is the slave
> above his master. It is enough for the scholar that he
> should be as his teacher, and the servant that he should
> be as his master. If they have called the master of the
> house Beelzebul, how much more shall they so call the
> members of his household.'

IT is Jesus' warning to his disciples that they must expect what happened to him to happen to them. This sentence was well known to the Jews: 'It is enough for the slave to be as his master.' In the later days, they were to use it in a special way. In AD 70, Jerusalem was destroyed, and destroyed so completely that a plough was drawn across the devastation. The Temple of God and the holy city were in ruins. The Jews were dispersed throughout the world, and many of them mourned and lamented the terrible fate which had befallen .

442

them personally. It was then that the Rabbis said to them: 'When God's Temple has been destroyed, how can any individual Jew complain about his personal misfortunes?'

In this saying of Jesus, there are two things.

(1) There is a *warning*. There is the warning that, as Christ had to carry a cross, so also the individual Christian must carry a cross. The word that is used for *members of a household* is the one Greek word *oikiakoi*. This word has a technical use: it means *the members of the household of a government official*, that is to say, the official's *staff*. It is as if Jesus said: 'If I, the leader and commander, must suffer, you who are the members of my staff cannot escape.' Jesus calls us not only to share his glory but to share his warfare and his agony; and we do not deserve to share the fruits of victory if we refuse to share the struggle of which these fruits are the result.

(2) There is the statement of a *privilege*. To suffer for Christ is to share the work of Christ; to have to sacrifice for the faith is to share the sacrifice of Christ. When Christianity is hard, we can say to ourselves not only: 'We are treading where the saints have trod'; we can also say: 'We are treading where the feet of Christ have trod.'

There is always a thrill in belonging to a noble company. The novelist Eric Linklater, in his autobiography, tells of his experience in the disastrous March retreat in the First World War. He was with the Black Watch, and they had emerged from the battle with one officer, thirty men and a piper remaining of the battalion. 'The next day, marching peacefully in the morning light of France along a pleasant road we encountered the tattered fragments of a battalion of the Foot Guards, and the piper, putting breath into his bag, and playing so that he filled the air like the massed bands of the Highland Division, saluted the tall Coldstreamers, who had a drum or two and some instruments of brass, that made also a gallant music. Stiffly we passed each other, swollen of chest, heads tautly to the right, kilts swinging to the answer of the swagger of the Guards, and the Red Hackle in our bonnets, like the monstrance of a bruised but resilient faith. We were bearded and stained with mud. The Guards – the fifty men that were left of a battalion – were button-bright and clean shaved – we were a tatter-demalion [ragged and disorderly] crew from the coal mines of Fife and the back streets of Dundee, but we trod quick-stepping to the brawling tune of "Hielan' Laddie", and suddenly I was crying with a fool's delight and the sheer gladness of being in such company.' It is one of life's great thrills to have the sense of belonging to a goodly company and a goodly fellowship.

When Christianity costs something, we are closer than we ever were to the fellowship of Jesus Christ; and if we know the fellowship of his sufferings, we shall also know the power of his resurrection.

THE KING'S MESSENGER'S FREEDOM FROM FEAR

Matthew 10:26–31

'Do not fear them; for there is nothing which is covered which shall not be unveiled, and there is nothing hidden which shall not be known. What I tell you in the darkness, speak in the light. What you hear whispered in your ear, proclaim on the housetops. Do not fear those who can kill the body, but who cannot kill the soul. Rather fear him who is able to destroy both soul and body in Gehenna. Are two sparrows not sold for a penny, and not one of them shall light on the ground without your Father's knowledge? The hairs of your head are all numbered. So then do not be afraid; you are of more value than many sparrows.'

THREE times in this short passage, Jesus bids his disciples not to be afraid. In the King's messengers, there must be a certain courageous fearlessness which marks them out from others.

(1) The first commandment is in verses 26–7, and it speaks of a double fearlessness.

(a) They are not to be afraid because there is nothing covered that will not be unveiled, and nothing hidden which will not be known. The meaning of that is that *the truth will triumph*. 'Great is the truth,' ran the Latin proverb, 'and the truth will prevail.' When James VI threatened to hang or exile the reformer Andrew Melville, Melville's answer was: 'You cannot hang or exile the truth.' When Christians are involved in suffering and sacrifice and even martyrdom for their faith, they must remember that the day will come when things will be seen as they really are; and then the power of the persecutor and the heroism of Christian witness will be seen at their true value, and each will have its true reward.

(b) They are not to be afraid to speak with boldness the message they have received. What Jesus has told them, they must tell to others. Here in this one verse (verse 27) lies the true function of the preacher.

First, preachers must *listen*; they must be in the secret place with Christ, that in the dark hours Christ may speak to them, and that in the loneliness Christ may whisper in their ear. No one can speak for Christ who has not heard Christ speak; no one can proclaim the truth who has not listened to the truth; for we cannot pass on that which we do not know.

In the great days in which the Reformation was coming to birth, the English scholar John Colet invited the famous Dutch reformer Erasmus to come to Oxford to give a series of lectures on Moses or Isaiah; but Erasmus knew he was not ready. He wrote back: 'But I who have learned to live with myself, and know how scanty my equipment is, can neither claim the learning required for such a task, nor do I think that I possess the strength of mind to sustain the jealousy of so many men, who would be eager to maintain their own ground. The campaign is one that demands, not a tyro [novice], but a practised general. Neither should you call me immodest in declining a position which it would be most immodest for me to accept. You are not acting wisely, Colet, in demanding water from a pumice stone, as Plautus [the Roman dramatist] said. With what effrontery shall I teach what I have never learned? How am I to warm the coldness of others, when I am shivering myself?'

Whoever would teach and preach must first in the secret place listen and learn.

Second, preachers must speak what they have heard from Christ, and they must speak even if their speaking is to gain them the hatred of others, and even if, by speaking, they take their lives in their hands.

Truth is ·not popular, for, as Diogenes said, truth is like the light to sore eyes. Once Bishop Latimer was preaching when King Henry VIII was present. He knew that the king would not relish what he was about to say. So in the pulpit he soliloquized aloud with himself. 'Latimer! Latimer! Latimer!' he said, 'be careful what you say. Henry the king is here.' He paused, and then he said: 'Latimer! Latimer! Latimer! be careful what you say. The King of Kings is here.'

Those who have a message speak to other men and women, but they speak in the presence of God. It was said of John Knox, as they buried him, 'Here lies one who feared God so much that he never feared the face of any man.'

Those who bear Christian witness are the men and women who know no fear, because they know that the judgments of eternity will correct the judgments of time. Christian preachers and teachers are men and women who listen with reverence and who speak with courage, because they know that, whether they listen or speak, they are in the presence of God.

THE KING'S MESSENGER'S FREEDOM FROM FEAR – THE COURAGE OF THE RIGHT

Matthew 10:26–31 (*contd*)

(2) The second commandment is in verse 28. To put it very simply, what Jesus is saying is that no punishment that others can ever lay upon us can compare with the ultimate fate of one who has been guilty of infidelity and disobedience to God. It is true that human beings can kill the physical body; but God can condemn a person to the death of the soul. There are three things that we must note here.

(a) Some people believe in what is called *conditioned immortality*. This belief holds that the reward of goodness is that the soul climbs up and up until it is one with all the immortality, the bliss and the blessedness of God; and that the punishment of evil men and women, who will not mend their ways in spite of all God's appeals to them, is that their souls go down and down and down until they are finally obliterated and cease to be. We cannot erect a doctrine on a single text, but that is something very like what Jesus is saying here.

The Jews knew the awfulness of the punishment of God.

> For you have power over life and death;
> you lead mortals down to the gates of Hades and back
>   again.
> A person in wickedness kills another,
> but cannot bring back the departed spirit,
> or set free the imprisoned soul.

(Wisdom of Solomon 16:13–14)

During the killing times of the Maccabaean struggle, the seven martyred brothers encouraged each other by saying: 'Let us not fear him who thinks he is killing us, for great is the struggle of the soul and the danger of eternal torment lying before those who transgress the commandment of God' (4 Maccabees 13:14–15).

We do well to remember that the penalties which human beings can exact are as nothing to the penalties which God can exact and to the rewards which he can give.

(b) The second thing which this passage teaches is that there is still left in the Christian life a place for what we might call a holy fear.

The Jews knew well this fear of God. One of the Rabbinic stories tells how Rabbi Jochanan was ill. 'His disciples went in to visit him. On beholding them he began to weep. His disciples said to him, "O Lamp of Israel, right-hand pillar, mighty hammer! Wherefore dost thou weep?" He replied to them, "If I was being led into the presence of a human king who today is here and tomorrow in the grave, who, if he were wrathful against me, his anger would not be eternal, who, if he imprisoned me, the imprisonment would not be eternal, who, if he condemned me to death, the death would not be for ever, and whom I can appease with words and bribe with money – even then I would weep. But now, when I am being led into the presence of the King of kings, the Holy One, blessed is he, who lives and endures for all eternity, who, if he be wrathful against me, his anger is eternal, who, if he imprisoned me, the imprisonment would be for ever, who, if he condemned me to death, the death would be for ever, and whom I cannot appease with words or bribe with money – nay more, when before me lie two ways, one the way of the Garden of Eden and the other the way of Gehenna, and I know not in which I am to be led – shall I not weep?"'

It is not that the Jewish thinkers forgot that there is love, and that love is the greatest of all things. 'The reward of him who acts from love', they said, 'is double and quadruple. Act from love, for there is no love where there is fear, or fear where there is love, except in relation to God.' The Jews were always sure that in relation to God there was both fear and love. 'Fear God and love God, the law says both; act from both love and fear; from love, for, if you would hate, no lover hates; from fear, for, if you would kick, no fearer kicks.' But the Jews never forgot – and neither must we – the sheer holiness of God.

And for the Christian the matter is even more compelling, for our fear is not that God will punish us, but that in response to his love we may cause only distress and grief. The Jews were never in any danger of sentimentalizing the love of God, and neither was Jesus. God is love, but God is also holiness, for God is God; and there must be a place in our hearts and in our thoughts both for the love which answers God's love, and the reverence, the awe and the fear which answer God's holiness.

(c) Further, this passage tells us that there are things which are worse than death; and disloyalty is one of them. If people are guilty of disloyalty, if they buy security at the expense of dishonour, life is no longer tolerable. They cannot face other people; they cannot face themselves; and ultimately they cannot face God. There are times when comfort, safety, ease and life itself can cost too much.

THE KING'S MESSENGER'S FREEDOM FROM FEAR – GOD CARES!

Matthew 10:26–31 (contd)

(3) The third commandment not to fear is in verse 31; and it is based on the certainty of the detailed care of God. If God

cares for the sparrows, surely he will care for men and women.

Matthew says that two sparrows are sold for a penny and yet not one of them falls to the ground without the knowledge of God. Luke gives us that saying of Jesus in a slightly different form: 'Are not five sparrows sold for two pennies? Yet not one of them is forgotten in God's sight' (Luke 12:6). The point is this – two sparrows were sold for one penny. (The coin is the *assarion*, which was one-sixteenth of a *denarius*; a *denarius* was the average day's pay for a working man.) But if the purchaser was prepared to spend two pennies, he got not four sparrows but *five*. The extra one was thrown into the bargain as having no value at all. God cares even for the sparrow which is thrown into the bargain, and which by human reckoning has no value at all. Even the forgotten sparrow is dear to God.

The point is even more vivid than that. The Revised Standard Version – and it is a perfectly correct translation of the Greek – has it that not one sparrow will fall to the ground without the knowledge of God. In such a context, the word *fall* makes us naturally think of *death*; but in all probability the Greek is a translation of an Aramaic word which means to *light* upon the ground. It is not that God marks the sparrow when the sparrow falls dead; it is far more; it is that God marks the sparrow every time it lights and hops upon the ground. So it is Jesus' argument that if God cares like that for sparrows, he will care much more for men and women.

Once again, the Jews would well understand what Jesus was saying. No nation ever had such a conception of the detailed care of God for his creation. Rabbi Chanina said: 'No man hurts his finger here below, unless it is so disposed for him by God.' There was a Rabbinic saying: 'God sits

and feeds the world, from the horns of the buffalo to the
eggs of the louse.' Rabbi Hillel has a wonderful interpretation of Psalm 136. That psalm begins by telling the story in
lyric poetry about the God who is the God of creation, the
God who made the heavens and the earth, and the sun and
the moon and the stars (verses 1-9); then it goes on to tell
the story about the God who is the God of history, the God
who rescued Israel from Egypt and who fought her
battles for her (verses 11-24); then finally it goes on to
speak of God as the God 'who gives food to all flesh'
(verse 25). The God who made the world and who controls
all history is the God who gives us food. The coming of our
daily bread is just as much an act of God as the act of creation
and the saving power of the deliverance from Egypt. God's
love for us is seen not only in the omnipotence of creation
and in the great events of history; it is also seen in the
day-to-day nourishment of our bodies.

The courage of the King's messengers is founded on the
conviction that, whatever happens, they cannot drift beyond
the love of God. They know that their times are forever in
God's hands; that God will not leave them or forsake them;
that they are surrounded forever by God's care. If that is so –
of whom then shall we be afraid?

THE LOYALTY OF THE KING'S MESSENGER
AND ITS REWARD

Matthew 10:32-3

> 'I too will acknowledge before my Father everyone who
> acknowledges me before men. I too will deny before
> my Father who is in heaven everyone who denies me
> before men.'

HERE is laid down the double loyalty of the Christian life. If people are loyal to Jesus Christ in this life, Jesus Christ will be loyal to them in the life to come. If they are proud to acknowledge that Jesus Christ is their Master, Jesus Christ will be proud to acknowledge that they are his servants.

It is the plain fact of history that if there had not been men and women in the early Church who in the face of death and agony refused to deny their Master, there would be no Christian Church today. The Church of today is built on the unbreakable loyalty of those who held fast to their faith.

Pliny 'the Younger', the governor of Bithynia, writes to Trajan, the Roman emperor, about how he treated the Christians within his province. Anonymous informers gave information that certain people were Christian. Pliny tells how he gave these men the opportunity to invoke the gods of Rome to offer wine and frankincense to the image of the emperor, and how he demanded that as a final test they should curse the name of Christ. And then he adds: 'None of these acts, it is said, those who are really Christians can be compelled to do.' Even the Roman governor confesses his helplessness to shake the loyalty of those who are truly Christian.

It is still possible to deny Jesus Christ.

(1) We may deny him with our *words*. It is told of J. P. Mahaffy, the famous scholar and man of the world from Trinity College, Dublin, that when he was asked if he was a Christian, his answer was: 'Yes, but not offensively so.' He meant that he did not allow his Christianity to interfere with the society he kept and the pleasure he loved. Sometimes we say to other people, practically in so many words, that we are church members, but not to worry about it too much; that we have no intention of being different; that we are prepared to take our full share in all the pleasures of the world; and that

we do not expect people to take any special trouble to respect any vague principles that we may have.

As Christians, we can never escape the duty of being different from the world. It is not our duty to conform to the world; it is our duty to be transformed out of it.

(2) We can deny him by our *silence*. A French writer tells of bringing a young wife into an old family who had not approved of the marriage, although they were too conventionally polite ever to put their objections into actual words and criticisms. But the young wife afterwards said that her whole life was made a misery by 'the menace of things unsaid'.

There can be a menace of things unsaid in the Christian life. Again and again, life brings us the opportunity to speak some word for Christ, to utter some protest against evil, to take some stand, and to show what side we are on. Again and again on such occasions, it is easier to keep silence than to speak. But such a silence is a denial of Jesus Christ. It is probably true that far more people deny Jesus Christ by cowardly silence than by deliberate words.

(3) We can deny him by our *actions*. We can live in such a way that our life is a continuous denial of the faith which we profess. Those who have given their allegiance to the gospel of purity may be guilty of all kinds of small-scale dishonesties and breaches of strict honour. Those who have undertaken to follow the Master who bade us take up a cross can live a life which is dominated by attention to their own ease and comfort. Those who have entered the service of him who himself forgave and who bade his followers to forgive can live a life of bitterness and resentment and variance with others. Those whose eyes are meant to be on that Christ who died for love of men and women can live a life in which the idea of Christian service and Christian charity and Christian generosity are conspicuous by their absence.

A special prayer was composed for the Lambeth Conference of 1948:

> Almighty God, give us grace to be not only hearers, but doers of thy holy word, not only to admire, but to obey thy doctrine, not only to profess, but to practise thy religion, not only to love, but to live thy gospel. So grant that what we learn of thy glory we may receive into our hearts, and show forth in our lives: through Jesus Christ our Lord. Amen.

That is a prayer which every one of us would do well to remember and continually to use.

THE WARFARE OF THE KING'S MESSENGER

Matthew 10:34-9

> 'Do not think that I came to send peace on earth: I did not come to send peace, but a sword. I came to set a man at variance against his father, and a daughter against her mother, and a daughter-in-law against her mother-in-law; and a man's enemies shall be the members of his own household. He that loves father or mother more than he loves me is not worthy of me; and he who does not take up his cross and follow after me is not worthy of me. He who finds his life will lose it; and he who loses his life for my sake shall find it.'

NOWHERE is the sheer honesty of Jesus more vividly displayed than it is here. Here he sets the Christian demand in its most forceful and uncompromising form. He tells his disciples exactly what they may expect if they accept the commission to be messengers of the King. Here in this passage, Jesus offers four things.

(1) He offers a *warfare*; and in that warfare it will often be true that the enemy will be members of a person's own household.

It so happens that Jesus was using language which was perfectly familiar to the Jews. The Jews believed that one of the features of the day of the Lord, the day when God would break into history, would be the division of families. The Rabbis said: 'In the period when the Son of David shall come, a daughter will rise up against her mother, a daughter-in-law against her mother-in-law.' 'The son despises his father, the daughter rebels against the mother, the daughter-in-law against her mother-in-law, and the man's enemies are those from his own household.' It is as if Jesus said: 'The end you have always been waiting for has come; and the intervention of God in history is splitting homes and groups and families into two.'

When some great cause emerges, it is bound to divide people; there are bound to be those who answer, and those who refuse, the challenge. To be confronted with Jesus is necessarily to be confronted with the choice whether to accept him or to reject him; and the world is always divided into those who have accepted Christ and those who have not.

The bitterest thing about this warfare was that people's enemies would be from their own households. It can happen that people love their family so much that they may refuse some great adventure, some avenue of service, some call to sacrifice, either because they do not wish to leave them, or because to accept it would involve them in danger.

The New Testament scholar T. R. Glover quotes a letter from Oliver Cromwell to Lord Wharton. The date is 1st January 1649, and Cromwell had in the back of his mind that Wharton might be so attached to his home and to his wife that he might refuse to hear the call to adventure and to battle, and might choose to stay at home: 'My service to the dear little lady; I wish you make her not a greater temptation than she is. Take heed of all relations. Mercies should not be temptations; yet we too often make them so.'

It has happened that some have refused God's call to adventurous service because they allowed personal attachments to immobilize them. Richard Lovelace, the Cavalier poet, writes to his Lucasta, 'Going to the War':

> Tell me not (Sweet) I am unkind,
>   That from the nunnery
> Of thy chaste breast, and quiet mind,
>   To war and arms I fly.
>
> True; a new mistress now I chase,
>   The first foe in the field;
> And with a stronger faith embrace
>   A sword, a horse, a shield.
>
> Yet this inconstancy is such,
>   As you too shall adore.
> I could not love thee (Dear) so much,
>   Loved I not honour more.

It is very seldom that people are confronted with this choice; they may well go through life and never face it; but the fact remains that it is possible for loved ones to become in effect enemies, if the thought of them keeps us from doing what we know God wants us to do.

(2) He offers a *choice*; and we have to choose sometimes between the closest ties of earth and loyalty to Jesus Christ.

John Bunyan knew all about that choice. The thing which troubled him most about his imprisonment was the effect it would have upon his wife and children. What was to happen to them, bereft of his support? 'The parting with my wife and poor children hath often been to me in this place, as the pulling the flesh from my bones; and that not only because I am somewhat too fond of these great mercies, but also because I should have often brought to my mind the many hardships, miseries, and wants that my poor family was like to meet with, should I be taken from them, *especially my poor blind child*, who lay nearer my heart than all I had besides. O the thought of the hardship I thought my blind one might go under, would break up my heart to pieces . . . But yet, recalling myself, thought I, I must venture you all with God, though it goeth to the quick to leave you; O I saw in this condition, I was a man who was pulling down his house upon the head of his wife and children; yet thought I, I must do it, I must do it.'

Once again, this terrible choice will come very seldom, in God's mercy to many of us it may never come; but the fact remains that all loyalties must give place to loyalty to God.

THE COST OF BEING A MESSENGER
OF THE KING

Matthew 10:34-9 (*contd*)

(3) Jesus offers a *cross*. People in Galilee knew very well what a cross was. When the Roman general Varus had broken the revolt of Judas of Galilee, he crucified 2,000 Jews, and placed the crosses by the wayside along the roads to Galilee. In the ancient days, the criminal did actually carry the cross-beam of his cross to the place of crucifixion, and the men to whom Jesus spoke had seen people staggering under the weight of their crosses and dying in agony upon them.

The truly great, whose names are on the honour roll of faith, knew very well what they were doing. After his trial in Scarborough Castle, the Quaker George Fox wrote: 'And the officers would often be threatening me, that I should be hanged over the wall . . . they talked much then of hanging me. But I told them, "If that was it they desired, and it was permitted them, I was *ready*."' When John Bunyan was brought before the magistrate, he said: 'Sir, the law [the law of Christ] hath provided two ways of obeying: The one to do that which I in my conscience do believe that I am bound to do, actively; and where I cannot obey it actively, there I am willing to lie down and to suffer what they shall do unto me.'

Christians may have to sacrifice their personal ambitions, the ease and the comfort that they might have enjoyed, the career that they might have achieved; they may have to lay aside their dreams, to realize that shining things of which they have caught a glimpse are not for them. They will certainly have to sacrifice their will, for Christians can never again do what they like; they must do what Christ likes. In Christianity there is always some cross, for it is the religion of the cross.

(4) He offers *adventure*. He told them that those who found life would lose it; and those who lost life would find it.

Again and again, that has been proved true in the most literal way. It has always been true that many people might easily have saved their lives; but, if their lives had been saved, they would also have been lost, for no one would ever have heard of them, and the place they hold in history would have been lost to them.

The Greek philosopher Epictetus says of Socrates: 'Dying, he was saved, because he did not flee.' Socrates could easily have saved his life, but if he had done so, the real Socrates would have died, and no one would ever have heard of him.

When John Bunyan was charged with refusing to come to public worship and with running forbidden meetings of his own, he thought seriously whether it was his duty to flee to safety, or to stand by what he believed to be true. As all the world knows, he chose to take his stand. T. R. Glover closes his essay on Bunyan thus: 'And supposing he had been talked round and had agreed no longer "devilishly and perniciously to abstain from coming to Church to hear divine service," and to be no longer "an upholder of several unlawful meetings and conventicles to the great disturbance and distraction of the good subjects of the kingdom contrary to the laws of our sovereign lord the king"? Bedford might have kept a tinker the more – and possibly none of the best at that, for there is nothing to show that renegades make good tinkers – and what would England have lost?'

There is no place for a policy of safety first in the Christian life. Those who seek first ease and comfort and security and the fulfilment of personal ambition may well get all these things – but they will not be happy; for we were sent into this world to serve God and one another. It is possible to hoard life if we wish to do so. But that way, we will lose all that makes life valuable to others and worth living for ourselves. The way to serve others, the way to fulfil God's purpose for us, the way to true happiness is to spend life selflessly, for only thus will we find life, here and hereafter.

THE REWARD OF THOSE WHO WELCOME THE KING'S MESSENGER

Matthew 10:40-2

'He who receives you, receives me; and he who receives me, receives him that sent me. He who receives a prophet because he is a prophet will receive a prophet's reward; and he who receives a righteous man because

> he is a righteous man will receive a righteous man's
> reward. And whoever gives one of these little ones a
> drink of cold water because he is a disciple – this is the
> truth I tell you – he will not lose his reward.'

WHEN Jesus said this, he was using a way of speaking which the Jews regularly used. The Jews always felt that to receive a person's envoy or messenger was the same as to receive that person. To pay respect to an ambassador was the same as to pay respect to the king who had sent him. To welcome with love the messenger of a friend was the same as to welcome the friend. The Jews always felt that to honour a person's representative was the same as to honour the person who had sent the representative. This was particularly so in regard to wise men and to those who taught God's truth. The Rabbis said: 'He who shows hospitality to the wise is as if he brought the first fruits of his produce unto God.' 'He who greets the learned is as if he greeted God.' If people are truly of God, to receive them is to receive the God who sent them.

This passage sets out the four links in the chain of salvation. (1) There is God, out of whose love the whole process of salvation began. (2) There is Jesus, who brought that message to men and women. (3) There are the human messengers, the prophets who speak, the good people who are examples, the disciples who learn, who in turn all pass on to others the good news which they themselves have received. (4) There are the believers, who welcome God's messengers and God's message and who thus find life to their souls.

In this passage, there is something very lovely for every simple and humble individual.

(1) We cannot all be prophets, and preach and proclaim the word of God; but those who give God's messenger the simple gift of hospitality will receive no less a reward than that prophet. There are many who have been great public

figures; there are many whose voices have kindled the hearts
of thousands of people; there are many who have carried an
almost intolerable burden of public service and public
responsibility, all of whom would gladly have borne witness
that they could never have survived the effort and the demands
of their task, were it not for the love and the care and the
sympathy and the service of someone at home, who was
never in the public eye at all. When true greatness is measured
up in the sight of God, it will be seen again and again that
those who greatly moved the world were entirely dependent
on someone else who, as far as the world is concerned,
remained unknown. Even prophets must eat and be clothed.
Let those who have the often thankless task of making a home,
cooking meals, washing clothes, shopping for household
necessities or caring for children never think of it as a dreary
and weary chore. It is God's greatest task; and they will be
far more likely to receive the prophet's reward than those
whose days are filled with committees and whose homes are
comfortless.

(2) We cannot all be shining examples of goodness; we
cannot all stand out in the world's eye as righteous; but those
who help such people in their work will receive equal reward.

The folklorist and writer of short stories, H. L. Gee, has a
lovely story. There was a young boy in a country village who,
after a great struggle, reached the ministry. His helper in his
days of study had been the village cobbler. The cobbler, like
so many of his trade, was a man of wide reading and far
thinking, and he had done much for the boy. In due time, the
young man was licensed to preach. And on that day, the
cobbler said to him: 'It was always my desire to be a minister
of the gospel, but the circumstances of my life made it
impossible. But you are achieving what was closed to me.
And I want you to promise me one thing – I want you to let

me make and cobble your shoes – for nothing – and I want you to wear them in the pulpit when you preach, and then I'll feel you are preaching the gospel that I always wanted to preach standing in my shoes.' Beyond a doubt, the cobbler was serving God as the preacher was, and his reward would one day be the same.

(3) We cannot all teach the child; but there is a real sense in which we can all serve the child. We may not have either the knowledge or the technique to teach, but there are simple duties to be done, without which the child cannot live. It may be that in this passage it is not so much *children in age* of whom Jesus is thinking as *children in the faith*. It seems very likely that the Rabbis called their disciples *the little ones*. It may be that in the technical, academic sense we cannot teach, but there is a teaching by life and example which we can all offer.

The great beauty of this passage is its stress on simple things. The Church and Christ will always need their great orators, their great shining examples of sainthood, their great teachers, those whose names are household words; but the Church and Christ will also always need those in whose homes there is hospitality, on whose hands there is all the service which makes a home, and in whose hearts there is the caring which is Christian love; and, as Robert Browning wrote in 'Pippa Passes', 'All service ranks the same with God.'